COLD WAR SOUTHEAST ASIA

PEOPLE'S REPUBLIC
OF CHINA (PRC)
Yunnan
Guangxi
Guangdong
REPUBLIC
OF CHINA
(TAIWAN)
Phu Thong
Viet Bac
Hanoi
BURMA
Sam Neua
NORTH
VIETNAM
Plain of
Jars
Hainan
Vientiane
LAOS
Yangon
Isan
Savan-
nakhet
Luzon
THAILAND
Manila
SOUTH
VIETNAM
Bangkok
Preah Vihear
CAMBODIA
PHILIPPINES
Phnom
Penh
Saigon
Betong
Ipoh
BRUNEI
N. Borneo/
Sabah
Aceh
MALAYSIA
Kuala
Lumpur
Sarawak
Borneo
SINGAPORE
Sumatra
Kalimantan
Sulawesi
INDONESIA
Jakarta
Java
Surabaya
Yogyakarta
Madiun
Dili
Timor

COLD WAR SOUTHEAST ASIA

EDITED BY **MALCOLM H. MURFETT**

Marshall Cavendish
Editions

For Nicolas

Published in 2012 by Marshall Cavendish Editions
An imprint of Marshall Cavendish International
1 New Industrial Road, Singapore 536196

Other Marshall Cavendish Offices:
Marshall Cavendish Ltd. PO Box 65829, London EC1P 1NY, UK • Marshall Cavendish Corporation. 99 White Plains Road, Tarrytown NY 10591-9001, USA • Marshall Cavendish International (Thailand) Co Ltd. 253 Asoke, 12th Flr, Sukhumvit 21 Road, Klongtoey Nua, Wattana, Bangkok 10110, Thailand • Marshall Cavendish (Malaysia) Sdn Bhd, Times Subang, Lot 46, Subang Hi-Tech Industrial Park, Batu Tiga, 40000 Shah Alam, Selangor Darul Ehsan, Malaysia

National Library Board Singapore Cataloguing-in-Publication Data:

Cold War Southeast Asia / edited by Malcom H. Murfett. – Singapore :
Marshall Cavendish Editions, c2012.
p. cm.
Includes bibliographical references and index.
ISBN : 978-981-4382-14-4 (pbk.)
1. Cold War – Political aspects – Southeast Asia. 2. Southeast Asia – Politics and government – 1945- I. Murfett, Malcolm H.
DS526.7
959.053 – dc23 OCN781340443

Cover photograph: LBJ Library, photo by Yoichi Okamoto
Printed in Singapore by Fabulous Printers Pte Ltd

CONTENTS

PREFACE

This volume of essays on the Cold War in Southeast Asia grew out of a series of very popular public lectures held on a monthly basis at the National Library in Singapore from September 2008 to May 2009. Enthusiastically supported by the Asia Research Institute, the Department of History at the National University of Singapore, and the History Channel, the evening lectures downtown played to full houses drawn from a wide cross-section of the general public.

Public lectures are a wonderful way of giving back to the community. It was heart-warming to see packed lecture rooms and a lively audience that really participated in the Q&A sessions following the lectures. I hope there will be more such initiatives in the future.

Once we had completed the nine lectures, I began to think of supplementing the original contributions with a number of invitations to scholars who could shed light on the political situation in those states that we hadn't had the opportunity of covering in the original series. Their contributions have helped to provide additional insights into the wider region in the years after the end of World War II when the spectre of communism was stalking the stage.

As always, acknowledging the help of others in the preparation of a book is both fitting and appropriate. My fellow authors and I have benefited greatly from the knowledge and wisdom offered to us by a group of talented librarians and archivists in research centres dotted around the world. We are especially indebted to the following institutions for their records, without which this book would never have seen the light of day: Air Force Historical

Research Agency (US), Maxwell Air Force Base, Alabama; Archives New Zealand, Wellington; Australian War Memorial, Canberra; Commonwealth Relations Office, London; Dwight D. Eisenhower Presidential Library and Museum, Abilene, Kansas; Filipinas Heritage Library, Makati; National Archives of Australia, Canberra; The National Archives of the UK, Kew Gardens, London; SAFTI Military Institute Library, Singapore; University of the Philippines Archives, Manila; US Army Combined Arms Center, Fort Leavenworth, Kansas; US Army Military History Institute, Carlisle, Pennsylvania; US National Archives, Washington, D.C.

All copyright material drawn from both public records and private collections is reproduced by permission of the relevant authorities identified in the notes.

In addition, Ang Cheng Guan wishes to thank the publisher of *Kajian Malaysia* for permission to quote from his article, 'Vietnam in 1948: An International History Perspective', which appeared in the journal in 2009 (vol. 27, nos 1 and 2, pp. 61–84).

Once again, I am indebted to Melvin Neo, the managing editor of Marshall Cavendish International (Asia), and to Justin Lau, our publishing editor, both of whom it has been a privilege to work with on this latest project of ours.

I'm also very happy to acknowledge the painstaking work of Stephanie Williams, who compiled the index with considerable distinction and admirable speed.

A final word of gratitude must go to the Lee Foundation in Singapore, which has consistently supported the editor in his research activities over more years than he cares to think about!

Malcolm H. Murfett
Singapore
25 January 2012

INTRODUCTION

Agreement on who or what caused the Cold War remains elusive—smoking guns do exist but there are rather too many of them for us to make much sense of who really pulled the trigger and brought this geopolitical reality about in the first instance. All that can be safely agreed upon is that a deep hostility between the communist and democratic states of the world had become a grim fact of life for millions of people in the years after the ending of the Second World War.

Victory in war for the Grand Alliance had come at an enormous price. Once Hitler's Nazi state had been eclipsed in Europe in May 1945 and Imperial Japan had been bombed into seeking an immediate armistice in mid-August, the rationale for the original formation of the Grand Alliance no longer applied and the tri-national grouping of the UK, US, and USSR swiftly fell apart. While the British, beset by financial and economic problems, swiftly subsided into the ranks of the also-rans, the Americans and the Soviets emerged as the two superpowers intent on leading their ideological allies and client states into the post-war period. Having won the war neither had any intention of losing the peace thereafter.

By 1947–48 the term 'Cold War', first used by George Orwell, had entered political discourse. Much like Churchill's phrase, 'Iron Curtain', it soon became popularly applied to life in post-war Europe—representing as it did an unrelenting struggle for power, influence and territory between the proponents of capitalism and communism, democracy and totalitarianism.

Although the Cold War had been spawned in Europe, it certainly did not remain confined to that continent. Instead it spread over the globe like an ideological pandemic in the post-war years, conjuring up emotive vistas of decolonisation, struggles for independence and nationalistic fervour, as well as civil wars that were often aided—clandestinely and openly—by the superpowers and their proxies.

Since 1947, official American policy towards the Soviet Union had been one of containment short of war; but the same geostrategic principles did not necessarily prevail elsewhere. This soon became clear when conflict broke out into active military engagements in Asia in the late 1940s and early 50s; in Central America in the early 1950s; and in many African states in the following decades. Whether it was civil war, major campaigns against foreign states, guerrilla or tribal warfare, the Cold War remained a convenient shorthand expression for many of these military confrontations even though there was little that was 'cold' about them.

Apart from the mountains of literature on the Vietnam War and innumerable references to the 'domino theory' that Eisenhower and others were so concerned about in the 1950s, the role of the Cold War in Southeast Asia has not been subject to much scrutiny. It is high time, therefore, to address this particular shortcoming, and that is what this volume of essays seeks to do.

We begin by looking at Vietnam in 1948, a year that represents a significant turning point in the Southeast Asian version of the Cold War. In his essay, Ang Cheng Guan illustrates that 1948—already a dramatic year for Cold War tension in Europe—was also a transformative year in Vietnam because it saw the evolution of what had previously been a colonial war into a conflict that carried much greater Cold War significance. Ang traces how Vietnam's national struggle for liberation became caught up with the global rivalry between the communist and non-communist world.

In Malaya, 1948 was also the year of two significant events: the outbreak of a communist insurgency that would only end 41 years later, and the declaration of the Malayan Emergency—events that have often been presented as part of the Cold War between the world powers. But in fact, as Cheah Boon Kheng shows, the Emergency was dictated not so much by ideological factors as by local elements. The British were using the Cold War bogey for their own purposes, Cheah explains. Inclined to put two and two together to make more than four, His Majesty's Government in London couldn't fathom the idea that a communist insurgency could begin anywhere in Southeast Asia without approval, support and direction from Beijing or Moscow. For them a conspiracy rather than a coincidence was at hand. It is fascinating to see how politicians can become convinced of a material fact when it is actually only supposition. Things haven't changed, as the hunt for Weapons of Mass Destruction in Iraq during the Blair premiership proved beyond all reasonable doubt.

Where the Philippines was concerned, the greatest immediate challenge of its newly acquired independence was to recover from the destruction brought about by the war. The year 1946 found it highly vulnerable and dependent upon the continued goodwill and aid from Washington. Its strident anti-communism was evident from the outset of the Cold War. While the default mechanism was reliance upon the US military, those views began to change, as Ricardo Jose shows in his wide-ranging essay on Manila's foreign and defence policies from 1946 to 1986. A sense of dissatisfaction with being taken for granted by Washington arose as the years passed and led to Filipino leaders exploring other avenues of support in the search for more effective policies. Whether they found any is a moot point. In those early post-war years Filipinos could find sympathy with the old, but surely not apocryphal, British sentiment about the Americans being "over-paid, over-sexed, and over here". As the US military lost its way and became bogged down in an unwinnable war in Vietnam, Ferdinand Marcos released himself from the constraints of democracy and began forging a more obviously independent foreign policy. Nixon *et al* might complain, but the resident of the Malacañang Palace sensed that the force was with him and that the prevailing currents of the Cold War could be best negotiated on his terms. They were—for a time.

Military alliances have frequently proven to be more effective on paper than in reality, but SEATO took this shortcoming to another degree altogether. Formed in 1954, the Southeast Asia Treaty Organization brought together the US, UK, Australia, France, New Zealand, Pakistan, the Philippines and Thailand, with hopes of being the NATO of Southeast Asia. Brian Farrell's meticulous examination of SEATO's plans for dealing with the strategic threat facing the region reveals the quite staggering extent to which the war planners were prepared to go in thwarting China's rise to power within the Asian continent. It is difficult not to feel a sense of rising incredulity as one studies the details of 'Plan 4', which coolly and dispassionately addressed the use of tactical nuclear strikes by the US and UK against the People's Liberation Army whenever and wherever it threatened to raise its multitudinous head beyond the borders of the PRC. SEATO planners and their political bosses obviously hoped that these surgical strikes against formidable conventional forces both in southern China and northern Vietnam wouldn't escalate into some global thermonuclear conflict, but they couldn't guarantee that a first-strike capacity would 'seal the deal' in their favour. After all, who knew what would happen once the lid to Pandora's Box had been ripped open in this extraordinary manner? Anything was possible. Nuclear deterrence might be viable, but what if it wasn't? For all the work lavished upon it, Plan 4—an exercise in profound futility—passed into counterfactual history as another grisly what-might-have-been. One can only breathe a sigh of intense relief at its singular demise.

While SEATO was geared to intercept and repel communism in Southeast Asia by military means, the British government envisaged a diplomatic 'Grand Design'. By amalgamating its colonies—Malaya, Singapore, Sarawak, Brunei and North Borneo—

into a single political entity, it hoped to bring them strength in unity in a vulnerable region supposedly characterised by a set of potentially falling dominos. Lee Kuan Yew, the astute but irascible Singaporean lawyer who swept into power at the head of the People's Action Party government in 1959, never doubted that size mattered. He was convinced that a merger with Malaya made the most sense. His older, more regal and urbane equivalent in Kuala Lumpur, Tunku Abdul Rahman, was much less enthusiastic about diluting his Malay community's national identity by welcoming a potentially radical Chinese diaspora into their midst. Tan Tai Yong's essay explores why the Tunku changed his mind and embraced an enlarged union in 1963. It was a decision, of course, he lived to deeply regret.

Whereas Malaysia and Singapore were spared by their geographical location from being in the front line against the actual or perceived communist threat in the region, the same could not be said of Thailand, whose borders were contiguous with those of Indochina for over 2000 km and behind which danger was acknowledged to lurk. For the fiercely independent and anti-communist Thais, the idea of any kind of foreign oppression—whether ideologically or militarily induced—was anathema. Wishing to keep all destabilising influences at bay, the regimes that held sway in Bangkok in the 1960s became convinced that they must become actively involved in the war effort going on to the north and east of them. Such was the level of the military support the Thais rendered the anti-communist cause that the Americans were wont to describe Thailand as their "unsinkable aircraft carrier". For once it wasn't hyperbole. After all, Thailand wasn't content to just put 12,000 men symbolically into the field against the Viet Cong in South Vietnam; they had nearly double that number engaged in covert operations in Laos, where their presence was vital to the maintenance of the anti-communist cause in their neighbouring buffer state. Sutayut Osornprasop's essay on how this long-running clandestine engagement began reveals the lengths to which the Thais were prepared to go to secure their objectives in the fierce struggle for supremacy within Laos.

Indochina is also the focus of Bruce Lockhart's account of how Cambodia and Laos fared in the elusive search for neutralism while the Vietnam War raged beyond their borders. Mutual mistrust was never far from the surface of official relations between the US and the keenly sensitive, periodically undiplomatic Norodom Sihanouk of Cambodia. Presidents could come and go in the US, but relations with Phnom Penh remained fraught. US enmity for the unreliable and intemperate Khmer prince sank to far greater depths than the qualified disdain that the Eisenhower administration reserved for the more inscrutable Souvanna Phouma of Laos. In the early years of the Indochinese imbroglio the Lao prince was seen as being woefully naive and easily manipulated by leftist influences. Over the years that attitude was gradually replaced by a grudging respect for this quintessential political survivor, who came to be seen as the key figure in holding Laos together in the heavy turbulence accompanying the struggle against communism in the region.

Before the onset of WWII, the US Army had largely ignored Southeast Asia as a potential theatre for military operations. Even the American colony of the Philippines was seen as a Pacific concern and not strictly an Asian one. Little apparently changed in the immediate post-war years until the region was 'rediscovered' by President Truman, the Joint Chiefs of Staff and the National Security Council in 1949 as a likely focus for Cold War struggle and intrigue. In his essay, 'Before the Quagmire', Brian Linn considers how US Army officers proposed to deal with the political and military threat being posed by the communists in a relatively unfamiliar world with a 'broken army' and a feckless SEATO. Much needed to be done to fix the US Army and make it a more robust fighting unit. Even then it looked a tough assignment to arrest communism around the globe. Worse still, those within the military whose gaze fell upon Southeast Asia admitted it was a task that was totally beyond the countries within the region. It followed, therefore, that since Southeast Asia couldn't be left to its own devices, and the fall of the region to communism was beyond the pale, what practical alternative was there left for the US military but to involve itself in defending South Vietnam?

Unlike the Americans, who felt increasingly drawn into Southeast Asia, the British tried everything they could to go in the opposite direction. Harold Macmillan, the inheritor of the post-Suez mess in 1957, sensed that the 'wind of change' blowing through Africa by the early 1960s—bringing in its wake accelerated decolonisation and the inauguration of newly independent states—would spill over to the littoral states of Southeast Asia, where remnants of the British Empire co-existed rather uneasily with one another and with the dominant power in the region, Indonesia. Acknowledging that communism remained a threat on the horizon, Macmillan embraced decolonisation on a grand scale as the best means of reducing the UK's military responsibilities in the region. Ironically, however, as Malcolm Murfett demonstrates, orchestrating something less than the whole—Brunei choosing to remain outside the enlarged state of Malaysia—left neither Moscow nor Beijing quaking in their boots, but was still more than enough to set the Indonesians off on their campaign of *Konfrontasi.* As a result, the British were once again forced to gird their loins, reach for their wallet, and ramp up their military to keep the Indonesians from reconfiguring the region in their own image. Notably successful in doing this, the British still needed the hostile Sukarno regime to implode before *Konfrontasi* became a thing of the past. Thereafter, the Wilson government acrimoniously managed to renege on its obligations to the Americans as well as their own former equatorial subjects and churlishly left both to tackle the communist menace on their own. It was not quite what the term 'special relationship' is meant to imply.

If the flamboyant Sukarno thought that dabbling with communism gave him added force in dealing with both his external enemies and internal foes, he was dramatically disabused of this notion in the months following the Untung coup in September 1965. His successor, General Soeharto, was under no such illusions. In her account of the 'New Order' government that replaced Sukarno's exercise in 'Guided Democracy,' Dewi Fortuna Anwar charts how Soeharto first sidelined the 'father of the nation' and then exercised ruthless power in Jakarta and throughout the archipelago for the next 32 years. Soeharto didn't need any coaching in loathing the communists and was only too willing to crush them and those thought to be fellow travellers in the aftermath of the 1965 coup. Over the following years Western capitals, who should have known better, generally turned a blind eye to the excesses and rampant corruption of the Soeharto regime. Pragmatism won out; the West appreciated that Indonesia could be relied upon as the leading anti-communist bastion in ASEAN. This argument also helps to explain why the West appears to have given their unspoken encouragement to the Indonesians to invade East Timor after the Portuguese withdrew their colonial administration from Dili in 1975. Soeharto, therefore, played the anti-communist card with great Javanese aplomb. It served him well.

In the last essay of this volume, Merle Ricklefs, who has done so much to advance the cause of Southeast Asian studies over a storied career, looks back on the Cold War and poses a crucial, overarching question: to what degree should the Cold War be held responsible for changing things in the region? His answer, typically robust and scholarly, is that the influence of the Cold War can be vastly overstated. Apart from anything else, only the US of the three superpowers was a consistent player in the region and a conspicuously unsuccessful one at that. Its client states benefited from its prolonged largesse and nimbly exploited the existing geopolitical circumstances to suit themselves. Sadly, US investment in these states rarely advanced the cause of true democracy. For many years it was often sufficient for these recipients of American aid merely to flourish the tokens of anti-communism to ensure that their paymasters would continue to support them regardless of their serious domestic shortcomings. Once the Soviet Union fell and the Cold War passed into history in the early 1990s, however, the world looked a radically different ideological place and new rules applied, as the Soeharto regime was to discover to its cost in 1998.

Before looking more closely at those countries of Southeast Asia that were caught up in the Cold War, it must be acknowledged that Burma—the largest of all the mainland states in the region and the one most devastated by the campaigns fought on its territory in World War II—was not one of them. Once it had thrown off the colonial yoke and attained its independence from the British in January 1948, Burma sought to project an external image of positive neutralism and genuine nonalignment in which ideology wouldn't feature. After entering the United Nations in April 1948, Burma became progressively disenchanted with international organisations, joining only the Colombo Plan (1952), the Asian Development Bank (1973) and ASEAN (1997), and avoiding SEATO, MAPHILINDO and ASA altogether. It would even eventually withdraw from the Non-Aligned Movement in 1979. Although pilloried by the Western media for a string of human rights abuses, rampant corruption, active involvement in the drug trade and pitiful economic development, Burma was at least consistent in its foreign relations throughout the Cold War. It wished neither to become a satellite of any of the big powers (PRC, US, let alone the Soviet Union) nor be drawn into any of their 'proxy wars'. Burma steered this non-confrontational course adroitly from the time that the PRC was founded in October 1949 and was always cognizant of its geographical vulnerabilities thereafter. A pithy Burmese expression encapsulated the issue starkly: "[W]hen China spits we swim down the Irrawaddy." Even so, one suspects that the key to the Burmese 'success' in keeping out of the Cold War lay more with the PRC being willing to play ball with this notion in the short to medium term rather than on the sublime Buddhist pacifism of U Nu, or the pragmatic xenophobic suspicion of Ne Win. In a sense, Burma was the 'elephant in the room' during the Cold War. China didn't feel threatened by it and the West came to abhor it.

While Burma successfully resolved not to be "caught under the clash of swords", the other nations of Southeast Asia were not so fortunate. Whether one loved it or loathed it, the Cold War couldn't merely be wished away from the region, as the absorbing essays in this volume will now reveal.

2

THE ORIGINS OF THE COLD WAR IN SOUTHEAST ASIA: THE CASE OF VIETNAM

Ang Cheng Guan

1948 has often been said to be a turning point for Southeast Asia. In that year, many of the region's communist parties—specifically those in Burma, Malaya, Indonesia and the Philippines—switched from a broad united-front strategy to armed revolt. The Moscow-controlled World Federation of Democratic Youth had in February organised the Southeast Asia Youth and Student Conference in Calcutta, to which the countries of the region had sent delegations. The influence of the 'Calcutta Conference' has been hotly debated: Did Soviet directives disseminated at the conference lead to the revolts in the various Southeast Asian countries, as the 'orthodox' school believes? Or were there in fact no instructions from Moscow—the 'revisionist' argument—and the revolts were parochially motivated, unconnected with the conference?[1] This chapter examines the case of Vietnam, which sent a delegation to Calcutta, and for whom 1948 appears to be the year their struggle for liberation assumed a new ideological complexion—shifting from a nationalist/anti-colonial basis to include communist/anti-capitalist sentiment—the year it became conjoined with the global Great Power rivalry of the Cold War.[2]

1. Roundtable on the Sixtieth Anniversary of 1948: Reassessing the Origins of the Cold War in Southeast Asia, organised by the Asia Research Institute, National University of Singapore (10–11 July 2008). Some of the papers of the roundtable were published in the *Journal of Southeast Asian Studies*, vol. 40, no. 3 (Oct 2009) and in *Kajian Malaysia*, vol. 27, nos 1 and 2 (Dec 2009).

2. It is instructive to read Wang Gungwu, 'The Limits of Decolonisation' in Marc Frey et al. (eds), *The Transformation of Southeast Asia: International Perspectives on Decolonisation* (Armonk, NY: M.E. Sharpe, 2003), chapter 17.

Background

On 2 September 1945, some three weeks after the Japanese surrendered to the Allies in the Pacific War, Ho Chi Minh proclaimed the birth of the Democratic Republic of Vietnam (DRV) at Ba Dinh Square in Hanoi. This was possible because earlier in March the Japanese had removed French control over Indochina and at the same time did not prevent Ho and his associates from taking power. Ho's government was soon able to consolidate control over North and Central Vietnam, when Chinese (Kuomintang) troops, who had been charged at the Potsdam Conference with the task of disarming Japanese troops north of the 16th parallel, withdrew in March 1946. Ho's government was unable, however, to control the South (Cochin China), as the French were able to regain power there with the support of the British, who had been charged with disarming Japanese troops south of the 16th parallel. The weakness of Ho's provisional government and the intransigence of the French—who had no intention at all of relinquishing control over Indochina—resulted in a series of abortive negotiations between March and September 1946, eventually culminating in the First Indochina War, or what the Vietnamese call the 'War of Resistance against the French,' which began on 19 December 1946.

The eve of 1948

On 7 October 1947, the French launched a major offensive into the Viet Bac, the area between the Chinese border and the Red River, described by Nguyen Khac Vien as "the very cradle of the resistance".[3] This campaign, dubbed Operation *Lea*, lasted until the end of 1947. Its aim, in the words of the commander-in-chief of the French Army in Indochina, General Jean-Étienne Valluy, was to "pursue the Vietminh into their lair", to seize the heart of the Viet Minh stronghold—some 8000 sq km of mountainous and forested terrain—and hence consolidate French dominance not only in the urban/delta areas and cities (which they already controlled) but

3. Nguyen Khac Vien, *Vietnam: A Long History* (Hanoi: The Gioi Publishers, 1993), p. 263.

throughout North Vietnam, particularly the northern border area. In this operation, Ho Chi Minh narrowly escaped capture and he and his colleagues were forced to move out of the Viet Bac area, in which he had based himself since December 1946.

The French operation ultimately failed to eliminate the Viet Minh; it did, however, force them to abandon any plans for a conventional war against the French and to resort to guerrilla warfare. As Jacques Dalloz put it, the Viet Minh were "severely tested, but had not been forced to capitulate by a model campaign". As for the French, the fact that Operation *Lea* was not an unqualified success dashed their hopes of ending the war in one stroke.[4]

Meanwhile, in November 1947, a coup took place in Bangkok that ousted Pridi Panomyong and his Seri Thai (Free Thai Movement) allies. Pridi had been strongly supportive of the DRV's anti-colonial struggle. With Bangkok as their headquarters, Vietnamese representatives had been at the forefront in the formation of the Southeast Asian League, whose aim was to resist the return of European colonialism. An informal organisation that included representatives from Thailand, Vietnam, Cambodia, Laos, Burma, Malaya, Indonesia and the Philippines residing in Bangkok, the league was established on 8 September 1947. Evidently there had been plans to convene a special meeting to discuss foreign policy matters in light of the changing regional and international environment as well as the need for a regional institution. This had to be jettisoned, however, because of the November coup.[5]

Following the coup, Pridi was replaced by Phibun Songkhram (or, Pibulsongkram), the former prime minister, who had a track record of being anti-communist. As described in 'An Internal History of the Communist Party of Thailand': "At the end of 1947, the fascist military group again rose to power. American influ-

4. Jacques Dalloz, *The War in Indochina, 1945–54* (Dublin: Gill and Macmillan, 1990), p. 97. Also, see William J. Duiker, *Ho Chi Minh: A Life* (New York: Hyperion, 2000), pp. 408–10.

5. Christopher E. Goscha, *Thailand and the Southeast Asian Networks of the Vietnamese Revolution, 1885–1954* (Surrey: Curzon, 1999), pp. 260, 282. For details, see chapters 6 and 7.

ence began to dominate Thailand. In 1948, the Thai fascist military group signed a treaty of economic and military assistance with America. From then on, America was the number one external enemy of Thailand."[6]

For the Viet Minh, the loss of the Southeast Asian League as a consequence of the coup was one thing. But, as pointed out by Christopher Goscha, more deleterious to their cause was the possible loss of the Viet Kieu (overseas Vietnamese) and trading networks in Thailand, which had been so critical to sustaining their struggle against the French.[7]

The year 1948

The Viet Minh leadership entered 1948 with these problems hanging over their heads. There is consensus among Vietnamese historians that from 1948 onwards the Viet Minh gradually seized the initiative from the French, culminating in their victory in the 1950 Border Campaign, one of the major turning points in the War of Resistance against the French (First Indochina War).[8] But that is an evaluation in hindsight. A recent study is perhaps more accurate in suggesting that in 1948, "no major maneuver operations took place; troops were dispersed in small posts for local security. The 'War on the roads' was initiated on the Tonkin/China border, as the VM repeatedly ambushed convoys serving French posts along RC (Route Coloniale) 4 and RC 3bis, and mounted probing attacks on small garrisons."[9]

According to the official Vietnamese history, in the wake of Operation *Lea*, the Party Central Committee convened an enlarged session on 15 January 1948, where it laid down the strategic plan

6. 'An Internal History of the Communist Party of Thailand' (first drafted in 1974, updated in 1978), translated from the Thai by Chris Baker, *Journal of Contemporary Asia*, vol. 33, no. 4 (2003): 510–41.

7. Goscha, *Thailand*, pp. 282–3.

8. Lien-Hang T. Nguyen, 'Vietnamese Historians and the First Indochina War' in Mark Atwood Lawrence and Fredrik Logevall (eds), *The First Vietnam War: Colonial Conflict and Cold War Crisis* (Cambridge, MA: Harvard University Press, 2007), chapter 3.

9. Andrew Wiest (ed.), *Rolling Thunder in a Gentle Land: The Vietnam War Revisited* (Oxford: Osprey Publishing Ltd, 2006), p. 40.

for 1948.[10] Anticipating that the French would ramp up their operations in the North and consolidate their control of the South, the Viet Minh leadership resolved to "smash the enemy's winter offensive in Bac Bo [northern Vietnam] and to foil the mopping up operations in Nam Bo [southern Vietnam]" through "a people's war" in enemy-controlled territories. The objective was to "destroy the enemy's isolated positions and narrow their zone of occupation", to drive the French out of Viet Bac, in particular the provinces of Bac Can, Cao Bang and Lao Cai.

To achieve this, the main force was divided into "independent companies along with armed propaganda teams to penetrate deep into enemy-controlled areas, to set up political bases, to develop the militia force and to start a guerrilla war". Indeed, guerrilla warfare would now be the main form of fighting while mobile warfare would play a secondary role. Through this, the leadership hoped that they would be able to gradually rebuild their regular army and that the balance of forces would eventually tilt in their favour. To ensure that there was effective command and control of the guerrilla war, the Central Committee consolidated the seven zones in Bac Bo into three inter-zones (1, 3 and 10); the four zones in Trung Bo (central Vietnam) would become inter-zones 4 and 5; and in Nam Bo, there would be three inter-zones (7, 8 and 9). The Saigon-Cholon zone would be designated a special zone. The most difficult task was how to convey effectively the Central Committee's decisions down to the local level—1948 was described as "a year when the war raged everywhere".[11] At least two major cadre conferences were convened, in May and August 1948, and another in January 1949, to disseminate the January 1948 decisions.

In July 1948, the Supreme Defence Council, under the chair-

10. '40 Years of Party Activity', *Vietnam Documents and Research Notes*, no. 76, p. 123; *The 30-Year War 1945–1975, Volume 1: 1945–1954* (Hanoi: The Gioi Publishers, 2000), pp. 135–6; *Ban Nghien Cuu Lich Su Dang Trung Cong, Nam Muoi Nam Hoat Dong Vua Dang Cong San Viet Nam* (Hanoi: Nha Xuat Ban Su That, 1982), pp. 98–9; *Lich Su Quan Doi Nhan Dan Viet Nam, Tap I* (Hanoi: Nha Xuat Ban Quan Doi Nhan Dan, 1977), pp. 331–4.

11. *The 30-Year War 1945–1975, Volume 1: 1945–1954*, p. 135.

manship of Ho Chi Minh, was established. The objective was "to achieve a unified, concentrated leadership over all fields of resistance work." More than a hundred representatives from the battle zones, army generals and senior officials of the Defence Ministry-Army High Command met in Viet Bac in mid-July, at the 5th Military Conference, to evaluate and exchange views and experiences of the resistance war. Some key conclusions reached at this conference were (a) the Vietnamese way of fighting so far could be described as 'mobile guerrilla warfare', distinct from guerrilla warfare in that the forces involved were much larger and the objective was annihilation and not attrition; (b) there was a need to remain close to the people—"The terrain might be temporarily lost, but by remaining close the people, the lost terrain could be regained"[12]; (c) there were supply/logistics difficulties in some areas; and (d) it was not yet a 'war of movement' (which was the eventual goal) because the Vietnamese soldiers were still poorly trained, ill-equipped and technologically inferior to the enemy. Combat was therefore restricted or confined to tactics such as encirclement, ambush, surprise raid, or combinations of these forms.

Until July 1948, Viet Minh troops were unable to attack any platoon-size positions. The change came in the battle at Phu Thong (located along Highway 3 from Cao Bang) on 25 July 1948, when the Viet Minh 11th Battalion succeeded in assaulting the French post, defended by a hundred or so legionaries. The operation won commendation from the party's Central Committee and the 11th Battalion was renamed the Phu Thong Battalion. According to the Viet Minh official history, it was the 11th Battalion "which ushered in the movement to wipe out small enemy garrisons at the threshold of the season of military deeds in the autumn-winter of 1948".[13]

But such successes were limited. The Viet Minh revolutionary leaders had little military training, according to David Elliot, and had to learn through trial and error; "surprising military

12. Ibid., pp. 141–2.

13. Ibid., pp. 141–5.

success[es] were followed by crushing defeats, but each time the revolutionaries regrouped, [they] analyzed their performance and set about devising a new response to overcome the difficulties".[14] Citing a French military observer, William Duiker noted that after Operation *Lea* the conflict became a "war of stagnation".[15]

The second problem that the Vietnamese communist leadership had to tackle in 1948 was the fallout of the coup in Thailand.[16] In an attempt to protect its Thai operations, General Nguyen Binh sent a personal letter of congratulations to the new prime minister, Phibun Songkhram, on 10 February, "as part of a well-calculated bid to maintain Thai sympathy at this crucial point in the supplying of the south".[17] Besides extending the good wishes of the Vietnamese, Binh also played on Thai antipathy towards the French. This apparently succeeded and, at least initially, Bangkok allowed the Vietnamese to continue their activities in Thailand. The Vietnamese communist leadership sent one of its most senior members, Hoang Van Hoan, to Thailand to manage the delicate situation. Hoan arrived in northeast Thailand in May 1948 and while there, established the Overseas Working Bureau, whose function would be to support the resistance in Vietnam from the west, via Laos and Cambodia.[18]

Phibun's goodwill, however, did not last beyond 1948. Immediately after the coup, Phibun had asked for US military and monetary support to strengthen the Thai army. The United States was initially reluctant because Washington viewed Phibun as a war-

14. David W.P. Elliot, *The Vietnamese War: Revolution and Social Change in the Mekong Delta 1930–1975* (Armonk, NY: M.E. Sharpe, 2007), p. 62.

15. Duiker, *Ho Chi Minh*, p. 411.

16. For a brief account of internal Thai politics in 1948, see Paul M. Handley, *The King Never Smiles: A Biography of Thailand's Bhumibol Adulyadej* (New Haven: Yale University Press, 2006), pp. 90–3.

17. Ibid., p. 283. For details, see pp. 283–4. The best account is Daniel Fineman, *A Special Relationship: The United States and Military Government in Thailand, 1947–1958* (Honolulu: University of Hawaii Press, 1997).

18. Thomas Engelbert and Christopher E. Goscha, *Falling Out of Touch: A Study on Vietnamese Communist Policy Towards an Emerging Cambodian Communist Movement, 1930–1975* (Clayton: Centre of Southeast Asian Studies, Monash University, 1995), pp. 35–6. Also see Hoang Van Hoan, *A Drop in the Ocean: Hoang Van Hoan's Revolutionary Reminiscences* (Beijing: Foreign Languages Press, 1988), part 5.

time enemy, Thailand having been an ally of the Japanese during the Pacific War. In order to change the view of the Americans and also to garner patronage and support, Phibun gradually burnished his reputation as being anti-communist and anti-Chinese. Those in the northeast of Thailand who were seen as either opponents of his government or else pro-Pridi were specially targeted and charged with plotting the separation of the northeast to be incorporated into a communist-dominated Indochina.[19] Thus, very quickly, "from viewing him in 1947 as a fascist inimical to US interests," writes Daniel Fineman, "the Americans had come to see him by late-spring 1948 as a friendly leader".[20] In April both the United States and Britain recognised Phibun's government. Within a year of assuming power, therefore, Phibun had changed his policy towards the Vietnamese communists and now vigorously clamped down on their activities in Thailand.[21]

The combination of military stalemate and changes in Thai political complexion had implications for the Vietnamese communists' relations with the Khmer Issarak (Cambodia) and the Lao Issara (Laos). Prior to Phibun, both the Khmer Issarak and Lao Issara movements had had the support of the Pridi regime as well as the Vietnamese communists, with Bangkok serving as the base for their activities. The Viet Minh mission in Bangkok directed the resistance movements in Cambodia and Laos. In the early years of the resistance, as Motoo Furuta described, "joint Cambodian-Vietnamese and Laotian-Vietnamese forces were at the core of the Khmer Issarak and Lao Issara, respectively".[22] However, because the Vietnamese communists had been preoccupied with their own liberation struggle against the French, they were until now unable

19. For details, see Chris Baker and Pasuk Phongpaichit, *A History of Thailand* (Cambridge: Cambridge University Press, 2005), pp. 144–5, and David K. Wyatt, *Thailand: A Short History* (New Haven: Yale University Press, 1984), pp. 266–8.

20. Fineman, *A Special Relationship*, p. 61.

21. Engelbert and Goscha, *Falling Out of Touch*, pp. 37–8.

22. Motoo Furuta, 'The Indochina Communist Party's Division into Three Parties: Vietnamese Communist Policy towards Cambodia and Laos, 1948–1951' in Takashi Shiraishi and Motoo Furuta (eds), *Indochina in the 1940s and 1950s* (Ithaca: Cornell Southeast Asia Program, 1992), p. 146.

to control and direct their counterparts in neighbouring Cambodia and Laos. The military stalemate forced the Vietnamese communists to extend their operations into Cambodia and Laos, which became "crucial second lines of defence" for Vietnam. At the same time, the deprivation of Thai support for the Khmer Issarak and Lao Issara led the Cambodians and Laotians to turn even more toward Vietnam for support.[23]

Apart from military strategy, the enlarged session of the Party Central Committee in January 1948 had also discussed political, economic and cultural issues. The Vietnamese communist leadership endorsed the view of the Cominform (formed in September 1947) that the world was divided into two opposing blocs, East and West, and that the Vietnamese communist resistance against the French belonged to the democratic camp of the East-West struggle.[24] Subsequently, at the August 1948 conference, the leadership redefined the Indochinese revolution as a "new democratic revolution". As Motoo Furuta noted, "through 1947 the ICP [Indochinese Communist Party] had accepted the definition used by Mao Zedong when he introduced the concept in 1940. As redefined, however, 'new democratic revolution' meant a 'people's democratic revolution' possessing the potential to evolve into socialism under communist-party direction".[25] But constrained by the ongoing armed conflict with the French, the leadership judged that it was premature to reveal their true communist colours as it would "expose it to assault from international anti-communist reactionary forces and would stir up domestic unrest among participants in the united front."[26]

In a recent article, Tuong Vu pointed out that the Indochinese Communist Party in the January and August plenums had adopted a more aggressive land policy and a more proletarian party, and that there was already "a deep and unbridgeable gap" between the communist and non-communist groups in the coa-

23. For details, see ibid., pp. 147–53.
24. Ibid., p. 156.
25. Ibid., p. 155.
26. Ibid., p. 157.

lition that "would be irreversible"[27]; but with regard to political strategy, however, it appears that the focus continued to be consolidating the unity among the population through broadening the national united front as well as securing the support of the socialist countries and "progressive, peace-loving forces of the world".[28] It is worth noting that in the spring and summer of 1947, Ho Chi Minh sent Vice-Minister Pham Ngoc Thach to Bangkok to explain Viet Minh policy to the Americans. The choice of Thach, who had served as the Vietnamese liaison to the US intelligence operative in Saigon in the autumn of 1945, could be interpreted as "an effort to capitalize on what the Vietnamese viewed as a positive encounter with the United States".[29] On 12 December 1947, the Party Central Committee circulated an internal directive explaining that "because the American threat has not been direct, statements in our media should be friendly with the United States and we should make use of the Vietnamese-American Friendship Association to favourably publicise us".[30] George Abbot, the American consul in Saigon, reporting in early 1949, found it "peculiar" that the Viet Minh had not indulged in as much anti-American propaganda as had been expected.[31] Indeed, from 1947 to early 1950, the DRV's news media avoided any criticism of Washington.[32]

27. Tuong Vu, '"It's time for the Indochinese Revolution to show its true colours": The radical turn of Vietnamese politics in 1948', *Journal of Southeast Asian Studies*, vol. 40, no. 3 (Oct 2009): 519–42. Tuong asked the question why the ICP did not break immediately with the non-communists in 1948 and follow the radical path adopted by the other Southeast Asian countries. Hopefully, this article answers his question.

28. *Ban Nghien Cuu Lich Su Dang Trung Cong*, pp. 98–9.

29. Robert S. McNamara, *Argument Without End: In Search of Answers to the Vietnam Tragedy* (New York: Public Affairs, 1999), p. 81; Mark Philip Bradley, *Imagining Vietnam and America: The Making of Postcolonial Vietnam, 1919–1950* (Chapel Hill: University of North Carolina Press, 2000), p. 150.

30. Nguyen Vu Tung, 'The Chinese Factor in the relationship between the Democratic Republic of Vietnam and the United States 1949–1968' (unpublished paper, The Norwegian Nobel Institute, 1995), pp. 8–9. The Vietnamese-American Friendship Association was formed on 17 October 1945. Tung quoted from Party Documents, Volume 4 (Hanoi: compiled and internally circulated by the Nguyen Ai Quoc Party High School, 1964).

31. Andrew J. Rotter, *The Path to Vietnam: Origins of the American Commitment to Southeast Asia* (Ithaca: Cornell University Press, 1987), p. 101.

32. Nguyen Vu Tung, 'The Chinese Factor', pp. 8–9. Nguyen cites personal interviews with Vietnamese researchers in

In addition to the United States, the Viet Minh also tried to enlist the assistance of the Kuomintang (KMT) government in Nanjing (Nanking). Twice in 1947 Ho Chi Minh sent a Viet Minh delegation to Nanjing but both times they failed. The mission led by Nguyen Duc Thuy which left for China during Operation *Lea* returned to Viet Bac in late spring 1948. The failure of the second attempt to reach Nanjing was also Ho's last attempt to connect with the KMT. After the fall of Manchuria to the Chinese communists in October 1948, Ho dropped further requests for KMT support.[33]

The Calcutta Conference, February 1948

Against this backdrop, the Calcutta Conference of Youth and Students of Southeast Asia Fighting for Freedom and Independence[34] convened from 19 to 26 February 1948. Because this conference placed much emphasis on the use of violence, contemporary analysts linked the conference to the communist-led insurgencies that erupted in Burma, Malaya and Indonesia soon after. In the case of Vietnam, as we have noted, the war had already started in December 1946.

The Vietnamese delegation to the conference was given the honour of delivering the keynote message, which in the event was a detailed discussion of the Vietnamese experience in guerrilla warfare.[35] While the military focus of the report seemingly gelled with the general tenor of the conference, the Vietnamese position actually differed from the consensus position. The Calcutta Conference issued a political thesis that reiterated the Zhdanov inter-

Hanoi and party documents compiled and circulated by the Nguyen Ai Quoc Party High School. The most detailed account of the DRV's attempts to cultivate the Americans in 1947 is found in Bradley, *Imagining Vietnam and America,* chapter 5.

33. For details, see King C. Chen, *Vietnam and China 1938–1954* (Princeton: Princeton University Press, 1969).

34. See Ruth McVey, *The Calcutta Conference and the Southeast Asian Uprisings* (Ithaca: Cornell Modern Indonesia Project, 1958).

35. Vietnam was represented at the conference by a delegation of seven Viet Minh military officers, which, as Ruth McVey has suggested, was perhaps the reason for the military emphasis in the report. But given that the Vietnamese communists had only

pretation of the international situation[36]; it condemned the Indian socialists for openly preaching "the illusion that socialism may be achieved by constitutional means" and called upon the communists to forge a "Democratic Front of all militant sections and honest revolutionaries to launch the final struggle to win real freedom and democracy". But, according to Ruth McVey, "the Vietnamese delegates showed no inclination to accept the meeting's declaration as law". Indeed, they denied its most important point—the rejection of all compromise with imperialism—instead approving of the Indian and Burmese path toward independence. They were apparently unrepentant in spite of criticism. "Upon returning from the conference the Vietnamese expressed irritation at the attempts to impose the international line on the Vietnamese movement."[37] The Vietnamese steadfastly maintained that the "struggle for independence and democracy takes on a different character according to the actual conditions prevailing in each country".[38]

The Calcutta Conference, then, did not have any immediate effect on the Viet Minh experience. This is not to say that the Vietnamese communist leadership did not subscribe to the view of a world divided between the socialists led by the Soviet Union and the imperialists led by the United States. Indeed, the ICP had anticipated the two camps as early as their Eighth Plenum in May 1941.[39] But while some quarters within the Viet Minh leadership supported Andrei Zhdanov's 'two camp' theory, the general consensus was inclined towards the pragmatic view that the bourgeoisie could still be harnessed against the anti-imperialist movement as part of a front led by the communist party.

recently engaged the French militarily, it was not surprising that the Vietnamese report focused on their military experience and current condition. See ibid.

36. Cited in M.R. Masani, *The Communist Party of India: A Short History* (London: Derek Verschoyle, 1954), pp. 89–90, 281–2 note 4, 283 note 5.

37. Ibid., p. 23.

38. Ibid., p. 15.

39. I am grateful to Tuong Vu for sharing with me his paper, 'From Cheering to Volunteering: Vietnamese Communists and the Coming of the Cold War, 1940–1951', which was subsequently published in Christopher E. Goscha and Christian F. Ostermann (eds), *Connecting Histories: Decolonization and the Cold War in Southeast Asia, 1945–1962* (Stanford: Stanford University Press, 2009).

This strategy would change in 1949 but the slow shift was already discernible from 1948. To better understand the reasons for the change and the process, we now need to turn to the involvement of the United States, Soviet Union and China.

The United States, Soviet Union and China

Washington had for some years been concerned about the communist character of Ho Chi Minh's government.[40] It had received intelligence reports of DRV contact with Moscow and the Chinese Communist Party headquarters in north China, and of Viet Minh cadres being trained by the Soviets and the Chinese communists. In fact, as early as 1946, the US consul in Saigon warned that should the Viet Minh manage to evict the French, Indochina would be vulnerable to capture by international communism.[41] The DRV's attempts to convince the Truman administration of its moderate stance in 1947, in hope of garnering American support, were unsuccessful.

At the beginning of 1948, neither Washington nor London had yet formed a coherent policy towards the First Indochina War. Recent scholarship generally agrees that it was developments in China in 1948 and 1949[42] rather than in Vietnam that led Washington to focus more intently on the danger of communism in Southeast Asia (just as the British gradually became more willing to support the French following the communist insurrection in Malaya from 1948). This gradual change of attitude from ini-

40. Scholarship in the English language on Vietnam between 1944 and 1950 is relatively scanty compared to the historiography of the Indochina Wars post-1950, particularly after the United States became involved. See Mark Atwood Lawrence, *Assuming the Burden: Europe and the American Commitment to War in Vietnam* (Berkeley: University of California Press, 2005); Bradley, *Imagining Vietnam and America*. See also Robert J. McMahon, *The Limits of Empire: The United States and Southeast Asia Since World War II* (New York: Columbia University Press, 1999), chapter 2; William J. Duiker, *Sacred War: Nationalism and Revolution in a Divided Vietnam* (New York: McGraw Hill, Inc., 1995), p. 60.

41. For details, see Lawrence, *Assuming the Burden*.

42. For the historiography of Sino-US relations, see Warren I. Cohen (ed.), *Pacific Passage: The Study of American-East Asian Relations on the Eve of the Twenty-First Century* (New York: Columbia University Press, 1966), chapters 1, 7 and 9.

tial sympathy for the anti-colonial struggle in Southeast Asia can be discerned from the Department of State policy paper of 27 September 1948, which addressed the need to eliminate communism in Southeast Asia and to foster governments friendly to the United States. With regard to Vietnam, the difficulty was how to support both the interests of the French and at the same time fulfil the aspirations of the Vietnamese people, how to strengthen the position of the nationalists and weaken the communists. The paper however offered no clear solution as to how to achieve a win-win situation for both the French and the Vietnamese, though it recognised that a French withdrawal would lead to communist domination of Vietnam, and possibly even Chinese Communist domination.[43]

By the end of 1949, however, the United States began to place Vietnam in the context of a West-versus-East, democracy-versus-communism dichotomy. This was clearly spelt out in a Pentagon paper, 'The Position of the US with respect to Asia' (NSC 48/2), dated 30 December 1949.[44] Washington's changed attitude had serious implications for Vietnam. In February 1950, Washington recognised the French-created Bao Dai government and also pressured Bangkok to recognise it, which it did, under Phibun, the following month.

In May 1950, Washington finally gave its support to the French war effort in Indochina. Between 1945 and 1948, recalled Luu Doan Huynh, the Americans had been more or less neutral about the war in Vietnam—"maybe not 100 percent. Maybe 80 percent neutral.... To us, 80 percent neutral was acceptable." Huynh pinpointed 1950, "not before, not after", as when the American "downfall" began.[45] To the Vietnamese communists, 1950 was the year

43. William J. Duiker, *U.S. Containment Policy and the Conflict in IndoChina* (Stanford: Stanford University Press, 1994), pp. 66–7.

44. See *The Pentagon Papers: Senator Gravel Edition*, Volume 1 (Boston: Beacon, 1971); Yano Toru, 'Who Set the Stage for the Cold War in Southeast Asia?' in Yonosuke Nagai and Akira Iriye (eds), *The Origins of the Cold War in Asia* (Tokyo: University of Tokyo Press, 1977), pp. 321–37.

45. McNamara, *Argument Without End*, p. 81.

the United States intervened in Vietnam. In the words of Nguyen Khac Huynh, "After this 'intervention', the Vietnamese people perceived both the French and the Americans as the enemy."[46]

With regard to Soviet assistance to the Viet Minh, the current scholarly consensus is that there is still no evidence to support this. Ilya Gaiduk, who studied the Soviet sources on the Vietnam War, advised those who are searching for the origins of Soviet involvement in the Indochina conflict to pay particular attention to what happened in Moscow in late 1949 and early 1950, noting that nothing significant in Soviet-Vietnam relations happened before that.[47]

Despite its professed sympathy for the struggles of national liberation, Moscow never paid much attention to Southeast Asia during this period. Indeed the Soviets had been apprehensive that the Viet Minh's war of resistance against the French would adversely affect the political prospects of the French Communist Party (FCP) in France. Both British and American intelligence were hard-pressed to find any concrete evidence of Soviet-Viet Minh connections. As an Office of Intelligence Research report submitted in the autumn of 1948 tersely remarked, "if there is a Moscow-directed conspiracy in Southeast Asia, Indochina is an anomoly [*sic*] so far."[48]

Moscow was apparently critical of Ho Chi Minh's insistence on maintaining the united-front approach and also his dissolution of the Indochinese Communist Party in November 1945.[49] There were no Soviet contacts with Ho until 1949, according to William Duiker, and Stalin was skeptical that the Viet Minh could win the war against the French and doubtful, too, whether Ho was a genuine Marxist-Leninist.[50] It was only with Mao's strong recommendation that Moscow eventually recognised the DRV on 30 January

46. Ibid., pp. 78–9.
47. Ilya V. Gaiduk, *Confronting Vietnam: Soviet Policy Toward the Indochina Conflict, 1954–1963* (Stanford: Stanford University Press, 2003), p. 1.
48. Rotter, *The Path to Vietnam*, p. 101.
49. William J. Duiker, *The Communist Road to Power in Vietnam* (Boulder: Westview Press, 1996), p. 142.
50. See Duiker, *Ho Chi Minh*, pp. 418–23, 648–9 notes 29 and 30.

1950—after Beijing had done so—and willingly left the Viet Minh to the guidance of the Chinese.[51]

We must now turn to the all-important Sino-Vietnamese connection in this puzzle. Chinese accounts acknowledged that Vietnamese and Chinese communists became much closer after the 1917 October Revolution in Russia. Much of Ho's early revolutionary activities were conducted in the Guangxi (Kwangsi) border area, which served as the base for the Vietnamese communists. As King Chen noted, the Viet Minh's sanctuary in the border areas between Vietnam and China—Guangxi and Yunnan—and the co-operation between the Vietnamese and Chinese communists were important factors that made it possible for the Viet Minh to survive the French attacks in 1947–48.[52]

On the Chinese Communist side, during the War of Liberation (Chinese Civil War, April 1927 to May 1950), when the Guangdong-Guangxi and Yunnan-Guangxi detachments encountered difficulties from the KMT attacks, they moved into the Viet Minh-liberated areas.[53] One such case is worth highlighting. In 1946, the First Regiment of the Southern Guangdong People's Force, which was the main CCP force in Guangdong-Guangxi, moved into Vietnam to avoid the KMT attack. It was a small and poorly equipped regiment. While in Vietnam, where they remained till August 1949 at the request of Ho, the regiment helped to train the Viet Minh troops, specifically officers, and to set up an intelligence system. By July 1947, over 830 Viet Minh cadres had been trained. An overseas-Chinese self-defence force numbering over 1000 was also created and subsequently incorporated into the Viet Minh army.[54] However, Hoang Van Hoan (who was the DRV's first ambassador

51. For an account of Soviet-Viet Minh relations 1945–50, see Christopher E. Goscha, 'Courting Diplomatic Disaster? The Difficult Integration of Vietnam into the International Communist Movement (1945–1950)', *Journal of Vietnamese Studies*, vol. 1, nos 1 and 2 (Feb/Aug 2006): 59–103.

52. Chen, *Vietnam and China 1938–1954*, pp. 192–5.

53. Journal of International Studies editorial board, 'Facts about Sino-Vietnamese relations', *China and the World* (1979), p. 99.

54. Qiang Zhai, *China and the Vietnam Wars, 1950–1974* (Chapel Hill: University of North Carolina Press, 2000), pp. 11–12.

to China) recalled that between 1947 and 1949, the military situations in Vietnam and China made Sino-Vietnamese communication very difficult.[55] Chinese sources confirm that ties between the two parties were limited between 1945 and 1949. There is also no evidence of any substantial Chinese technical assistance during this period.

A new phase in the Viet Minh's international linkages emerged in the first half of 1948.[56] After pursuing a strategy of cultivating both communists and non-communists in the region, the Viet Minh leadership in mid-1948 strengthened its ties with the Chinese communists, who at the same time were taking a growing interest in Southeast Asia and the Viet Minh in particular. This phase of improving relations between the Chinese communists and the Viet Minh was marked by cross-border collaboration between the two sides. In his message to the 5th Cadres Conference (8–16 August 1948), Truong Chinh observed that the French were becoming more dependent on the American imperialists. He anticipated that the eventual victory of the CCP would have a major positive impact on the Vietnamese resistance struggle. This did not mean that the Viet Minh would rely on 'outsiders', but a united front of the Vietnamese and Chinese communists would certainly be better able to resist the American-French imperialists.[57]

According to Chinese Communist accounts, their War of Liberation reached its "decisive phase" in the autumn of 1948. Victory, however, was not yet a foregone conclusion. Significantly, total KMT military strength still exceeded that of the PLA. The CCP leadership led by Mao Zedong decided to throw caution to the wind and launched three consecutive major campaigns from September 1948: the Liaoxi-Shenyang campaign, the Huai-Hai

55. Hoang Van Hoan, 'Distortions of Facts about Militant Friendship between Vietnam and China is Impermissible', *Beijing Review* (7 Dec 1979), p. 12.

56. Laura Calkin, 'Sino-Vietminh Relations 1948–1952', unpublished PhD thesis, SOAS, University of London, 1990.

57. Truong Chinh, 'We Struggle for Independence and Democracy', distributed at the Fifth Central Cadres Conference, 8–16 Aug 1948, in *Lich Su Quan Doi Nhan Dan Viet Nam, Tap I*, pp. 334–5.

campaign and the Beijing-Tianjin campaign. On 23 April 1949, the PLA finally captured Nanjing, the KMT capital. The military success of the Chinese communists was fortuitous for their Vietnamese counterparts. Not only was their military struggle against the French at a stalemate,[58] in late 1948 they were also under great pressure to relocate their Bangkok-based liaison headquarters.[59] Chinese Communist military forces gave substantial operational assistance to the Viet Minh for the first time in early 1949. Before the First Regiment returned to southern China in autumn 1949 it helped create the first PAVN (People's Army of Vietnam) division in August 1949.[60]

While the Chinese Civil War was still going on, and even when the Chinese communists appeared to be winning, especially after taking Manchuria in October 1948, Ho remained very cautious and discreet about Sino-Vietnamese relations (although, as noted earlier, after the fall of Manchuria, he ceased requests for KMT support).[61] Up till late August 1949 he appeared neutral—despite the fact that his colleagues had on various occasions remarked that the success of the Chinese communists would be positive for the Viet Minh. The current consensus among scholars is that the Chinese Communist victory in 1949, together with the founding of the PRC on 1 October 1949, was a critical turning point in the Vietnamese colonial struggle. Shortly after 1 October, Ho Chi Minh dispatched two envoys, Ly Bich Son and Nguyen Duc Thuy, to Beijing to seek Chinese assistance.[62] It is also from late 1949 that the Vietnamese-French war took on a significant international dimension and became part of the wider Cold War struggle.

The DRV and the PRC established official diplomatic relations on 18 January 1950. According to Nguyen Vu Tung, based on his interviews with Vietnamese researchers in Hanoi in 1994, Beijing

58. Elliot, *The Vietnamese War*, pp. 70–1; Duiker, *U.S. Containment Policy*, p. 87; Nguyen Khac Vien, *Vietnam: A Long History*, p. 267.

59. Engelbert and Goscha, *Falling Out of Touch*, pp. 38–9.

60. Zhai, *China and the Vietnam Wars*, p. 12.

61. For details, see Chen, *Vietnam and China 1938–1954*.

62. Zhai, *China and the Vietnam Wars*, p. 13.

pressured a reluctant Ho Chi Minh into it. Ho had gone to Beijing in January 1950 not to establish diplomatic relations but to seek aid. He wanted to avoid having to explicitly take sides for fear of inviting US military intervention in Vietnam. In fact, in his interviews with Andrew Roth and Salt Sanders in the autumn of 1949, Ho had told the two American journalists that the DRV would follow the Swiss model of neutrality.[63] Ho also did not offer his congratulations to the PRC until November 1949. We are not able to compare the Chinese and Vietnamese accounts until the Vietnamese side allows access to its archives on this period. What we can say is that, reluctantly or otherwise, the establishment of diplomatic relations between them marked the categorical acceptance of Zhdanov's 'two camp' theory and spelt the end of the strategy, tactical or otherwise, of cultivating broad support from both communists and non-communists alike. On 17 April 1950, the CCP Central Military Commission ordered the formation of the Chinese Military Advisory Group (CMAG) to assist the Viet Minh.[64] By 1951, Truong Chinh for the first time made the claim that the balance of forces between the democratic and imperialist camps had tipped in favour of the former.[65] Also in 1951, the Indochinese Communist Party—which had been dissolved in 1945—re-emerged as the Lao Dong, or Vietnam Workers' Party.

Conclusion

In 1948, the resistance war against the French was still the top priority for the Vietnamese, although the differences between the coalition partners were already apparent—if not "irreversible" as Tuong Vu would argue.[66] The colonial struggle was at a stalemate

63. Nguyen Vu Tung, 'The Chinese Factor', pp. 5–6

64. See Zhai, *China and the Vietnam Wars*, chapter 1; Chen Jian, 'China and the First Indo-China War, 1950–54', *China Quarterly*, no. 133 (Mar 1999): 85–110.

65. Report to the Second National Congress of the Vietnam Workers' Party, February 1951, Truong Chinh, *Selected Writings* (Hanoi: Foreign Languages Publishing House, 1977), p. 235, cited by Gareth Porter, 'Hanoi's Strategic Perspective and the Sino-Vietnamese Conflict', *Pacific Review*, vol. 57, no. 1 (Spring 1984), p. 11 note 12.

66. Tuong Vu, 'It's time for the Indochinese Revolution to show its true colours'.

and the prognosis for the long term was not favourable to the Vietnamese communists. Increasingly, the Vietnamese communist leadership had to take into cognizance the Cold War environment developing around Vietnam even as they single-mindedly pursued national liberation. Though it would only become clear two years later, 1948 indeed marked the transformation from a purely colonial war into a Cold War struggle. That said, let us end on a cautious note. As Shawn McHale put it as recently as 2006, Vietnam scholars are "still grappling to understand the internal dynamics of Vietnam in this period", not to mention the larger "regional and international contexts of the war".[67]

67. H-Diplo Roundtable (2006) on Lawrence's *Assuming the Burden*.

3

THE COMMUNIST INSURGENCY IN MALAYSIA, 1948–1989: WAS IT DUE TO THE COLD WAR?

Cheah Boon Kheng

When communist insurgents in Malaya launched an armed revolt in 1948 and the British colonial government declared in the same year a state of Emergency, the events were initially projected in the mass media along Cold War lines. Contemporary interpretations suggested that the Malayan Communist Party had received instructions from Moscow to revolt, that it was all part of the global onslaught of communism. But to what extent was this true? The Cold War reading asks us to frame these developments in the international context of the Cold War, especially the ideological conflict between the US and the Soviet Union; but the reality is that while in Europe and America the Cold War was indeed at the forefront of national politics, foreign affairs and defence, in British-ruled Malaya and Singapore it was not so. In fact, as this chapter examines, whether with regard to the insurgency's origins, Britain's handling of the Emergency or the experience of the Malayans, the events of this period were more closely related to a complex interaction of *local* issues.

The Cold War perspective

The global conflict was a 'cold' war in that the two sides of the ideological divide were engaged in propaganda, rhetoric and diplomacy, but stopped short of a real war, largely because of the huge nuclear arsenals each side had developed and amassed, and which they hesitated to use against each other (though they did get involved in small-scale 'proxy' wars). This Cold War paradigm, though initially promulgated in the media, was hard to reconcile, however, with local realities, as the insurgency involved a wider range of local issues: the ongoing struggle for Malaya's independence from British rule; the curtailment of freedom, human rights and democracy, and disruption of public life[1]; ethnic urbanisation in the form of the 'New Villages'; the emergence of a military regime under General Gerald Templer; and a 'shooting war' in the jungle. As a result, in the Malayan public's experience of the events, the Cold War perspective did not take root.

It was a localised 'hot war,' not a large-scale war like the Korean War, which the Americans and other members of the United Nations became involved in. British policy of keeping the Americans out of Malayan affairs came into play, so that the insurgency in Malaya was a localised, and not an international, problem. In July 1950, in line with its policy of 'containing' communism (which had become more pressing after China's fall to the communists in October 1949), the US State Department sent out a high-level, top-secret mission, headed by John F. Melby, to Southeast Asia.[2] In talks with British officials in Malaya—including the commissioner-general for Southeast Asia, Malcolm MacDonald—the Melby mission enquired what the US could do to assist Malaya's fight against the communist insurgents. A request was made for military aid. However, when the mission visited London, the British government appeared rather lukewarm to US involvement, as it regarded Malaya as a British sphere of influence.[3] Whereas prior

1. To deal with the Emergency regulations, the British government introduced a series of draconian measures: coercive powers of detention, arrests, deportations and banishments, the registration of the entire population, control of publications, assembly and societies, and the imposition of the death penalty for anyone carrying unauthorised firearms.

2. See Pamela Sodhy, 'America's Melby Mission to Southeast Asia in 1950: The Case of Malaya', *JEBAT* (History Journal of the Universiti Kebangsaan Malaysia), 18 (1990): 263–87.

3. See ibid. London's cold response to the Melby mission's offer of US military aid seems to contradict Philip Deery's account of US rejection of military assistance to Malaya made earlier by a British police official in

to 1951 the British official view was inclined to accept the Soviet conspiracy theory, afterwards they changed their view and played down the suggestion of external involvement in the MCP's decision to take up arms.[4] British officials in Malaya thereafter were not encouraged to pursue US military aid further. Fortunately for Britain, the Korean War caused a 'boom' in Malaya's rubber and tin prices, and the increased revenue helped it to finance the fight against the communists.[5]

The Cold War perspective had first been presented on 18 June 1948, when MacDonald, in a radio broadcast explaining the background to the state of emergency in Malaya, charged that Moscow had given instructions to the Malayan communists to resort to a campaign of violence, "of the gun and knife". He claimed it was all a plot of international communism. But he did not say that the MCP had launched an armed rebellion.

These assertions—of Soviet inspiration and Cold War expansionism—were thereafter echoed in various forms by the British government in Malaya and in London.[6] From the 1950s this Cold War view became the 'orthodox' view of the communist uprising in Malaya.[7] Scholars writing during the early Cold War years such as Virginia Thompson and Richard Adloff, Victor Purcell, Harry Miller, Lucian Pye, J.H. Brimmel, and Alex Josey, among others, all held this view.[8]

Malaya to the US consul in Kuala Lumpur on 22 June 1948, soon after the outbreak of the communist insurgency. The request was made at a low government level, but apparently did not go up to London. See Philip Deery, 'Britain's Asian Cold War?' *Journal of Cold War Studies*, 9, 1 (2007): 29–54.

4. See R.B. Smith, 'China and Southeast Asia: The Revolutionary Perspective 1951', *Journal of Southeast Asian Studies*, XIX (1).

5. For a detailed account of the unexpected economic benefits for Malaya brought on by the Korean War, see Richard Stubbs, *Hearts and Minds in Guerrilla Warfare: The Malayan Emergency 1948–1960* (Singapore: Oxford University Press, 1989), pp. 107–14.

6. See the papers in the *UK Parliamentary Debates*, 23 July 1948, and the papers of then British secretary of state Arthur Creech Jones on Moscow's role, cited by John Deery in his article, 'Britain's Asian Cold War?' op. cit. See also Virginia Thompson and Richard Adloff, *The Left Wing in Southeast Asia* (New York: William Sloane, 1950), p. 54, for the view that British policy on Malaya was influenced by MacDonald's conviction that external Soviet pressure had determined the MCP's action.

7. Yeo Kim Wah, cited in Anthony Short, 'Correspondence', *Journal of Southeast Asian Studies*, vol. 1, no. 2 (Sep 1970), p. 155.

8. See Thompson and Adloff, *The Left Wing in Southeast Asia*; Victor Purcell, *Malaya:*

However, till today there is no documentary evidence to prove that Moscow gave the MCP instructions to start such a campaign of violence. The escalating violence—mark, not rebellion—was an action that the communist-led trade unions launched in 'self-defence' and on their own initiative in retaliation against 'provocation' by employers, the police and the government, claimed Chin Peng, the MCP's former secretary-general, in his autobiography. He asserted that the killings were not sanctioned by the Central Committee, and they "amounted to a serious mistake" on the part of the members involved, forcing the party onto the "defensive." It was not intended to mark a prelude to the MCP's planned revolt.[9]

Furthermore, he denied that the rebellion, which was in response to the Emergency, was Moscow-directed, and said that at no point, either prior to or during the Emergency, did he have contact of any nature whatsoever with the Soviet Union. He never sought Russian aid and no Russian, or agent of Moscow, ever approached him personally, or the MCP, with offers of aid.[10]

The debate

The Soviet archives are opening up, yet no researcher has unearthed any evidence to support the British administration's Soviet conspiracy theory.[11] Recent scholarship, based on the latest research evidence, continues to be skeptical of the Cold War perspective

Communist or Free? (Stanford, CA: Stanford University Press, 1954); Harry Miller, *The Communist Menace in Malaya* (New York: Praeger, 1955); Lucian W. Pye, *Guerrilla Communism in Malaya: Its Social and Political Meaning* (Princeton, NJ: Princeton University Press, 1956); and J.H. Brimmell, *The Malayan Communist Party: A Short History* (Singapore: Donald Moore, 1956).

9. Alias Chin Peng, *My Side of History*, as told to Ian Ward and Norma Miraflor (Singapore: Media Masters, 2003), pp. 202–5, 222. The escalating violence, initiated by the MCP-dominated trade unions, was a fallout that the MCP did not anticipate, as it went too far. Chin Peng said it grew out of a remark by a visiting Australian communist, Lawrence Sharkey, who had suggested to the party that one of the ways in which Australian trade unionists had handled strike-breakers was to resort to militant action.

10. Alias Chin Peng, *My Side of History*, p. 247.

11. This was revealed by L.M. Efimova of the Moscow State Institute of International Relations at a roundtable on the Cold War, held at the Asia Research Institute, National University of Singapore, 10–11 July 2008. In her paper, 'New Russian Evidence on the Calcutta Youth Conference (Feb. 1948), and Soviet Policy toward Indonesia', Efimova declared that recently declassified archival

and reinforces the findings of an earlier group of researchers who also rejected that notion.[12]

One fact that seems to be lost on those who advance the Soviet conspiracy theory is that the Malayan Emergency was declared *before* the MCP launched its armed revolt. This has led to some confusion in their view of the sequence of events, in which the industrial violence and the outbreak of the MCP's armed rebellion are regarded as one and the same thing. The revolt, in fact, was not launched until about two weeks *after* the Emergency was declared. Only then did the MCP's ex-members association of its wartime guerrilla force (the Malayan People's Anti-Japanese Army), call up its members to rearm and fight the British. Armed units based in rural areas were joined by cadres who had abandoned their undercover roles in the city and town areas and fled helter skelter. It was only in July 1948—about a month later—that the British authorities realised an armed communist rebellion was under way and officially banned the party. Scholars advancing the Cold War perspective, therefore, are really speculating on the Moscow angle, or accepting British Cold War propaganda.

In the 1950s and 1960s this Cold War view was challenged by a group of scholars who demonstrated that local conditions, more than Soviet directives, had determined not only the origins of the communist insurgency in Malaya, but also the other communist insurgencies which occurred almost simultaneously in Burma, Indonesia and the Philippines. The first attack was made in 1958 by Ruth McVey, who studied the four communist uprisings in Southeast Asia. As a specialist with early access to the Soviet archives, McVey found no evidence of Moscow's instructions to the MCP.

documents of the Central Committee of the All-Union Communist Party (of Bolsheviks), or CC-AUCP, in Moscow, do not corroborate the Soviet conspiracy theory.

12. See the following works: Deery, 'Britain's Asian Cold War?'; Anthony J. Stockwell, '"A widespread and long-concocted plot to overthrow government in Malaya"', *Journal of Imperial and Commonwealth History*, 21, 3 (1993): 66–88; Anthony J. Stockwell, 'Chin Peng and the Struggle for Malaya', *Journal of the Royal Asiatic Society*, 6, 1 (2006): 279–99; T.N. Harper, *The End of Empire and the Making of Malaya* (Cambridge: Cambridge University Press, 1999), pp. 94–114.

She also argued that internal events in each of the respective countries were more important than any instructions by Moscow (allegedly issued at two Indian Communist Party congresses in Calcutta in February 1948) to Asian communist parties to start a revolt:

> The opportunity and incentive for Communist rebellion were already present in the countries where revolt occurred. It thus does not seem likely that the two-camp message [consisting of 'imperialists' and 'anti-imperialists' as proclaimed by Soviet official Andrei Zhdanov] lit the revolutionary spark in Southeast Asia, though it may well have added extra tinder which caused it to burn into flame.[13]

In Malaya the British authorities declared a state of emergency largely because they were unable to control the escalating industrial disputes and attacks on and murders of Chinese and European miners, planters and labour contractors that had occurred in the states of Penang, Selangor and Johor from April to June 1948. In his 1970 study, Michael Stenson established that these incidents were perpetrated by communist-led unions, in retaliation against the arrest and imprisonment of communist union leaders by the British, and police firing on strikers and demonstrators on a number of occasions, which had resulted in fatalities on the protestors' side.[14] Stenson's research, therefore, added weight to McVey's view that local conditions caused the revolt. He also showed that the British administration had adopted selective use of banishment orders in Singapore against trade union and communist organisers accused of sedition or violence. The government was also accused, by left-wing political groups like the Malayan Democratic Union, of having colluded with employers and the police in breaking up workers' strikes, and in imposing trespass laws in late 1947

13. Ruth T. McVey, *The Calcutta Conference and the Southeast Asian Uprisings* (Ithaca: Cornell Modern Indonesia Project, 1958), p. 24.

14. See M.R. Stenson, *Industrial Conflict in Malaya: Prelude to the Communist Revolt of 1948* (London: Oxford University Press, 1970), pp. 231–3.

to remove trade union organisers from rubber estates and other commercial premises.

The incidents of April–June 1948 culminated in the killing of three European planters in the Sungei Siput area of Perak state on 16 June. It was these killings that forced the British administration to declare a state of emergency.

MCP on the defensive

The Sungei Siput murders did not, however, mark the start of the communists' armed rebellion. At their Central Committee meetings earlier in March and May, the MCP had originally decided to start their armed revolt in September 1948, but these plans were not completed. It was the Emergency that pre-empted events towards that end.

The government's intelligence agency, the Malayan Security Service (MSS), had failed to uncover details of the March and May plans for revolt, let alone the June 1948 murders. It was abolished, and in its place two police intelligence agencies, known as the Special Branch, were established, one in peninsular Malaya and one in Singapore. Problems plaguing the MSS and British intelligence in Malaya at this time included the lack of expertise in Chinese languages, in coping with the challenge posed by the mainly Chinese-led MCP.[15] After the uprising, the Special Branch came to the view that Soviet influence, as opposed to influence from the Chinese Communist Party, was negligible in Malaya, and although the Soviets gave verbal support to the Malayan uprising in 1948, trade came before politics.[16] The Special Branch view, which contradicted Malcolm MacDonald's account of the industrial violence, was also released to the international media. The *Sydney Morning Herald* of 18 June 1948 reported: "The officers (security officials)

15. Leon Comber, *Malaya's Secret Police 1945–60: The Role of the Special Branch in the Malayan Emergency* (Singapore: Institute of Southeast Asian Studies, 2008), p. 46.

16. Leon Comber, 'The Origins of the Cold War in Southeast Asia: The Case of the Communist Party of Malaya (1948–1960)—A Special Branch Perspective', *Kajian Malaysia*, vol. 27, nos 1 and 2 (2009): 39–60.

declared there is no evidence that Russia or any other overseas body is directing the challenge to the Malayan Government."[17]

On the other hand, the MCP, itself caught by surprise, reacted to events initiated by the British administration instead of determining or initiating them, and thus, as rightly observed by Anthony Stockwell, "stumbled into revolution".[18] The British administration, acting blindly in the dark, and unaware that the MCP had been planning an armed revolt, thereby gained a psychological advantage.

For the MSS, its biggest setback was the loss of its most important agent, Lai Tek, who had been planted in the MCP in the 1930s and had become its secretary-general. He had survived the Japanese Occupation by working with the Japanese Kempeitai police, and had then resumed his services with the British police after the war. But in 1947 he was unmasked by Chin Peng at a Central Committee meeting, and fled to Bangkok, where he was eventually killed. According to a Special Branch authority, "the MSS was deprived of an important source of intelligence about the CPM [Communist Party of Malaya] at the highest possible level, which placed it at a considerable disadvantage".[19] In view of this disclosure, one can only surmise that MacDonald was resorting to bluff and propaganda when he charged that the industrial violence in June was Moscow-directed, without having obtained any hard evidence from the intelligence agencies.

In his autobiography, Chin Peng reveals that the Emergency created chaos and confusion within the MCP's ranks,[20] and that instead of launching major attacks on British targets, the party was on the defensive. All their experience and revolutionary-warfare theory confirmed that guerrilla forces should determine the time and location of all attacks and that they should strike where the

17. *Sydney Morning Herald*, 18 June 1948.

18. Stockwell, 'Chin Peng and the Struggle for Malaya'; see also Stockwell, '"A widespread and long-concocted plot to overthrow government in Malaya"'.

19. Comber, *Malaya's Secret Police 1945–60*, p. 32.

20. Alias Chin Peng, *My Side of History*, p. 226.

enemy was at its weakest. They had intended to operate the early phase of armed struggle via nine concurrent insurgencies—one in each of the Malayan states—and planned to set up two jungle base areas. But the details were never finalised as the party was thrown into disarray by the declaration of the Emergency and their forces were now on the run.

Without any reference to Chin Peng, some individuals in state committees and some former military commanders quickly reorganised and took the initiative to launch attacks. A group of about a hundred guerrillas stormed the Batu Arang coal mine in Selangor state. Chin Peng himself was in hiding at a tin mine in Ipoh and escaped through the back door as a police party closed in on him. After rejoining a guerrilla unit in the Pahang jungle, he ordered the guerrillas to try and set up a liberated area by launching a heavy attack on Gua Musang in the northern state of Kelantan. On 17 July 1948 they captured the town, including the police station, where the entire police staff was taken hostage. British military reinforcements soon arrived and after a five-day battle recaptured the town. The government then banned the party.

The MCP decided to continue its efforts to establish liberated areas in both the northern and southern regions of the peninsula. In this rush of events, the party announced that its ultimate aim was the establishment of the People's Democratic Republic of Malaya. In hindsight, Chin Peng admitted that this was a critical mistake. What it should have done was to announce their aim of fighting for the broad concept of independence. "Our battle cry," he said, "should have been: Independence for Malaya and all Malayans who want independence."[21]

I have presented this sequence of events to show that at the outbreak of the communist insurgency, the MCP had received no directives from the Soviets, and its insurgency did not have a Cold War motive, although British propaganda tried to give it a global Cold War slant.

21. Ibid., p. 238.

The Cold War influence from 1951 onwards

From 1951 onwards, however, the situation changed and the MCP's armed revolt began to take on a true Cold War dimension. Not only did it re-establish contact with the Chinese Communist Party (CCP), it also got in touch with the Communist Party of the Soviet Union (CPSU), both of which started to influence it and involve it within the global Cold War conflict. Much of this involvement was not publicised, however, and therefore not widely known to the public, but has now been revealed through the memoirs of MCP participants, including Chin Peng's, on which the following account is largely based.[22]

In 1951 the MCP's Central Committee issued its 'October 1st 1951 Resolution', which adopted a change of strategy. Guerrillas were ordered to get closer to the people and to reduce military activities that would affect or disrupt the people's livelihood. There was to be no more slashing of rubber trees, no confiscating of identity cards, no burning of buses or attacking of civilian trains. The war was still going badly for the MCP, however, especially as the Briggs resettlement plan cut off the guerrillas' food supplies. The police Special Branch and the security forces had also succeeded in disrupting the MCP's communication lines.[23] By 1953 the guerrilla forces had retreated from most parts of the peninsula to the Betong Salient near the Malay-Thai border.

In the same year Chin Peng sent a cadre, Ah Hai, who was suffering from tuberculosis, to China for treatment. He then received a message from the CCP requesting a senior member of the MCP to be sent to Beijing for important discussions. Chin sent Siao Chang, a Central Committee member. Thus Ah Hai became the first official contact with the Chinese communists since the outbreak of the insurgency, and, after arriving in Beijing in 1953, Siao Chang also gained considerable experience dealing with high-level

22. Besides Chin Peng's memoirs, those of other leaders also reveal contacts with the CCP and CPSU; see *Memoir Abdullah C.D.*, vols 1, 2 and 3 (Petaling Jaya: SIRD, 2007), and *Memoir Shamsiah Fakeh: Dari AWAS ke Rejimen Ke-10* (Petaling Jaya: SIRD, 2007).

23. Comber, *Malaya's Secret Police 1945–60*, p. 167.

leaders, enjoying easy and regular access to the decision-making levels of the CCP, and travelling to Moscow to confer with top Kremlin men.

In 1954, the Cold War influence began to set in. Both Ah Hai and Siao Chang had become "strongly influenced by the advice they had been receiving from both Peking and Moscow"—advice that the Party look favourably at peace negotiations to resolve the ongoing conflict.[24]

Owing to this CCP-Soviet intervention, the party was to make the first overture for peace talks to end the state of emergency in Malaya. Ah Hai and Siao Chang drafted a paper hinting at this line. An overseas left-wing comrade was chosen to present the paper at a conference of delegates from British Empire communist parties held in London in early 1954, and the British media picked it up. "The document appeared to imply that the CPM was looking for a new strategy to fight for independence other than through armed struggle," revealed Chin Peng,[25] who claimed he had been completely unaware of this change of policy taken by Ah Hai and Siao Chang in Beijing. Nevertheless, he and the Central Committee followed suit once they received communication from the two men.

This change of policy eventually led Chin Peng to hold talks with Malaya's newly elected Chief Minister Tunku Abdul Rahman at Baling in Kedah state, near the Malay-Thai border, on 28–29 December 1955. The talks ended in failure, however, as the Chief Minister rejected the MCP's two demands: recognition of the party, and no police screening for its members who laid down their arms.

Just before Chin Peng had left his jungle hideout to attend the talks, an emissary from China had arrived with a message entitled 'Joint Written Opinion of the CPSU and the CCP', addressed to him from both the Communist Party of the Soviet Union and the Communist Party of China.[26]

24. Alias Chin Peng, *My Side of History*, p. 352. 25. Ibid., p. 352. 26. Ibid., p. 353.

The two major communist parties had been influenced by developments at the international level and in Malaya. The first of these involved the Geneva talks on ending the war in Indochina, which had taken place from May to July 1954 and concluded with accords covering an end to fighting in Vietnam, Laos and Cambodia. The other was the Bandung conference on peaceful co-existence held in April 1955. It was apparent that the two major parties calculated that the communist side could try to secure advantages or concessions through talks while having breathing space and preparing the ground for a long-drawn-out war.

Matters were also getting complicated for the MCP as events in Malaya had already led to the holding of general elections, the installation of an elected government under Tunku Abdul Rahman's multi-racial Alliance Party, and the prospect of the end of British rule and independence for Malaya.

The joint message, therefore, contained four points and advocated negotiations and a peace settlement with the Malayan authorities. First, it pointed out that Malaya had no common frontier with a socialist state. Second, the MCP's struggle had failed to form a broad front across all races. Third, there was an extreme imbalance in military strength between "the MCP and the enemy", which meant there was little hope of achieving victory. Finally, there was a clear suggestion that the MCP should wind up their armed struggle and concentrate on political struggle instead.[27] The advice given to the MCP was to advance "peaceful co-existence" within the larger context of the Cold War.

The MCP's failure to secure a 'peace' settlement at the Baling Peace Talks led to the stagnation of guerrilla activities. The Malayan government started declaring 'white areas' in Malaya (i.e. areas free of guerrilla activities). Chin Peng has admitted that the MCP was by then militarily defeated.[28] Demoralisation set in. Guerrillas started to surrender, or were allowed to return to their

27. Ibid., p. 367.

28. Ibid., p. 286.

homes. On 31 August 1957 Malaya achieved its independence. The Central Committee began to debate its future and finally decided to wind up its armed struggle, prepare for the demobilisation of guerrillas and allow party members to return to the political struggle.

This new line bore fruit for MCP cadres in the general elections held in Singapore in May 1959. Chin Peng had ordered the party in Singapore to give electoral support to Lee Kuan Yew's left-wing People's Action Party (PAP), which had been branded a communist 'united front' organisation by the government. The PAP's victory led to the formation of a government in which communist cadres were given appointments as political secretaries and parliamentary secretaries. In July 1960 Malaya's Alliance government announced the end of the state of emergency.

Cold War directions: MCP resumes armed struggle

In December 1960, owing to his ill-health and fears that the secret of his hideout had been breached and that he would be assassinated, Chin Peng left for Beijing. Ah Hai took over command of the MCP and the guerrilla forces at the border. On his way to the PRC, Chin Peng held talks in Hanoi with Vietnamese leaders. Once in Beijing he discussed party matters with CCP leaders. All advised him to reverse the MCP's demobilisation policy and resume the armed struggle; revolutionary warfare would eventually defeat Western imperialism in the global conflict.

In 1959 North Vietnam had agreed to continue training MCP members in revolutionary warfare as well as support its overland (cross-country) communications and supply network. While in Hanoi, Chin Peng secretly learnt from the Vietnamese for the first time about the Sino-Soviet ideological split (which had occurred in Moscow seven months earlier) and he discovered that the Vietnamese communists were trying to remain neutral.

In 1961 he held talks with CCP leader Deng Xiaoping, who also advised the MCP to resume the armed struggle. Southeast Asia,

Deng told him, was to undergo monumental changes. The region was becoming "ripe" for communist armed revolution and the MCP should "take advantage of the opportunities that would be presenting themselves throughout Southeast Asia".[29] Deng assured the MCP of financial support. Chin Peng passed the message to the party's Central Committee at the border and they agreed to resume the armed struggle in 1961. Chin Peng then visited Moscow to attend the 44th anniversary of the Russian Revolution and the Soviet Congress, where he listened to Soviet leader Nikita Khrushchev in his element denouncing the enemies of communism.

In August 1964 Chin Peng visited Hanoi again, at the invitation of the Vietnamese communists, who enquired about the progress of the party's resumed armed struggle. In October Khrushchev was overthrown and the Sino-Soviet ideological split came out in the open.

MCP's alignment with CCP's 'world revolution' policy

In 1964 the CCP's supreme leader, Mao Zedong, met Chin Peng and Musa Ahmad, the MCP chairman, as well as other party officials, to find out their stand on the Sino-Soviet ideological dispute. They all declared support for Mao's line. Soon they became caught up in Mao's Cultural Revolution, which they regarded as an important development in the evolution of world communism.

In the period 1968–69 the MCP split into three factions due to purges, executions and charges of infiltration by enemy agents within the party. The CCP intervened, but failed to resolve the conflicts.

In 1969 US President Richard Nixon set in motion the process of *détente* by withdrawing American troops from South Vietnam. In 1971 he recognised and then visited Communist China. In 1974 Malaysia's Prime Minister Tun Abdul Razak followed suit, and met Mao, and diplomatic relations were established between the

29. Ibid., pp. 428–9.

two countries. The following year Cambodia and Laos fell into communist hands.

With Mao's death in 1976, China under Deng Xiaoping embarked on a policy of economic reforms and liberalisation, and began to moderate its stance towards the Soviet Union. Many of Mao's 'revolutionary' policies were abandoned. Deng also decided to downgrade relations with fraternal communist parties in Southeast Asia, going to the extent of asking the MCP to close down its broadcasting station, Suara Revolusi ('Voice of Revolution'), which was based in China. He explained that China did not wish to offend the governments of Singapore and Malaysia. The station was later moved to southern Thailand and began broadcasting under a new name, Suara Demokrasi ('Voice of Democracy').

The end of the MCP drew near. In 1981 Deng urged Chin Peng to seek avenues for a peace accord with Malaysia. In 1987 both MCP factions—the MCP (Marxist-Leninist) and the MCP (Revolutionary)—surrendered to the Thai authorities. In 1988 the Malaysian and Thai governments both made peace initiatives to the rump MCP under Chin Peng. The CCP gave the go-ahead. In February 1989 negotiations began, and a peace accord was signed on 2 December, under which the party laid down its arms and ended its 41-year insurrection.

Public perceptions: the insurgency not 'Cold War'

Since 1989 a public review of the communists' role has been under way in Malaysia. This has taken place largely in an atmosphere of greater openness and transparency. There have been attempts by left-wing groups to rehabilitate former communists into Malaysian society by presenting them as patriots and nationalists and by looking at some positive aspects of their past activities. On the other hand, there have been statements by the Malaysian government, politicians, ex-servicemen's and police associations criticising the MCP's activities in the past, especially its acts of terrorism, assassinations and murders.

But in all this, hardly any reference has been made to the Cold War and the global conflict between communism and Western liberalism or democracy.

The Malaysian government, in prohibiting Chin Peng from returning to Malaysia from Thailand, where he now resides, has been more concerned with the possible repercussions, especially among present and former members of the police and the armed forces who fought the communists over the 41-year period. Excluding Chin Peng, many former members of the MCP, especially Malays, have been allowed to return to Malaysia.

Chin Peng in 2008 lost his appeal in the High Court against the government's ban on his return, although this had been agreed to in the 1989 peace accord.[30] In fact, one of the key issues at the talks then had been whether the Malaysian government would recognise the MCP's role in accelerating the independence process; the accord was only signed after the Malaysian government representative announced that it would not "deny or dispute" the party's contribution to independence.[31] The communists' role in fighting for independence has been recognised by no less than Malaysia's first prime minister, the late Tunku Abdul Rahman:

> Just as Indonesia was fighting a bloody battle, so were the communists of Malaya who, too, fought for independence. With the difference that the communists of Malaya were not the indigenous people of this country and they were fighting to set up a communist regime which the believers in the faith of Islam [i.e. the Malays] could not support nor could those orthodox people, who believed in democracy and freedom. So the struggle for the independence of this country was carried out by the communists alone and they fought a subversive as well as a shooting war, losing many of their men and at the same time killing many of our men and the Commonwealth soldiers. The battle continued for

30. See the report in *The Star* (Malaysia), 21 June 2008, p. 32.

31. Alias Chin Peng, *My Side of History*, p. 490.

> 12 years [i.e. 1948–60] and would have gone on had not the British government yielded to our demand for a general election as a step towards independence.[32]

Two former deputy prime ministers, the late Tun Dr Ismail Abdul Rahman and Tun Ghafar Baba, have also publicly acknowledged the contributions and struggles of the "left-wing movement" towards nationhood. This often loaded expression usually includes socialists or those linked to the communist movement as well.

Malay attitudes towards both the communist and left-wing movements have been changing over the years. While critical of their deeds, especially assassinations and acts of terrorism, many Malays are now willing to accept that without their armed struggle against the British, Malaya's independence could not have been achieved in 1957. Even the religious Party Islam (PAS), on the eve of Malaysia's 49th anniversary of independence celebrations in 2006, declared: "History cannot ignore the fact that the Communist Party of Malaya had also played a role in fighting for the independence of this country." It described the communist movement's armed struggle as "a patriotic war", and hailed the party's Malay members, Rashid Maidin and Abdullah C.D., as "patriots and heroes".[33]

In the same year, however, former prime minister, Mahathir Mohamad, in his foreword to a book on the 1989 MCP-Malaysia 'peace' accord, which his government had brokered, expressed a rather ambivalent attitude towards the communists' role in fighting for national independence:

> The MCP claims that they fought for Malaysia's independence. There could be some legitimacy when the British still ruled the country. But after independence in 1957 that claim becomes meaningless. The Malayan Communist Party fought against Independent Malaysia with the same ferocity it did against colonial Malaysia.

32. See Tunku Abdul Rahman, *Lest We Forget: Further Candid Reminiscences* (Singapore: Eastern Universities Press, 1983), p. 34.

33. The statement was issued in the party organ, *Harakahdaily.net*, 27 Aug 2006.

However, he acknowledged that the Malay communists in the CPM had joined the party despite it being predominantly Chinese, and despite "suffering discrimination in the jungle and in the camps, in order to have access to arms to fight against the British for independence, in what they believed to be a reasonable chance of success".[34]

Conclusion

Although the United States and the Soviet Union carved out their spheres of influence at the end of the Second World War, Malaya did not become an area of competition. In terms of propaganda and rhetoric, Britain sided with the US in the Cold War, and tried to present its counterinsurgency campaign in Malaya from 1948 onwards as part of that global conflict. But, increasingly, it forestalled American intervention in its own sphere of influence and did not want to turn the communist insurgency into a global conflict. It treated the communist insurgency in Malaya as its "internal problem" as well as a colonial problem.

The Cold War perspective and propaganda that Britain projected became complicated and distorted, clouded further by the challenges it faced from Malayan nationalism and its own decolonisation agenda. Communism was an extreme form of nationalism, but it did offer to many people in Malaya hopes of an end to colonial subjugation and humiliation. The MCP's armed struggle was seen as a courageous fight against British colonialism, despite any psychological fear of communism that British propaganda might have aroused in the people.

In any case, the Emergency created harsh conditions for the people in Malaya as the British government introduced draconian measures and even a military regime to combat militant communism. As presented above, the Malayan public's view of the com-

34. See foreword by Mahathir Mohamad in Collin Abraham, *'The Finest Hour': The Malaysian-MCP Peace Accord in Perspective* (Petaling Jaya: SIRD, 2006), pp. xii–xiv.

munist insurgency was, therefore, a complex and multi-focal one, in which the Cold War perspective was not dominant.

The origins of the communist insurgency were determined by local factors, and not by any directives from Moscow. The declaration of the state of emergency was due to the British government's attempt to check spiralling industrial violence. It pre-empted the communists' plans for armed revolt, caught them unprepared, and caused chaos in their ranks, so that they stumbled into revolution. Failing to take the initiative, the MCP "miscalculated and bungled," and, admitted Chin Peng, "a critical moment was lost, never to be regained."[35]

Despite the MCP's involvement in the Cold War politics of the Soviet Union and Communist China from 1954 onwards—reported mainly in the MCP's clandestine radio broadcasts—such news was dismissed officially as subversive propaganda threatening national security, and the Malayan public was discouraged from listening in to the broadcasts.

Consequently, the 'Cold War' dimension receded further into the background.

35. Alias Chin Peng, *My Side of History*, p. 286.

THE PHILIPPINES DURING THE COLD WAR: SEARCHING FOR SECURITY GUARANTEES AND APPROPRIATE FOREIGN POLICIES, 1946–1986

Ricardo T. Jose

The Philippines emerged from the Second World War destitute—its cities in ruins, its economy destroyed, the agricultural cycle derailed and the population reduced by one million. Its prewar defence plans—begun in 1935 by the Philippine Commonwealth government—were now obsolete; to raise a modern national defence force in its current impoverished state was an impossibility. Thus when independence was declared on 4 July 1946 it became imperative for the government of the Republic of the Philippines to see to the immediate security of the nation against external threats. Since the Philippines had remained loyal to the US during the war, and had been the only American colony in Asia, Filipinos felt that the two countries enjoyed 'special relations', and thus it was to the US that the Philippines turned for rehabilitation and military assistance, and on whom it would find itself locked in an increasingly unhappy reliance in the subsequent years of the Cold War.

The early years

Faced with dire circumstances in 1946–47, when the Americans proposed to continue operating their military bases on Philippine soil, the plan was welcomed by the administration of Manuel

A. Roxas, the republic's first president. The bases would provide protection from external military threats; the Philippine government would seek a guarantee to ensure this.[1]

Filipinos—especially the leaders, from President Roxas on down—knew of the Four Freedoms and the Atlantic Charter, and viewed the war as between democracies and totalitarian states. Thus, what Filipinos and Americans fought for during the war was essentially one and the same. As the Cold War set in, it was easy to identify ideologically with the emerging 'Free World' as opposed to the communist umbrella.

The priorities of the government were rehabilitation and reconstruction, though the country was also divided over the issue of collaboration with the Japanese, and, to a lesser extent, guerrilla atrocities during the war. Peace and order was difficult to restore, owing in large part to the proliferation of unlicensed firearms. There were rumblings in the agricultural sector and labour unions for more adequate share of crops and better pay. One of the larger guerrilla groups in Luzon during the war was the left-leaning Hukbo ng Bayan Laban sa Hapon (People's Army Against Japan), shortened to Huks, composed mainly of farmers and labourers. Its leaders were inspired by Soviet Russia and Marx, and the organisation had received training and advice from Chinese Communists. Thus, as the Philippines began its existence as a politically independent state, it was inevitably drawn into a close alliance with the US, politically, economically, militarily, and ideologically.

President Roxas, a reserve officer in the Philippine Army who had participated in the Philippine defence campaign in 1941–42, and who was a close friend of General Douglas MacArthur, believed that the realities of the post-war world—particularly in terms of security and economy—dictated that the closest possible ties between the Philippines and the US were necessary and had

1. This portion is based on Milton W. Meyer, *A Diplomatic History of the Philippine Republic: The First Years, 1946–1961* (Claremont, CA: Regina Books, 2003; reprint of 1965 work) and Nick Cullather, *Illusions of Influence* (Stanford: Stanford University Press, 1994).

to be developed. Roxas publicly praised the Americans and saw in them an example to emulate, a leader to follow. Because the Philippines had been an American possession, the US had the obligation —most Filipinos felt—to help the Philippines rise from the ashes of war. In his inaugural address on 4 July 1946, Roxas reminisced on the good fortune that had brought the Americans to the Philippines in 1898, and urged the Filipino people to have absolute faith in the goodness of America, wherein lay faith in democracy, in the future and in the Philippines. "Our safest course," he announced, "is in the glistening wake of America, whose sure advance with mighty prow breaks for smaller craft the waves of fear."[2]

Foreign relations in the early years of the Philippine Republic have been dubbed by Pacifico Castro as the period of 'initiation', covering the years 1946–57.[3] A dominant theme was the maintenance of close US and Philippine relations, which many Filipinos considered 'special relations'. Close ties with the US were to be expected, not only because the Americans had recognised Philippine independence peacefully (although there were many motives involved), but more especially because the two countries had been allies during World War II. Most Filipinos were euphoric over the end of the war, even amidst the death and destruction, and the Americans were seen as liberators and friends.

The Philippines had little experience in handling its own foreign affairs. Even in the transition years before World War II, when the Philippine Commonwealth government was allowed a great degree of autonomy, the US held on to formal diplomatic relations. During the war, the Commonwealth government went into exile, and had some hands-on experience in the founding years of the United Nations; but it had no professional diplomats and no government agency for foreign affairs.

2. Roxas's inaugural address is published in full in Manuel Roxas, *Speeches, Addresses and Messages as President of the Philippines* (Manila: Bureau of Printing, 1954), Volume I, pp. 141–52; quoted portion is on p. 150.

3. Pacifico A. Castro, 'Towards an Integrated Philippine Foreign Policy', *State of Philippine Society* (Manila: Foreign Service Institute, 1982), p. 10.

With political independence in 1946, one of Roxas's first acts was to create the Department of Foreign Affairs, to set the nation's own foreign policies. During the period of initiation, the Philippine government—headed first by Roxas, then Elpidio Quirino—set out a foreign policy built on four pillars[4]: (1) commitment to the United Nations; (2) continued ties with the United States; (3) maintenance of friendly relations with its neighbours; and (4) devotion to world peace. In practice, the Roxas administration prioritised close relations with the US, although it also quickly established formal relations with the Republic of China, Spain and the United Kingdom.

The first formal treaty entered into by the Philippine republic was the Treaty of General Relations with the United States, signed by Roxas and the outgoing high commissioner and incoming ambassador, Paul McNutt, shortly after the independence ceremonies. The treaty marked the official withdrawal of American sovereignty, control and jurisdiction over the Philippines, except those military and naval bases allowed under the Tydings-McDuffie Act, which would remain under American control for the mutual protection of the US and the Philippines. In the treaty, the US formally recognised the Republic of the Philippines.[5]

Roxas's policy speeches placed close relations with the US as his primary foreign policy priority, officially setting the tone for Philippine foreign policy and relations with the US for the next ten years. By staying with America, and following what it did, Roxas felt that American prosperity would rub off on the Philippines—he essentially placed all his eggs in one basket, hoping for massive amounts of American aid.[6]

4. Benjamin B. Domingo, *The Re-making of Filipino Foreign Policy* (Quezon City: Asian Center, University of the Philippines, 1993), p. 27.

5. Haydee B. Yorac (ed.), *Philippine Treaty Series, Volume I 1944–1948* (Quezon City: Law Center, University of the Philippines, 1968), pp. 217–20; also see Meyer, *A Diplomatic History*, pp. 32–4.

6. A survey of Roxas's speeches shows marked consistency in his reliance on and praise of the US.

The US emerged from World War II as one of the two superpowers in the world, but already imminent was an ideological and political showdown with the USSR, as communist movements began to rise up in the world. Conditions in the world made it ripe for nationalistic movements to clamour for and fight wars for independence. Given its military and economic power in a torn and dislocated world, the US saw itself as the world's policeman and took upon itself the responsibility of preventing the spread of communism and safeguarding the 'Free World'. Not all of the 'Free World', however, was democratic, and several of the old European powers were still colonial powers with holdings in Asia. As the nationalistic movements struggled for independence, they echoed the sentiments of the American Revolution of 1776, but the anger was directed against the United States' wartime allies such as France and Britain. Some of the nationalists could gravitate to the communists, but to support them and keep them away from communism might mean antagonising old friends. Thus arose the dilemmas of the nascent Cold War.

As a world power, the US would place priorities on and looked with concern at Europe and China, whereas the Philippines—according to one American observer—was so excited at being liberated and becoming independent that the US did not have to do too much in those early post-World War II years.

Early US and Philippine security agreements

One reason for seeking extreme closeness with the US was the desire to prevent the Philippines from getting involved in another war. Although the US had not been able to defend the country in 1941, the reality of the post-war world was that another war could start any time, given the tensions arising from the Cold War. Communist takeovers in Europe and Asia seemed to be part of a world plan for communist domination, which would not spare the Philippines. Internally, the Huks, who had risen up against the old social order—particularly when their representatives in the national congress were not allowed to take their oaths and were unseated—were seen as part of this communist danger.[7]

Furthermore, since the weapons for war had grown to levels of great complexity and cost, the prewar national defence plan, which had been shown to be defective, was itself outmoded. But to build a modern military establishment would be way too expensive for the republic, given the limited revenues of the government. A solution to the problem was to keep US bases on Philippines soil. As long as these remained, they could provide security against external threats.

As a result, Roxas, in his inaugural address as president, proclaimed that the first plank of Philippine foreign policy was the closest cooperation with the US in "all matters concerning our common defence and security". In fact, just prior to the Philippines' independence, the US transferred $100 million worth of weapons and military equipment.

To formalise the status of the bases, on 14 March 1947 the Philippines and the United States signed the Military Bases Agreement (MBA). Through the MBA, whose aim was to "promote their mutual security and to defend their territories and areas", the Philippines granted the US the right to maintain and use specified bases (13 in the original agreement) for a period of 99 years. The US was free to determine how to use the bases, in accordance with military necessity. The agreement made provision for the enlargement and addition of bases, provided appropriate negotiations and mutual agreements were reached. For its part, the US would respect Philippine sovereignty, particularly in cases involving its servicemen. In practice, the US did not have to notify the Philippine government of weapons in the bases (including nuclear weapons), or on the use and operations of its military forces.[8]

7. This section is based on Meyer, *A Diplomatic History*; Cullather, *Illusions of Influence*; Cesar P. Pobre, *History of the Armed Forces of the Filipino People* (Quezon City: New Day, 2000); and Bonifacio S. Salamanca, *Towards a Diplomatic History of the Philippines* (Quezon City: University of the Philippines Press, 1996), pp. 148–66.

8. Yorac, *Philippine Treaty Series*, Vol. I, pp. 357–70.

Technically, the MBA was not a treaty, and the US Senate never ratified it. But Roxas chose to treat the agreement as a treaty, and had it ratified on 26 March 1947 by the Philippine Senate.

While the Philippine government viewed the US bases as a solution to their problem of military security, the Americans also benefited from the arrangement. The bases would allow them to station American forces in the Philippines, which could protect their interests—in the Philippines as well as the wider region. They would be vital for projecting American presence in Asia, and blocking the spread of communism into the region. The US needed alliances with friendly countries to build up the so-called 'Free World' against communism, and the bases thus worked to the mutual benefit of the Philippines and the United States.[9]

Complementing the MBA was the Military Assistance Agreement, which was signed a week after the MBA, on 21 March 1947. This agreement obliged the US to provide the Philippine Armed Forces with ships, aircraft, military vehicles, weapons, military equipment and supplies, services and training. However, the title to nonexpendable items—ships, aircraft, vehicles, arms and equipment—was to remain with the US.[10] The original pact was good for five years, after which a supplementary agreement extended its life; it could, should the need arise, be terminated by either country.

The pact also provided for the establishment of the Joint US Military Advisory Group (JUSMAG), which would provide technical and professional advice and assistance on military affairs. JUSMAG was composed of US Army, Navy, and Air Force officers and enlisted men, with the Philippine government paying special allowances, official travel expenses, and also living expenses for

9. However, the US also recognised the strategic value of Okinawa and Japan to US interests, to the point that Japan outweighed the Philippines in strategic importance. See Yuko Ito, 'Postwar US Military Policy and the "Japanese Factor"' in Ikehata Setsuho and Lydia Yu-Jose (eds), *Philippines-Japan Relations* (Quezon City: Ateneo de Manila University Press, 2003), pp. 308–14.

10. Full text in Yorac, *Philippine Treaty Series*, Vol. I, pp. 387–91.

their families. The Philippine government was also responsible for providing appropriate buildings, office spaces and residences for JUSMAG personnel (which were much better than those of the Armed Forces of the Philippines officers). Its top officials were given diplomatic immunity.[11] JUSMAG also set the number of soldiers and officers to be trained and advocated an organisational structure closely following US lines. It recommend Filipino officers to train in US service schools such as the Infantry School, the Armor School, the Quartermaster School and others.

Among the policies JUSMAG recommended, and which the Philippines accepted, was the development of the Philippine armed forces into an organisation focusing on maintaining internal security. Since the external security functions were too expensive and taxing for the Philippines, the US became the de facto armed force against external threats, while the armed forces of the Philippines became responsible for maintaining security within the country. As a result, the dependency relationship continued, and the Philippines did not develop a true independent national defence organisation.

As the agreements were carried out, some sobering realities were noted by the Philippines. While the MBA was concluded for the mutual security of the signatories, there was nothing in it that assured the Philippines of automatic assistance from the US in case the Philippines was attacked by a third power. The absence of such a clause proved to be a point of controversy and an irritant in US-Philippine relations. The Philippines pressed for a more concrete assurance of automatic reaction, but the US, fearing it might get involved in a conflict where its interests were not particularly threatened, refused to commit. The Filipinos also found that the military vehicles and weapons they received from the Americans, although functional, were not state of the art and many were US surplus. The Philippine Air Force was given P-51 fighter-bombers,

11. Pobre, *History of the Armed Forces*, pp. 370–1.

some of which saw practical use in the campaign against the Huks, and C-47 transports, but no medium bombers or jet aircraft. The Philippine Navy was given submarine chasers, minesweepers, and LSTs, but no destroyers or fleet units. The Philippine Army received M4 Sherman tanks but not later models.[12] In a sense, these weapons were suitable for internal security purposes and were less expensive to maintain, but they were less powerful compared to what the Republic of China, Japan and Latin American countries received.

Roxas's closeness with the US was shown not only in the bases and military agreements, but also in forging an agreement that allowed the US to represent the Philippines in countries where the Philippines did not have diplomatic posts. At times, Philippine interests were even subordinated to US interests insofar as world security was concerned[13]: it was felt that whatever ensured a peaceful world augured well for the Philippines in the long run. Roxas viewed US and Philippine interests, especially in the field of security and anti-communist ideology, as being virtually identical. Critics with the benefit of hindsight later called him an 'American boy', but Roxas—having seen war first-hand and aware of the difficulties of raising an independent Philippine armed forces—had virtually no other option at the time.

Not all Philippine foreign policies were identical with the United States'. One policy the Philippines pursued in the UN was to support the struggle for independence. Having itself been a colony, it took on the mantle of championing decolonisation in the world. It quickly recognised India and expressed support for the Indonesian war of independence, as well as for Palestinian independence. Anti-colonial nationalism was a tradition Filipinos were well familiar with. These postures, however, distanced the Philippines from France and Britain.[14]

12. See annual reports of the Chief of Staff of the Philippine Armed Forces, 1946–1949.

13. Domingo, *The Re-making of Philippine Foreign Policy*, p. 97.

14. Meyer, *A Diplomatic History*, p. 70–1.

Apart from the lack of a clear pledge from the US to defend the Philippines, there were other irritants growing between them. One was the failure of the US government to recognise all Filipinos who had fought in the war; several thousands were denied their rightful benefits. Another was the one-sidedness of the trade agreement, which allowed for Americans to enjoy equal rights in exploiting Philippine natural resources and in owning land in the Philippines, but not for Filipinos in the US. On top of that, the war damage amount estimated by the Philippine government had not been fully paid by the US.

But the threat of war—from inside or outside—hung over the Philippines during the Roxas administration, and this remained a paramount fear whereas the irritants could be toned down. The Huks posed a serious threat to internal peace and security; Roxas took a strong anti-communist stand versus the Huks, using the armed forces—equipped with US weapons and equipment—against them. As the Chinese Civil War heated up, hundreds of Chinese refugees began pouring into the Philippines. Not all were checked by the Philippine immigration authorities, and there was a growing fear that communists were among them. The Philippine anti-communist stand led to its support of the US containment policy. It did not recognise the Soviet Union, and labelled communist supporters as subversive.

Roxas died of a heart attack in, ironically, the US base at Clark Field in April 1948. He was succeeded by his vice-president, Elpidio Quirino, who opted to continue placing the US as the top priority in Philippine foreign relations. Quirino, on taking office, described the US as the Philippines' best friend. He essentially continued Roxas's foreign policies, although he sought more comprehensive security arrangements and more concrete American promises of assistance in case of war. At the end of what would have been Roxas's fourth term, in 1949, Quirino ran for president and won—in what some have described as the dirtiest election in the Philippines up to that time.

Early plans for a regional grouping

With a new mandate, and partly reacting to criticism that Philippine foreign policy was too US-centred, Quirino specifically outlined a more regional policy focusing on Asia and the Pacific. He proclaimed the Philippines' support for Asia and its peoples, particularly their struggle for independence.[15] He would try to put into effect one of the four planks of foreign policy, namely friendly relations with neighbouring countries.

Under his predecessor the Philippines had opened formal relations with the Republic of China, attempting to address issues involving Chinese in the Philippines. In July 1949, Quirino invited Chiang Kai-shek, just before the Communist takeover of mainland China, for a meeting in the Philippine summer capital of Baguio to discuss closer economic and cultural ties.[16]

But Quirino ultimately had higher goals: a regional bloc that could promote cooperation. At the Conference on Indonesia held in New Delhi in January 1949, the Philippines had aired the idea of an Asian grouping, and proposed establishing a small secretariat in New Delhi or Manila. No consensus was reached on the subject, however.[17] What Quirino envisaged was a non-military alliance, nominally non-communist but allowing for true nationalist movements. He felt, for example, that Ho Chi Minh was a true nationalist; and when Mao Zedong took over mainland China he kept an open mind on recognising the government there and kept lines open with Premier Zhou Enlai. He initially tried to stay neutral and even publicly stated that he did not care whether China or Japan turned communist, as long as conditions in the Philippines were stable. He did, however, regard the Communist Chinese in the Philippines who aided the Huk rebellion as a threat, and spoke out against them in his 4 July 1949 speech.[18]

15. Domingo, *The Re-making of Philippine Foreign Policy*, p. 29.

16. Meyer, *A Diplomatic History*, pp. 146–7.

17. Ibid., pp. 142–3.

18. Ito, 'Postwar US Military Policy', pp. 319–24. Also see David W. Mabon, 'Elusive Agreements: The Pacific Pact Proposals of 1949–1951', *Pacific Historical Review* (May 1988), and Meyer, *A Diplomatic History*, pp. 139–58.

Quirino hoped to bring the US into the planned alliance, but the US indicated that it was disinclined to join. Nonetheless, he announced Philippine sponsorship of a conference in Baguio in May 1950, to which Australia, Pakistan, India, Ceylon, Thailand and Indonesia were all invited.[19] Neither the Republic of China in Taiwan (which wanted to be invited) nor South Korea were invited due to the potential military character they might bring to the proceedings. During the conference, Quirino announced that the first task at hand was to identify mutual interests. The conference could also go into discussing how to deal with common internal problems through collective action, and initiating the machinery for a concrete base of regional cooperation. The conference came up with a resolution recommending that the participating governments take common measures to promote commercial and financial interests, and to unite their efforts to facilitate cultural progress and social well-being. The participating nations also agreed that no political measures be discussed, and the conference stayed away from military and anti-communist topics.

This initiative for a regional bloc and collective, non-military cooperation was laudable—but ahead of its time. Political and military issues were very real as the Cold War deepened. None of the major powers, especially the US, lent support to Quirino's plan, and it eventually fell by the wayside. He was further disappointed to find out that the US, Australia and New Zealand had inked their own agreement, not knowing that the US did not in fact consider as urgent the Philippines' external defence beyond existing agreements.[20] He sensed that US interest in the Philippines was waning.

Seeking US guarantees

Even as Quirino pursued his idealistic regional bloc, the contradiction of keeping US military bases while trying to voice neutrality became stark. The anti-communist movement in the Philippines—

19. This would be Indonesia's first international conference as an independent nation.

20. Ito, 'Postwar US Military Policy', pp. 321–4.

through the military and civic campaign to subjugate the Huks, as well as the harassment of left-leaning speakers and writers—grew strong. In 1950, the Philippine Congress created the Committee on Un-Filipino Activities (later Anti-Filipino Activities), seemingly aping its US counterpart. Radicals and communist-sympathisers were investigated. The Philippine government continued seeking more concrete promises from the US in the event it was attacked, but while many public statements were made in the US to this effect, there was nothing in writing.

The invasion of South Korea by North Korea in 1950 brought the Cold War to one of its tensest moments. South Korea and the US were caught by surprise. Japan, still under American administration after the end of World War II, could not get involved, and the Philippines was the closest anti-communist country that could provide military assistance, even though its armed forces were battling the Huks. The Americans requested Philippine military support—and even borrowed Philippine Army tanks before Philippine troops were sent. The Philippines, willing to show its readiness to defend a neighbouring country against communist aggression, as well as to show its loyalty to the US and to uphold its commitments to the United Nations, decided to send a battalion combat team, complete with tanks. It was one of the first to show unity with the US, as well as to support the United Nations in this peace-keeping operation.[21]

The Philippines maintained its quest for an ironclad security guarantee with the US. In early 1951, the Philippine government felt it would become part of a regional military alliance in the Pacific, along with the US, Australia and New Zealand. But it was

21. The Philippine Expeditionary Force to Korea was a controversial issue, and has been subjected to different interpretations. Conservative Philippine views had it as fulfilling Philippine responsibilities in Asia as well as with the UN, while revisionists have pointed to US pressure to send military forces. Recent research shows that Quirino and members of his administration saw this as an opportunity to engender a friendlier attitude in the US Congress. See Meyer, *A Diplomatic History*, pp. 129–31, and Ito, 'Postwar US Military Policy', p. 319. Pobre discusses the military side of Philippine participation.

disappointed when it was not invited to the meetings, the result of which was a three-power alliance, ANZUS. The exclusion of the Philippines from this alliance meant that a separate, black-and-white promise by the US to aid the Philippines in case of armed attack was needed.

In response to the Philippines' clamouring for a clear US stand, President Harry S. Truman declared that the US would "act accordingly" should the Philippines be attacked by an outside power. He added that an armed attack on the Philippines would be considered by the US as dangerous to its own safety. Secretary of State Dean Acheson further added that the US would not tolerate any aggression against the Philippines from "any quarter".[22] But there was still no guarantee in writing. Claro M. Recto, chair of the Philippine senate committee on foreign affairs, deemed Truman's and Acheson's statements insufficient; he and other Filipino political leaders wanted clearer and more binding military guarantees from Washington—Quirino wanted a pledge similar to that the US gave its NATO allies. Recto declared that the "irreducible minimum" should be a formal treaty—not an executive agreement—in which the Americans categorically guaranteed an automatic declaration of war should the Philippines be attacked.[23] The Filipinos felt, moreover, that their acceptance (though grudging) of the Japanese Peace Treaty, together with their participation in the Korean War, gave them leverage to seek a more definitive US commitment to defend the Philippines.

The result was the Mutual Defense Treaty, signed on 30 August 1951—a year after the Korean War started. The treaty was reportedly agreed upon because of the "historic relationship" between the US and the Philippines, which brought the two countries "together in a common bond of sympathy and mutual ideals to fight side by side against imperialist aggression during the last war", and their "common determination to defend themselves

22. Domingo, *The Re-making of Philippine Foreign Policy*, p. 155.
23. Ibid.

against external armed attack". The treaty conceded that "an armed attack in the Pacific Area on either of the Parties would be dangerous to its own peace and safety"; in such an event, the country not under attack pledged "to meet the common dangers in accordance with its constitutional processes". The treaty was ratified by the Philippine senate, after much debate, six months later, on 31 March 1952.[24] Although this was the clearest promise yet made by the US, it still fell far short of the automatic declaration of war the Filipinos wanted, and thus was considered to be a letdown.

The Mutual Defense Treaty created a Mutual Defense Board, which provided for closer liaison and consultations over security matters, but it did not officially meet until 1958. Even so, there was still no clear promise of defence from the US.

Mounting irritation between the Philippines and the US

Meanwhile, thorny problems regarding the bases became more serious, particularly the question of jurisdiction over crimes committed by American servicemen. Cases of Filipinos being shot like dogs without warning and cases of mistreatment of Filipinos by Americans led to calls to re-examine the bases issue, and to resolve whether Philippine courts had the right to try the Americans. Anti-American sentiments were triggered, with Senator Jose B. Laurel, among others, arguing that the US was taking Filipino loyalty for granted and not doing enough about developing the relationship. He called for reducing the base leases from 99 years to 50 years. This would indeed result in negotiations, but these would not succeed until the 1960s.[25]

Other irritants arose from the extension of free-trade relations with the US and having to amend the constitution to allow parity for Americans in owning land and exploiting Philippine natural resources, failing which rehabilitation funds would be withheld. In addition, the Philippines never got the full amount it claimed

24. Full text in Yorac, *Philippine Treaty Series*, II.

25. Meyer, *A Diplomatic History*, and Salamanca, *Towards a Diplomatic History*.

for war damages; neither were veterans of World War II fully recognised. A further insult was the Rescission Act of 1946, which removed most of the benefits Filipino veterans could hope for from the US.

The question of Japan

One plank of Philippine foreign policy was friendly relations with its neighbours, further clarified by Quirino as support for and close cooperation with Asian nations. This included Southeast Asia, but not Japan. Philippine policy was to ensure that Japan would never again be a threat to world peace, which would come about through genuine political and economic reform. At a suitable time, the Philippines was willing to welcome a democratic and non-militaristic Japan as a friendly neighbour, but its immediate priority, having suffered grievously from the Japanese occupation, was to obtain early and equitable reparations for war damages caused by Japan. The Philippines also sought justice through war crimes trials, participating in the International Military Tribunal for the Far East in Tokyo, and holding its own Class C war crimes trials in Manila.[26]

The Philippines continually insisted that Japan pay reparations, primarily at the Far East Commission (FEC), based in Washington, which gave policy guidelines to the Allied—but in practice American—government of Japan. Carlos P. Romulo, the Philippine representative in the FEC, called for Japanese factory machinery and other equipment be transferred to the Philippines as part of the reparations.[27]

The US at first supported the Philippine claims, hoping to remove Japan's ability to make war and to decentralise industries

26. The most thorough coverage of the Filipino participation in the Tokyo trials is by Hitoshi Nagai, 'The Tokyo War Crimes Trial' in Ikehata and Yu-Jose (eds), *Philippines-Japan Relations*, pp. 261–98. For Philippine war crimes trials, see Ricardo T. Jose, 'The Philippine War Crimes Trials, 1947–1949' in *Remembering World War II in the Philippines*, (Manila: National Historical Institute, 2007), Vol. II, pp. 65–80.

27. This section based on Ito, 'Postwar US Military Policy'; Carlos P. Romulo, Report

in Asia. As the Cold War developed, however, particularly after the fall of China to the communists, the Americans began eyeing a strong Japan as an ally, who might serve as a bulwark against the expansion of communism. In order to achieve this, Japan's industries would have to be rehabilitated. In order to help Japan stand up, the US discouraged further Philippine reparations claims.

The need for an allied and economically stable Japan became more imperative to the Americans once the Korean War broke out. The US decided that the Allied occupation should be ended and a formal treaty ending World War II be signed, allowing Japan to re-enter the family of nations as an independent, democratic country. It pressured the Philippines to attend the peace conference at Washington and to sign the peace treaty. The treaty as proposed by the US dropped all claims for reparations in the interests of a stable, free Asia. This US line caused anti-American protests, which reached their peak when John Foster Dulles, Truman's special ambassador, visited Manila to try to persuade the Philippine government to accept the peace treaty. The Philippines signed the treaty reluctantly, but only after getting changes that allowed reparations claims to be pursued after the signing of the treaty. The Americans discouraged this, but the Philippines would push through its claims.

Criticism of the pro-US policy

Although official policy was to maintain close ties with the US—and speeches by Filipino diplomats at international conferences almost always spoke highly of the US—opposition to this policy, led by Recto, was growing stronger. Recto questioned the Philippines' "mendicant" foreign policy, and criticised as being unfair

on the Peace Treaty with Japan (unpublished, 1951); Lydia Yu-Jose, 'Philippine-Japan Relations: The Revolutionary Years and a Century Hence' in Aileen Baviera and Lydia Yu-Jose (eds), *Philippine External Relations: A Centennial Vista* (Manila: Foreign Service Institute, 1998), pp. 310–12; Takushi Ohno, *War Reparations and Peace Settlement: Philippines-Japan Relations, 1945–1956* (Manila: Solidaridad Publishing House, 1986).

and one-sided the US economic and security policies towards the Philippines. By 1956, a great outburst of nationalism was sweeping the Philippine legislature, calling for re-examination of all treaties with the US.[28]

Recto, who had served as foreign minister in the 1943 Philippine Republic established by Japan, emerged as one of the key leaders in this nationalistic movement. The 1943 republic's president, Jose P. Laurel, was also strongly opposed to the unquestioning alliance with the US, and the ideological blinds which cut the Philippines off from its Asian neighbours.[29] Recto and Laurel criticised the close US-Philippine relationship as not being nationalistic, since dependence on the Americans made the Philippines subservient to the US. The presence of American bases on Philippine soil could well attract attacks rather than deter them; and with the American flag flying over them and the lands under US lease not under Philippine government jurisdiction, the bases made a mockery of Philippine independence. During the discussion of the MBA in 1947, critics of the agreement pointed out that these allowances to the Americans encroached on Philippine sovereignty, and that the 99-year period was simply too long. Supporters of the MBA pointed out that the savings the Philippine government would reap from not having to buy expensive military hardware could be put to better use for economic development. MBA critics maintained that the bases only deepened Philippine dependence on the US, and would result in a weak national armed force.

The Mutual Defense Treaty was also criticised by Recto as being an "empty declaration", because it did not provide for automatic US military reaction in case the Philippines was attacked. He and other critics noted the ambiguity with which it was writ-

28. Meyer, *A Diplomatic History*, pp. 173–81.

29. A thorough discussion of Recto's ideas can be found in Emerciana Yuvienco Arcellana, *The Social and Political Thought of Claro Mayo Recto* (Manila: National Research Council of the Philippines, 1981).

ten: following "constitutional processes" could take time and did not guarantee that the US would support the Philippines in war.

The Philippine administration also came in for criticism for being a US puppet—following its master loyally without pride or dignity—as did Filipinos for being brainwashed into adopting American ways and being infected with a colonial mentality, losing their Asian identity in trying to copy things American. (On the other side of the coin, both the Soviet Union and the People's Republic of China also called the Philippines a US puppet.) Non-aligned Asian nations such as Indonesia also tended to look askance at the Philippines' pro-US posture.

The Military Assistance Agreement was criticised by Senator Carlos P. Garcia—a World War II guerrilla officer and later president of the Philippines—for making the Philippine armed forces an appendage of the US. He had urged safeguards in the agreement, but was outvoted.[30]

Ferment

With the Huks posing a very real threat to take over Manila, Quirino appointed as his secretary of national defence in 1950 an energetic World War II veteran in the Philippine Congress, Ramon Magsaysay. Almost overnight, morale in the military shot up. The government campaign against the Huks turned aggressive; Huk leaders were soon captured and the backbone of the communist uprising broken. The victory was made possible through a potent combination of Magsaysay's personality, effective use of professional Filipino officers and psychological warfare.[31]

Magsaysay went on to decisively defeat Quirino in the 1953 presidential election. Staunchly anti-communist, charismatic, and widely popular among the Filipinos, he was considered by the US the perfect president during the Cold War. He opened the gates

30. Meyer, *A Diplomatic History*, p. 42.

31. The classic scholarly political biography of Magsaysay is Jose V. Abueva, *Ramon Magsaysay: A Political Biography* (Manila: Solidaridad, 1971).

of Malacañang Palace—the presidential residence—to the people, and set up a system for any Filipino to report grievances to the government via one-centavo telegrams. He subverted the Huks' battle cry of 'Land for the Landless' by offering them land if they surrendered. The communist menace in the guise of the Huks was destroyed.

Magsaysay moved the Philippines closer to the US orbit by taking the opportunity to hold a summit conference in Manila in September 1954. The result was the Manila Pact, which created the Southeast Asia Treaty Organization (SEATO). Coming just months after the fall of Dien Bien Phu in Vietnam, SEATO was the United States' answer to the communist tide in Asia, although only two countries were really from Southeast Asia—the Philippines and Thailand. The other members were former colonisers or their allies—the US, Great Britain, France, Australia and New Zealand, with Pakistan added.[32]

In a sense SEATO was similar to the alliance Quirino had hoped to forge five years earlier, except that it had no teeth. Like the Mutual Defense Treaty of 1951, SEATO member states would react to a threat on any member only in accordance with their respective constitutional processes. Unlike NATO, there was no provision for automatic retaliation. While there were joint military exercises, in practice SEATO was not a military alliance.

The Philippine armed forces did benefit from the alliance to a limited extent. In 1955, the Eisenhower administration turned over T-33 jet trainers to the Philippine Air Force (PAF), bringing it to the jet age. Two years later, F-86 fighters were transferred to the PAF (though it must be noted that by this time the US was already using more modern aircraft and the F-86s were already obsolescent).[33]

32. A fuller discussion of SEATO from the Philippine standpoint is in Meyer, *A Diplomatic History*, pp. 226–40, and Cullather, *Illusions of Influence*, pp. 141–5.

33. Cullather, *Illusions of Influence*, pp. 134ff; Pobre, *History of the Armed Forces*, p. 382. The PAF was proud of its fighters nevertheless, and organised an aerobatic exhibition team called the Blue Diamonds.

Magsaysay saw the communist threat in Asia as a threat against the Philippines, and authorised the dispatch of an all-Filipino civic team made up of doctors and nurses to Vietnam, in a programme called Operation *Brotherhood.* When Communist China shelled the Quemoy and Matsu islands of Taiwan, Magsaysay voiced concern and supported the US stand to defend the islands if necessary. Other Filipinos supporting the anti-communist line considered any criticism of the pro-American policy—or even liberal ideas exploring the roots of peasant unrest—as a form of subversion, and had writers of such sentiments investigated. Any thought of opening relations with the USSR or the People's Republic of China was deemed equally suspect.[34]

But despite the strong anti-communist—and pro-US—stand of the Magsaysay administration, there was another line of thought emerging. The various problems and irritants in the Philippine-US relationship, as well as disappointment on the Philippine side that their loyalty to the Americans had not been recompensed by US actions, led to moves to re-examine US-Philippine relations. This was part of a growing nationalist trend led by Recto and Laurel, which criticised the existing policy as being over-dependent on the US and prioritising geopolitical concerns over Philippine problems. Recto particularly singled out the bases, claiming that they were magnets for attack rather than deterrents; he also argued that special relations between the US and the Philippines were non-existent: the Americans had their own interests and these did not always work for the Philippines' benefit. Rather than rely on the US, Recto argued for a more Asian orientation.

Nationalism and regionalism—these were the new ideas that Recto and Laurel, among others, espoused in order to transcend the ideological conflict of the Cold War. Nationalism found expression in prioritising Philippine needs over large-scale geopolitical

34. A number of writers and professors of the University of the Philippines were among those accused of subversion, among them Leopoldo Yabes, who wrote an in-depth analysis of the peasant problem in the Philippines.

concerns. Magsaysay, even though he was pro-American, could not dismiss the rising tide and did call for a review of the bases agreement, with an eye to shortening the duration of the leases and granting more authority to Philippine authorities with respect to crimes committed by American servicemen. The review was also in response to increasingly brazen American attempts to enlarge the bases and station nuclear weapons in them. The review came to naught, but it did show that not all Filipinos were happy with the bases.[35] Incidentally, a more reciprocal trade agreement was also negotiated under the Magsaysay administration; the Philippine panel was led by no less than Laurel.

In 1955, non-aligned nations, including the People's Republic of China, met for the first time in Bandung, Indonesia. The Philippines recognised the historicity of the event and the opportunity to have its voice heard in an Asian gathering. Romulo, a veteran diplomat, advised Magsaysay that Philippine attendance was especially important, lest it become the outcast of Asia. But the Philippines could not attend as a regular participant because of its ties with the US. With US bases on Philippine soil, the Philippines could not claim that it was non-aligned. Romulo was allowed to attend only as an observer. The presence of Communist China in the conference was problematic, too, given the Philippines' anti-communist stance, and Romulo was instructed not to commit any act that might be construed as recognising the PRC.[36] Romulo saw the importance of the conference and wrote about it; he had been extremely pro-American before but would later change his stand and opt for a more pro-Asian policy.

The two trends—pro-American anti-communism, and nationalism coupled with regionalism—would continue through the late

35. Cullather, *Illusions of Influence*, pp. 134ff; Salamanca, *Towards a Diplomatic History*, pp. 110–32.

36. Severo Canete Madrona Jr., 'Respectable Independence: The Foreign Policy of Carlos P. Garcia, 1957–1961' (unpublished MA History thesis, University of the Philippines, 2002); Carlos P. Romulo, *The Meaning of Bandung* (Chapel Hill: University of North Carolina Press, 1956); Meyer, *A Diplomatic History*, pp. 221–5.

1950s and early 60s. But it was still too early for an Asian policy to surface formally. In 1954, the undersecretary of foreign affairs, Leon Ma Guerrero, spoke about an Asia for Asians. He was severely criticised for this, since the phrase smacked of the slogan the Japanese had used in World War II, which had such disastrous consequences. Magsaysay distanced himself from Guerrero, who was then made ambassador to London, far away from trouble.[37]

The two trends pointed to a reality that had always been there but not given attention. The Philippines, having been a colony of Spain and the US, had close cultural, educational, religious and political links to the West. But the Philippines was geographically in Asia. Diplomat Salvador P. Lopez wrote of this conflict in the Philippine identity:

> Torn between the opposing tropisms of ideology and geography, the Filipino has become so ambivalent as to be almost schizophrenic. He is in Asia but not of it; he wants to belong to Asia but is aware that he is not fully accepted by his fellow Asians. There is in consequence something frenetic about his efforts to prove his Asianness; he is even willing to listen to the cultural nationalists and purists who urge him to discard the Western trappings of his life as well as the Western furniture of his mind and soul.

The emerging question was: should the Philippines stick with its old ally, even with all the problems and disappointments of that alliance, or should the country seek other directions, towards Asia?[38]

Towards 'respectable independence'

The sudden death in March 1957 of Magsaysay in a plane crash cut short his administration. Garcia, his vice-president and foreign secretary, took over and essentially continued Magsaysay's policies.

37. Meyer, *A Diplomatic History*, pp. 190–5.

38. Salvador P. Lopez, 'New Directions in Philippine Foreign Policy', *Army Journal* (Jun 1977), p. 6. In earlier years, Romulo, echoing another view, wrote about how the Filipinos were superior to other Asians, combining the best of the two worlds.

When Garcia won a full term in the November elections, however, he placed more emphasis on Philippine needs. Larger geopolitical and ideological concerns would have to take second place as the Philippines tackled its own problems, while projecting a "respectable independence" to the world. The Philippines had not recognised the Soviet Union or the People's Republic of China, neither of which had recognised the Philippines. The USSR and PRC had branded the Philippines a US puppet, and other Asian nations reportedly were suspicious of the Philippines' close ties with the US. These opinions hurt, and Garcia was conscious of them, thus his determination to improve the Philippines' image with more nationalistic policies. Still, Garcia rebuffed early Russian attempts to open relations; imports from communist countries were also banned.[39]

Garcia was acutely aware of the failure of the US to live up to its obligations, as seen from Filipino eyes. The veterans' recognition and benefits issue still festered—he knew this only too well, having been a guerrilla during the war and having participated in veterans' recognition talks with the US. The failure of the Americans to pay for all war damage claims, total US authority in the bases and environs (the Philippine government did not know whether nuclear weapons were in the bases, nor did it know US plans for the bases) and other related issues rankled. While Germany had managed to negotiate a status of forces agreement with the US in US bases in Germany, such an agreement had never been negotiated in the Philippines.

Garcia's foreign secretary in his full term as president was Felixberto Serrano, who was close to Recto. Philippine foreign policy shifted then from almost total dependence on the US to a more Asian and Philippine policy. The Asian policy gave rise to the Association of Southeast Asia (ASA), which included the Philippines, Thailand and Malaya. Launched in Bangkok in 1961, ASA

39. For details, see Madrona, 'Respectable Independence', pp. 99–110; also see F. Landa Jocano, *Philippines—USSR Relations* (Metro Manila: NDCP Foundation, 1988), pp. 42–3.

was non-military and non-ideological; instead it was meant as a venue for economic and cultural cooperation.[40]

Garcia also strengthened ties with Japan, with whom the Philippines had finally inked a reparations agreement in 1956, which led to ratification of the peace treaty, enabling formal diplomatic relations to be resumed.[41]

Playing down the impact of the Cold War, Garcia clarified that the Philippine stance on the Quemoy and Matsu islands was only moral support for the US, and did not mean that the Philippines would actually send troops.[42]

On the local front, Garcia launched the 'Filipino First' programme. Basically economic in nature, this programme gave strength to Filipino businessmen and industrialists through government assistance. The public was urged to buy Filipino products rather than imports. The programme hurt the Americans, who considered it as being enacted against them. Garcia maintained that it was the only way to get the Philippine economy on its feet.

While recognising the importance of the US to the Philippines, Garcia called for a re-examination of Philippine policy towards the Americans. In his inaugural address in December 1957, he stated that his administration was determined to "preserve and enhance our historic relation of friendship with the United States" but added that this was to be "based on equality, mutuality of interest and community of ideals". He pushed for a re-examination of the bases agreement, with the end in view of gaining greater Philippine authority over them. Military assistance from the US, he declared, was a matter of right and not privilege.[43]

The US took Garcia's stand as being too demanding, and the bases talks collapsed. It curtly rejected Garcia's stand that assistance was a matter of right. Considering the various crises then

40. Madrona, 'Respectable Independence', pp. 77–9; Meyer, *A Diplomatic History*, p. 269.

41. For details on these negotiations, see Ohno, *War Reparations*.

42. Madrona, 'Respectable Independence', p. 164.

43. Domingo, *The Re-making of Philippine Foreign Policy*, p. 31; Madrona, 'Respectable Independence', pp. 111–15.

going on, what was happening in the Philippines was small fry. The resulting impasse has been called, by Pacifico Castro, the period of *immobilisme*.[44]

Garcia ran for a second term but lost. He was succeeded by Diosdado Macapagal. Macapagal did not pursue ASA, nor did he carry on the 'Filipino First' programme. Instead he pushed for a resolution of Philippine war debt payments in the US Congress; when the bill failed to pass, he cancelled a planned state visit to the US and instead went to Spain. He also changed the date of Philippine independence from 4 July 1946 to 12 June 1898, when Filipinos had proclaimed their independence during the revolution against Spain. Macapagal also terminated the agreement that allowed the US to represent the Philippines in countries where the Philippines had no diplomatic mission. When a treaty banning nuclear tests in the atmosphere, in outer space and underwater was up for signing in Moscow in 1964, Macapagal designated Pakistan to sign for the Philippines, since the Philippines did not have ties with the Soviet Union.[45]

Growing dissatisfaction with the US over limited military assistance, among other grievances, pushed Macapagal to strengthen relations with Europe and Africa. In Southeast Asia, Macapagal joined with the leaders of the neighbouring states in creating the concept of Maphilindo (Malaysia, Philippines, Indonesia). Macapagal would state that the "Filipinos are an indubitably Asian nation".[46] Maphilindo would collapse, however, when the Philippines' claim to Sabah strained relations to breaking point and torpedoed the proposed confederation. Furthermore, border clashes between Malaya and Indonesia in Borneo brought forth the realisation that local wars might be just as threatening as the ideological wars of the Cold War.[47]

44. Madrona, 'Respectable Independence', pp. 119–35; Domingo, *The Re-making of Philippine Foreign Policy*, p. 18.

45. Proclamation No. 28, 12 May 1962, published in the Official Gazette; Diosdado Macapagal, *The Philippines Turns East* (Quezon City: Mac Publishing House, 1966), p. 9.

46. Macapagal, *The Philippines Turns East*.

47. Carlos L. Albert, 'The War Next Door: A Filipino at Borneo Frontline',

Despite its stronger nationalist and regionalistic stand, the Philippines remained anti-communist. In 1960, during the 15th Session of the United Nations General Assembly, the Philippine delegate to the United Nations, Lorenzo Sumulong, challenged Nikita Khrushchev's proposed declaration to grant independence to colonial countries, by urging that it include those states with paper independence, including peoples of Eastern Europe swallowed by the Soviet Union. It was at this point that Khrushchev removed his shoe and began banging it on his table. Khrushchev ridiculed Philippine independence and called the Philippines a stooge of the US. Sumulong insisted on replying and defended the Philippines.[48] He was congratulated by several members of the General Council.

But calls grew louder for a more independent foreign policy, one that transcended the Cold War. In 1964, Salvador P. Lopez, then the secretary of foreign affairs, urged the revision of the Philippine policy towards the Soviet Union and other Eastern European states. He was the first high government official to do so. He also advocated an Asian policy that took into account the emergence of China as a power in Asia. Lopez also recommended the Philippines' excessive dependency on the US be reduced by developing a "new foreign policy leverage and broadening our options in international affairs".[49] This would be taken seriously by the next administration.

Ferdinand Marcos took over as president in December 1965. During his first term, he maintained a strong US policy, and hosted an international summit conference. The summit, attended by US President Lyndon B. Johnson, produced the Manila Declaration to help Vietnam in late 1966. Johnson obtained a commitment from Marcos to send a Philippine contingent to Vietnam, even though

Philippines Herald, 6–10 July 1965. (Interestingly, this series was reprinted by Malaysia's Department of Information.) Baviera and Yu-Jose (eds), *Philippine External Relations: A Centennial Vista*, passim.

48. Madrona, 'Respectable Independence', pp. 199–203.

49. Lopez, 'New Directions in Philippine Foreign Policy', p. 7.

Marcos had promised during the election that he would not do so. Marcos did send a Philippine force, the Philippine Civic Action Group (PHILCAG), to Vietnam, but they did not fight in the front lines. In return for this, the US provided the Philippine armed forces with engineering equipment and F-5 fighter aircraft, among others. In this sense, Marcos was following the old policy of close alliance with the US.[50]

But the dispatch of PHILCAG touched a raw nerve among Philippine students and intellectuals, and the Vietnam War became the subject of heated debates and demonstrations, many of which became violent. Despite the growing tensions, Marcos was able to get the Philippines aboard the Association of Southeast Asian Nations (ASEAN) in 1967.

Marcos had stated in his inaugural address that the Filipinos were a people strong and free, who traced their ancestral roots to Asia. The Filipinos were proud of their Oriental heritage as well as Western culture, said Marcos, paving the way for a multi-linear, omni-directional foreign policy.

A new foreign policy

By the late 1960s, the brinksmanship diplomacy of the 1950s was over and *détente* was being practised. The superpowers were talking with each other and negotiating arms control. But the Vietnam War simmered on, even as new weapons were developed.

The Philippines began to face new domestic issues, among them anti-American and anti-government student and labour demonstrations. An anti-government communist movement was revived—the Communist Party of the Philippines (CPP) with its armed wing, the New People's Army. (The CPP derived its inspiration from Mao Zedong, while the Huks had been followers of the Russian, Marxist form of communism.) Militant Islam began to rear its head in the form of the Moro National Liberation Front.

50. Cf. Domingo, *The Re-making of Philippine Foreign Policy*, Pobre, *History of the Armed Forces*.

These forces gave Marcos reason to worry, but the US bases did not provide much support. The bases were busy with Vietnam and other US interests in Southeast Asia, not domestic Philippine problems. It had become obvious that Philippine and American interests did not always coincide. To Lopez, the objective of the US was to remain a power in Asia, which is what the bases were in the Philippines to ensure. But the purpose of the Philippines was to become a credible Asian nation, "living in peace with its neighbors and assisting in the maintenance of a just a durable peace in the region". The US bases tended to complicate the issue, even as the Philippines did not have strong armed forces.[51]

The ideological barrier was already being challenged by the Philippine Congress, which sent a mission to the Soviet Union and Eastern Europe in 1967 to explore possible trade relations. The mission recommended the removal of all barriers between the Philippines and socialist countries. Actual if limited trade began soon after.[52]

Faced with severe domestic problems, Marcos declared martial law in September 1972. Without a Congress to deal with, Marcos was able to craft a new and more independent foreign policy. He declared that this new policy was pragmatic, flexible, non-ideological, and beneficial to both the Philippines and those states with which it was engaging, but with Philippine interests ever at the fore. He opened embassies in Eastern Europe, and followed this up with state visits to China and Soviet Russia. Formal relations with the PRC were started in June 1975, while relations with the USSR were reached in 1976. Ever pragmatic, the Marcos administration opened formal relations with Vietnam in 1976—just a year after the Vietnam War ended.[53]

51. Lopez, 'New Directions in Philippine Foreign Policy', p. 7.

52. *The Enverga Report on the Exploratory Mission to the Socialist Countries in 1967* (Manila: Congress of the Republic of the Philippines, 1968), p. 72. Manuel S. Enverga was then chairman of the House Committee on Foreign Affairs.

53. For specific dates and treaties, see *Philippine Diplomacy: Chronology and Documents 1972–1981* (Manila: Foreign Service Institute, 1981), pp. 48–9, 251–3.

This change in diplomacy reflected not only Marcos's and his diplomats' views of how this innovative foreign policy was to be carried out, but also the changing balance of power in Southeast Asia. After the Vietnam War, the US was no longer the military power it was held to be, and the time was ripe to renegotiate the bases agreement—stressing Philippine authority and American assistance (Marcos used the term 'rent'; the Americans maintained that what they gave was 'aid'). The Philippine flag was now allowed to fly over the bases, while the bases themselves would have a Filipino base commander (at least in name).

The new balance of power and the opening of relations with communist countries gave Marcos leverage to gain more concessions from the US. If US military assistance was not forthcoming, the Philippines would seek it elsewhere. As a result, the Philippine armed forces sourced light tanks from Britain, trainer aircraft from Italy, and trucks from Romania. Marcos also pushed for a more self-reliant defence posture and established a government arsenal in Bataan to manufacture ammunition and spare parts.[54] Furthermore, Marcos engineered agreements between Australia and New Zealand regarding Special Warfare Exercises in 1982. Philippine defence was no longer the monopoly of the United States.

Marcos also took advantage of the discord between China and the Soviet Union; he was careful to open relations with both countries. Not only did Marcos provide for a counterbalance for one or the other, but he also could use these relations as leverage towards the US.[55]

In order to ensure fuel security, as well as help forge a solution to the Muslim separatism movement in Mindanao, Marcos actively sought the cooperation of Libya and Saudi Arabia.

By 1975, Marcos publicised the guidelines for his new foreign policy, prioritising, in order, ASEAN relations; relations with

54. Pobre, *History of the Armed Forces*, pp. 501–2. Spare parts and non-interchangeable components, however, remain a problem.

55. Lopez, 'New Directions in Philippine Foreign Policy', p. 7.

Socialist states, especially the Soviet Union and China; closer identification with the Third World; continuing beneficial relations with Japan; supporting Arab countries in their struggle for a just and enduring peace in Middle East; and finding a new basis, "compatible with the emerging realities in Asia, for a continuing healthy relationship with the US". Marcos moved towards non-alignment, even with the US bases still on Philippine soil.[56]

Marcos, however, overused his powers, and his administration turned into a dictatorship—which the US nevertheless felt constrained to support until the last moment. His removal in 1986 did not, however, spell the end for the foreign policies that he, and the best Filipino diplomats, had crafted.

Epilogue

After long negotiations, in 1966 the Military Bases Agreement was reduced to 25 years thereon, subject to negotiation; in 1991 the Philippine Senate voted against extending the leases on the bases. The Military Assistance Agreement, on the other hand, was extended in 1950 for 3 years, and in 1953 extended indefinitely. It is at present still in force. In the 1990s, the US and the Philippines signed the Visiting Forces Agreement—assuring US forces access to the Philippines. The Cold War is now over, but its legacies live on in the Philippines.

56. Domingo, *The Re-making of Philippine Foreign Policy*, pp. 35–6.

5

ALPHABET SOUP AND NUCLEAR WAR: SEATO, CHINA AND THE COLD WAR IN SOUTHEAST ASIA

Brian P. Farrell

In September 1966 the Southeast Asia Treaty Organization (SEATO) published its report for the past year, in which it reiterated the alliance's central purpose—"to halt China's long-term aspirations for the domination of Asia."[1] Ten years before, SEATO had begun to plan the military defence of Southeast Asia against Chinese aggression, envisaging as a worst-case scenario a massive military invasion of the 'Treaty Area' by the armed forces of the People's Republic of China. The strategic plan it adopted in 1962 to face that threat, Plan 4, assumed the United States of America and United Kingdom would use nuclear weapons to destroy multiple targets in southern China and Southeast Asia, to defeat any such Chinese onslaught. But the plan was overtaken by events even as it was adopted. Plan 4 turned out, in fact, to be a metaphor for SEATO and the Cold War at large.

In September 1954 the US, the UK, Australia, France, New Zealand, Pakistan, the Philippines and Thailand signed the Manila Pact, or Southeast Asia Collective Defence Treaty (SEACDT), out of which SEATO would eventually be created. Its declared purpose was to organise collective security to contain Chinese Communist expansionism in the region. But for the British, an equally important motive was to enhance their influence on American defence policy. And the problem at hand was not overt Chinese aggression

1. 'SEATO Report 1965–1966' (8 Sept 1966), The National Archives, UK (TNA): FCO 15/393.

but rather Southeast Asian communist political and military subversion, especially in successor states carved out of former French Indochina. The interplay between these three factors—the Chinese threat to the region, American policy, and communist challenges within the region—shaped the evolution of SEATO, until the massive American military intervention in the war in Vietnam in 1965. For the British, this triangle defined SEATO within their national policy. This came out most strongly in the contingency planning that produced Plan 4.

The British played an important role in shaping Plan 4, trying hard to relate it to wider collective security problems. Closer examination of their efforts sheds important light on three questions. How did SEATO plan and prepare to fight major war in Southeast Asia? What can these plans and preparations tell us about Western perceptions of the Cold War and the use of nuclear weapons? And what can they tell us about SEATO as an instrument of collective security? This chapter will show that Plan 4 exposed three things. Western thinking about nuclear weapons and military strategy evolved over time, but could not reconcile the worst-case threat to Southeast Asia with the very different attacks it actually suffered. The Americans were willing to use SEATO if possible but resolved to use force as they saw necessary, to defend the partition of 1954. Finally, the British felt obliged to support military plans to contain China they did not see as viable in order to try to retain something they saw as essential: influence over American conduct of the Cold War.

The partition of Vietnam in 1954 by the Geneva Agreements framed SEATO's effort to contain communist expansion in Southeast Asia. It also revealed the different priorities influencing that effort. The UK played a leading role in orchestrating the Geneva Agreements, and along with the Soviet Union agreed to act as co-sponsor for their implementation. The British government diplomatically recognised the PRC and its communist government as accomplished facts the West must deal with. The US on the other hand only 'took note' of the Geneva Agreements, warned all parties that it reserved the right to respond to any violation of them, and did not recognise the PRC or its communist government as legitimate. The British promoted the Manila Pact to try to bridge this divergence with the Americans over how to respond to French defeat in Indochina, and how to contain China. They knew only an American commitment would make collective security in Southeast Asia possible. But they also worried the Americans might provoke avoidable confrontation, and sought to retain influence on American policy. Australia and New Zealand faced a similar balancing act. Both now regarded Southeast Asia as fundamental to their own security. Both pursued a policy of forward defence that, due to limited means, could only be effective if it rested on British and American engagement.[2]

The SEACDT complicated matters by combining Western and Asian powers in a collective security partnership. The Asian members saw SEATO as a means to obtain American aid. Pakistan, a geographical stretch to begin with, sought only to win support in its fraught relationship with India. Thailand regarded itself as a front-line state whose security should be SEATO's top priority. The Philippines, already a junior military partner of the US, wanted more attention to its internal security concerns. Then there was France. Humiliated in Vietnam, disengaging from Indochina, the French sought to save as much face and preserve as much influence as possible—as well as remain in touch with American policy in the region. Nor can it be said the American motive was disinterested. When possible American military intervention to rescue French forces in Dien Bien Phu was discussed in spring 1954, one precondition not satisfied was that American forces must not act unilaterally. If other allies were concerned about the situation, they

2. Daniel Fineman, *A Special Relationship: The United States and Military Government in Thailand, 1947–1958* (Honolulu: University of Hawaii Press, 1997), pp. 193–6; Ronald B. Frankum, *The United States and Australia in Vietnam 1954–1968: Silent Partners* (Lewiston, NY: Edwin Mellen, 2001), chapter 3; P. Busch, *All the Way with JFK? Britain, the US and the Vietnam War* (Oxford: Oxford University Press, 2003), pp. 36–7.

must put their money where their mouth was. President Dwight D. Eisenhower and Secretary of State John Foster Dulles saw the Manila Pact as a means to legitimise, at home and abroad, any further American effort to contain communism in Southeast Asia.[3]

Eisenhower and Dulles certainly had a point. The Western military presence in the region was denounced as 'neocolonialism' by states such as Indonesia and India. Despite having Asian signatories, the SEACDT was condemned as a ploy to extend Western hegemony. This criticism was ramped up in spring 1955 at the Bandung Conference, which inaugurated the so-called Non-Aligned Movement. President Sukarno of Indonesia singled out the pact as interference in Southeast Asian efforts to decolonise without being dragged into the Cold War. The Americans were undaunted. They spelt out a strategic line of containment to emphasise how important regional partners were to this new coalition. The signatories added a Protocol declaring they would consult not only about any threat to any member state but also any threat to "designated" states: Cambodia, Laos, and "the free territory under the jurisdiction of the State of Vietnam". The Protocol States and the partition of Vietnam became the front line of containment. Thailand welcomed this commitment, which also suited the Philippines and the Commonwealth allies as providing forward defence for their own national interests. But Pakistan sought to enlarge the area seen as threatened; France resented being displaced in its former colonies; and the British fretted about how to contain China while also restraining the Americans.[4]

The British hoped the SEACDT could be the instrument of containment, because they did not think an effective anti-communist government could emerge in South Vietnam. Simply declaring the intention to contain communism might suffice, without forc-

3. Frankum, *The United States and Australia in Vietnam*, chapter 2; J. Prados, *Operation Vulture* (New York: Ibooks, Inc, 2002).

4. J. Mackie, *Bandung 1955: Non-Alignment and Afro-Asian Solidarity* (Singapore: Didier Millet, 2005); Frankum, *The United States and Australia in Vietnam*, chapters 3 and 5; Karl Hack, *Defence and Decolonisation in Southeast Asia: Britain, Malaya and Singapore 1941–68* (Richmond: Curzon, 2001), chapters 5–6.

ing the allies to make problematic commitments. But John Foster Dulles saw things differently. Dulles refused to settle for a political promise resting on no tangible commitments. He played his part to develop the North Atlantic Treaty Organization (NATO) from a declaration of intent to an integrated military alliance with standing joint forces, a coalition command structure, and agreed plans. This was collective security and deterrence with teeth—a development the British supported, in Europe. They did not believe such a model would fit in Southeast Asia. Dulles agreed this new alliance should not lead to military integration with standing joint forces or a coalition command structure. He wished to preserve American freedom of action in this more fluid strategic theatre. But he did want to build something more substantial to make the deterrent more effective—to "put red blood in the blue baby".[5] His answer was to turn a treaty into a coalition, with a structure that could at least guide and focus any action it might take.

Dulles used Article V of the SEACDT to forge his instrument. The article enabled signatories "to provide for consultation with regard to military and any other planning as the situation obtaining in the Treaty Area may from time to time require". Thanks to his pressure the signatories decided in February 1955 to establish SEATO. The idea was not to replicate NATO; an attack on one member was not automatically considered an attack on all, but only an act to which all members would respond as they saw fit—as was attack on any Protocol State. National forces would not be placed under any standing SEATO command. The Americans insisted on retaining freedom to act. That made their allies more interested in measures the Americans were ready to consider—measures to make SEATO a potentially viable military instrument to "deter and if need be defeat" any communist attack on the Treaty Area.[6]

5. 'Relations between SEATO, CENTO and NATO', DEA Brief (3 Apr 1963), Archives New Zealand (hereafter ANZ): EA 1, W 2668,

6. The phrase comes from Damien Fenton's forthcoming book, *SEATO and the Defence of Southeast Asia 1955–1965: Caging the Red Dragon*. Fenton's work will be the standard study of SEATO and the Cold War, and it inspired my own interest in the subject of this paper.

The most important were arrangements to provide military advice to SEATO governments, and contingency plans by which SEATO might wage war. Such steps could transform the coalition from a political agreement to a military alliance ready, if necessary, to take the field.

The new coalition thus developed a formal administrative structure.[7] Its headquarters were located in Bangkok, to underline the importance of the regional partners. The Council of Ministers became the highest authority, the body through which member governments would make policy decisions. It would rely on a Military Advisers Group (MAG), consisting of senior military officers from each member state, for military advice. These officers reflected the degree to which each member committed to SEATO: France and Pakistan sent lower-ranking officers, whereas the American adviser was the Commander-in-Chief Pacific (CINCPAC), the British adviser the senior officer based in Singapore. The MAG assumed that realistic coalition war plans could only be forged by a standing coalition planning staff. However, the wheels of bureaucracy took time. Not until March 1957 did the coalition open its Military Planning Office (MPO). Staffed by officers from all member states, the MPO's primary responsibility was to draft contingency plans by which SEATO could respond to attacks on the Treaty Area. This gave the coalition a formal standing body that could think through strategic problems and choices. It also provided another forum in which to discuss national agendas. And it certainly gave SEATO the potential to wage coalition warfare. But member states agreed they must start by establishing fundamental strategic principles. This could be done faster by ad hoc conferences than by waiting for SEATO bureaucracy to take shape. As a result the MPO inherited American 'strategic concepts'. These concepts became the foundation for SEATO's grand strategy.

7. Fenton, *SEATO*, chapter 3; Leszek Buszynski, *SEATO: The Failure of an Alliance Strategy* (Singapore: Singapore University Press, 1983), chapter 2.

The fact that the MPO had to work with inherited ideas highlighted some constraints that shaped its work from the start. American power was so preponderant that any plans must reflect both American intentions and capabilities. This meant that SEATO plans must be refined by efforts to influence American plans. The divergence between national agendas remained wide enough that it was faster to build on an American draft than to produce a combined plan. SEATO plans started from an American national plan to defend Southeast Asia against a major invasion, adopted in February 1955. The plan rested on six points. The Protocol States would be defended. Local ground forces would lead the defence on the ground, supported by American mobile strategic forces, especially air and naval, in reserve. The "enemy" coast, loosely defined to include both China and northern Vietnam, would be blockaded. Air strikes using nuclear weapons would destroy "strategic targets" in "enemy territory". American ground forces would spearhead a counteroffensive to expel enemy forces from friendly territory. Finally, the Americans, through CINCPAC headquarters, would work through SEATO channels to connect allied forces to their plans.[8]

This plan formed the basis of 'strategic concepts' accepted by SEATO planners at an ad hoc conference in Singapore in June 1956. The worst-case scenario was open invasion of the Treaty Area by China's People's Liberation Army (PLA). War plans to meet this scenario would be developed from four concepts. SEATO would resist any armed attack on the Treaty Area by North Vietnamese or Chinese forces, whether regular or presented as 'volunteers', as the Chinese did in Korea in 1950. SEATO forces would engage the enemy in the Protocol States, to provide forward defence for Thailand. Nuclear weapons would be used if deemed militarily necessary and politically acceptable; it was assumed this would not provoke Soviet intervention. And SEATO military strategy would

8. Fenton, *SEATO*, chapter 4.

involve four stages. First SEATO forces, both regional and "out of area", would take up defensive positions. Meanwhile, nuclear weapons would be used on targets in enemy territory, to interdict routes of movement and supply. Second, friendly lines of supply would be secured. Third, SEATO forces would counter-attack, to destroy enemy forces and retake lost territory. Finally, SEATO forces would invade North Vietnam, both from Laos and by amphibious invasion from the sea, to destroy the People's Army of Vietnam (PAVN) and by implication the Democratic Republic of Vietnam (DRV).[9]

Every state drafted contingency plans as part of the process by which they related military power to foreign policy. It was more difficult for coalitions to make such plans, because they had to try to harmonise national agendas and capabilities. Contingency planning was central to 'strategic foreign policy'. Governments that wanted the option to use military force had to identify in advance broad principles by which armed forces might be moved, equipped, supplied, sustained, and directed—and objectives they might be ordered to achieve. The US was a global power with global interests. It had to relate plans for waging war in one region to global policy for the Cold War. The US and UK had to balance regional commitments such as NATO and SEATO because they drew from the same finite pool of armed forces. For a nascent coalition such as SEATO, drafting such plans would address several objectives. Making plans could indicate what military capabilities each partner was willing and able to commit to the coalition. Every other partner hoped to use SEATO planning to identify American intentions and capabilities. Making plans could also indicate what priorities the coalition might agree, and reveal any differences in intelligence appreciations. Finally, making plans could spark concrete measures to strengthen the economy, infrastructure and defences of a given member, for example Thailand.

9. Ibid.

Nuclear weapons were still a new and uncertain factor in waging war and making plans. The US and the Soviet Union had only recently introduced the far more destructive hydrogen bomb, or thermonuclear weapon, into their arsenals. By 1956 American grand strategy rested on nuclear deterrence—the so-called 'New Look' policy. The Americans distinguished between the use of hydrogen weapons and atomic weapons at all levels, from grand strategy down to battlefield tactics. The broadest distinction was to define the nature of military conflict in the most basic possible manner: 'general war' was taken to be global total war involving the Soviet Union, in which all available weapons would be used; 'limited war' was defined as *any* lesser conflict. NATO and SEATO adopted this distinction, which was so broad it did as much to confuse as focus planning. This became evident when planners set to work on SEATO's scenarios. It might be possible to engage PAVN ground forces in Laos without requiring forces NATO needed in Europe, or provoking global political uproar; but attacking targets in China, with any type of nuclear weapons, seemed certain to provoke greater consequences. However, prevailing American and NATO warfighting doctrine now accepted the utility of so-called battlefield or tactical nuclear weapons, delivered by heavy artillery, surface-to-surface missiles, and even smaller ordnance. Doctrine drew a distinction between both scale and target. Smaller weapons with less destructive power, aimed neither at cities nor at homeland strategic targets, but at forces in the field and their supply lines, could be used without provoking escalation to global war. This assumption was widely debated, but meanwhile it shaped American and NATO strategic planning. Soviet conventional forces were formidable; Chinese forces were large and also taken seriously. Matching such manpower would impose grave economic and political strain on the US and its allies, in Europe and Asia. The nuclear deterrent, extended to smaller battlefield weapons, made it seem possible to deter and if necessary defeat communist aggression with smaller conventional forces, posing less risk of mutual annihilation. Such US-sponsored economy of force was transferred from NATO to SEATO, which wrote it in as a planning assumption from the start. There would never be enough conventional forces available to defeat a full-scale invasion of the Treaty Area—but nuclear weapons could fill that gap.[10]

The Singapore conference in June 1956 gave the Australians their first closer look at American ideas for defending Southeast Asia in open war. The Australian Joint Planning Committee (JPC) duly noted that the whole concept for the worst case "was dependent upon the use of nuclear weapons where appropriate".[11] Australian planners noted that thermonuclear weapons were not being considered for SEATO use. The NATO thermonuclear deterrent would contain the Soviet Union, which meant "atomic weapons could be used in a limited war without provoking global war". They also noted that the list of targets for nuclear attacks was directly connected to military operations in the Treaty Area. The 25 first-priority targets included 18 airfields in south China and North Vietnam, as well as port and transportation facilities in south China. The purpose of these attacks would be to isolate communist ground forces invading Thailand and the Protocol States. Two things stood out: the assumption enemy ground forces would converge on Thailand from Burma, Laos and North Vietnam, so SEATO must plan to engage all three axes of advance as far forward as possible; the assumption that SEATO must use nuclear weapons to defeat any major invasion of the Treaty Area, whether by China or North Vietnam. Uncertainty drove this discussion. For example, assuming that using atomic rather than hydrogen weapons would not provoke global war prompted the wry hope that the communists agreed, otherwise "our assumption ... might be falsified." The point was to try to reduce uncertainty. Global

10. L. Freedman, *The Evolution of Nuclear Strategy* (New York: St Martin's Press, 1983); Henry Kissinger, *Nuclear Weapons and Foreign Policy* (New York: W.W. Norton, 1969 [1957]).

11. 'JPC Discussions on 10 July 1956' (11 July 1956), National Archives of Australia (hereafter NAA): A 1838, TS 688.

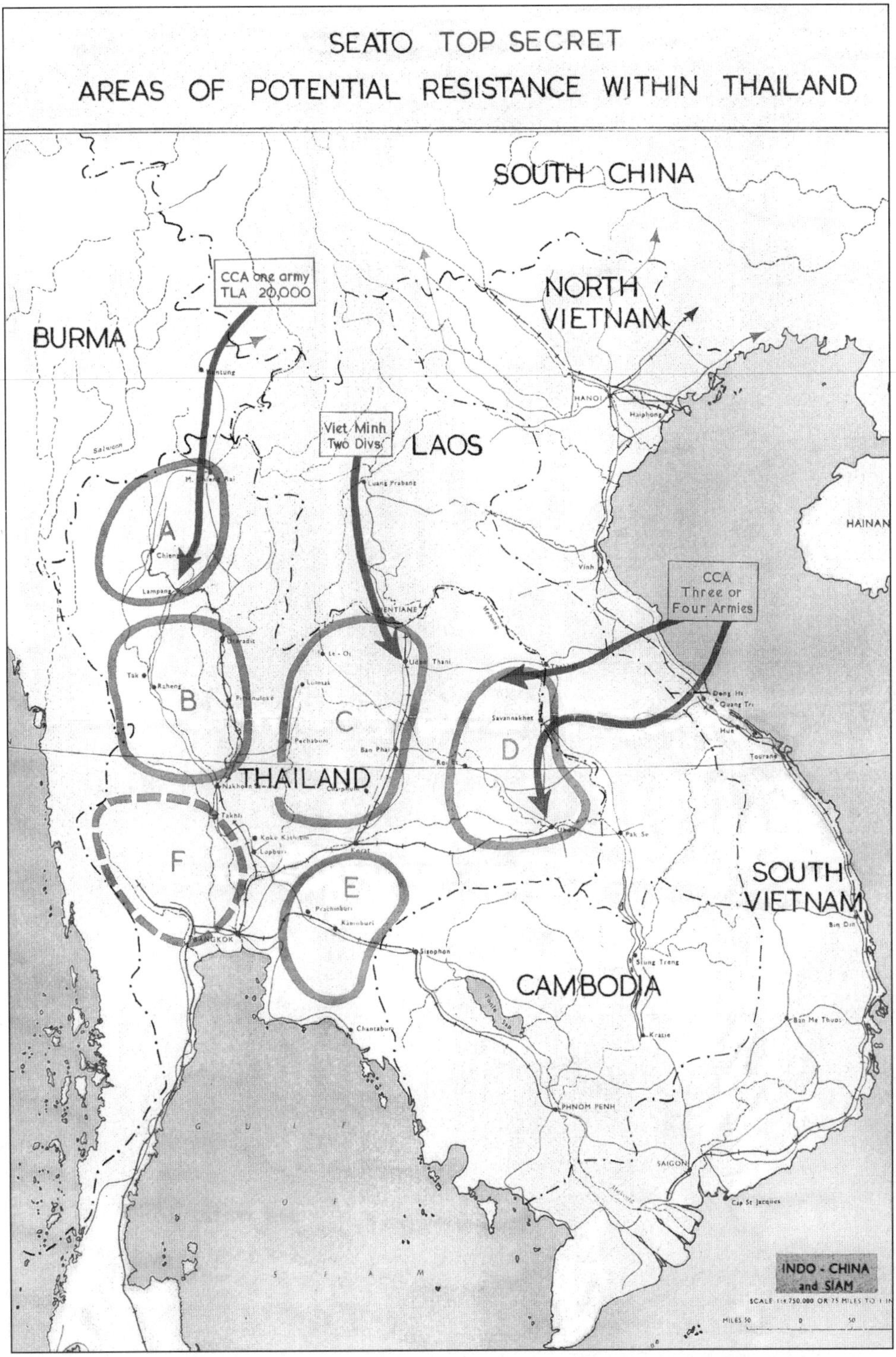

▲ *SEATO: Areas of Potential Resistance within Thailand*. Map accompanying the Report of the Third SEATO Military Staff Planners Conference in Singapore, Australian JPC Report No. 46/1956 (13 July 1956), National Archives of Australia: A 1838, TS 688.

war and major war in Southeast Asia were the greatest threats to Australian security, which ultimately rested on American intentions; therefore, the more specific SEATO plans became the better for Australia.[12]

Pakistan argued that SEATO should study the threat to the Treaty Area in global war. They wanted to bring West Pakistan inside SEATO plans, and learn more about American strategy. The British objected on two grounds: security within SEATO "is not sufficiently high to permit of frank discussion" and focusing on global war "would be likely to divert attention from more immediate threats of subversion and limited war". The Americans agreed, arguing that because they carried greater burdens they required freedom to plan and act—and they shared British concerns about security. And the Australians agreed that "armed action, under conditions which do not permit it to be identified as overt aggression, by organized bands or groups responsive in varying degrees to foreign control or direction", was a problem SEATO must study carefully. On the other hand, no SEATO plans could be realistic without knowing what forces the Americans and British could commit.[13]

The sticking point was clear: the British and Americans disagreed about what SEATO could do in the Protocol States, especially Vietnam. Notwithstanding American intentions, British diplomats warned the South Vietnamese government that because any advance on Hanoi might provoke a much wider war the British "would not therefore even contemplate such planning".[14] Such tensions could be kept at bay so long as threats did not seem immediate, and plans were not ready to be confirmed as formal commitments. But nothing stands still. Rising Cold War tensions, plus changing national defence policies, complicated SEATO's effort to

12. 'Defence Committee Discussion: Report of the Third SEATO Military Staff Planners Conference Singapore June 1956' (19 July 1956), NAA: A 1838, TS 688. See also Map One, attached to the report.

13. 'SEATO Concept for the Defence of Southeast Asia in Global War', JPC Report 58/1956 (7 Nov 1956), NAA: A 1838, TS 688/27/8 part 3.

14. Australian Legation Saigon to DEA, Savingram 2 (26 Jan 1957), NAA: A 1838, TS 688/27/8 part 3.

define strategic plans, but increased pressures to do so. Chinese harassment of the offshore islands lying between Taiwan and the mainland triggered a serious crisis. Chinese efforts to modernise the PLA, supported by Soviet assistance, were worrying. Mao Zedong's 'Great Leap Forward' raised concerns about Chinese stability and intentions, as did his rhetoric denouncing American imperialism, dismissing the nuclear deterrent as a "paper tiger", and demanding more aggressive resistance to "imperialism". Trouble also arose in the Protocol States. The DRV supported communist Pathet Lao military and political pressure against the Laotian government. By spring 1959 the American government grew alarmed about the situation in Laos. Meanwhile the British made some sweeping defence policy changes. The 1957 Defence White Paper reoriented grand strategy, shifting from relying on national service conventional forces to greater emphasis on thermonuclear weapons and the nuclear deterrent. But it would take time to upgrade bases in the Far East, to make it possible to deploy Royal Air Force bombers and Royal Navy aircraft carriers that formed the nuclear deterrent. It would also take time to decide how to compensate for reductions in British conventional forces and still meet commitments from NATO to SEATO, and beyond. The government launched a full-scale review of British overseas defence policy—but MPO planners in Bangkok set the pace.[15]

MPO plans became a forum in which member states tried to reorient SEATO to their own agenda. Work began in spring 1957 on the Plan 1 scenario of a DRV invasion of Thailand and the Protocol States. But by late 1959 members directed the MPO to pursue as first priority a plan to intervene in Laos to confront the Pathet Lao, who were being covertly supported by the DRV. This evolution was important. Plans were adjusted, superseded or discarded according to what seemed necessary—but that depended not only

15. Chen Jian, *Mao's China and the Cold War* (Chapel Hill: UNC Press, 2001); Michael Carver, *Tightrope Walking: British Defence Policy Since 1945* (London: Hutchinson, 1992); Michael Dockrill, *British Defence Since 1945* (Oxford: Blackwell, 1989).

on threat perceptions but also national priorities. The need to spell out force requirements, to make plans realistic, clashed with reluctance to make firm commitments. The need to plan counter-insurgency intervention provoked concerns about political consequences, in the region and at home. Plans involving nuclear weapons provoked arguments about priorities, commitments and consequences. Plans came to represent SEATO efforts to balance clashes between different national concerns and objectives.

Plan 1 was soon discarded as unrealistic on the grounds that the DRV could not launch such a bold challenge without direct Chinese support. Plan 2 replaced it, envisaging a DRV invasion openly reinforced by the Chinese. Concerns about Vietnam prompted Plan 3, to meet a DRV attack on South Vietnam, covertly supported by the Chinese. But trouble in Laos prompted the Americans to champion Plan 5, the counterinsurgency intervention in Laos. This alarmed the British. They feared that Western military intervention in such a politically ambiguous conflict could destabilise the Protocol States, and wreck the Geneva Agreements. On the other hand the Thais insisted SEATO must study this threat on their border more seriously. Meanwhile, Pakistan and the Philippines complained their concerns were not being addressed by any MPO study. These pressures boiled over in September 1959. Plan 3 was already discarded as unrealistic, for reasons similar to Plan 1. The MAG agreed to direct the MPO to work on Plan 5 as first priority. But it also agreed to proceed with another plan, one that "amounted to a new catch-all contingency plan against communist conventional aggression in the SEATO region": Plan 4.[16]

The British knew they had time to reflect before any such plan could be adopted. But they also knew things were becoming more complicated. Before British forces could support SEATO in mis-

16. 'Report of the SEATO Intelligence Ad Hoc Committee Meeting November 1957', DC Agenda Item g (19 Feb 1958); 'SEATO Intelligence Assessments and Resulting Changes in SEATO Military Planning', Tange to Plimsoll (27 Feb 1958), NAA: A 1838, TS 688/27/3; Fenton, *SEATO*, chapter 5.

sions ranging beyond the defence of Malaya and Singapore, they first had to upgrade their airbases, particularly Butterworth and Tengah. Upgrading work triggered a debate about whether storing nuclear weapons there might provoke a local backlash. Singapore was still under British control. But Malaya was now a sovereign state and ally, whose government publicly discouraged entanglement with SEATO, and declared the bases should be used only to defend Malaya from direct attack. Nevertheless the British had already adopted one contingency plan ignoring any such restriction: *Mastodon*, calling for responding to a major crisis by flying out three squadrons of medium bombers—from the so-called V bomber force—from the UK. Such aircraft formed the backbone of the British strategic nuclear deterrent. They could launch nuclear strikes at long range. To buy some time, the British combined with the Americans in 1958 to stall the MPO. They persuaded SEATO to direct the MPO to draft outline plans only, "leaving detailed studies, as may be determined necessary, to be undertaken subsequently". It would also "produce detailed logistic and movement studies designed to investigate capabilities within the theatre of operations designed to sustain SEATO operations envisaged in [Plan 2]".[17]

In autumn 1959 the Americans and British decided to buy more time by another change in direction. This time they persuaded the MPO to discard Plan 2, in favour of the more ambitious Plan 4. This would address Pakistani, Filipino and Thai demands to be included in the worst-case scenario. Work now focused on Plan 4 and a new Plan 6, a revived scenario for North Vietnam invading South Vietnam. The MPO was to concentrate on the counterinsurgency Plan 5, but also develop these new scenarios for 'limited war'. Fenton rightly notes the Americans and Brit-

17. Commonwealth Relations Office (CRO) to UK High Commissioner Canberra, Circular Z 6 (30 Jan 1958), CRO to UK High Commissioner Canberra, Telegram 203 (30 Jan), TNA: PREM 11/3277; 'Note for Record' (1 Oct 1958), Dean to Brook (29 Oct), 'Airfields in Malaya and Singapore' (30 Oct), TNA: CAB 21/4431; DC 'Notes on 8th SEATO Military Advisers Conference' (19 Mar 1958), NAA: A 1838, TS 688/27/3.

ish expected to avoid having to declare force contributions to the worst-case scenario "for at least a couple of years".[18] But there was a catch. Using Plan 4 to buy time meant the plan would in the end take shape. It did so through the earlier work on Plan 2, revolving around nuclear weapons.

Assumptions defining Plan 2 led directly to nuclear weapons. SEATO assumed the communists would try to dominate Southeast Asia by "a combination of political action, subversion and insurgency". But should that fail North Vietnam would invade the Protocol States and possibly Thailand, supported as necessary by China. D-Day would be the day PAVN forces invaded either Laos or South Vietnam. SEATO defensive strategy would "take into account the effects of air attacks with conventional and nuclear weapons on North Vietnam and subsequently on China". The USSR would not intervene. The Protocol States would defend themselves and request SEATO help, making all facilities available. Most important:

> Permission will be given for nuclear weapons to be used on suitable targets wherever they might be. Air attacks on selected targets in North Vietnam, on the Chinese mainland and Hainan Island, using nuclear and conventional weapons, will be undertaken as soon as aggression by [North Vietnam] and the Chinese Communists, respectively, is detected.[19]

These assumptions rested on two themes: the communists would have the military initiative, so their ground forces would attack before SEATO strategic power could pre-empt them; therefore power must destroy the infrastructure through which the enemy would prosecute any strategic advance. Topping the target lists were airbases, ports, railway lines and stations, bridges, roads, sup-

18. Extract from 'Report by Australian Military Adviser to the 9th SEATO MA Conference September 1958' (3 Dec 1958), NAA: A 1838, TS 688/27/3; Fenton, *SEATO*, chapter 5.

19. Australian JPC Agendum 22/58, 'Concept of Operations for Defence against initial Viet Minh Aggression and subsequent Chinese Communist Intervention' (17 Feb 1958), NAA: A 1838, TS 688/27/3.

ply depots and troop staging areas. The Americans identified 50 targets that warranted nuclear strikes, plus another 75 for which conventional weapons should suffice, in northern Vietnam and southern China. SEATO would stop the communist invasion by destroying its supply lines, reinforcements and axes of advance, after which it would counterattack.[20]

The 1956 discussions defined some problems nuclear strikes would encounter. The arsenal theoretically available ranged from the countervalue megaton thermonuclear weapons, one of which could obliterate a major metropolitan centre by itself, to the low-yield ten-kiloton 'tactical' nuclear weapons. If SEATO refrained from using high-yield weapons near major cities, but insisted on destroying targets in and around such cities, it must risk multiple strikes using multiple sorties—exposing its bomber force to attrition—rather than rely on a single pulverising attack. No one could be certain whether multiple attacks by smaller weapons would be less likely to provoke escalation, or international outrage, than one major attack. Planners assumed dense jungle would inhibit blast, heat and radiation from nuclear attacks, enough to dilute their effectiveness against enemy ground forces on the march. They also assumed the enemy would anticipate nuclear attacks and adopt countermeasures. These would include prepositioning supplies in dispersed dumps, dispersing combat forces as much as possible, and adopting the lightest possible scales of transport, weapons and equipment. Indeed, SEATO intelligence assumed the PLA would deploy a "light infantry division"—a formation not in fact identified in its Order of Battle—to operate, without heavy armour or mechanised transport, in Southeast Asian conditions. SEATO must prepare to cope with an initial enemy onslaught that enjoyed some self-sufficiency and freedom to manoeuvre, and deploy accordingly for a defensive battle.[21]

20. 'Attack on Selected Targets of the Chinese Mainland in support of military operations in the Treaty Area' (July 1956), NAA: A1209/23, 1957/5853; Fenton, *SEATO*, chapter 5.

21. Australian JIC memo, 'A study on the

SEATO must launch a strategic air offensive as soon as possible, using both nuclear and conventional weapons. The first wave of air attacks on targets in North Vietnam would be carried out by D plus 3. Meanwhile 'local' ground forces would fight delaying actions to hold the 17th parallel in Vietnam, and block advances through the mountain passes from North Vietnam into Laos. Naval and air forces would interdict enemy movements while 'external' ground forces deployed around Danang, and on the western bank of the Mekong River in Laos and Thailand. Chinese intervention would trigger Phase 2. SEATO would reply with conventional and nuclear air strikes on targets in southern China, on Hainan island, and on troop concentrations, while ground forces fought delaying actions in Laos and South Vietnam. In Phase 3 SEATO would send in further 'external' reinforcements and escalate its air offensive, ranging from direct support of ground forces to "nuclear attacks on suitable troop concentrations, and an increasing scale of attack on selected targets in South China and North Vietnam". In Phase 4 SEATO would counterattack on the ground, clear friendly territory, and launch an amphibious assault on North Vietnam, to sever enemy lines of communication. A final phase would involve advancing into enemy territory "if necessary".[22]

Meanwhile however, Plan 5 and the crisis in Laos rewrote the worst-case scenario. Internal subversion, covertly assisted by North Vietnam and China, made it politically more difficult for SEATO to defend the Protocol States. Without open invasion, public opinion at home and abroad was prone to condemn what could appear to be Western interference in civil strife. This could delay SEATO intervention to the point where only the use of nuclear

effects of nuclear air attacks upon selected logistic targets in south China and North Vietnam' (9 Feb 1956), NAA: A 1838, TS 688/18 part 1; Fenton, *SEATO*, chapter 5.

22. Australian JPC Agendum 22/58, 'Concept of Operations for Defence against initial Viet Minh Aggression and subsequent Chinese Communist Intervention' (17 Feb 1958), JPC Report 15/1958, 'Concept of Operations for Defence against initial Viet Minh Aggression and subsequent Chinese Communist Intervention' (21 Feb), NAA: A 1838, TS 688/27/3.

weapons might still prevent communist victory. Such a connection would of course trump the American and British decision to concentrate on Plan 5 in order to delay completing Plan 4. The root problem was clear. The allies agreed China and North Vietnam were determined to overrun mainland Southeast Asia. They agreed their adversaries could choose from a range of strategies to pursue that goal. But they disagreed about whether SEATO could intervene militarily in Laos without doing more harm than good. The question was now urgent: what plans could SEATO endorse that would give the coalition a realistic chance to contain various threats, without compromising the alliance? Planning for the most immediate problem, counterinsurgency, was criticised by members who feared any such operation would backfire. Planning for the most dangerous problem—general invasion—was impeded by members reluctant to confirm what they could commit to any such operation. Some stakeholders felt connections between the scenarios could not be ignored. Others felt they could not be accepted. MPO plans were now a litmus test as to whether SEATO could become a viable instrument for collective security.

Plan 5 focused on a de facto partition of Laos, through SEATO intervention, to confine communist expansion well east of the Mekong River valley. The British and Americans broadly agreed the goal should be to establish a neutral but stable Laos. But the Americans were more willing to intervene militarily if necessary, whereas the British preferred to try to persuade the Soviet Union to broker a diplomatic neutralisation. The British felt deploying forces in Thailand might provoke conflict in Laos. The Americans argued failing to do so would damage Thai confidence in SEATO. They had a point. The Thai government did treat SEATO's approach to the problem in Laos as a credibility test. That underlined the connection between plans for counterinsurgency and plans for limited war: credibility and cohesion.

The British government examined the same connection during a searching reappraisal of global strategy for the next decade. One general agreement stood out from the start: during the 1960s British military commitments in Asia must be reduced, in order to reduce government spending. Beyond that, three main questions focused a long discussion in London. What were British interests in Southeast Asia and how important were they to British global policy? What threatened British interests in the region? Finally, how could the British best protect their interests and deter the threats? The Foreign Office set the tone for the review, arguing that communist insurgency in the region was the most serious threat, but it was underpinned by "the background exercise of Chinese power". The communist powers were prepared to wait for insurgencies to bear fruit, with good reason. Corruption, inefficiency and frustrated expectations undermined developing states in the region, reinforced by Chinese intimidation "to deter them from taking steps to build up an effective system of collective security". Regional governments might give in to Chinese pressure "if they were not confident of our readiness to come to their assistance".[23]

Recommendations emerged from three discussions: the importance of Southeast Asia, the limits of British capabilities, and the connection to global priorities. The Treasury was blunt: British economic returns from the region barely matched British spending, especially military spending, in the region. The FO replied that, above and beyond a general British interest to uphold containment and collective security in the region, and to preserve close ties with the Commonwealth allies, it was necessary to "maintain a political and military presence in the area sufficient to enable us … to retain our influence on United States policy decisions". If the nuclear deterrent must underpin Western military strategy to contain China, then "in order both to play our full part in this strategy and to retain our influence on United States policy decisions, the United Kingdom should make a contribution in support

23. 'Chinese and Russian Penetration of South and South East Asia', DSE(60)3 (17 June 1960), TNA: CAB 134/1644.

of the United States nuclear deterrent forces, in addition to maintaining conventional forces in the area".[24]

The Chiefs of Staff connected their review of global strategy to this Southeast Asia discussion, warning "it was not possible to undertake commitments 'on the cheap'". The UK should support SEATO, but should not "become involved in large scale land operations in Southeast Asia", because it could not commit enough ground forces to play a major role in such operations. If China intervened, "allied forces would either be overrun by weight of numbers or be compelled to use nuclear weapons". An interdepartmental Committee on Future Developments in Southeast Asia (DSE) discussed these reports in July. It drew an optimistic conclusion:

> The maintenance of a political and military presence in South East Asia might contribute to the retention of our influence on United States policy. Politically it might enable us to act as a restraining influence on United States activities in South East Asia and on her attitude towards China. Our membership of SEATO and the fact that we were the only white nation with a foothold in South East Asia would probably incline the Americans to consult us on major policy issues affecting the area.... Our presence in South East Asia would thus contribute to our general aim of trying to ensure that American forces and resources were used in the most sensible manner throughout the world.[25]

The British now began to take into account changes in American strategic thinking, spurred on by the approaching presidential election later that year. The Americans were showing more interest in conventional forces "since their realization that massive retaliation was not adequate for all situations". This raised interest in the network of British bases and forces overseas. On the other hand Brit-

24. 'United Kingdom Economic and Financial Interests in South and South East Asia', DSE(60)9 (1 July 1960), 'United Kingdom Obligations and Policies in the Area', DSE(60)11 (6 July), TNA: CAB 134/1644.

25. 'The Military Position', DSE(60)5(Revised) (7 July 1960), Minutes, DSE (8 July 1960), TNA: CAB 134/1644.

ish forces were too small to tip the balance in limited war, and kept a low profile in order not to aggravate regional tensions between SEATO and non-alignment. That left one alternative: "the need to involve the United States in our affairs might make it desirable for the United Kingdom to have a strategic nuclear capability in the Far East, thus strengthening our right, moral or otherwise, to be consulted by the Americans on matters of major policy."[26]

The British cabinet posed the direct question on 5 August: "How important is it from the point of view of our relations with the Far Eastern nations and with the United States of America that the United Kingdom should make an independently controlled contribution to the nuclear strike capacity of the West in the Far East?"[27] The answer came from the services, through their 'Working Party on the Use of Nuclear Weapons'. China would only be deterred from military invasion of Southeast Asia if it was convinced the West would launch nuclear strikes on the Chinese homeland in retaliation. Because tactical nuclear weapons could not seriously delay any major invasion after it began, it made no sense to provide them to British ground forces. The issue was what contribution the UK could make to the strategic deterrent. In that respect "the United States forces alone are adequate to deter the Chinese". However, the UK must remain involved in regional security for its own sake, remain connected to Australia and New Zealand, and above all retain some influence over American policy. The Americans would not pay attention to British concerns unless the British helped tackle common problems. Recent discussions with CINCPAC "have shown [his] great interest in the coordination of nuclear targets between the British and US forces". But the discussions reached a dead end: the British could not commit forces to any campaign against China because as yet they had no nuclear weapons in the region. Therefore, "there is no direct mili-

26. Minutes, DSE (15 July 1960), 'Future Level of Expenditure in South and South East Asia', DSE(60)19 (2 Aug), TNA: CAB 134/1644.

27. 'Defence Committee Remits', DSE(60)20 (5 Aug 1960), TNA: CAB 134/1645.

tary requirement for Britain to contribute to the Allied strategic nuclear deterrent in the Far East, but there are good political reasons for her doing so."[28]

The DSE reported on 5 November 1960. It listed "to contain Communism" as the first objective the UK shared with its allies. Beyond protecting British territories, contributing to the strategic deterrent against China and to SEATO operations were the main roles for British military forces in the Far East. During the 1960s the British commitment to the region must be reduced, for economic and political reasons. But the commitment must remain because the threat would. China was not likely to deliberately provoke open war but sought to confront the West, and was prone to miscalculate. Southeast Asia was volatile contested space, with weak governments and political frictions that could be exploited by either side in the Cold War. The US must play the lead role to contain this threat. The region must rank behind higher priorities in British global strategy, but withdrawal was unthinkable. Commitments in one region could not be isolated from those in another without undermining the cohesion on which collective security must rely everywhere. In Southeast Asia that now meant deploying nuclear weapons: "For general political reasons—influence with the United States, the Commonwealth connection, and our status as a power with a worldwide stake in stemming Communist expansion—the United Kingdom must make a contribution to the nuclear deterrent against China." The committee preached to the converted. In October Prime Minister Harold Macmillan and his cabinet had decided the UK must contribute to "the strategic nuclear deterrent" against China, to seek British influence over American strategy in the region.[29]

Five days after this report John F. Kennedy was elected president of the United States. This guaranteed that the rethinking

28. 'The Use of Nuclear Weapons' (23 Aug 1960), TNA: DEFE 7/2382.
29. 'Final Report', DSE(60)30(Final) (3 Nov 1960), TNA: CAB 134/1645; 'Nuclear Strike Planning in the Far East', COS(62)131 (27 Mar 1962), TNA: CAB 163/22.

of American grand strategy would continue. Changes in American strategy would of course decisively influence SEATO contingency plans. Communist pressure in Indochina focused attention on the relationship between decolonisation, nuclear weapons and military strategy. Kennedy came into office convinced that the 'Third World' was now the main front in the Cold War. Europe faced military and political stalemate. An armed truce held fast in Korea. But the growing number of African and Asian states emerging from the dismantling of European empires faced a choice between the Western alliance, the Soviet bloc, and possibly non-alignment. The Eisenhower grand strategy to rely on nuclear deterrence, linked through a connecting web of military alliances, did not deter communist tactics to foment subversion and insurgency in the Third World, covertly aided and abetted by the Soviet Union and the PRC. But many observers saw such conflicts as civil wars driven by internal rivalries. If the only thing the US could do to prevent communist victories in such conflicts was to launch nuclear strikes on the Soviet Union and China, it might face strident pressure to accept local defeat rather than start global war. Kennedy reoriented American grand strategy, moving away from relying on the threat of massive nuclear retaliation, towards building up a capability for "flexible response".[30]

Flexible response meant increasing the range of strategic choices the US could make to deter or defeat communist aggression. It included both stronger conventional forces and greater willingness to use tactical nuclear weapons, to raise the "threshold of escalation"—the point at which conflict might escalate to global war. This rejuvenated American military interest in limited-war scenarios, with direct consequences for SEATO. But it did so amidst growing global tension, as the communist powers directly challenged the resolve of the new American government to wage

30. Lawrence Freedman, *Kennedy's Wars: Berlin, Cuba, Laos and Vietnam* (Oxford: Oxford University Press, 2000); Freedman, *The Evolution of Nuclear Strategy*; Fenton, *SEATO*, chapter 5.

the Cold War. Regarding Southeast Asia, Eisenhower went out of his way to warn Kennedy that communist subversion in Laos was only the first phase in a communist campaign to subvert the wider region.[31]

This warning coincided with the resumption of armed struggle in South Vietnam in December 1960. The challenge to the Republic of Vietnam (ROV) ostensibly came from within, from a National Liberation Front (NLF) opposed to Ngo Dinh Diem's government. The NLF was in fact Hanoi's instrument to implode its southern enemy, to complete the unification of Vietnam under communist rule. North Vietnam tried to present its onslaught as a southern civil war. They hoped to avoid the mistake of 1950, when a crude invasion of South Korea by the regular army of North Korea made it easy to justify Western military intervention. The Kennedy administration did not know that in January 1961 the Committee for State Security—the Soviet national security and intelligence agency, better known by its acronym KGB—persuaded the Soviet government to adopt a grand strategy for waging more aggressive Cold War in Asia and Africa. The Soviets sensed opportunities to exploit passions generated by decolonisation and resentment of the West. They also felt the need to rebut Chinese criticism that they were too timid to confront "American imperialism".[32] What Kennedy did see was generally more aggressive communist pressure in the 'Third World', including Southeast Asia. He resolved to confront the challenge, by more flexible grand strategy. Plan 4 evolved within that context.

The first British response to this changing situation came during staff talks in Australia in February. Admiral of the Fleet The Earl Mountbatten of Burma, British Chief of the Defence Staff (CDS), attended in person, and threw the proverbial hand grenade into the ring. Tension in Laos undermined Asian confidence

31. Freedman, *Kennedy's Wars*, chapters 2, 3 and 5.

32. Christopher Andrew and Vasili Mitrokhin, *The Mitrokhin Archive II: The KGB and the World* (London: Allen Lane, 2005), pp. 9, 40.

in Western commitment. To maintain confidence in SEATO the coalition must now produce more ambitious plans that identified larger force requirements. But the British could not provide such forces, nor did they think the coalition should assume a moral obligation it could never fulfill. Plan 4 pointed up the problem. It was not realistic as it stood, because the coalition could not defeat any determined Chinese offensive "without the immediate use of nuclear weapons". This issue should now be forced, in order to provoke "a complete reappraisal of SEATO planning for limited war". The dilemma was now clear. The earlier decision to pursue Plan 4 "as a technical exercise" now could not connect with the desire to use it to reassure Asian allies "that their own interests are not being overlooked in the concentration on plans for protection of the Protocol States". The political need for delay and ambiguity now collided with the military need for clarity and realism. In Plan 4 this meant nuclear weapons and force declarations.[33]

Mountbatten's outburst reflected British concerns that they were being strategically compromised. British interests remained wide enough for Macmillan's government to feel it could not allow the UK to become too obviously dependent on American power—but commitments stretched beyond capabilities, undermining any claim to be treated as a principal. The grand strategy reorientation of 1960 included the decision to adopt the American Skybolt air-launched ballistic missile as the weapon to equip the next generation of the nuclear deterrent. British weapons programmes were cancelled in favour of Skybolt, which would arm the V bombers after reaching production in the mid-1960s. This economising measure made it even more important to offset dependence through contribution.[34] Just how difficult that could be was indicated when the JIC, on 4 May, discussed a very basic issue: 'Knowl-

33. Minutes, ANZAM DC (22 Feb 1961), NAA: A 1838, TS 688/27/8 part 3; DEA Brief, 'SEATO Military Planning' (10 Mar), ANZ: EA 1, W 2668-120/2/5 part 2; DEA to NZ High Commissioner Ottawa, Visit of Earl Mountbatten (28 Apr 1961), ANZ: LONB, 106/7/1 part 1.

34. For the Skybolt controversy, see Freedman, *The Evolution of Nuclear Strategy*, ch. 20, and Dockrill, *British Defence Since 1945*.

edge of the Deployment of U.S. Forces'. The Director of Military Intelligence (DMI) put it carefully:

> [H]e was greatly concerned at our lack of knowledge of the deployment of U.S. military forces at any particular moment and this could be a very relevant factor in appreciating the situation in time of emergency. At times when the policies of the United States and British Governments were divergent this knowledge could be of vital importance.

Understated language did not bury the point: if British grand strategy relied on partnership with the Americans, but the British did not know where American military forces were, let alone what they were doing, they would find it difficult to influence their ally or respond effectively to fast-moving events. The JIC even wondered whether to resort to covert means to obtain the necessary information.[35]

The JIC decided not to jeopardise the partnership by spying on American military movements, but the Foreign Office emphasised how necessary it was to know about them—not least because they frequently provoked countermeasures from the Soviets and Chinese, and the British did not want to be caught off-guard. The COS decided to seek the necessary information as quietly as possible through established liaison channels, to avoid unwanted American attention and awkward questions. Nothing more starkly spotlighted how crucial American intentions were to British strategic planning or how vulnerable the British felt as a result.[36] This sensitivity shaped British approaches to Plan 4, amidst rising tensions in Laos.

The MPO agreed to place force declarations for Plan 4 on the agenda for the MAG meeting in October. More fighting in Laos produced another truce but it collapsed in May, destabilising

35. JIC Minutes, Confidential Annex (4 May 1961), TNA: CAB 159/35.

36. JIC Minutes, Confidential Annexes (11 May, 8 June, 13 July 1961), TNA: CAB 159/35.

the weak royal government and army. The Americans and Soviets stepped up covert support to their proxies. The Americans also flexed their muscles, deploying forces in Thailand to deter the Pathet Lao and reassure the Thais. SEATO allies cautiously followed suit, the British and Australians each deploying a fighter squadron. American planners examined possible military intervention, including the use of tactical nuclear weapons, to prevent a communist takeover. The deteriorating situation prompted them to invite Admiral Sir David Luce, C-in-C Far East Fleet, to review the problem with Admiral Harold Felt, CINCPAC. In response the British carefully considered two issues: the possible consequences of a communist takeover in Laos, and the likely consequences of SEATO using nuclear weapons to stop this.

The JIC decided on 8 June to concentrate on the Plan 5 concept: how best to partition Laos. This assumed that trying to clear all of Laos, especially by using nuclear weapons, would provoke wider war, or destroy SEATO politically in Asia, or both. This was reinforced by a JIC Far East (JICFE) report on the Royal Laotian Army (RLA) that did not mince words. The RLA:

> have not, and have never had, a military capability to resist determined attack... could not on their own hold Luang Prabang or Pakse against Pathet Lao attack.... Training and re-equipment alone will not have a significant effect on PLA capability in the foreseeable future. Moreover, in view of the inherent lack of Lao military qualities we do not envisage any real improvement in the long term.[37]

This squarely contradicted optimistic American assessments of the RLA and its prospects, and therefore of SEATO options. But as Luce prepared to meet Felt, Mountbatten pointedly reminded him, on 20 June, about the other side of the equation: "You should

37. JIC Minutes (8 June 1961), TNA: CAB 159/35; CDS to BDCCFE, COSSEA 27 (20 June 1961), JICFE Report, 'Capabilities of the Royal Laotian Army', n.d. (June 1961), NAA: A 1838, TS 688/27/6/6 part 2.

know that Ministers attach great importance to demonstrating to the Americans our continuing whole-hearted support for planning for military intervention in Laos."[38] Luce's mission was to persuade his counterpart to agree SEATO should only intervene in Laos if the RLA collapsed, and at most aim to carve out a buffer zone to screen the Thai border—carefully distant from Vietnam, China, and any serious escalation.

Luce met Felt on 22 June. He knew Felt did not want his hands tied by SEATO political caution, but understood the value of quiet prior agreement with the British. Luce concentrated on finding common ground on practical operational matters, notably by agreeing SEATO intervention forces would inevitably come in direct contact with the Pathet Lao. This established some rapport with Felt, who warmed up enough to admit he strongly doubted any ceasefire would hold, and anticipated having to intervene. Luce thought Felt paid lip service to American optimism about the RLA, but noted his insistence American airpower would prevent or defeat any Viet or Chinese intervention. When Felt offered to have his planners discuss details with Luce's staff, Luce "accepted with alacrity". Other British officials noted Felt's desire to "make the DRV sorry they came to Laos" and felt he inclined towards "an entirely military solution". But they agreed the meetings were productive, indicating what SEATO forces might do if they went into Laos. They were optimistic, because they thought Felt was prepared to accept willingness to plan for modest intervention as better than standing still while Laos collapsed. If his minimum met a British maximum a SEATO consensus might emerge, aiming to avoid a wider war over Laos.[39]

This modest professional rapport came in time to influence British efforts to 'put up or shut up' for Plan 4. The JIC argued that using nuclear weapons to prevent a communist takeover in

38. Ibid.

39. 'Report by Admiral Sir David Luce', DCC(FE)(61)182 (25 June 1961), CRO to UK High Commissioner Canberra, Telegram 1842 (11 July), CinCFEF to CDS (23 July), NAA: A 1838, TS 688/27/6/6 part 2.

Laos was likely to produce such a damaging political backlash against the Western powers, especially in the Commonwealth and Asia, that SEATO probably could not use them without destroying itself as a coalition. But because their use was "cardinal to SEATO strategy"—a clear reference to Plans 4 and 6—this had wide ramifications for collective security.[40] Ironically, British progress in urging caution in Laos now pushed forward the worst-case scenario. When the MPO scheduled another discussion on Plan 4 for 20 June, the British 'men on the spot' called time on the long review in London.

The British Defence Coordination Committee Far East (BDCCFE) supported Mountbatten's call to force the issue of Plan 4. They underlined some realities the British must face to preserve the coalition:

> ...without the use of nuclear weapons the force requirements for the Plan could not be met. Thus Plan 4, which is designed to combat the threat for which SEATO was mainly created, would not be viable. The knowledge of this could have far-reaching implications. Any attempt by the UK to have the Plan written on a basis of conventional weapons only, might, therefore, have most unfortunate effects.

This view from the theatre dismissed fears of an Asian backlash to plans to use nuclear weapons, arguing neutral states must already know this was the only way SEATO could defeat a determined Chinese invasion. The COS agreed. They stipulated that regarding nuclear strike operations the MPO should only "suggest types and locations of targets which would need to be attacked", and not become involved in detailed strike planning and execution. With that caveat, they argued the British must be ready "to declare forces including nuclear capability" to Plan 4, or risk losing any standing in SEATO.[41]

40. JIC Minutes (8 June, 6 July 1961), TNA: CAB 159/35.

41. DCDS to Minister of Defence, 'SEATO MPO Plan 4/61 Nuclear Planning' (14 and 15

The Americans now stepped up pressure to complete Plan 4, proposing to define its aims very aggressively:

> To inflict a decisive defeat on the communist armed forces and to bring about an early cessation of hostilities under conditions representing a net advantage to the Free World, these conditions to include as a minimum the recovery of lost territories, the liberation and control of North Vietnam by friendly forces, and the reunification of Vietnam under governmental control aligned to the Free World.[42]

The Australian JIC chipped in with an important argument. SEATO was necessary in order to enable American military power to deploy in Southeast Asia. American power was the only major obstacle that blocked communist domination of Southeast Asia. Logically "the collapse of SEATO is therefore an important communist objective in Southeast Asia." The communist powers preferred to succeed by insurgency in Laos and would accept a diplomatic settlement that left them predominant there. The PRC and DRV would intervene to rescue the Pathet Lao, if necessary, or to deal SEATO a mortal political blow, if possible. They would wait to see what happened at the forthcoming conference in Geneva. But they were emboldened by SEATO hesitation over Laos, would intervene if SEATO did, and did not fear SEATO would use nuclear weapons over the issue. All this, plus Thai frustration with the British and French in particular, meant SEATO must now show some resolve. That meant completing a realistic Plan 4.[43]

June 1961), TNA: DEFE 13/542. The BDCCFE was a co-ordinating committee combining the senior civilian and service authorities in the region, to advise on and implement British strategy and policy. It replicated the cabinet and committee system used in London. In November 1962 it was replaced by a unified service headquarters, Far East Command.

42. Australian JPC Agendum No. 7/61, 'SEATO MPO Plan 4/61 and Theatre Estimate Proposed National Amendments' (18 Apr 1961), NAA: A 1838, TS 688/27/8 part 3.

43. 'The Likelihood of War up to the End of 1966', JIC(Aust)(61)2 Final (May 1961), 'The War Potential of Communist Countries in Asia up to the End of 1966', JIC(Aust)(61)20 Final (June 1961), NAA: A 1209/1961/6; 'Probable Communist Reactions to SEATO Intervention in Laos', Australian JIC Note 4/8/14 Annex C (16 June 1961), NAA: A 1838, TS 688/27/6/6 part 2; Australian Embassy Bangkok to DEA, Telegram 395 (23 June 1961), NAA: A 1838, TS 688/27/8 part 3.

Nuclear weapons inspired both an agreed outline plan and a challenge to that plan. In July the French military adviser urged his colleagues to prepare an alternative estimate of forces required for Plan 4, assuming nuclear weapons would not be used. When the MAG met in Bangkok on 3 October, Felt duly gave way and agreed the MPO should produce an alternative non-nuclear Plan 4 estimate. But, as Fenton rightly argued, Felt did so because the Americans assumed the alternative numbers would only reinforce the argument: SEATO could not defeat a full-scale invasion without using nuclear weapons.[44] British and Australian attitudes reinforced this apparent American flexibility. Both went to Bangkok intending to fall in line behind the Americans, which meant declaring contributions to a nuclear Plan 4.

Macmillan's government agreed in June to authorise Luce to nominate British forces for Plans 4 and 6. For Plan 6, this meant not ruling out nuclear weapons. For Plan 4, this meant assuming they would be used from the outset, but not agreeing in advance to using them automatically. The agreed formula was clear: "SEATO forces will be prepared to use nuclear weapons on suitable enemy targets if the situation demands. This does not imply the automatic use of nuclear weapons and will be dependent on political agreement." But the formula was also cosmetic. The operations sketched out by the plan, the forces required to conduct them, rested squarely on assuming nuclear weapons would be used. For the British this meant emphasising their nuclear contribution. This posed two problems. The British shared American reluctance to discuss details regarding nuclear weapons and strike plans within SEATO at large. They feared security leaks, political controversy, and constraints on freedom to act in a crisis. The British also wanted to follow the American lead and place only air defence, plus ground forces, directly under SEATO command; naval and

44. Fenton, *SEATO*, chapter 5; CDS to Minister of Defence, Telegram 537 (8 Oct 1961), NAA: A1209, 1961/1098.

air striking forces would support SEATO operations, but remain under national command. These were, of course, the forces that would launch nuclear strikes. But this would expose the British ground force contribution as painfully small: one infantry battalion plus support arms, from within the 28th Commonwealth Brigade Group, based in Malaya. This would contribute little to the five divisions of 'external' ground forces Plan 4 would require.

To address these problems, the COS suggested the UK should declare it would contribute nuclear strike forces to support Plan 4 but retain them under national control; this meant withholding details and conducting strike planning "outside the MPO". It was thought it would remind the MAG that British global military commitments must be considered when reviewing force nominations. It should spell out in detail British naval forces nominated to support SEATO—which amounted to the entire Far East Fleet—to enhance the impression of commitment. And it should include 3rd Commando Brigade in the naval contribution, to participate in the planned amphibious invasion of North Vietnam. This would make the ground force contribution seem a bit larger. The conditions attached to nuclear forces would prod the Americans to suggest joint strike planning, while reassuring them they could do so without compromising security. The Commando contribution went beyond what the cabinet had endorsed. The COS argued the increase would impress the Americans—and the commitment "can be properly made even in the light of the current examination of military strategy". Surely this reassurance underlined British determination to stay in line with the Americans? To emphasise this, London authorised Luce to declare the command status of British conventional forces "in line with any American declaration". Swallowing their qualms, the British opted to use Plan 4 for leverage. They hoped to parlay concessions on a contingency plan into greater influence on American policy towards Indochina.[45]

45. CDS to Minister of Defence, 'SEATO MPO Plans 4 and 6' (6 Sept 1961), 'Declaration of Forces under SEATO Plans' (29 Sept), TNA: DEFE 13/542.

Australian planners spelt out their views regarding nuclear weapons for Plan 4 in detailed comments on its Concept of Operations. The force requirements stipulated only what SEATO required to stop the communist advance, not additional ground, air and naval forces it would need to counterattack. These would be much greater without nuclear weapons. The Australians stressed the need to deny the Lao Bao Pass to the enemy for as long as possible. This pass was one of only two major routes communist ground forces could use to advance from North Vietnam into southern Laos. By denying it SEATO could keep them at bay while building up its own forces in Thailand and Laos, and preparing its amphibious invasion. If the enemy seized it, SEATO's whole plan would be jeopardised. At least two divisions would be needed to deny the pass, but they would be worn down fairly quickly in battle. The implication was clear. This was precisely the kind of high-priority target that nuclear strikes could reach faster, deny more effectively, and economically, than ground forces. A US Air Force general described how this would work:

> Picture a situation where an enemy is using rain force to conceal his movement. Let's assume that there is a 60-mile choke point in this forest created by two mountain ridges. The enemy will have to pass through this choke point en route to his objectives. Sixteen nominal-yield nuclear weapons, air burst, would create a debris belt 58 nautical miles long and almost four miles wide. The corridor would be effectively blocked. Jungle-trained troops moving on foot would have great difficulty crossing the debris belt. Even if they tried to clear a path or road through the debris corridor, they would have to concentrate men and machinery or animals, and another nuclear target would be provided. If you created such a belt behind these advancing troops as well as in front of them, you would have an effective trap. Using nuclear weapons this way, you would only kill enemy troops and jungle animals.... A single nominal-yield nuclear weapon, air burst, will clear a forest area about 8000 feet in radius. To get a similar effect with napalm

> would require 8000 sorties of F-100 aircraft.... I don't have to go into detail to describe to you the logistical tail involved... to support this kind of operation.[46]

The MAG conference in Bangkok from 3 to 5 October marked a turning point for Plan 4 and SEATO. Felt balanced his concession to study a non-nuclear scenario by persuading his allies to nominate forces to Plan 4 for both scenarios. American contributions dwarfed the 'external' allies combined: more than four divisions out of the five required, plus the 7th Fleet and the 13th Air Force. The air forces indicated the imbalance, both between the Americans and their allies and the two scenarios. Using nuclear weapons, SEATO would need 70 land-based and 50 carrier-borne bombers, supported by 165 land-based and 60 carrier-borne fighters. British nuclear-capable bombers could however amount to more than a third of that category, if they deployed the V bomber squadrons. But without nuclear weapons, SEATO would need 260 land-based and 50 carrier-borne bombers, supported by 240 land-based and 150 carrier-borne fighters—and only the Americans could provide the increase. The MAG did not discuss Plan 5, but did direct the MPO to prepare a plan for counterinsurgency in South Vietnam. The Australians summed up the general view: the meeting was very positive, because American determination visibly encouraged the Asian allies.[47]

Little wonder. But there was a serious problem. During 1961 the Kennedy administration strove to prop up the royal government in Laos, deployed forces in Thailand, and stepped up American military support for South Vietnam. Now it pledged to provide SEATO with enough forces to make Plan 4 realistic—provided it relied on nuclear weapons. That indicated resolve to

46. 'SEATO MPO Plan 4B/61', DC Agendum 74/1961 (11 and 14 Sept 1961), NAA: A 1209, 1961/315, part 1; R.S. Horowitz, *The Ramparts We Watch* (Derby, CT: Monarch Books, 1964), pp. 22–3.

47. CDS to Minister of Defence, Telegram 537 (8 Oct 1961), 'Possible Australian Force Contributions for SEATO Plans 4 and 6', DC Report 93/1961 (14 Sept 1961), NAA: A 1209, 1961/1098; 'SEATO MPO Plan 4B/61', DC Agendum 74/1961 (14 Sept 1961), NAA: A 1209, 1961/315, part 1.

deter or if necessary defeat any level of communist aggression. This induced its Asian allies to expect the coalition to honour its pledges and respond vigorously to any further communist pressure in the Treaty Area. But for the UK, Australia and New Zealand the Plan 4 consensus rested in fact on diplomacy resolving the crisis in Laos, and domestic counterinsurgency containing the threat in Vietnam. The British committed themselves to Plan 4 as a calculated risk, assuming they would never need to redeem it. This was reasonable for one risk: nuclear war with China. It was much less reasonable if it meant backsliding on what Asian allies now expected: SEATO would reinforce American determination to contain communist expansion by any means necessary, ranging from counterinsurgency intervention to 'limited' war using nuclear weapons. Flexible response meant vigorous response. The Americans intended to contain communism without resorting to limited war—but Plans 4 and 6 indicated how far they might go to contain it if necessary. Approving Plan 4, and agreeing to plan for counterinsurgency in South Vietnam, committed SEATO to live up to its original premise: the coalition must either follow where the Americans led, to defend the partition of 1954, or fall apart in disarray.

In 1962 the Americans threw down the gauntlet. In February they retitled their adviser force in Vietnam the Military Assistance Command Vietnam, and increased its strength. In March, Secretary of State Dean Rusk concluded an agreement with Thai Foreign Minister Thanat Koman that put SEATO on notice. The Rusk-Thanat Agreement declared that the Manila Pact commitments could be exercised bilaterally as well as collectively; in other words the Americans would act on their own to defend Thailand—thus by implication Indochina—if SEATO balked. Rusk reminded the Australians on 9 May that American policy was to strengthen conventional forces, in order to raise the threshold beyond which nuclear weapons must be used to prevent defeat. But he also admitted that so far the Americans had no clear idea even in NATO how to define that threshold—and "had done no similar thinking about

Southeast Asia". Rusk insisted the US "is not straining at the leash to make early use of nuclear weapons in Asia", but if push came to shove it would put security considerations first and override Asian opinion, "which, he believed, would not greatly increase the 'agony of decision' which fell upon the United States in these matters".[48]

Setbacks in Laos forced the Americans to accept in July the controversial Geneva Accords. The Accords 'neutralised' the country under a shaky coalition government, and required all foreign forces to withdraw. Thailand denounced them, rightly convinced Viet communist forces would not withdraw, and the coalition would rapidly fall under Pathet Lao domination. SEATO's timidity made the Thais doubt it could be relied on at all.[49]

The conflict in Vietnam also intensified, prompting American pressure for allied assistance there. This prompted Australian Prime Minister Robert Menzies to raise Plan 4 with Robert McNamara, the American secretary of defence, on 18 June. McNamara sang a somewhat different tune:

> the United States fully understood the high cost, including the lasting hostility of Asian opinion, of a decision to use nuclear weapons.... [T]here was a high probability that there would be no resort to nuclear weapons in any Southeast Asia combat. In any case it would not be for a field commander to decide to use nuclear weapons, whether tactical or strategic.

This perhaps helped confirm the decision in July to send an Australian Army Training Team to South Vietnam. But comments Rusk made, regarding what the Americans might do before resorting to nuclear weapons, indicated the clear intent to take the fight to the enemy:

48. Australian Embassy Washington to DEA, Telegram 1071 (30 Apr 1962), DEA to Australian Embassy Washington, Telegram 1158 (15 June 1962), NAA: A1209, 1962/432; Attachment to JPC Agendum No. 88/63 (1 July 1963), Australian War Memorial (hereafter AWM): 122/69/2016.

49. Fenton, *SEATO*, chapters 6–7; Busch, *All the Way with JFK?*, pp. 21–8.

> [The US] might well want to make an early conventional attack of a harassing kind into enemy territory as a warning and deterrent—for example, if time came when it had to be accepted that there were North Vietnamese troops invading South Vietnam, answer might be to attack points in North Vietnam from the air.[50]

The Australian government could not miss the implication, as it sent advisers into South Vietnam. Their American ally was ready to fight fire with fire; if necessary they would pre-empt a Plan 4 conflict by escalating the conflict in Vietnam.

On 22 March the British COS authorised Luce to "open discussions with Americans on co-ordination of nuclear strike plans in support of SEATO Plan 4". The COS noted they were reviewing "problems related to nuclear strike planning in the Far East".[51] In fact, the British decision to stay in line with the Americans, by committing nuclear weapons to Plan 4, caught them without a settled policy regarding nuclear weapons and grand strategy. They opted to address that problem by trying to orchestrate joint planning with the Americans.

The decision to equip the V bomber force with Skybolt missiles prompted the British to review their strategy for waging nuclear war. The root problem was familiar: too many commitments, too few resources. The COS set up two bodies to advise them on how the UK could wage nuclear war: the Nuclear Strike Co-ordinating Committee (NSCC), and the Joint Interservices Group for the Study of All-Out Warfare (JIGSAW).[52] In February 1962 the NSCC reported that because there was no British strategy for nuclear war with the PRC, they could not determine a "target system suitable for attack" against it. The COS clarified one issue on 13 March: there would be no separate British national strategy

50. Attachment to JPC Agendum No. 88/63 (1 July 1963), AWM: 122/69/2016; DEA to Australian Embassy Washington, Telegram 1158 (15 June 1962), NAA: A 1209, 1962/432.

51. CDS to CinC's Committee Singapore, COSSEA 11 (22 Mar 1962), TNA: CAB 163/22.

52. Memo, Price to Hunt (9 Jan 1962), 'The United Kingdom Nuclear Deterrent', JIC(62)10 (Terms of Reference) (11 Jan), TNA: CAB 163/22; JIC Minutes, Confidential Annex (11 Jan 1962), TNA: CAB 159/37.

for nuclear war with China; British policy was to contribute to an allied deterrent in the Far East. However, they did not know whether joint planning had been done with the Americans, particularly with their Strategic Air Command (SAC). The obvious question produced a quick NSCC answer: "no nuclear planning on a national basis in respect of China itself has so far taken place; nor has there been any liaison with the United States in this field." The 1960 discussions with the Americans regarding Plan 4 "were abandoned until we were in a better position to declare a genuine nuclear capability in the Far East". This had now been done. That made it possible to ask the JIC to identify a suitable target system for strikes against China, for Luce to use as a basis for discussion with the Americans. But on 20 March the COS decided it would be easier to "ask the Americans how our forces could be fitted into their plans", given there would be no independent UK plan for the Far East. The invitation to discuss Plan 4 could be used to raise the wider issue of global strategy with SAC. Luce was duly authorised to approach Felt, and because Macmillan was scheduled to meet Kennedy in April the COS decided to prepare a brief for the prime minister, to "show that we were capable of a useful contribution in the Far East".[53]

This prompted a discussion about how to approach the Americans. It revolved around three points: the need for information about American intentions, the possible consequences of American actions, and the leverage, or lack thereof, provided by British contributions. Everyone agreed nuclear strikes against China through Plan 4 might lead to wider war. Some saw that connection as more opportunity than difficulty—the opportunity to learn more about wider American intentions. In that light the COS changed their minds on 27 March, authorising Luce to discuss "co-ordination of

53. 'Progress Report by the NSCC', COS(62)116 (9 Mar 1962), COS Minutes, Confidential Annex (20 Mar), TNA: DEFE 7/2382; COS Minutes, Confidential Annex (13 Mar 1962), 'Nuclear Strike Planning in the Far East' (16 Mar), TNA: CAB 163/22.

the strategic plan against China", and directing the JIC to provide a basis for discussion. Mountbatten's staff argued that because British forces could only reinforce their larger ally in any attack against China "it would be sufficient to tell the Americans what we can do and merely see how we can fit in with their existing target system". The COS nevertheless concluded the JIC must prepare a British proposal for a target system, otherwise American planners would not be willing to go into details.[54]

The JIC agreed to start by producing a study of China's vulnerability to nuclear strikes. But the FO raised another concern. The Americans were pledged to defend the Nationalist government in Taiwan, whereas the British were not. Plans that committed British forces to attacks on China might drag the UK into an unwanted war over Taiwan. The Ministry of Defence connected the dots. The brief for the prime minister should stress that the British commitment to discuss "tactical nuclear strike planning for SEATO Plan 4" with the Americans could not be separated from British readiness to contribute to "the strategic deterrent against China", as both stemmed from the decision to contribute to that deterrent. The danger of war over Taiwan was trumped by an optimistic rationale for contributing to the deterrent: "to get so involved with the Americans in the Far East that we should be able, where necessary, to apply the brakes." The prime minister should tell Kennedy the British were ready to discuss details, and list the forces the British intended to contribute.[55]

It was obvious the British were not strong enough to pursue an independent military strategy in the region. As a result, they could not formulate a realistic grand strategy without consulting the Americans. This left planners in London working without

54. CDS to Prime Minister, 'Nuclear Planning in SEATO' (21 Mar 1962), TNA: DEFE 13/542; 'Nuclear Strike Planning in the Far East', COS(62)131 (27 Mar), TNA: CAB 163/22; Wright to CDS, 'Nuclear Strike Planning in the Far East' (29 Mar), COS Minutes, Confidential Annex (29 Mar), TNA: DEFE 7/2382.

55. JIC Minutes (5 Apr 1962), TNA: CAB 159/37; de la Mare to Benwell (3 Apr), Benwell to Wilkinson (5 Apr), TNA: DEFE 7/2382.

co-ordination. That was emphasised by a memo to the JIC on 9 April, informing it that a JIGSAW study on China's vulnerability to nuclear strikes was nearly complete. Further evidence came from another body working on nuclear strategy, the British Nuclear Deterrent Study Group, whose task was to consider a "successor deterrent force" for the 1970s. The group pointed out to Mountbatten that the British could not promise to deploy forces or weapons in the Far East until they decided what deterrent force they would maintain overall. But there was only one pool from which to draw, and Europe came first: "the forces required to deter China are thus provided from within the total of our main strategic deterrent force, and planning is based on the assumption that contingencies will not occur in Europe and the Far East at the same time." Therefore, the prime minister should not be in any hurry to spell out details to President Kennedy. The COS duly agreed to advise Macmillan "he should avoid any commitment quoting numbers or squadrons or aircraft or megaton weapons", and hope Luce could make some progress.[56]

The British decision to pledge nuclear weapons to Plan 4 was a calculated risk, hoping to reap some political benefits without having to pay any military price. The prizes were information about American plans and intentions, and influence over American policy; the risk was to commit the UK to a conflict it might not support, by pledging forces it might not be able to deploy, to reinforce an ally on whom it depended. This happened despite the methodical and comprehensive manner in which the Macmillan govern-

56. 'Nuclear Strike Planning in the Far East' (9 Apr 1962), TNA: CAB 163/22; CDS to Minister of Defence, 'Strategic Nuclear Deterrent against China' (16 Apr), TNA: DEFE 13/542; COS Minutes, Confidential Annex (17 Apr), DEFE 7/2382. The decision to restrict British nuclear weapons in the Far East to the airborne strategic deterrent prompted the COS to terminate, in March, an ongoing study in Singapore: JP(62) Note 4 (26 Jan), COS(62)99 'Control of Nuclear Weapons in the Tactical Land Battle in the Far East' (8 Mar). But this decision came five months after British forces were nominated for SEATO Plan 4, eight months after the decision to focus on the strategic deterrent. That speaks to the lack of co-ordination in British strategic planning for the Far East before autumn 1962.

ment and its advisers reviewed British strategy and policy. It also happened despite an obvious historical precedent warning about the danger of just such a calculated risk. Before the Second World War, the British based their grand strategy for defending the Far East on a plan to dispatch forces they could only spare if the situation in Europe was quiet. They did this to be able to pledge to defend the region, to maintain influence with allies. The result was of course military disaster in 1942. Now they planned to do something similar, for a similar reason, pursuing similar political goals, by again accepting a military risk. None of the men who made this decision were stupid; quite a few were personally involved in Second World War decisions and their consequences. Nothing more starkly underlined how important they felt it was for the UK to secure as much influence as possible over American strategy.

British forces that could be deployed for "the strategic offensive against China" were identified after the 1960 decision to deploy nuclear weapons in the Far East. The RN deployed one fleet aircraft carrier East of Suez carrying nuclear weapons, with a complement ranging from 14 to 34 strike aircraft; from 1964 they would deploy two carriers. Preparations to store nuclear weapons at bases in Singapore and Malaya were nearly completed. The RAF contributed one light-bomber squadron, operating from Singapore or Butterworth; later that year it would be equipped with nuclear weapons. Under *Mastodon* it would be reinforced by three V bomber squadrons sent from the UK.[57] The weakness of the concept was of course the fact the medium bombers could only deploy if Europe was quiet, and they provided the really heavy striking power. The merit was that if SEATO did have to implement a nuclear Plan 4, and British forces were deployed, they would definitely increase its punch. This persuaded the British to use this

57. 'Nuclear Strike Planning in the Far East', COS(62)131 (27 Mar 1962), TNA: CAB 163/22; Matthew Jones, 'Up the Garden Path? Britain's Nuclear History in the Far East, 1954–1962', *International History Review*, XXV, no. 2 (June 2003); R. Moore, 'Where Her Majesty's Weapons Were', *Bulletin of the Atomic Scientists*, 57, no. 1 (2001).

commitment as a lever to gain influence with the Americans.

Luce met Felt at another MAG meeting in Bangkok on 4 May. Their discussion vindicated the British approach in one sense, but also indicated the allies had work to do to co-ordinate strategy in SEATO. Felt declared that while he was willing to discuss bilateral nuclear strike planning for Plan 4, he had not yet been instructed to do so. And first he needed to know whether the British had established what they promised in 1960: a resident nuclear capability in the theatre. Felt asked whether British nuclear weapons were now stockpiled in the theatre, how quickly a combat-ready bomber force could redeploy from the UK, how many targets the British were planning to strike, how far their bombers could strike and with what payload. Luce saw the point of this cross-examination: "to discover the earnestness of our intentions and indeed to decide whether any designation of target areas or actual targets to the UK force would be of value to him." His answers pleased Felt, who agreed they could start by having planners discuss target lists, and then "warming to the subject, gave me some unsolicited information". The British discovered that the Americans intended to execute Plan 4 without drawing on the heavy bombers of SAC, relying on the striking power of the Pacific Fleet and the land-based 13th Air Force. The Americans believed they could defeat China without committing their main global deterrent force. Felt hoped the British did not plan to strike all their targets at once, because "to lessen the chances of extending the conflict only a few should be used initially; we should then await the reaction".[58] This indicated the Americans intended to refrain from throwing a 'knockout punch,' to try to control the escalation of any SEATO conflict with China. The message was not lost on the British: if you want to sit at this table, buy a chair.

58. 'Coordination of Nuclear Strike Planning in support of SEATO Plan 4', Annex to COS 666/21/5/62 (May 1962), TNA: CAB 163/22; 'Nuclear Strike Planning in the Far East', Annex to COS 1575/2/11/62 (Oct 1962), TNA: DEFE 7/2382.

Such encouragement naturally persuaded the British to continue to discuss Plan 4. So did broader events. There were encouraging signs of a rift between the Soviets and Chinese. Their dispute might not remove the threat to Southeast Asia, but could hamper Chinese efforts to develop nuclear weapons. The British also hoped the agreement to neutralise Laos might provide a model for Indochina as a whole. But they knew American patience was running low. The Rusk-Thanat Agreement was ominous, as was the situation in Vietnam. If the Americans decided they no longer required SEATO to provide political cover for military intervention in mainland Southeast Asia, this would reduce the means by which the UK could influence American policy. That made it even more important to work Plan 4. Macmillan did not raise the issue of nuclear strategy in the Far East with Kennedy, to allow his advisers to obtain more information first.[59] Ironically, the more the British learned about American intentions, the more it complicated their thinking.

Confusion persisted on one point: was there any important distinction between nuclear attacks on China as part of Plan 4 and as part of strategic nuclear deterrent operations? Treasury efforts to save money produced one interesting answer: no, at least not regarding British forces required and the cost of using them. Both campaigns would require the same forces, ground support and overall expenditure. But the language of the reply pointed to the source of confusion: expenditure on "the strategic nuclear deterrent against China" was identical to that required for "the tactical support of SEATO". This suggested there was after all some military distinction between Plan 4 operations and a "strategic strike against China", notwithstanding the fact the same British force would execute both. The only possible distinction was the crucial issue of Plan 4: could SEATO use nuclear weapons against China without escalating the conflict to a higher level of violence?

59. JIC Minutes (31 May 1962), TNA: CAB 159/37; 'Nuclear Strike Planning in the Far East' (27 June), TNA: DEFE 7/2382.

The only possible answer was yes, so the COS stuck to the script. In November Mountbatten declared that the problem of how to control nuclear strikes launched to support Plan 4 was "a different problem from the question of our contribution to the strategic nuclear deterrent against China". The British had not yet worked out standard procedures by which to control nuclear strikes, either in NATO or SEATO. Now that they had a better idea what the Americans had in mind regarding China, such procedures must be defined as soon as possible.[60]

The British gained that better idea in meetings with Felt's planning team in August and October, in Hawaii and Singapore. They found that American planners definitely wanted British assistance for Plan 4 nuclear strikes against China. Because they would not draw on SAC heavy bombers, there were important targets out of range of the carrier-borne and land-based strike aircraft under CINCPAC control. These targets were however within range of carrier-borne aircraft launched from the Indian Ocean, as well as British bases in Malaya and Singapore. The Americans proposed to define geographic areas of responsibility for SEATO nuclear strikes, and assign targets in Burma, southwest China and the island of Hainan to the British. British planners confirmed that their aircraft could reach all the designated targets, and welcomed the suggestion to operate their carrier from the Indian Ocean, closer to British bases. They did not ask why the Americans needed help to strike Hainan, which lay within range of bases in Okinawa and Guam as well as their Pacific-based carriers. One might infer that the reason was that CINCPAC forces were already fully committed to numerous targets in China and the Treaty Area? The plan to include nuclear attacks against Chinese forces advancing through Burma ran contrary to coalition governments' reluctance to authorise operations in Burma, unless

60. Wright to Peck (14 May 1962), Peck to Wright (15 May), TNA: DEFE 7/2382; CDS to Minister, 'Nuclear Strike Planning in Support of SEATO Plan 4' (22 Nov 1962), TNA: DEFE 13/542.

the Burmese requested help. Planners could in fairness leave that problem to higher authority. But the British responded quickly when the Americans noted the Australians were "greatly interested in nuclear strike planning", and asked the British to brief them. The Americans could have done this themselves. The British could not but interpret this as further evidence that supporting American plans produced more information and influence than keeping them at arm's length. Indeed, it seemed that Plan 4 as the Americans conceived it was not possible without the participation of British nuclear strike forces. That revelation prompted the British to try to resolve several problems: how best to attack China; how to control any such campaign; and how best to relate Plan 4 to "strategic deterrent operations" in a way that conformed to British policy ends and military means. The essential issue was clear: could either campaign be conducted "without escalation into Global War"?[61]

Nuclear strategy had so far been treated as a distinct problem, addressed by ad hoc bodies: the NSCC, JIGSAW, and the Joint Global War Committee (COSJGW), designed to supervise JIGSAW by combining the COS and Chief Scientific Adviser. The rationale for this approach was of course the fact the UK had never waged war using nuclear weapons. But that, as noted, led to unnecessary duplication of effort. COSJGW pulled the threads together on 31 October. It decided to integrate nuclear strategy directly into the formulation of grand strategy, and clarify ideas regarding strategy against China. It dissolved itself and JIGSAW, replacing them with the Long-Term Study Group (LONGSTUD), reporting to the CDS and Chief Scientific Adviser. But first it reviewed two JIGSAW studies: the study of Chinese vulnerability, and a study of how the army might use tactical nuclear weapons in South-

61. Luce to Mountbatten (31 July 1962), Benwell to Wright (6 Nov), Secretary to COS, 'Nuclear Strike Planning in the Far East' (13 Nov), TNA: DEFE 7/2382; CDS to Minister, 'Nuclear Strike Planning in Support of SEATO Plan 4' (22 Nov), TNA: DEFE 13/542. The British delegation, designated the UK Nuclear Planning Team, was drawn from Far East Fleet and Far East Air Force staff officers stationed in Singapore.

east Asia. The tactical nuclear weapons study was rendered obsolete by the 1961 decision to rely on airborne weapons, but this did not stop the committee from remarking that it underestimated the effect nuclear interdiction strikes would have on communist ground force movements. The China study focused on "the weight and pattern of attack on China which would be required to induce breakdown". "Breakdown" was meant literally: the weight and type of attack that would physically destroy the ability of the enemy to wage war. The problem was referred to the JIC.[62]

The JIC produced its assessment of how to use what were still called "certain tactical nuclear forces to SEATO" in December. The term really did not apply. The JIC rebutted the JIGSAW study on the cardinal point: what the Chinese might still be able to do after suffering SEATO nuclear strikes, and how "this might be dealt with". The main premise was simple: the kind of attack that would cripple the war-making potential of a Western enemy would not necessarily achieve 'breakdown' against China, because China was different. Its backwardness would make it harder for SEATO to neutralise. The PLA remained essentially an infantry force that relied much less on war-making industry than NATO armies did, especially when conducting 'guerrilla-type' operations. It could also draw on a vast reserve force scattered throughout its huge population to conduct such operations. And the neighbouring states it might attack were themselves "somewhat primitive and thinly populated". The conclusion was sober: a campaign of nuclear strikes designed to destroy China's war-making industry would no doubt leave the PLA unable to fight the kind of war it fought in Korea—but "would not necessarily remove the potential for considerable guerrilla activity against the countries of Southeast Asia". Using nuclear weapons against strategic targets in

62. COSJGW Minutes (31 Oct 1962), TNA: CAB 163/22. This is an extract from COSJGW minutes, identified as recording discussions from the third meeting in 1962 of that body. Large sections of the extract have been deleted, and this author did not locate any organised collection of COSJGW minutes in any other file series in The National Archives. See also Jones, 'Up the Garden Path.'

China would prevent the PLA from overrunning the Treaty Area by invasion, but might not stop it from launching guerrilla war to pursue the same objective. The ramification was more than sober: because Chinese reserve forces were so large and widespread, the only way SEATO might destroy them would be "a major nuclear attack designed to cover all, or most of, the country with lethal fall-out". Such an 'annihilation attack', aiming to kill 85 per cent of the Chinese population, would require as many as 4000 one-megaton warheads. But even this could not guarantee to destroy 85 per cent of Chinese "ground force potential". The crucial fact was stark: the Chinese army was ultimately the Chinese population, so to cripple one you must kill the other. This was such a non-starter, from every angle, that it seems fair to assume the JIC used an analysis of extremes to identify what was realistic. The Americans did not then have so many thermonuclear warheads—and would never use them all on China even if they did. Any such attack on the Chinese nation would make a mockery of the argument that SEATO was only trying to 'contain' China in a 'limited' war, and almost certainly destroy the political position of the Western powers in Asia. If you could not cripple the enemy you must find another way: "containment of China's ground force potential by nuclear attack would have to include the interdiction of all routes from China to neighbouring countries. Provision might also have to be made for the neutralisation of residual air and sea support."[63]

This conclusion fit the Plan 4 concept of operations. But this did not dissuade the Director of Air Intelligence from challenging it. However, while he chastised the report for using the straw man argument by spelling out how many weapons were required to annihilate China, his own rebuttal was contradictory. He did not think it would be necessary to interdict all routes from China to Southeast Asia with nuclear weapons, because the large number of nuclear attacks on China should both cripple it physically

63. Thorneycroft to Macmillan (7 Dec 1962), TNA: DEFE 7/2382; 'Nuclear Strike Planning in the Far East', JIC/1924/62 (13 Dec), TNA: CAB 163/22.

and plunge it into a grave political crisis. Just when much of the population would be in shock, the ability of a centralised system of government to enforce control would be crippled. This would focus attention on internal survival rather than 'military adventure', and make it very difficult for surviving military forces to operate. Even a calibrated offensive would hurt China too much to allow it to hit back. Yet he argued it was unwise not to target command and control centres for nuclear attack. If any remained intact "they might well be able to organize the remaining war potential in the country and so launch significant operations against Western forces in the area". Just how they might do this if China was in turmoil, as described above, was not made clear. Nevertheless the report sent to the COS was amended by ambiguity: "We cannot assess whether significant guerrilla activity would be started but it is possible that [PLA] forces deployed in areas contiguous to SE Asian countries would employ such tactics," and "A direct attack against ground force personnel would be prohibitive in terms of numbers of nuclear weapons. It would appear, therefore, that to contain China's ground force potential it might be necessary to carry out interdiction of routes from China to neighbouring countries in SE Asia."[64]

What then can we learn from drinking this alphabet soup of abbreviations? What by 1963 was the situation regarding SEATO and Plan 4? As a war plan, it did not change: whether the PLA came in open invasion or as swarms of guerrillas, SEATO would stop them by nuclear strikes against their axes of advance, centres of supply, support bases, and concentrations of forces. From the British point of view there were slightly more pros than cons. American frustration over Laos, determination to support South Vietnam, and willingness to guarantee Thailand all pointed to serious risk. The British could be pulled into a double-jeopardy

64. Director of Intelligence (Air) to Secretary JIC, 'Nuclear Strike Planning in the Far East' (19 Dec 1962), 'Nuclear Strike Planning in the Far East', JIC/1955/62 (21 Dec), TNA: CAB 163/22.

conflict in mainland Southeast Asia—one that domestic opinion saw as internal, ambiguous and unnecessary, but then escalated into a more dangerous war. Or they could destroy SEATO by refusing to support further confrontation, which could persuade the Americans to ignore it—and close the channel of information and influence it provided. But on the positive side of the ledger, as an item of high policy, Plan 4 remained important because it was important to the Americans—and for which they clearly needed British help.

The British also saw Plan 4 as a useful counterweight to American pressure for help on the ground in Vietnam, and threats to act unilaterally—"if worst comes to worst you can count on us, let's keep consulting." Plan 4 envisaged very aggressive military operations indeed, notably to reunify Vietnam by force. But the Americans clearly regarded it strictly as a contingency plan, to broadly outline the military strategy by which SEATO would respond to what now, given the rift between China and the Soviet Union, seemed less likely than ever: a Chinese invasion of the Treaty Area, using the main force of the PLA. Plan 4 would require nuclear strikes. But the Americans now seemed confident they could contain communist expansion without having to resort to it. And even if they did, nuclear strikes would be restricted to targets directly related to operations in Southeast Asia; that might leave some political wiggle room. More important for the British, they could credibly promise to hold their end up—in a campaign they thought would never come off.

This must be seen as both calculated risk and trying to make a virtue out of a necessity. Plan 4 was inherently dangerous. It took a leap of faith to assume there would be any real distinction between attacking any part of China in order to protect Southeast Asia and attacking it for 'strategic deterrent' reasons. It took an even larger leap of faith to assume using nuclear weapons on China or in Southeast Asia, regardless of the circumstances, would not either provoke wider war, or destroy the Western political position in Asia, or both. But it seemed clear, despite McNamara's reassurance, that if push ever did come to shove SEATO could not hold the Treaty Area without using nuclear weapons. Yet it also seemed clear how the Americans intended to solve that problem. They would pre-empt it by winning the war in Vietnam, to deter a wider war all over the Treaty Area. And they still hoped SEATO could help them accomplish this. This hope, plus American willingness to discuss nuclear strategy, convinced the British they had no choice. As long as the value of a seat at the American table offset the risks they ran to stay there, they should try to keep SEATO operating. That had to include supporting Plan 4—fraught as it was. The whole exercise indicated how difficult it was to contain both a serious adversary and a stronger ally. British aspirations to 'apply the brakes' were indeed debunked, when the Americans transformed the war in Vietnam.

6

THE COLD WAR AND THE MAKING OF SINGAPORE

Tan Tai Yong

In the 1950s and early 1960s, as Singapore joined the ranks of Asian colonies awaiting eagerly, or pushing impatiently for, independence from colonial rule, it found itself caught up in a tumultuous swirl of events both regional and international—the withdrawal of the Europeans from Asia, the rise of nationalism, sometimes accompanied by violent revolution, and a global ideological polarisation which found the capitalist and communist countries of the world facing off in a state of Cold War. This chapter traces Singapore's political progression from Crown Colony to independence, and explains how Cold War considerations fundamentally influenced the actions of the various parties fighting to determine the political future of Singapore. Ultimately, the need to secure the strategic advantage of the Singapore base dictated both the manner of its independence—through Malaysia—and its domestic political form and shape, the legacy of which is felt to this day.

Introduction

Independence for Singapore was never thought conceivable. Whether to the British—having developed the island colony from a largely uninhabited backwater in the early nineteenth century to a busy port-city a hundred years later—or to the nationalist politicians who had emerged by the 1950s, ready to take over the mantle of local government, it was unthinkable that Singapore could exist as a separate and independent city-state once the British left.

Even Lee Kuan Yew, and his People's Action Party (PAP), which has dominated Singapore politics since self-government in 1959, fought in the early years on the platform of a Malayan nationalism, to make Singapore part of a wider Malayan Federation. Their efforts, which were eventually realised when Malaysia was formed in September 1963, were abetted by a departing British colonial power concerned that the strategic island state—and the naval base—would be lost (to the British cause) if Singapore were left to its own devices. Yet, within two years of attaining independence as part of Malaysia—and despite the whole idea of Singapore having once been thought a "man-made [one] ... [created] by the fancy of planners and map-makers in London"[1]—Singapore was out on its own.

Singapore's curious birth as a nation-state was, to a large extent, determined by regional flows and global events.[2] Singapore had always been a commercial centre that survived, and occasionally thrived, on its ability to organise trade, regionally and internationally. It is now known that Singapore had since the 14th century been part of an intricate trading network linking the Persian Gulf, the Straits of Melaka and the South China Sea, not so much as an export port for its Malay hinterland, but more as an emporium for East-West trade and a port linking the archipelago to the world markets in China, South and West Asia and Europe.[3] When a former prime minister of Singapore spoke of "the need

1. Han Fook Kwang, Warren Fernandez and Sumiko Tan, *Lee Kuan Yew: The Man and His Ideas* (Singapore: Singapore Press Holdings and Times Editions), p. 67.

2. I have argued elsewhere that Singapore's emergence and growth as a nation-state cannot be understood solely from the way the city-state's history has traditionally been conceived, that is, along internal lines, and based mainly, if not solely, on the time-worn trajectories of administrative, political and national historical narratives. See Tan Tai Yong, 'Singapore's Story: A port city in search of hinterlands' in Arndt Graf and Chua Beng Huat (eds), *Port Cities in Asia and Europe* (London: Routledge, 2009), pp. 207–19. This linear, progressive—and now dominant—narrative of the Singapore story may have served the young city-state well in terms of its nation-building endeavours, but it obscures the impact of events beyond its shores that, in profound ways, shaped the evolution of Singapore from classical emporium to city-state.

3. See Kwa Chong Guan, Derek Heng and Tan Tai Yong, *Singapore: A 700-Year History—From Early Emporium to World City* (Singapore: National Archives of Singapore, 2009), pp. 19–32.

to widen [Singapore's] hinterland, to build Singapore as the hub for the greater Asian region"—a 7-hour hinterland[4]—it is quite evident that the underlying plot of the Singapore story, as a functional and at times critical node in multiple overlapping networks, has not changed since the 14th century.

Decolonisation and Cold War in Asia

The impact of events beyond its shores in the aftermath of World War II would have a profound effect on Singapore's political fate. When the European powers returned to their erstwhile colonies after the war, hoping to "rediscover the grandeur of an imperial past", they were faced with a different reality.[5] A combination of post-bellum political and economic fatigue in the European capitals, a dramatically altered post-war landscape, and the rise of indigenous nationalisms across the region were spurring a wave of decolonisation. The Dutch lost their empire in the East Indies in the wake of a revolutionary movement that culminated in the declaration of the independent state of Indonesia in 1949. The French withdrew from Indochina under similarly ignominious circumstances, ousted by the determined Viet Minh communist revolutionaries. The experience of the British, however, was different. When Britain realised its hold on the Indian Empire was no longer tenable, it quick transferred power and staged an orderly withdrawal. The mess and bloodshed caused by the decision to 'divide and quit' the subcontinent in 1947 notwithstanding, Anglo-Indian relations remained warm in the wake of decolonisation. The retreat from India did not suggest that Britain was about to relinquish its position as a world power and retire from empire. Indeed, in the Southeast Asian colonies, which were still critical for Britain's global interests and responsibilities, the plan was to stay on

4. Prime Minister Goh Chok Tong's speech at the National Day Rally, University Cultural Centre, National University of Singapore, 19 Aug 2001.

5. Matthew Jones, *Conflict and Confrontation in Southeast Asia, 1961–65: Britain, the United States and the Creation of Malaysia* (Cambridge: Cambridge University Press, 2001), p. 1.

for an indefinite period. Malaya was especially valuable because it was the world's primary producer of rubber and tin, both critical dollar-earners for the Sterling area, while Singapore's command of the vital sea-lanes of the Indian Ocean, South China Sea and the Southern Pacific made it a vital lynchpin of Britain's long-term security considerations and defence obligations in the region, especially in relation to Australia and New Zealand. In considering self-government and eventual independence for these colonies, stability and security, within the colonies and for the region as a whole, were of paramount importance.

Southeast Asia was a disparate region, comprising several territories large and small, and politically undeveloped in most cases. British strategic interests, and the ways in which the colonies were linked, required that London take a regional approach in developing its policies there.[6] The consolidation of regionalism—based on security pacts, policy co-ordination and economic cooperation—was regarded as essential to the security of the region, and its natural corollary was the coming together, eventually, of the British territories of Southcast Asia to form a regional bloc. The idea of a federation of proximate, if disparate, territories as an objective of British policy in post-war Southeast Asia had indeed been discussed in London as early as 1945. The appointment of Malcolm MacDonald as commissioner-general in Southeast Asia with authority over the governors of the individual territories in Singapore, Malaya and the Borneo territories soon after the end of hostilities in those parts was essentially aimed at preventing these dependencies from drifting off in different directions. An ultimate union of the British territories in Southeast Asia quickly became, in the immediate post-war years, a long-term objective of British policy in the region. In 1952, the assistant under-secretary of state responsible for the Hong Kong and Pacific and Southeast

6. See Nicholas Tarling, '"Some Rather Nebulous Capacity": Lord Killearn's Appointment in Southeast Asia', *Modern Asian Studies*, 20, no. 3 (1986), p. 559.

Asia departments of the Colonial Office recorded, in a memorandum on 'Malaya', that "from 1945 onwards it has been Colonial Office policy that there should be closer association between (a) The Federation and Singapore, and (b) the Borneo territories; and there was also hope that there would ultimately be a Union of the Malaysian and Borneo territories".[7] Indeed, in the 1940s and early 1950s it had seemed that it was part of Britain's grand plan for the region that there would be no "apportioning of self-government to the territories individually, but in blocs".[8] Regionalism seemed to offer the best solution to British policy-makers who had to contend with the pressures of having to plan for eventual (and hopefully an orderly) withdrawal from the region on the one hand, and, on the other, having to ensure stability in the region, particularly in the context of defence and security in Asia generated by Cold War considerations.

By the early 1950s, the Cold War had come to Asia. China turned communist in 1949, the effects of which were soon felt in many parts of Southeast Asia. Communist revolutionaries fought for power in Indochina and Indonesia, and a communist-inspired insurrection broke out in Malaya in 1948, prompting the British to impose a state of emergency to maintain their grip on this key colony in Southeast Asia. British plans for regionalism had to be put on hold—or at least now delivered piecemeal—when Malaya was singled out for independence in 1956. By granting Malaya independence, the British sought to remove the anti-colonial cause from communist agitation and to place the country in the hands of moderate, anti-communist politicians who would be sympathetic to British interests there. The independence of Malaya may have consolidated an anti-communist force in the region, but the under-

7. Minute by J.J. Paskin on the question of closer constitutional association between the Federation of Malaya and Singapore, 10 Dec 1952, in David Goldsworthy (ed.), *British Documents on the End of Empire*, Series A, Volume 3, *The Conservative Government and the End of Empire, 1951–1957, Part II: Politics and Administration* (London: HMSO, 1994), p. 377.

8. Greg Poulgrain, *The Genesis of Konfrontasi: Malaysia, Brunei, Indonesia, 1945–65* (London: Hurst, 1998).

lying concern of containment of communism was still foremost in British preoccupations in the region.

In June 1960, following British Prime Minister Harold Macmillan's initiative to review Britain's overseas policy, an interdepartmental sub-committee on 'Future Developments in Southeast Asia' under the chairmanship of the former commissioner-general of Southeast Asia, Sir Robert Scott, was established to "review the likely course of developments in the region during the next ten years as well as British aims and the means to secure them".[9] The Scott committee produced a summary report in mid-October and its final report in November. According to the report, Southeast Asia—the area defined in the study as being bounded by Pakistan in the west, Japan in the east and Indonesia to the south—"will continue to be a major source of conflict in the East/West struggle". The report assumed that "China will, in terms of power, increasingly overshadow the area ... and will seek to expel the West from Formosa, Japan, Korea and Indochina by all means short of overt armed aggression, and will generally seek to weaken the West throughout Asia and in Africa and Latin America".[10] It believed that the major countries that were "free" would not defect to the communist bloc, but it was crucial that they continue to receive Western support, including "military backing, without which they are unlikely to maintain their independence".[11] In this regard, British general aims were very much in line with fundamental Cold War concerns: "containment of communism"; "maintenance of western influence"; "preservation of peace and reinforcement of non-communist societies"; "fostering of trade, political stability and economic development".[12] While America was obviously taking the lead in Southeast Asian defence through SEATO, Britain would be obliged to play its part in supporting

9. 'Future Developments in Southeast Asia', gist of report by the Committee on Future Developments in SE Asia, D(60)50 (12 Oct 1960), The National Archives of the UK (hereafter TNA): CAB 131/24, in Anthony J. Stockwell (ed.), *British Documents on the End of Empire*, Series B, Volume 8, *Malaysia* (London: Stationery Office, 2004), p. xlvii.

10. Ibid.

11. Ibid.

12. Ibid.

this security arrangement. At the same time, its dependencies in Southeast Asia had to be protected through appropriate internal security arrangements and external defence assurances against the Chinese Communist threat. In the Malayan region, the security arrangements that would obviously contribute to the "strategic deterrence against China" included the Anglo-Malayan Defense Agreement (1957) and the ANZAM Agreements with Australia and New Zealand. Here, Cold War calculations shaped the "temper, pace, and ultimate outcome" of decolonisation in Southeast Asia.[13] British regional actions were now part of a bigger global plot: "the maintenance of Western influence ... [in order] to play a significant part in countering Communist penetration in the area."[14] This had been a consistent theme since the early 1950s. In 1952, his American counterpart, Secretary of State Dean Acheson, reminded British Foreign Secretary Anthony Eden that "the western powers must do what we can to save Southeast Asia [from the communist threat]".[15]

That Southeast Asia would come to feature in the global contest for power and influence between the United States and Soviet Union stemmed from two major post-war developments: the emergence of the United States as the foremost power in the region from 1945, and the rise of Communist China in 1949. Post-war Southeast Asia featured in American strategic thinking in a number of ways. The military bases in the Philippines were crucial to American ambitions to maintain its "posture and presence as a Pacific power". Furthermore, the Americans believed that accessibility to commodities that were in abundance in the region—rubber, tin and oil—had to be maintained if the global economy was to recover quickly from the effects of the war. American concerns

13. Robert J. McMahon, 'The United States and Southeast Asia in an Era of Decolonization, 1945–1965' in Marc Frey, Ronald W. Pruessen and Tan Tai Yong (eds), *The Transformation of Southeast Asia: International Perspectives on Decolonization* (Singapore: Singapore University Press, 2004), p. 213.

14. 'Future developments in Southeast Asia'.

15. McMahon, 'The United States and Southeast Asia in an Era of Decolonization', p. 214.

also stemmed from a generalised fear of the communist threat, and the conviction that the region would only be stable and safe when political powers were in the hands of moderate local nationalists[16]; communism should not be allowed to spread in the region. This was a challenge to regional order, as anti-colonial revolutionaries seemed determined to fill the void left by the departing European colonial powers.

The communist contagion became a distinct worry when Mao Zedong's Chinese Communist Party emerged victorious from the civil war against the Guomindang (Kuomintang). When Chiang Kai-shek's forces retreated to Taiwan, all of mainland China came under communist rule. The communist victory in China was seen as a failure of the Americans' Chinese policy but the problem obviously did not end there. The birth of Red China inspired anti-Western, anti-colonial revolutionaries all over Asia, and the threat thus posed made containment in the region a vital part of the US global Cold War strategy. As the Americans saw it, revolutionary outbreaks, if not prevented or contained, would lead to instability and chaos that would spread through Asia like a disease. Economic stability, political order and the transfer of power to moderate anti-communist nationalists were regarded by the Americans as crucial tactics in stemming the spread of communism in Asia. After the loss of China to communism, successive US presidents knew that any semblance of weak or indecisive policies in the face of communist challenges anywhere in the world could hurt them politically, both domestically and internationally. Allies and friends had to be assured that the Americans were not likely to balk at any challenge mounted by the communists; consequently American policies and actions in Southeast Asia—including its support of the Sukarno regime in Indonesia, support of the French against the Viet Minh, formation of SEATO, dispatch of land forces to Indochina—were all aimed at reassuring non-communist regimes in

16. Ibid., p. 213.

the region of unremitting US support for their contest with the communist foes.[17]

The Cold War and the 'Grand Design'

Like the Americans, British policy-makers accepted that the transfer of power to moderate, non-communist allies, however gradual, would eventually keep its dependencies in line with and staunchly supportive of British interests. By the mid-1950s, the logic behind territorial consolidation of its dependencies had become increasingly compelling: a Southeast Asia that was facing uncertainties—with trouble in Burma, Indochina and Indonesia—could do well with a stable, pro-British core, on which British strategic and economic interests could be secured even after the formal decolonisation of the region. A British plan, known as the 'Grand Design', grew out of those considerations and aspirations.

The concept of the 'Grand Design' was based on a longstanding desire of British policy to see its Southeast Asian colonies—Malaya, Singapore, Sarawak, Brunei and North Borneo (Sabah)—amalgamated into a single political entity as a necessary condition for independence. Since the end of the war, planners in Whitehall had envisaged, as a first phase, the merger of Singapore with the Federation of Malaya; this would be followed by the grouping of the colonies of Sarawak, North Borneo and the protected state of Brunei into a bloc; finally, the two regional blocs would be amalgamated into a single political unit. Throughout the 1950s, however, the amalgamation remained a vague concept, and it never really generated much interest or gathered its own momentum.[18] British governors and high commissioners spoke about the possibility of integration in conferences on the political future of British colonies in Southeast Asia, but the idea never obtained serious official consideration, nor were there any con-

17. Ibid., p. 217.

18. See Mohamed Noordin Sopiee, *From Malayan Union to Singapore Separation: Political Unification in the Malayan Region, 1945–65* (Kuala Lumpur: Penerbit Universiti Malaya, 1974), p. 128.

crete plans, detailing the timing and manner of the withdrawal of the British from the region, ever laid out or submitted as a firm policy proposal.

When the idea of consolidation reappeared in the early 1960s in the form of the 'Grand Design', it was clear that politics and security were foremost considerations. Only through the 'Grand Design', which would lead to a 'Greater Malaysia', were the British confident of granting self-government status to the Borneo territories and Singapore. A stable federation would reduce the dangers that small units might be affected piecemeal by subversive elements from within or outside their borders. Most importantly, the British viewed the formation of an anti-communist super-federation, and the securing of the Singapore base, as the surest way to provide stability in Southeast Asia and therefore minimise their internal security obligations in the region.[19] This would offer an effective, and affordable, peacetime policy of containing the communist threat as opposed to the more expensive approach of maintaining bases in preparation for war.[20] Commonwealth links—involving the defence of Malaya, Australia, New Zealand and Hong Kong—as well as British relations with the United States, especially in the context of the Cold War in Asia, would be enhanced through this initiative. Political stability would provide the necessary conditions for economic development, which in turn would foster trade between the West and Asia. The 'Grand Design' for a 'Greater Malaysia' would ultimately preserve British influence in post-colonial Southeast Asia, allowing her to maintain her position in the world and yet keep the balance of payments healthy and defence costs down. Thus, from the early 1960s, strategic interests, more than economic benefits, shaped British thinking about their position in Southeast Asia. The Cold War and the containment of communism, defence and security obligations in

19. Note to Prime Minister, 'Singapore, the Malayan Federation and the Borneo Territories' (17 Apr 1961), TNA: PREM 11/3418.

20. See Jones, *Conflict and Confrontation in Southeast East Asia*, pp. 18–19.

the region, and Anglo-American relations dominated policy thinking about the future of Southeast Asia.[21]

The economic value of the 'Grand Design' was less obvious. By 1960, rubber and tin were no longer essential to British balance of payments, and the balance sheet for the region indicated that more money was spent for political reasons "rather than for any prospect of financial gain".[22] As A.J. Stockwell and others have shown, while British businesses continued to dominate trade in Southeast Asia, the region's economic significance for Britain had been declining.[23] Moreover, there was little evidence to indicate that the British government and business interests took a unified approach to economic matters concerning the empire. The records and memoranda on the 'Grand Design' were largely silent on the economic benefits that the scheme would bring to Britain. British ministers were clearly more interested in "bases not markets, security not commerce, and international influence not investment opportunities".[24]

The 'Grand Design' did have another obvious advantage for the British: it would offer a satisfactory solution to the future of its strategic naval base in Southeast Asia. The Crown Colony of Singapore was a major area of concern because of disturbing signs, at least to the British, that left-leaning political forces were taking root and dominating the political arena in the island colony. Following constitutional talks in London in 1957, Singapore was on track for self-government, but the issue of the security of the base was still unresolved. British prognosis on the future of the Singapore base was relatively bleak. London had hoped that as Singapore progressed towards self-government and eventual inde-

21. Stockwell, *Malaysia*, p. xlviii.

22. 'Future Developments in Southeast Asia': Committee on Future Developments in Southeast Asia minutes (29 Sept 1960), DSE(60) 15th meeting, TNA: CAB 134/1644.

23. See Nicholas White, 'The Business and Politics of Decolonization: The British Experience in the Twentieth Century', *Economic History Review*, 53, no. 3 (2000): 544–64; and Anthony J. Stockwell, 'Malaysia: The Making of a Neo-Colony?' *Journal of Imperial and Commonwealth History*, 26, no. 2 (1998): 138–56.

24. Stockwell, *Malaysia*, p. xlvii.

pendence, a moderate, pro-British government that would ensure the security and accessibility of British bases there would govern it. However, if the communists were to gain political ground, as they were showing signs of doing in the 1950s, the British would lose their hold on this prized strategic asset in Southeast Asia, with possible dire consequences for the security of the region, as well as Australia and New Zealand. The only way to secure the bases, so the British reasoned, was to ensure that Singapore would not turn 'red' and the best way of 'guaranteeing' this was to make sure that Singapore became part of the staunchly anti-communist Malayan Federation. The defence establishment in London, however, had their doubts about such an arrangement and were concerned that Singapore's integration with Malaya would restrict British access to the use of the military bases.[25] The Chiefs of Staff argued that the "run-down of British presence in Singapore would discourage friends and allies",[26] and that since Malaya was already an independent country there was no guarantee that the government in Kuala Lumpur, once they had secured Singapore, would continue to do the bidding of the British. Differences of opinion about the desirability of having the Singapore base under Malaysian control did not, however, diminish the eventual conclusion that "the 'Grand Design' was the last harmful of the possible developments".[27] A merger between Singapore and the Federation, and the subsequent incorporation of the Borneo territories, which were considered too "backward to survive on their own in the Cold War",[28] would do much, according to the calculations of British officials in the region, to secure a key area in Southeast Asia. Without a merger with Malaya, independence for Singapore was almost a non-starter. Although bound by an agreement to institute a constitutional review in 1963, four years after Singapore was granted

25. Ibid., p. xlix.

26. Ibid.

27. 'Defence implications of an association of the British Borneo territories with the Federation of Malaya and the State of Singapore', Report of Joint Planning Staff, JP(61)57 (17 July 1961), TNA: DEFE 4/137.

28. Anthony J. Stockwell, 'Malaysia: The Making of a "Grand Design"' *Asian Affairs*, XXXIV, no. 3 (Nov 2003), p. 238.

self-government, the British were convinced that they would not grant any further constitutional concessions to Singapore if the conditions were not right. The 1959 constitution had stipulated that should the United Kingdom and Singapore governments not arrive at a mutual agreement in a constitutional review by 1963, the current constitution would "continue in force".[29] The political dangers and security implications of an independent and politically unstable Singapore were clearly of major concern to London.

Securing the base: Singapore in 'Greater Malaysia'

Although Singapore had been separated from the other Straits Settlements and Malaya and established as a Crown Colony in its own right in April 1946, British officials were convinced that the island's long-term existence as a state on its own was hardly viable given its economic and trade dependence on the Malayan hinterland.[30] Indeed when the British decided to excise Singapore from the mainland, largely as a measure to ease the acceptance of the Malayan Union plan by the Malay politicians and the sultans,[31] the separation of the two territories was meant to be a temporary expedient; British officials expected their reunion in the not-too-distant future.[32] Once out, however, it was to prove difficult

29. *Report of the Singapore Constitutional Conference held in London in March and April 1957*, presented by the Secretary of State for Colonies to Parliament, by Command of Her Majesty (London: HMSO, 1957), Cmd. 147 para. 48(d).

30. Prior to 1867 the Indian Government administered Singapore, together with the Straits Settlements of Malacca and Penang. In that year, the Straits Settlements became a British Crown Colony. From 1942 to 1945 the Japanese occupied the island. Upon the restoration of civilian government at the end of the war, Singapore was detached from the other Straits Settlements to become a separate colony. In a White Paper published at that time (Cmd. 6724, Jan 1946), it was stated that "in considering the need for a closer integration in Malaya, His Majesty's Government consider that, at least for the time being, Singapore requires separate treatment.... It is recognised, however, that there were, and will be, close ties between Singapore and the mainland".

31. For the story of the Malayan Union, see Anthony J. Stockwell, *British Policy and Malay Politics during the Malayan Union Experiment, 1945–48* (Singapore: Malaysian Branch of the Royal Asiatic Society, 1979); and Albert Lau, *The Malayan Union Controversy, 1942–48* (Singapore: Oxford University Press, 1990).

32. Nicholas Tarling, *Nations and States in Southeast Asia* (Cambridge: Cambridge University Press, 1998), p. 77.

for Singapore to get back with the mainland again. After 1946, Malcolm MacDonald claimed that although the British were prepared to return Singapore to Malaya, Malay leaders had blocked the decision during the Anglo-Malay constitutional discussions in mid-1946.[33] When the Union experiment failed—its liberal citizenship provisions to non-Malays proved politically unacceptable to the Malay elites—and was replaced by a new arrangement in the form of the Federation of Malaya in 1948, the Malay political leadership continued to oppose the re-merger of Singapore, determined as they were to prevent "the submergence of the Malays by the economically superior and aggressive Chinese".[34]

While policy-makers in London doubted if Singapore could afford to stay out of Malaya for long, for the moment at least the retention of Singapore as a separate Crown Colony had its own logic. For Britain, direct control over Singapore would mean that it was able to retain continued use of the military bases there for the purposes of maintaining its strategic policy East of Suez.[35] Further, there was the concern that if Singapore were to be re-incorporated into Malaya, its economy, which was ultimately dependent on entrepôt and free-trade arrangements, would be threatened as Kuala Lumpur would in all probability bring the island into some form of customs union with the rest of the Federation. For the time being, therefore, it was decided in the interests of all concerned that Singapore should remain separate from the mainland. By 1948, even political parties in Singapore, many of which still saw an eventual merger with Malaya as the only way by which Singapore would ultimately achieve its independence, had come round to the view that under the existing conditions, merger with the Federation was perhaps inappropriate as an immediate political goal for Singapore. The most prominent party of the time, the Singapore Progressive Party (SPP), an elite, moderate and pro-

33. Ibid.

34. Yeo Kim Wah, *Political Development in Singapore, 1950–55* (Singapore: Singapore University Press, 1973), p. 14.

35. For this, see Chin Kin Wah, *The Defence of Malaysia & Singapore: The Transformation of a Security System 1957–71* (Cambridge: Cambridge University Press, 1983).

establishment party "without any mass support or an effective country-wide organization," had argued that "Singapore ... should press for self-government and then merge with the mainland [only] when the Federation Constitution had been liberalised to confer equal rights on the Malays and the pro-Malays".[36] The SPP leader, C.C. Tan, a Singapore-born and London-trained lawyer, explained that any form of merger at this stage with a pro-Malay Federation would retard the political progress of Singapore.[37] The SPP's main political rival, the Singapore Labour Party, formed by trade unionists and dominated by English-educated Indians, similarly felt that merger was not a serious option at this stage. Its president, Lim Yew Hock, warned that an immediate merger was tantamount to "tying a millstone around [Singapore's] neck".[38] All that these parties, as well as the Chinese economic interests in Singapore, would support at this point in time was for the concept of a loose Confederation of Malaysia that would comprise Malaya, Singapore and the North Borneo territories.[39] Consequently, from the immediate post-war period, Singapore, as a separate colony, proceeded to develop on its own, its directions and destiny divorced, for the time being, from those of mainland Malaya.

By the early 1950s, as political parties in Singapore sought progress towards eventual self-government for the colony, the question of merger with Malaya began to generate interest again. All major political parties had accepted the view that Singapore was not likely ever to achieve sovereignty existing on its own and it was necessary, as the rhetoric of self-rule and independence became more pronounced, that the question of merger now had to be addressed with a greater degree of urgency. Indeed, in the 1955 elections, following the adoption of the Rendel Constitution—which considerably increased the size of the legislative assembly,

36. Yeo Kim Wah and Albert Lau, 'From Colonialism to Independence, 1945–65' in Ernest Chew and Edwin Lee (eds), *A History of Singapore* (Singapore: Oxford University Press, 1991), pp. 124–5.

37. Ibid., p. 125.

38. *The Straits Times*, 26 Mar 1953, quoted in ibid.

39. See Yeo, *Political Development in Singapore,* pp. 44–9; and Sopiee, *From Malayan Union to Singapore Separation*, chapter 5.

the franchise and the number of political parties in Singapore—merger with the Federation became a prominent electoral issue, eliciting encouraging comments from several prominent politicians. In January 1955, campaigning to form the first government under the Rendel Constitution, C.C. Tan, in a perceptible shift from his earlier position, called for an early tie-up between Singapore and the Federation, declaring that before Singapore could expect complete independence, "the question of her relationship with the Federation must first be settled".[40] Tan, however, did not expect any immediate moves in that direction, and urged that politicians from both sides of the causeway should "refrain from interfering in each other's affairs".[41] The following month, Lim Yew Hock of the Labour Front[42] spoke of the necessity of "bringing the two territories into a coherent whole", and argued that independence for Singapore would "automatically follow merger".[43] In a manner characteristic of his flamboyant style, the Jewish lawyer and leader of the Labour Front, David Marshall, confidently declared in March 1955 that "there will be a union of the two territories within three years", a view which he said was based on information which he had gathered from London.[44] For all the keen rhetoric on merger in the Singapore political scene, the time was perhaps still not ripe for such a venture. The colony was still some way off in securing self-government—its next stage of political progress—and in any case, the Malayans had chosen to remain cool to any idea of union with Singapore. Tunku Abdul Rahman made clear his government's stand when he announced that "the question of merger [is] still a long way off and nothing much can be done about it until Singapore and the Federation achieve their [respective] independence".[45]

40. *The Straits Times*, 24 Jan 1955.

41. Ibid.

42. In July 1954, following the publication of the Rendel Report, the Singapore Labour Party sought to extend its organisational base by drawing former socialists together to form a Labour Front under the leadership of David Marshall.

43. *Straits Echo*, 7 Feb 1955.

44. *Straits Times*, 5 Mar 1955.

45. Sopiee, *From Malayan Union to Singapore Separation*, p. 110.

In the meantime, politics in Singapore took an interesting turn. Despite expectations that the pro-British and conservative SPP would emerge victorious in the 1955 elections and thus form the first government under the Rendel Constitution, it was the moderate democratic socialist Labour Front that surprised everyone with their performance at the polls. With no single party winning enough seats to form the government, the Labour Front, which won 10 of the 22 seats contested, went on to form a coalition government, with three additional seats from the Malay Union Alliance.[46] David Marshall became the first chief minister of Singapore.

Swept up by the euphoria of his strong election showing, the new chief minister took it upon himself to wrest early independence for Singapore from the British and staked his political reputation on the accomplishment of that task. He led an all-party delegation to London in April 1956 for negotiations. The talks, however, broke down, and a discredited Marshall returned to Singapore and resigned. Marshall had demanded full internal self-government by April 1957, and while he was prepared to leave foreign policy and defence in the hands of the British, he wanted a veto on defence and rights of consultation on foreign affairs.[47] Marshall had clearly misread British intentions and underestimated their concerns on the security of Singapore. The Colonial Office feared that Singapore might end up as an outpost of Communist China, and would not entrust security to a government it had no confidence could deal effectively with the communist threat. The British government was prepared to concede on most other areas—a fully elected assembly, citizenship, local control of trade and commerce—but would not compromise on security, in which they demanded the casting vote in the defence council.[48]

46. The Malay Union Alliance was a parliamentary coalition of UMNO (United Malays National Organisation) and the Malayan Chinese Association.

47. C.M. Turnbull, *A History of Singapore, 1819–1988*, 2nd edition (Singapore: Oxford University Press, 1989), pp. 257–8.

48. Ibid.

Lim Yew Hock, Marshall's colleague from the Labour Front government, succeeded him. Lim's tenure, from 1956 to 1959, was dominated by the government's head-on collision with the increasingly militant activists among the Chinese students, teachers and union leaders.[49] Communist agents in Singapore had been active in infiltrating Chinese youth groups and vernacular schools, and trying to influence labour unions and political parties such as the PAP. Their anti-British and anti-American sentiments resonated with Chinese-educated youths inspired by fervent nationalism and revolutionary ideals. A number of violent strikes and riots that took place in 1956 and 1957 were met with firm government reaction in the form of arrests without trial. Although concerned with the communist threat, the British decided to proceed with their plans for conceding self-rule for Singapore, reasoning that lack of progress in political devolution would simply feed the communist cause. Lim Yew Hock led a second all-party delegation to London for talks in March–April 1957, and succeeded where Marshall had failed in securing the promise of self-government for Singapore by 1959. Provisions for an extended franchise based on Singapore citizenship and a parliamentary system of government based on popular elections were eventually agreed upon. Defence and external affairs would, however, remain in British hands, and the British, Singapore and Malayan governments would jointly share responsibilities for internal security.[50]

Both Lim and Marshall, as chief ministers, had made repeated overtures to the Tunku, urging him to consider merger with Singapore. To them, this was the only way in which Singapore could realistically convince the British to grant independence to the colony. The Tunku chose, however, to turn a deaf ear to the requests. Although he liked Lim Yew Hock for the firm manner in which the latter had dealt with the militant Chinese students and workers in Singapore, once even describing his government as "courageous

49. Ibid.

50. *Report of the Singapore Constitutional Conference Held in London in March and April 1957.*

and good", he was still uncertain if the conditions for merger were right. His greatest worry was the danger of importing a large, radicalised Chinese population from Singapore into Malaya.

If indeed merger was to take place, it was not destined to happen under the auspices of the Labour Front government, as things turned out. The 1959 elections,[51] which ushered in the period of self-government for Singapore, were swept by the left-wing People's Action Party (PAP), which won 43 of the 51 seats contested, garnering 54 per cent of the overall votes. The old Labour Front, which had fallen apart and re-organised into a new Singapore People's Alliance Party, on the other hand, had lost the support of the Chinese-educated masses. With its party organisation fractured by internal dissent and public image tainted by the smear of corruption,[52] the party managed to win only four of the 39 seats contested.

The PAP campaigned throughout the 1959 elections on the pledge of bringing Singapore into a united Malaya. From its very inception in November 1954, the PAP had declared as one of its main objectives the ending of colonialism in Singapore through the establishment of "an independent [and non-communist] national state of Malaya comprising ... the Federation of Malaya and the Colony of Singapore".[53] Following the constitutional talks in London in 1957, Lee Kuan Yew, leader of the PAP, maintained his position that independence for Singapore was not possible until merger with the Federation was achieved, and just before the PAP

51. Singapore attained internal self-government in June 1959. The new constitution provided for a legislative assembly with 51 elected members and a cabinet responsible for the assembly. While the local government assumed responsibilities for domestic development such as labour, education, culture, finance, health and national development, the key portfolios of defence, external affairs and some internal security responsibilities remained with the United Kingdom, overseen by its commissioner in Singapore. An internal security council was set up, comprising the UK commissioner and five other members—two appointed by the UK, two by the prime minister of Singapore and one by the government of the Federation of Malaya.

52. Ibid.

53. 'An assessment of the present situation and the future outlook in Singapore', Department of External Affairs, Canberra, 20 Aug 1957, National Archives of Australia (hereafter NAA): A 1838/318, no. 3024/1/7, part 1.

fought the 1959 elections, he obtained an undertaking of full support, particularly from the pro-communists within his party whom he knew were ambivalent to the idea of re-integration with Malaya, for merger as the way to independence.[54] Having won the elections so convincingly, the PAP now believed that they had the mandate from the people to push vigorously for merger with Malaya, and promised that this would be achieved within their term of office.

Ever the pragmatic politician with a solid grasp of the realities of the day, Lee pursued merger based on his assessment of the problems that Singapore had to contend with as it moved towards political and economic independence. As far as he was concerned, separate independence for Singapore was a "dangerous illusion", and the island state would be "committing national suicide if [it] refused to merge in Malaysia".[55] Throughout the 1950s, the colony had been under mounting economic pressure brought about by the combination of an explosive rate of population growth and declining entrepôt trade. Its exports to the region had been dramatically reduced, owing to import restrictions on the part of many of its neighbours to protect their own industries, and entrepôt trade, the mainstay of its economy, was threatened by countries increasingly engaging in direct trading. Amidst all this, there was the further problem of ensuring that employment opportunities kept pace with population growth. If Singapore was to create enough jobs for its young and fast-growing population as well as cut its dependence on the entrepôt trade, its economy would have to embark on a course of rapid industrialisation. But for this to work, integration with the economy and markets of the Federation was crucial.[56] Finance Minister Goh Keng Swee saw this very clearly and commented, "whatever we do, major changes in our economy are only possible if Singapore and the Federation are integrated as one economy".[57]

54. Han, Fernandez and Tan, *Lee Kuan Yew*, p. 70.
55. Speech by Lee Kuan Yew at the luncheon of the Singapore National Union of Journalists, 24 May 1963.
56. Ibid.
57. Cited in Turnbull, p. 267.

Without some form of economic integration or common market, the Singapore and Malayan economies would find themselves in direct competition with each other, particularly in attracting foreign investors. Singapore, with its smaller workforce and higher production costs, had found that it was in a particularly disadvantageous position as many local companies, such as local rubber footwear firms, were moving out of Singapore into the Federation, where costs of production were much lower. In the Federation, these companies could also secure tariff protection for their products, which they could not under Singapore's free port economy. Although Singapore could hope to overcome some of these problems by taking action to restrict imports of goods that competed directly with the island's industries, this would put the island's free port status in question.[58] And while Singapore was having difficulties protecting its local industries from foreign competition, it found at the same time that the Federation's tariff barrier stood in the way of Singapore manufactured goods making it across the causeway into the Federation markets.

The Singapore government was therefore keen to establish an integrated industrial development programme with the Federation in the context of a common market. However, negotiations to that end had made little progress. The Federation government quite rightly recognised that as long as Singapore completely retained its free port status, while the rest of the Federation was imposed with a set of customs duties, market arrangements would only give a preponderant advantage to the latter. At present, the Federation had a normal range of tariffs on imported goods, including those bought from Singapore, while Singapore collected duties only on intoxicating liquors, tobacco and petroleum intended for domestic consumption. Goods manufactured in the Federation thus enjoyed free entry into Singapore, while goods made in Singapore had to pass through a tariff barrier before they could be marketed in the

58. 'Economic Relations between Singapore and Malaya', TNA: CO 1030/972.

Federation.[59] If Singapore were to remain wholly a free port while a common market was instituted, the Federation would have to open their own markets to Singapore manufactures in return for no further advantages in the Singapore market that they did not already possess. The Malayans, therefore, saw little rationale in having a common market with Singapore.

While the Singapore government had very strong and compelling economic reasons for merger, it was politics that propelled the PAP government to urgently seek an effective union with Malaya. From its early days, the PAP was "divided between two ideologically diverse factions with incompatible ends and means".[60] While Lee and a number of his moderate, English-educated comrades were committed to achieving an independent, democratic and socialist Malaya through open constitutional struggle, there was a rival faction within the party, comprising powerful union leaders like Lim Chin Siong, whose political aims were focused on the establishment of a socialist Malaya through radical political change, if necessary. This faction was believed to have communist and pro-communist members. In the first few years of the PAP's existence, for reasons of mutual political expediency, the two factions were able to forge a united front. Lee and the English-educated moderates needed the help of the Chinese-educated pro-communists members, with their control of the trade unions, cultural organisations and Chinese schools, to win the Chinese ground,[61] while the communist elements saw in the PAP a legitimate left-wing party and a convenient legal political vehicle on which to carry out their activities, gradually subverting Singapore and ultimately using the island as a base to foment a revolution in Malaya. Lee knew that his attempt to ride the 'communist tiger' was fraught with danger, and that once the British left, the two factions would have to scrap it out between themselves. By 1960,

59. Ibid.

60. Yeo and Lau, 'From Colonialism to Independence, 1945–1965', p. 133.

61. Lee Kuan Yew, *The Battle for Merger* (Singapore: Government Printing Office, 1962), p. 16.

while the moderates still controlled the party through the Central Executive Committee, there were growing signs that the influence of the pro-communists was growing stronger and more pervasive as Chinese chauvinism, fuelled by economic frustrations and the popular appeal of anti-imperialism (especially with the British enjoying full rights of occupation, control and use of the bases on the island), fed the popularity of the extreme left.

With the radical left stirring up an anti-colonial mood in Singapore, Lee knew that his political position would become increasingly tenuous as long as colonialism, or forms of colonial presence, was still evident in the island state. As an anti-colonial party, the PAP was obliged to end Singapore's status as a colony, but Lee and his government knew that without merger, it was not likely that the British would concede independence; and unless the government was able to make some progress with the Federation on either political merger or a common market and thus mark the road to independence with a degree of certainty, the pro-communists would continue to gain political mileage at the moderates' expense.[62]

While the gathering strength of Lee's political opponents made the securing of a merger agreement with the Malayans a matter of extreme importance for the PAP government, it was the very same question of merger that catalysed the seething tension between the pro-communist and the moderate wings of the PAP into an open conflict between the two groups.[63] All along, the extreme left-wing in the PAP had been fundamentally opposed to merger, which would see Singapore gaining independence as part of the Federation. For them and the communists, merger would mean internal security being placed in the hands of a rabidly anti-communist Kuala Lumpur government, which would certainly spare no effort in suppressing the communist movement in Singapore. Independence through merger would also remove in a single

62. Selkirk to Secretary of State (Colonial Office), 2 May 1961, TNA: CO 1030/979.

63. Lee Kuan Yew, radio broadcast, 25 Sept 1961.

stroke their continued excuse of couching their political struggle in the form of an anti-colonial struggle. However, for so long as the possibility of achieving merger seemed remote, the extremists had found it expedient to pay lip service to the idea. They were, after all, anti-colonialists who had regarded that the split between Singapore and Malaya was a colonial act that had to be rectified. However, should Lee have a breakthrough, they would be prepared to sabotage the enterprise by staging a revolt against the PAP leadership. Encouraged by the British, who stipulated that they were prepared to allow the pro-communists, whom they were ready to accept as radical non-communists, to form the government should they acquire power constitutionally—an act of subterfuge, according to Lee—the militants began to openly challenge Lee and the moderates for control of the party and the government.[64]

By 1960, Lee was clearly in a fix: without showing a stern hand in dealing with the militants, he was not likely to win the Tunku's confidence for merger; yet without the clear prospects of merger, Lee was in no position to politically defeat the militants that were out to get him. For the embattled prime minister of Singapore, the survival of his government and the future viability and stability of Singapore without merger was very bleak.[65] Indeed, the political survival of the PAP would soon be staked on that very issue. The longer the Malayans held out, the weaker would be his position. According to Philip Moore, the British acting high commissioner in Singapore, "the opposition to Lee was building up and he would find it increasingly difficult to carry Singapore with him in a merger with the Federation".[66] But up to 1961, Lee, despite his best efforts, was not having any luck with the Tunku.[67] Each time the Singapore government raised the issue, the Malayan premier would reject any suggestion that the Federation was prepared to

64. *Singapore Legislative Assembly Debates*, 20 July 1961, Col. 1668.

65. Note on 'Lee Kuan Yew, Merger and Malaysia' by British Secretary of State (n.d.), TNA: DO 169/249.

66. Note of Meeting on 26 June in Singapore, TNA: DO 169/26.

67. Han, Fernandez and Tan, *Lee Kuan Yew*, p. 280.

consider any form of merger with Singapore, and point out that Malaya had first to settle its own racial policies. For a long time the Tunku decided to shut his ears to all suggestions of merger,[68] and, not wishing to lead Singapore into thinking that merger was indeed on the cards, the Federation government, also to avoid drawing flak from the right-wing political ground in the Federation, would cautiously keep a safe distance from any proposals for common action that might be interpreted as the first steps towards a political merger of the two territories. With the position of the Tunku on a Singapore-Malaya merger made clear to him several times before, Lee knew that it would be naive of him to expect positive gestures from the Federation at this stage; but he was concerned that the Federation should at least keep alive the hope of eventual merger and not encourage the idea that Singapore could be independent on its own.[69] In a meeting with the British high commissioner to Malaya, Geofroy Tory, Lee explained that in speaking of merger, he was not trying to upset the Malaya or the Alliance government; he was simply expressing his belief that without Malaya, Singapore was nothing. He was, as it were, simply "putting his hand across the causeway and keeping hold of the Federation". He seemed genuinely to regard it as an essential part of the plan to contain and absorb communism in Singapore.[70] At present, he lamented, he was not even getting this minimal measure of assistance.

While the door across the causeway remained shut for the moment, Lee knew that he could not stop at rhetorical gestures, but had to continue creating tangible conditions in Singapore that would encourage the Tunku to be more favourably disposed to

68. M.J. Moynihan to Commonwealth Relations Office (12 Oct 1961), TNA: DO 169/30; and Tunku's speech in Parliament on 16 Oct 1961, as given to the press.

69. Note of meeting between UK delegation and Singapore delegation on Internal Security Council, which took place on Saturday, as enclosed in Acting UK Commissioner (Singapore) to Secretary of State (Colonial Office), 28 June 1960, TNA: CO 1030/977 no. 256.

70. Report of meeting between Lee Kuan Yew and Sir Geofroy Tory, UK High Commissioner (Kuala Lumpur), on 21 and 22 Dec 1959, TNA: CO 1030/972.

merger once the time was right.[71] Fundamentally, the PAP realised that it had to "resolve the ... fears which make the Malay majority in the Federation not want the Chinese majority in Singapore".[72] From its inception in 1954, the party had created a Malay Affairs Bureau, under the charge of an active Malay journalist, Othman Wok, who later became a cabinet minister. While on the Opposition benches between 1955 and 1959, the PAP had demonstrated its readiness to cooperate with the Federation government when Lee took the potentially problematic and unpopular position of supporting the institution of the Internal Security Council to control security in Singapore. Lee had then argued that as the PAP's ultimate aim was to effect merger between Singapore and Malaya, it was logical to recognise that the Federation would have a decisive voice in the affairs of Singapore, including its security.[73]

By 1960, despite the PAP's policies of conciliation and goodwill, the Tunku still remained cool to the idea of merger. The PAP government was becoming increasingly worried if it could hold on indefinitely to the line of independence through merger without any promise of concrete achievements. In the meantime, the government's position was further undermined by the loss of two by-elections in quick succession. The electoral defeats dealt a serious blow to the PAP government, which believed that its inability to make headway with merger would simply strengthen its rivals. With its position weakened, the PAP government would soon be subjected to increasing pressure from the pro-communist hard-liners to adopt the objective advocated by Marshall and never expressly abandoned by Lim Yew Hock: separate and outright independence for Singapore, or independence before merger. Both these courses of action could well postpone merger indefinitely. Lee, naturally, did not want this and indeed he was especially afraid of it, since he had the sense to see that an independent

71. *Petir,* 4th anniversary issue (Singapore, 1958).

72. People's Action Party, *6th Anniversary Celebrations Souvenir* (Singapore, 1960).

73. *Singapore Legislative Assembly Debates*, 8 Oct 1958, Col. 804.

Singapore, standing by itself, would rapidly be engulfed.[74] The line had to be drawn, and the PAP announced that at the 1963 constitutional review talks they would demand independence through merger with the Federation, or merger in a larger federation. Lee then confided to the British that the party would stand or fall by this.[75]

Ironically, the increasingly precarious position of the PAP government proved to be fortuitous for Lee and the moderates in an unexpected way. Watching with great interest from Kuala Lumpur, the Tunku began to realise that the moderates were rapidly losing ground, and unless he did something to bolster Lee's position, the government in Singapore would be taken over by the radical left. In April 1961, the Tunku informed Lee that while he was still strongly opposed to the idea of a direct merger between Singapore and the Federation, he was open to the possibility of bringing in the Borneo territories first if Singapore had to be taken in at a later stage.[76] Lee then spoke to Lord Selkirk, the British commissioner to Singapore, about the Tunku's ideas; Selkirk assured him that the British government was in favour of the 'Grand Design'—the overall amalgamation of the British colonies in Southeast Asia (including independent Malaya) into a single entity in principle, but he omitted details on what the authorities in London had in mind.[77] Indeed, in an earlier meeting with the governors of these territories in October 1959, the commissioner-general had recommended that discreet "encouragement should be given to the interests that the Prime Ministers of both the Federation and Singapore had been taking in the wider association with these territories".[78] Lee was now offered a way out of his impasse: as the PAP's declared aim of independence through merger with the Federation was

74. Selkirk to Macleod (15 Mar 1960), TNA: CO 1030/925.

75. Selkirk to Macleod (27 June 1961), TNA: CO 1030/980.

76. Record of conversation between Lee Kuan Yew and Selkirk (24 Apr 1961), TNA: DO 169/25.

77. Ibid.

78. Draft brief for Prime Minister's Conference (13 Feb 1961), TNA: CO 1030/978.

"vulnerable to destructive criticism from his political opponents because the Federation's attitude was so unforthcoming", he started to push for merger through a wider political association that would include the Borneo territories.[79]

By the middle of 1960, with no headway on the venture of a single merger between Singapore and the Federation, Lee had become increasingly attracted to the idea of a larger grouping both as a solution to his own dilemma and as a desirable development in its own right. Through the 'Grand Design', which could proceed on the basis of a Malaya-Singapore merger with the three Borneo territories coming in as a counterweight to the Chinese factor (which he knew the Tunku dreaded), Lee reasoned that he would probably have more success in talks with the Federation ministers.[80] The 'Grand Design', it seemed, was the only method by which the Tunku could be persuaded to accept Singapore. However, Lee was advised that it was politically inexpedient to switch his line too rapidly from merger to 'Grand Design', and any change on his part ought to be presented as an expansion rather than an abandonment of previous ideas.[81] British officials were concerned that too sudden a switch might be seen as an acknowledgment of defeat of the PAP's merger policy, which would have an adverse political effect on Lee's standing in Singapore.[82] Unsure of the Tunku's attitude, British officials were concerned that should Lee push his ideas of a 'Grand Design' too enthusiastically, he might "cause revulsion in the Federation and also excite alarm in the Borneo Territories".[83] However, after the Kuala Lumpur meeting of April 1961, and following the Tunku's request for Lee to draft a paper on the 'Grand Design', the British were more confident that the time was perhaps ripe for Lee to pursue the matter further.

79. Selkirk to Macleod (30 Jan 1961), TNA: CO 1030/973.

80. Proposals for a Wider Association between the British Borneo Territories, Singapore and the Federation of Malaya (n.d.), TNA: CO 1030/980.

81. Ibid.

82. H.T. Bourdillon to Melville (17 Dec 1960), TNA: CO 1030/973.148.

83. Ibid.

Lee was then advised by Philip Moore, deputy high commissioner in Singapore, that he should attempt to highlight the attractiveness of the 'Grand Design' as an option of "general interest to the entire Malaysian region", while making references to the "possible dangers to the Federation of a movement in Singapore for complete independence".[84]

In early May 1961, Lee produced his own paper on the 'Grand Design'. In it, he listed two alternatives for the constitutional future of the British territories in Southeast Asia. The first was for the territories to be given independence on their own, to function as separate, independent political units. He then pointed out that if this alternative developed, merger between Singapore and the Federation of Malaya would be abandoned as a political objective, and "power in Singapore would pass to a China-minded group with strong cultural and economic links with Communist China".[85] A pro-communist government would emerge that would eventually achieve independence for Singapore with the help of Communist China. With such a development, he warned that British interests and security in Southeast Asia would come under considerable threat, with a Chinese Communist base right in the heart of Southeast Asia. The repercussions would be felt in Malaya too. An independent Singapore would have to "pander to its 75% Chinese population and will end up with greater appeals to Chinese chauvinism and eventually all talk of Malayan culture, national language, national solidarity and nation-building will disappear with tremendous adverse repercussions on the Chinese in the Federation of Malaya".[86] The consequences would be frightening, according to him: "it would put to an end any hope of building a united multi-racial community in Malaya."[87]

84. Record of conversation between Lee Kuan Yew and Philip Moore (28 Apr 1961), TNA: DO 169/25.

85. Paper on the future on the Federation of Malaya, Singapore and the Borneo Territories by Lee Kuan Yew (n.d.), TNA: CO 1030/979.

86. Ibid.

87. Ibid.

The alternative was the establishment of a larger federation comprising the territories of Malaya, Singapore and the Borneo territories. This, to him, was the most satisfactory solution for the peoples of the territories concerned, and also one that the British could quite easily accede to. In broad terms, the scheme was to use the stable Malaya-based Federation government as the sheet anchor of the whole of this region. Each of these states could then be left to elect its own government based on its existing state arrangements, with the government of the Federation of Malaya, by virtue of its larger population, controlling the government of the larger federation. The seats in the Federation government would be apportioned in such a way as to give the Federation government an overwhelming majority,[88] and this would ensure that the "government of the Federation of Malaya [would] automatically control the government of the larger federation".[89] The powers of the larger Federation government should include defence, foreign affairs, police, security and such matters as currency and common economic development. To protect the susceptibilities of the Borneo peoples and the present balance of power between Singapore and the Federation of Malaya, provisions would have to be built into the constitution to ensure that voting by citizens of the respective three states could only be done in their own states. This safeguard would prevent upsets in the balance of power.[90] In subsequent discussions with British officials, however, Lee expressed reservations that the Borneo territories could be incorporated into the Malaysian Federation at once, since they were in a less advanced constitutional condition; the most that would be possible was for the British government to give the Malayan government an undertaking on the Borneo territories so that the process of merger between Singapore and Malaya would not be hampered.[91]

88. According to the paper, Malaya would be entitled to the 68 seats, with Singapore and the Borneo Territories taking 16 and 12 seats respectively. See ibid.

89. Ibid.

90. Ibid.

91. Moore to H.T. Bourdillon and Selkirk (6 June 1961), TNA: CO 1030/977.

The thrust of Lee's argument was clear: separate independence for Singapore was too much of a political risk for British as well as Malayan interests. Merger with the Federation did not only promise economic viability for the small island state, but more fundamentally, its survival in face of the communist threat. There was no doubt in the mind of Prime Minister Lee that "the Communists could only be beaten if it was clear that Singapore could not have independence except through merger".[92] But the position of his government, with whom the Tunku could still do business, was under the constant threat of the radical Left and rebels within the party. Unless the government's position was strengthened by its ability to achieve independence for Singapore through merger with the Federation, the moderates would fall, and if the communists were to come to power, the PAP would not be the only loser: Britain and Malaya would have to suffer consequences as well. He understood, however, that a straightforward merger between Singapore and the Federation would not be acceptable to the Malayan prime minister. Thus, a 'Greater Malaysia', incorporating the Borneo territories, was the solution that would satisfy all concerned.

By 1961, as the political situation in Singapore became increasingly threatening and desperate for the PAP, Lee decided that he had to appeal to Malaya's sense of self-interest in order to get the Tunku to respond more positively to his overtures. He thus decided to highlight the threat that Singapore would pose for Malayan security should the Tunku decide to keep Singapore out. He began arguing that the Singapore problem was an integral part of the wider Malayan problem, and that "it was easier if [the Tunku] were to include [Singapore] in his overall calculations ... than if he were to try to pass the problem child to the British".[93]

92. Note of a meeting between UK delegation and Singapore delegation on Internal Security Council, which took place on Saturday, as enclosed in Acting UK Commissioner (Singapore) to Secretary of State (Colonial Office), 28 June 1960, TNA: CO 1030/977 no. 256.

93. Ibid.

Gradually, as Lee explained, "the unpleasant facts were placed before the Federation Government.... What had been publicly known was that Malaya was vital to Singapore. But what we did not emphasize... was that Singapore was vital to their survival."[94]

By the middle of 1961, Lee's efforts seemed to pay off, and the Tunku began indicating that he had had a change of mind, when he spoke for the first time, in May 1961, of the need for political and economic association with Singapore. The stage was thus set. The governments of Singapore and the Federation of Malaya entered into a series of complicated and sometimes acrimonious negotiations, and, with British help and interventions, especially in facilitating the passage of the initially reluctant Borneo territories into the Federation, 'Greater Malaysia' materialised in September 1963.[95]

On the eve of merger, the British, Malayan and Singapore leadership joined hands in executing the coup de grace on the pro-communist forces in Singapore. Operation *Cold Store*, carried out in February 1963, was a security swoop ordered by the Joint Security Council of Singapore that led to the arrest and detention of some 130 communist sympathisers, including political, trade union and student leaders. The operation crippled the opposition to the PAP, and consolidated Lee Kuan Yew's hold on power in Singapore. The PAP's main rivals, the Barisan Socialis, never recovered from the arrests and fared dismally in the 1963 elections as many of its leaders were in detention.[96] The threat from the pro-communist elements thus removed, Lee Kuan Yew and his party became the dominant political force in Singapore.

The merger, through which Singapore gained independence, proved to be short-lived. Within two years, Singapore separated

94. *Singapore Legislative Assembly Debates*, 30 July 1963, Col. 301.

95. For the politics and negotiations leading to merger and the formation of Malaysia, see Tan Tai Yong, *Creating 'Greater Malaysia': Decolonisation and the Politics of Merger* (Singapore: ISEAS, 2008).

96. Matthew Jones, 'Creating Malaysia: Singapore Security, the Borneo Territories, and the Contours of British Policy, 1961–63', *Journal of Imperial and Commonwealth History*, 28, no. 2 (2000): 85–109, p. 104.

from Malaysia, under rather bitter circumstances, and became a sovereign state in August 1965.

Conclusion

Cold War calculations and security considerations were instrumental in determining the pace and process that led to the independence of Singapore in 1963. This is not to suggest that Britain and the United States, on their own, successfully orchestrated, through a 'Grand Design', an outcome in the Malayan region that would fundamentally serve their overarching political and economic objectives in the Cold War. While the formation of 'Greater Malaysia' in 1963 proved to be a happy result where British interests were concerned, local interests and developments had a part as well. The political battles in Singapore, the anti-communist orientation of the Malayan leadership, and the attempts at regional consolidation all played into the larger contexts of the Cold War in Asia, and brought about an alignment of powers and interests—American, British, Malayan and the PAP's—that eventually influenced the shape and content of Singapore politics from the mid-1960s. Were it not for the deep-seated fear of what a communist-controlled Singapore could do to a strategic naval base in a region where the Americans and British were vying against communist forces for supremacy in the Cold War, the political history of Singapore might have taken a very different turn.

7

THAILAND AND THE SECRET WAR IN LAOS: THE ORIGINS OF ENGAGEMENT

Sutayut Osornprasop

> Rare indeed is the capital located at the edge of the national territory, its city limit coincident with the frontier of another country. It was as if the Laotians, terrified of their North Vietnamese neighbors, had fled as far away from their threatening shadow as possible; as if the tactile presence of Thailand was an assurance of Laotian survival.[1]

Thailand was among the key players in the wars in Indochina, amidst the heat of the Cold War of the 1960s and 1970s. Staunchly anti-communist, situated at the centre of the Southeast Asian landmass, and sharing over 2000 km of its borders with Indochina, Thailand was of great importance to American military operations in Southeast Asia. During the wars, Thailand provided land for American-built and -operated air bases and army facilities; American fighters and bombers operating from these bases accounted for 80 per cent of the air attacks against North Vietnam and Viet Cong installations elsewhere in Indochina. The role of Thailand in the American war effort was so great that the Americans regarded Thailand as their "unsinkable aircraft carrier".[2]

Thailand's role in the wars in Indochina was not limited to passive support for the Americans or for fellow anti-communist

This chapter is based on Sutayut Osornprasop, 'Thailand and the American Secret War in Indochina, 1960–1974', PhD thesis, University of Cambridge, 2006.

1. Henry Kissinger, *Years of Upheaval* (London: Weidenfeld & Nicolson, 1982), p. 18.

2. R. Sean Randolph, *The United States and Thailand: Alliance Dynamics, 1950–1985* (Berkeley: Institute of East Asian Studies, University of California, 1986), p. 49.

forces in the region. In 1966, the Royal Thai government began to actively support the Vietnam War by dispatching two Royal Thai Navy vessels into service in South Vietnam. In July 1967, a combat regiment with over 2200 troops was sent to fight the Viet Cong in South Vietnam. By early 1968, this had been upgraded to full division strength, with 12,000 troops. To the general public, the assistance rendered to South Vietnam seems to be the most important contribution the Thais made to help prevent Indochina from falling to communist domination. However, this perception is not entirely correct.

With the declassification and release of US official documents and recent interviews with former diplomatic, intelligence and military officers directly involved in the conflicts, a striking fact has been revealed: the majority of Thai activities took the form of covert operations in Laos. At the same time that American military activities in South Vietnam scaled down from the late 1960s and ended with the withdrawal of its combat troops in 1973, Thailand's secret military activities in Laos, which had begun as early as 1960, gradually increased throughout the 1960s and early 1970s, finally reaching its climax in 1971–72, with over 23,000 clandestine Thai forces serving in Laos. This is twice the number of Thai forces on duty in South Vietnam at its peak.

Clandestine Thai military activities in Laos served two main objectives.[3] The original objective was to preserve the non-communist Royal Lao Government, which was severely threatened by the communist Pathet Lao and the North Vietnamese. The second objective, which became increasingly important in the late 1960s and early 1970s, was to support secretly the United States' military

3. Very few Thai people were aware of the fact that there were Thai forces in Laos. This was very much due to the sensitivity of the subject of foreign military operations in Laos, as under the 1962 Geneva Accord on Laotian Neutrality foreign forces were not supposed to exist on Laotian territory, except for a small number of French military officers commissioned to help train Laotian troops. Because the clandestine Thai military involvement in Laos took place under the military dictatorship regimes of Sarit Thanarat and Thanom Kittikachorn, all archives related to this subject have been deposited at the Supreme Command of the Thai Forces. None have been declassified.

activities in South Vietnam, and the existence of the South Vietnamese government, by interrupting the Ho Chi Minh Trail—the lifeline of the communists that ran through the dense jungles of Laos and the northeastern part of Cambodia, linking the revolutionary movement in the field with the supply base in North Vietnam. Given that there were half a million American troops in South Vietnam at the time, the Thai combat forces there were more of symbolic than military significance. Nevertheless, as the Royal Lao Army was weak and incapable of defending itself, and as there were no active US ground troops in Laos, there is no question that the clandestine Thai forces in Laos were vital, if not indispensable, to the survival of non-communist regimes in Indochina.

The genesis of covert Thai operations in Laos

Before one can understand the motives behind Thailand's involvement in the Secret War in Laos, we must first appreciate the historical, cultural, economic, and political backgrounds of the two countries. Of the three former French Indochinese countries, Laos stood out for its historical and strategic importance to Thailand. Historically, Laos had been under Thai suzerainty for hundreds of years; it was only after three aggressive actions and threats towards Thailand, in 1893, 1904, and 1907, that the whole of Laos was ceded to France. Strategically, Laos, lying like a dagger piercing into the heart of the Southeast Asian landmass, separated Thailand from China and Vietnam—effectively serving as a buffer state between Thailand and her potential enemies. As the border between Thailand and Laos is 1754 km long, Thailand had always paid a great deal of attention to what happened in this small, land-locked country. It is no wonder that Thailand was the first nation to establish a diplomatic mission in Laos after the small kingdom gained its independence from France in 1954.[4]

4. E.H.S. Simmonds, 'The Evolution of Foreign Policy in Laos', *Modern Asian Studies*, vol. II, no. 1 (1968), p. 10.

Laos shares common cultural, ethnic, linguistic and religious backgrounds with Thailand. The Laotians and the Thais living along the Mekong were kinsmen and used to cross the river freely as if the lands on both banks belonged to the same country. In essence, the Mekong acted as the 'conductor' rather than the 'insulator' of the interaction between the peoples from the two sides of the river. It was thus logical for Thai rulers to regard the Mekong valleys of Laos as integral parts of the Thai common security area, and the frontier of this common security area was thus extended to the eastern mountains dividing Laos from China and Vietnam.

Another leading cause for Thailand's concern about Laos was the population of Lao-speaking Thais. Their existence was mainly the result of centuries of forced migration of the Lao-speaking people from the Lao side across the Mekong to the Thai side every time a Lao ruler attempted to free his country from Thai overlordship. This strategy of the earlier Thai kings was practical in the days when maintaining a certain number of subjects was vital to the survival of the kingdom, and hence given top priority. In addition, given the history of rivalry between Thailand and Vietnam for domination of the Indochinese peninsula, this forced relocation of Lao-speaking people would not only deny the Vietnamese any significant manpower should it take over the Lao side of the Mekong, but the Thai kings could also deploy these relocated Lao-speaking people as front-line soldiers against external threats.[5]

However, the forced relocation of Lao-speaking people to Thailand would have an adverse impact in the post-war era, when nationalistic and chauvinistic sentiments grew strong. Former rulers of Thailand could not have predicted that Lao-speaking Thais would eventually outnumber Thai-speaking Thais on the Thai side of the Mekong, and moreover spread all over northeastern Thailand—the region popularly known as Isan. By 1960 Lao-speaking Thais represented a third of the country's population. This was,

5. Bangon Piyaphan, *Lao nai krung Rattanakosin* [The Lao in early Bangkok] (Bangkok: Samnakngan kongtoon sanap sanun kanwijai, 1998).

remarkably, at least six times more than the number of Lao-speaking people in Laos itself. The potential problems arising from the nationalistic sentiments of the Lao-speaking Thais were aggravated by the fact that Isan was the country's poorest region, mainly because of its lack of natural resources and an inhospitable climate. The poverty problem grew worse with decades of inadequate attention from the central government, as Isan contributed relatively little to the country's GDP and overall economic progress. Despite being the largest region of the country in terms of area, Isan was Thailand's backwater. Therefore, it was unclear where the allegiance of these Lao-speaking Thais in Isan lay. The Thai government was to realise that not all Lao-speaking Thais thought of themselves as Thais, and that these people were vulnerable to subversion from outside.

Even worse, during the First Indochina War, thousands of Vietnamese fled to northeastern Thailand for safety. By the end of the war, there were more than 40,000 Vietnamese refugees in Thailand. Most of them placed their sympathies with the Viet Minh and there is no question that many of them were Viet Minh spies. As the French lost the war and left Indochina for good in 1954, the Viet Minh's influence in the region grew significantly.

In light of all these factors, Laos, sandwiched between North Vietnam and northeastern Thailand, was naturally the key to the security of Thailand. It was thus natural for Bangkok to try its best to exert its influence on the weaker neighbour to ensure that the government in Vientiane was pro-Thai and would pursue a foreign policy compatible with that of Thailand.

It is important to note here that Bangkok's national policy at the time was to be anti-communist on the one hand, and to enhance an increasingly closer alliance with the United States on the other. With the arrival of the strict military dictatorship regime of Field Marshal Sarit Thanarat in the late 1950s, the anti-communist and pro-US policy of the Thai government was even more pronounced. The Thai ruling elites considered communism incompatible with the Thai way of life, given that Thai society was traditionally attached to the monarchy, Buddhism, and the patron-client relationship. Furthermore, the strengthening alliance between Thailand and the United States, in the eyes of the Thai leaders, was beneficial to Thai national interests. Both Thailand and the United States not only shared anti-communist sentiments in the Cold War, but Thai rulers also believed that the United States, emerging all-powerful from World War II, would be able to help Thailand withstand the threats from 'Red' China.

Similarly, the United States, committed to the 'domino theory', was apprehensive at the prospect of communist expansion southward into Southeast Asia; they regarded Thailand, the only independent country in Southeast Asia with a relatively stable economy and government, as the fortress against that threat. With their complementary foreign policy objectives, Thailand soon became the United States' most important ally on mainland Southeast Asia.

Laos crisis

Laos emerged from the First Indochina War politically divided. While some elements in Laos were impressed by the victory of the Viet Minh, others were suspicious of an emerging Vietnam, which had once dominated Laos. Still others wanted Laos to remain under French protection.[6] Unlike Thailand, where the rightist military rule was firmly established and the leftists were effectively eliminated from the political arena, in Laos three main political groupings—the leftists, the neutralists and the rightists—still relentlessly struggled for power and dominance.

The leftists, generally known as the Pathet Lao, received vehement support from the North Vietnamese and were based mainly in Sam Neua and Phongsaly provinces in the northeastern part of

6. It is interesting to note that Laotians, in proportion to the country's population, had the highest representation among the people from the three Indochinese territories fighting for the French against the Viet Minh during the First Indochina War.

Laos, adjoining Vietnam and China. The Pathet Lao's top man was the wily, half-Laotian, half-Vietnamese Kaysone Phomvihan, who maintained a subservient relationship with North Vietnam. However, the fact that Kaysone was the supreme leader of the Pathet Lao was kept strictly secret until the Pathet Lao gained full control of the kingdom in 1975. The reason Kaysone stayed behind the scenes was perhaps his lowly origins and lack of charisma—distinct shortcomings in a country that treasured royalty and nobility. More importantly, Kaysone's strong links with North Vietnam would have unveiled North Vietnam's hidden desire to use the Pathet Lao as their puppet. Kaysone's leadership was so secretive that no Communist Chinese leaders met him before 1970.[7] The public figurehead of the Pathet Lao was Prince Souphanouvong.[8] Even though Souphanouvong was not the top man of the Pathet Lao, it was estimated that he would have been number three or number four in the party. The prince was described as naturally brilliant, articulate, extroverted and physically robust.[9] He possessed enormous charismatic appeal and was highly popular among the Laotians for his nationalism.

At the centre of Laotian politics was the neutralist group led by Prince Souvanna Phouma, elder half-brother of Prince Souphanouvong. Souvanna Phouma, a French-educated engineer, was a political moderate who tried to sustain a coalition government that included the Pathet Lao faction. Many people regarded him as an adept, clever politician. But he was also perceived as naive and weak towards the communists, partly because of his expressed belief that his half-brother Souphanouvong was not a communist, and partly because he had appointed as his deputy Quinim Pholsena, an extreme leftist.[10]

7. Interview with Mark S. Pratt, 25 Mar 2005, Washington, D.C.

8. Martin E. Goldstein, *American Policy Towards Laos* (Cranbury, NJ: Associated University Presses, Inc., 1973), p. 68.

9. Ibid.

10. *Foreign Relations of the United States* (*FRUS*), *1961–1963, Laos Crisis,* Vol. XXIV, Memorandum of Conference with President Kennedy, Washington, 9 Mar 1961, p. 76, and John F. Kennedy Library (hereafter JFKL), Oral History Interview with Winthrop G. Brown, by Larry J. Hackham, Washington, D.C., 1 Feb 1968, p. 3.

The Laotian rightists were headed by General Phoumi Nosavan. Phoumi's military background and his expressed anti-communist stance had impressed the CIA and the American military personnel in Vientiane, and they considered him the key man who could save Laos from the communist advance. More importantly, General Phoumi was Thai Field Marshal Sarit's cousin-once-removed; he called Sarit 'uncle'. As both Sarit and Phoumi shared an anti-communist attitude and family ties, it is no wonder that Sarit was in full support of Phoumi, and would help him gain influence in Laotian politics. Following a rigged election and the use of dirty political tricks to oust his enemies, by the middle of 1960 Phoumi sat at the top of Laotian politics.

Although it seemed as if Phoumi's control over Laos was uncontested, as he was fully supported by the Thais and the Americans, the unexpected took place in the early hours of 9 August 1960. Having received instructions to move his troops through Vientiane to the north of Laos, Captain Kong Le, the commander of the Second Parachute Battalion of the Royal Lao Army (RLA), led his troops from his barracks and marched into Vientiane. But instead of passing the capital and heading north, his unit seized government offices, communications centres, airfields, arsenals, a power station, and took control of strategic points around Vientiane. It was a coup d'etat, and it was timed perfectly. Most of the Laotian ministers, as well as high-ranking military and civil officers, had flown to the royal capital of Luang Prabang the day before to confer with King Savang Vatthana on the arrangements for the cremation of the late King Sisavang Vong.

There was no effective opposition of any kind to the coup.[11] Shortly after Kong Le took control of the capital, he broadcast a heartfelt appeal over Radio Vientiane for an end to fraternal bloodshed caused by the civil war, for an end to corruption by gov-

11. Charles A. Stevenson, *The End of Nowhere: American Policy Toward Laos Since 1954* (Boston: Beacon Press, 1972), p. 92.

ernment officials, for the removal of all foreign forces from Laos, and for genuine Laotian neutrality. He also openly criticised the Americans.[12]

Only 26 years old at the time, Kong Le had never been involved in politics and was not generally known to the public. He was simply a young soldier who had long been in the front line of the RLA and who, according to an American record, had "fought bravely in the Pathet Lao engagements".[13] Because of Kong Le's bravery, honesty, intelligence, leadership, and down-to-earth behaviour, he was highly respected by, and was assured of loyalty from, his subordinates. He was a fine example of a first-rate Lao military leader at a time when many top-ranking military officers were considered corrupt, unscrupulous, and cowardly. Kong Le's battalion was regarded as the best trained, the best led, the best supported, and the most effective in the RLA.[14]

However, Kong Le's grave weakness was his naivety. His understanding of Cold War conflicts, the aims of the Pathet Lao, and the intentions of the North Vietnamese were too simplistic. Kong Le held the view that the conflicts and bloodshed in his country were purely generated by outside interference, especially that of the United States. He distrusted American and Thai claims that Laos was under serious threat from communist subversion, originating beyond the Lao borders. From his own experiences, he saw that Laotians were fighting brother Laotians, not the Viet Minh nor Communist Chinese.[15] He strongly believed that Laotians were intrinsically peaceful people, and disputes between Laotians could be solved by peaceful means.[16] He must have thought that without American intervention, bloodshed and conflicts

12. *Summary of World Broadcasts* (*SWB*), FE/407/B/2, Radio Vientiane, 9 Aug 1960.

13. *FRUS, 1958–1960, East Asia-Pacific region; Cambodia, Laos*, Vol. XVI, Memorandum of Discussion at the 455th Meeting of the National Security Council, Washington, 12 Aug 1960, p. 787.

14. *FRUS, 1958–1960, East Asia-Pacific region; Cambodia, Laos*, Vol. XVI, Vientiane to State Department, 2 Oct 1960, pp. 873–5.

15. *SWB*, FE/410/B/6, New China News Agency (NCNA), 12 Aug 1960.

16. Stevenson, *The End of Nowhere*, pp. 92–3, and Hugh Toye, *Laos: Buffer State or Battleground* (London: Oxford University Press, 1968), pp. 138–41.

between Laotians could be eliminated. Kong Le then approached the neutralist leader, Prince Souvanna Phouma, and asked him to become the new Lao prime minister.

The Kong Le coup came as a surprise to all, not least the Thais. Rumours circulated that the coup had been instigated by the Pathet Lao, North Vietnam, or even the French. We now know that the Kong Le coup was undertaken by the Second Parachute Battalion alone. There was no outside interference of any kind.[17] Even the Pathet Lao was caught by surprise when they first heard of the coup. They wondered why the parachute battalion, which was set up by the Americans, would turn against the Americans.[18]

It did not take long, however, for the coup to turn into a major regional crisis, as the Pathet Lao and the North Vietnamese, having their secret schemes in mind, quickly extended their support to the coup. Subsequent negotiations for a peaceful end to the conflict failed. The rightists soon took arms in their course to retake Vientiane, knowing that the Americans and the Thais were on their side. While mortar shells were fired into Kong Le's positions from the Thai side, the actual fighting took place at Paksane, a provincial town to the east of Vientiane. With superior numbers, better-equipped weapons, and ammunition, it was generally expected that Phoumi's forces would beat Kong Le's and retake Vientiane easily. Despite all the advantages, however, Phoumi's forces were scattered and shamefully withdrew from Paksane on 21 September, after putting up little resistance against Kong Le's troops.[19]

This unexpected incident, though very minor in terms of casualties caused, changed the course of the conflict in Laos.[20] It

17. Vientiane to Foreign Office, DF 1011/1 (21 June 1961), The National Archives of the UK (hereafter TNA): FO 371/159811.

18. Phoumi Vongvichit, *Nai Kwam Song Jam kong Phoumi Vongvichit* [In the memory of Phoumi Vongvichit], translated by Pitsanoo Janwitan (Bangkok: Nation Books International, 2003), p. 186.

19. *FRUS, 1958–1960, East Asia-Pacific region; Cambodia, Laos*, Vol. XVI, Memorandum of Discussion at the 460th Meeting of the National Security Council, 21 Sept 1960, pp. 859–60; and Vientiane to Foreign Office, DF 1015/611 (21 Sept 1960), TNA: FO 371/152354.

20. It was known later that some three companies of Pathet Lao troops had joined Kong Le's troops in defeating Phoumi at

became clear that Phoumi's forces were ineffective and lacked the willingness to fight. To the countries that extended their material support to Phoumi, the fall of Paksane indicated that supplying him with money, weapons, and ammunition was not enough. The only way to help Phoumi win the war seemed to be by sending foreign expeditionary forces to lead his troops in battle. But which country would take this risk?

Thailand was the only country that expressed publicly the possibility that Thai military forces could be sent to Laos. Shortly after the fall of Paksane, Deputy Premier Thanom stated to the press that "the Thai government is ready to use force if the situation in Laos threatens Thailand's security".[21] Prime Minister Sarit also made a public announcement asking Thai citizens to "prepare to sacrifice in defence of Thailand".[22] However, the ruling generals must have been aware that Thailand would be condemned by the international community if it took unilateral military action in Laos. Also, the intervention might provoke retaliation from Beijing and Hanoi, in which case it would have been too risky for Thailand to handle the matter alone. In the end, Bangkok and Washington decided not to overtly send troops to Laos, but to covertly provide Phoumi's troops with stiffeners from Thailand.

Enter the PARUs

Phoumi's embarrassing defeat at Paksane convinced Bangkok and the CIA that he would not be able to retake Vientiane on his own. It seemed that there was only one way to ensure success in retaking Vientiane, and that was to supply Phoumi secretly with a small number of Thai and American military advisers to lead Phoumi's forces into battle. On 28 October 1960, top policy-makers from the Pentagon and State Department met in Washington to dis-

Paksane. *FRUS, 1958–1960, East Asia-Pacific region; Cambodia, Laos*, Vol. XVI, Memorandum of Discussion at the 461st Meeting of the National Security Council, 29 Sept 1960, p. 868.

21. *Siam Rath*, 23 Sept 1960. General Thanom Kittikachorn also held the position of defence minister.

22. Ibid.

cuss the Laos crisis. They concluded that the United States was not yet ready to send American advisers to lead Phoumi's battalions into battle for fear of possible retaliation from Laos's communist neighbours and worldwide damage to American interests should their role be made public. But they came up with the idea that members of the Royal Thai Police Aerial Reinforcement Unit (PARU), Thailand's elite paratroopers, should be used as military advisers in Laos and attached to Phoumi's battalions.[23] Since Laotians and Thais tended to look alike and their languages were very similar, Thai military advisers could blend in well among the Laotian forces.

The PARUs would never have been introduced to this State-Defence meeting without the intervention of a Texan known as 'Bill' Lair. Born in 1924, Lair had served in the United States Army in Belgium, France, and Germany during World War II. He joined the CIA at the outbreak of the Korean War, and came to Thailand as a case officer in 1951. At that time the PRC had successfully consolidated their hold and gained effective control of southern China. The remnants of Chinese nationalist soldiers had fallen back across the borders into the northern part of Burma and Laos. There were fears that the Red Chinese were going to move further south into Burma, Laos, and possibly Thailand to eradicate any potential threats posed by the remnant Kuomintang (KMT) soldiers in the area. To prepare for this possible threat from the north, Bangkok and Washington agreed to cooperate and establish a guerrilla-warfare training programme for Thai personnel. In effect, these personnel would be trained to become the equivalent of the United States Special Forces today. Upon his arrival in Thailand, Lair was assigned to take charge of the programme. The graduates of this training programme would become part of the newly established PARU. What Lair was really proud of was that

23. *FRUS, 1958–1960, East Asia-Pacific region; Cambodia, Laos,* Vol. XVI, Editorial Note, Memorandum of Discussion at the State-JCS Meeting, 28 Oct 1960, pp. 933–4.

the PARU programme was one of the first of its kind in the world, pre-dating even the US Special Forces.[24]

Trained by the CIA, the PARUs were the best and most capable paratroopers in Thailand at the time.[25] Even though the nature of their work was more compatible with the military rather than the police force, the fact that the PARUs were part of the police was due to the complex nature of Thailand's domestic politics. During this period, real power lay in the hands of Police General Phao Sri-yanon and General Sarit Thanarat, the left- and right-hand men of Premier Field Marshal Plaek Pibulsongkram (or, Phibun Song-khram). Without direct control of the military or police forces, Pibulsongkram could retain his premiership only as long as he could handle the delicate balance of power between Phao and Sarit, or in other words, between the Royal Thai Police (RTP) and the Royal Thai Army (RTA). As American aid poured into Thailand, it was arranged that the RTA would receive aid from the Pentagon, while the RTP would receive aid from the CIA. Thus the CIA-funded PARU programme came under the supervision of the RTP; officially, then, these Thai 'Special Forces' were not soldiers but policemen.[26]

As the PARUs were created to engage in guerrilla warfare along the heavily forested border areas where roads were mostly non-existent, they were trained to be parachutists, and operated in small five-man or ten-man teams.[27] All PARUs had to learn how to survive in the jungle and how to live off the land for at least three months. Moreover, they were trained to handle and operate all kinds of light weapons, mortars, and explosives. Each PARU

24. Interview with James William Lair, 21 Feb 2005, Meridian, TX.

25. Ibid., and Memorandum from Brig. Gen. Edward G. Lansdale, Pentagon expert on guerrilla warfare, to Gen. Maxwell D. Taylor, President Kennedy's military adviser, undated but apparently from July 1961, *The Pentagon Papers: Senator Gravel Edition*, Volume 2 (Boston: Beacon Press, 1971, 1972), pp. 643–9.

26. Interview with Lair.

27. Interview with Vang Pao, 7 Apr 2005, Santa Ana, CA; and telephone interview with Rashane Kijavej, 22 June 2005. Police Colonel Rashane was a former PARU and close aide of Vang Pao.

team would have at least one radio/communications specialist and a medical technician. Most PARU trainees were recruited from frontier provinces all across Thailand, with many of them competent in the languages of Thailand's neighbours. According to Lair:

> We picked trainees from the Northeast who could speak Lao and Khmer. We picked some from the North and the West who could speak languages of the Burmese minorities. We also picked some from the South, who were Muslims and spoke Malay. We picked all over. We would fly over towns along the Thai border, with high schools. We would drop leaflets that we wanted boys at the age of 18–21 with high school education, and unmarried. A few days later a team would be dropped by parachutes to that town or village. It would be the first time for the villagers to see parachute jumpers. It was an effective way to attract crowds of people. Each town we visited there were at least fifty boys [who] came to us and we picked only five. They were all country boys. The city boys don't want to go and live in jungles.[28]

The first PARU base was in Lopburi province, north of Bangkok. Later, they were relocated to Hua Hin, by the Gulf of Thailand, some 200 km south of Bangkok. Hua Hin was more suitable for the PARU's training, for the surrounding areas offered all the kinds of terrain with which the PARUs would need to get familiar: beaches, sand dunes, plains and semi-steppe environments along the coastline, and rainforests, hills, and mountains further inland. Moreover, Hua Hin was not far from the Burmese border, giving the PARU first-hand experience in border operations.[29]

The standard of PARUs was high. They had to be young and physically fit; according to Lair, "if they are not good enough, they would be transferred to other police units. If they get older, they would be moved to other departments. We keep the age young." By 1960, there were approximately 300 PARUs. As they were retrained regularly and kept on alert status, they could be mobilised and

28. Interview with Lair.

29. Ibid.

deployed for combat operations as soon as they were given orders to do so.[30]

PARUs to Savannakhet

On 9 August 1960, as Lair was flying one of the C-47s and dropping two PARU teams over the Thai-Burmese border, he learned from the BBC radio news that Kong Le had taken over Vientiane. He suddenly realised that "now this was what PARU was preparing for". When he got back to Bangkok, he rushed to see Police Colonel Pranet Ritileuchai, the commander of the PARU. Lair had a close working relationship with Pranet, "as close as two human beings can be together". Pranet and Lair agreed with each other that "if something happens and we would have to do something which we think would be good for the Americans and for the Thais, we would do it no matter what our superiors say".[31]

Lair was different from most other CIA officers in Thailand. He had picked up the Thai language and culture rapidly. The fact that he married a Thai further deepened his attachment to the country. Thailand was his second home. The Thais trusted him. As he had worked faithfully for Thailand and devoted himself to the PARU programme, he was bestowed the prestigious rank of colonel in the RTP. Being a CIA case officer and a Thai Police colonel at the same time, Lair determined to do his best for the interests of Thailand as long as they did not conflict with the interests of the United States.[32]

Both Pranet and Lair recognised that the Kong Le coup offered the perfect opportunity for the utilisation of the PARUs to further the interests of Thailand and the United States in Laos. But the ultimate decision for any sort of PARU deployment had to come from Sarit, and it was not an easy task to persuade the Field Marshal to make such a decision. When Police General Phao went

30. Ibid., and Memorandum from Lansdale to Taylor, in *The Pentagon Papers*.

31. Interview with Lair.

32. Ibid.

into exile after the 1957 coup, Sarit had attempted to play down the role of the PARU, an organisation closely associated with his arch-rival. Sarit did not trust the PARU and wanted it disbanded. King Bhumibhol, however, saved the PARU. He recognised the value of the organisation.[33] But even so, Sarit did not appreciate the exceptional quality of the PARUs. Therefore, it was difficult to imagine that Sarit would easily agree to confer on the PARUs any missions of high national security.

The opportunity for the PARU eventually came in October, when Phoumi was preparing to retake Vientiane for the second time. The CIA decided to provide Phoumi with extra financial support. Lair duly volunteered to bring the money from Bangkok to Phoumi by himself. He knew that he needed to introduce the PARU to Phoumi, as Sarit would be more likely to approve PARU's deployment should the request come from Phoumi. Lair was further assured that with the big bag of CIA money he would be warmly welcomed by Phoumi.[34]

Lair flew to Savannakhet and met Phoumi on 19 October. He first explained to Phoumi that he came with the money to pay for Phoumi's troops, something that Phoumi was pleased to hear. Then, he told Phoumi about the PARU. He explained that he had five-man teams, with medical technicians and excellent communications specialists. Lair stressed that he would like to assign a team with each of Phoumi's five battalions. Phoumi told Lair frankly that he had no medical technicians and had bad communications. Clearly, Lair knew exactly what Phoumi needed, and he was able to convince Phoumi that the PARU could help him retake Vientiane.[35]

Indeed General Phoumi was impressed by PARU's potential and the news soon reached Field Marshal Sarit. As Lair and Pranet expected, Sarit did not trust the PARU, and wanted to put RTA

33. Ibid. At the time that Sarit was about to disband the PARU, an article written by a close aide to the king praising the PARU was published. As a result, Sarit did not further his efforts in liquidating the organisation, and left the PARU alone to its own devices.

34. Interview with Lair.

35. Ibid.

personnel in Laos. In November, Sarit assigned four army officers, headed by Colonel Chamnien Pongpirot, RTA Chief of Thai-Laos security affairs, to negotiate with Phoumi about further Thai military assistance. Accompanying Chamnien were Pranet and Lair. In Savannakhet, Colonel Chamnien told Phoumi in earnest that Sarit did not like the idea of deploying the PARU to Laos, and wanted to use the army. Then Phoumi asked Chamnien, "How long will it take before these army teams can be here?" Chamnien replied that it would take about one month before the army could be in Savannakhet. Chamnien's answer disappointed Phoumi. Phoumi turned to Pranet and asked the same question. Pranet humbly answered:

> Sir, let me go across the river right now. I will get one of those long-tail boats to go right over. I have a team over there which will send a message to Hua Hin, getting these five PARU teams to Savannakhet. They will be picked up at dawn and will be here by 10 o'clock tomorrow.[36]

Both Phoumi and Chamnien were struck by Pranet's answer.[37] But why was the RTA no match for the PARU in terms of combat readiness and effectiveness? The key to this weakness lay in the Thai military institution itself. The Thai absolute monarchy was abolished in 1932; civilian governments taking over political control from the king were unable to consolidate the hold that democratic processes had had on Thai politics for long.[38] Soon Thai politics

36. Ibid.

37. Ibid. Chamnien admitted to Lair that the RTA would not be able to get ready for such an immediate deployment.

38. For more information on Thai politics after the 1932 revolution, see Josiah Crosby, 'The Failure of Constitutional Government in Siam', *Asiatic Review*, 39, 140 (Oct 1942): 415–20; Josiah Crosby, *Siam: The Crossroads* (London: Hollis and Carter Ltd, 1945); Josiah Crosby, 'War and Militarism in Siam', *Great Britain and the East*, 61, 1726 (24 Jun 1944): 12–14; B.A. Batson, *The End of the Absolute Monarchy in Siam* (Singapore: Oxford University Press, 1984); Kenneth P. Landon, *Siam in Transition* (London: Oxford University Press, 1939); Judith A. Stowe, *Siam Becomes Thailand: A Story of Intrigue* (London: C. Hurst and Co. Ltd, 1991); Kobkua Suwannathat-Pian, *Thailand's Durable Premier: Pibul through Three Decades, 1932–1957* (Oxford: Oxford University Press, 1995); V. Thompson, *Thailand: New Siam* (New York: Institute of Pacific Relations, 1941); and Richard J. Aldrich, *The Key to the South: Britain, the United States, and Thailand during the Approach of the Pacific War, 1929–1942* (New York: Oxford University Press, 1993).

was dominated by Thai military generals, especially those in the army. Coups, instead of democratic elections, became the way to gain political power and attain to the highly respected post of prime minister. Thai military institutions became springboards for able soldiers to rise politically; captains, majors, and colonels all wanted to stay in big cities and get involved in politics, rather than stay deployed along the borders. More people joined the armed forces with politics in mind, rather than with a wish to become professional soldiers. Field Marshal Sarit was no exception.[39]

There is no wonder that Sarit was upset when he learned that the PARU outdid the army. According to Lair, Sarit said, in anger, "Get the police there, I don't give a damn about what would happen to them."[40] But he did approve the deployment of PARU to Laos after all. As five PARU teams arrived in Savannakhet the next morning, a new chapter in Thai-Lao relations had begun.

Thailand's Military Assistance and Advisory Committee

Bangkok's decision to dispatch the PARUs to Laos, where they would act as military advisers to Phoumi's forces, was a significant milestone in Thai history. It was the first time in the post-war era that the Thai government had its personnel attached to the armed forces of a foreign country.[41] Prime Minister Sarit decided to set up on 4 November 1960 a secret committee to supervise the whole of Thai covert operations in Laos. The committee was named Kana Kammakarn Tiprueksa Lae Chua Leua Tang Taharn ('Military Assistance and Advisory Committee'), or Kor Tor for short (after the Thai letters 'k' and 't'); Deputy Premier Thanom was appointed the head.[42] Interestingly, Thailand had hosted the

39. Interview with Lair.

40. Ibid.

41. With the exception of UN-sanctioned operations, i.e. the Korean War.

42. Interview with Saiyud Kerdpol, 1 Apr 2006, Nonthaburi. General Saiyud Kerdpol was assistant secretary of Kor Tor. Thanom was appointed as the head of this committee so that Prime Minister Sarit would be theoretically able to deny his government's involvement in the committee. However, practically, Sarit was represented in the committee by his close aide, Colonel Chalermchai Jaruwat, who acted as the secretary of Kor Tor.

United States Military Assistance Advisory Group (MAAG) since 1951, and had learned how to be a 'receiver' of military assistance and advice from the United States.[43] In 1960, the Thai government had the opportunity for the first time to be a 'giver' of military assistance and advice to a neighbouring country.

Nevertheless, the Thai military assistance to Laos was extraordinary in the sense that it had to be done covertly, especially with regard to the dispatch of Thai personnel to Laos. This was because the deployment was in violation of the 1954 Geneva Accords.[44] Bangkok insisted that their operations were "deniable." Each member of PARU personnel serving in Laos had to officially resign from his post in Thailand. Bangkok could thus deny that the PARU personnel were acting under the orders of the Thai government if they were killed in action or arrested by the enemy. When the PARUs successfully completed their tour of duty in Laos, their letters of resignation would be destroyed, and their official records would read as if they had never left their units in Thailand.[45]

PARUs in action

After Thailand and the United States stepped up their efforts to assist Phoumi and increase their financial, material, and manpower support to him, Phoumi's troops, with PARU teams as advisers and stiffeners, were able to advance towards Vientiane. As the troops came within striking distance of Vientiane, Souvanna Phouma allegedly delegated his powers to the 'High Command of the

43. Randolph, *The United States and Thailand*, p. 15. MAAG was later renamed Joint US Military Advisory Group or JUSMAG.

44. It is interesting to note that Washington at the time also established MAAG Laos and unlawfully maintained a certain number of military and CIA personnel in Laos. However, the United States was a superpower while Thailand was a small power. The Thai government not only feared that their country would be condemned by the international community had the presence of Thai paramilitary personnel in Laos become public knowledge, but also that it might provoke retaliation from the PRC and North Vietnam, in which case it would have been too risky for Thailand to handle the matter alone.

45. Interview with Jerdjamras Jitkaroonrat, 17 Mar 2006, Bangkok; and interview with Saiyud Kerdpol. Police Major General Jerdjamras was the leader of one of the first PARU teams deployed in Laos.

Army',[46] and left, on 9 December, with most of his cabinet, for exile in Phnom Penh.[47] It turned out, however, that it was not the 'High Command of the Army' that had taken charge of the government in Souvanna Phouma's absence but Quinim Pholsena, an extreme leftist member of his cabinet.[48] On 10 December, Quinim made a 24-hour trip to Hanoi. There, he made a firm deal with the Russians: in exchange for a formal alliance between Kong Le's troops and the Pathet Lao, the Russians would airlift into Laos arms and supplies for the resistance against General Phoumi's American-supplied troops.[49]

The Russians kept their promise and were quick to make deliveries. The next day four howitzers complete with ammunition were unloaded from two Soviet aircraft at Vientiane airport.[50] According to the US State Department, in the first half of December 1960 the Russians made at least 34 flights to Vientiane.[51]

The day after Souvanna Phouma left for exile in Cambodia, 40 out of 49 deputies of the National Assembly met in Savannakhet and passed a vote of no confidence against Souvanna Phouma. On 12 December the king signed a royal ordinance ousting Souvanna Phouma's government and transferring all powers to General Phoumi's Revolutionary Committee. Boun Oum was appointed the new Laotian premier.[52] Phoumi had won the political battle.

Despite the Soviet deliveries, Quinim and Kong Le's troops were not able to outfight the Thai-backed and better-equipped forces of Phoumi. On 16 December 1960, Kong Le's forces staged

46. Timothy N. Castle, *At War in the Shadow of Vietnam: U.S. Military Aid to the Royal Lao Government 1955–1975* (New York: Columbia University Press, 1993), p. 24.

47. *FRUS, 1958–1960, East Asia-Pacific region; Cambodia, Laos*, Vol. XVI, Vientiane to State, 9 Dec 1960, p. 1002.

48. *FRUS, 1958–1960, East Asia-Pacific region; Cambodia, Laos*, Vol. XVI, Paper prepared by the Assistant White House Staff Secretary, 12 Dec 1960, p. 1003.

49. Arthur J. Dommen, *Conflict in Laos: The Politics of Neutralization* (New York: Frederick A. Praeger, 1964), p. 167.

50. *FRUS, 1958–1960, East Asia-Pacific region; Cambodia, Laos,* Vol. XVI, Paper prepared by the Assistant White House Staff Secretary, 12 Dec 1960, pp. 1003–4.

51. Department of State Bulletin, 23 Jan 1961, pp. 114–15.

52. *FRUS, 1958–1960, East Asia-Pacific region; Cambodia, Laos,* Vol. XVI, Paper prepared by the Assistant White House Staff Secretary, 12 Dec 1960, p. 1004.

an orderly withdrawal from Vientiane, and control of the capital passed to Phoumi's victorious forces.[53] There is no doubt that Thailand, and especially the PARUs, contributed significantly to Phoumi's victory. Beijing claimed as early as late November that the United States "sent foreign soldiers to masquerade as troops of [the] Nosavan rebel clique [Phoumi's clique] so as to reinforce the strength of that clique".[54] Furthermore, the Indian weekly *Blitz* published a report from Bangkok that Thai Army divisions, under the control of US military "advisers", were massing in areas adjacent to Laos and assisting Phoumi's group. Some of the Thai troops had crossed the Mekong to the Laotian side.[55] Furthermore, Prime Minister Pham Van Dong of North Vietnam made a protest on 15 December 1960 to the co-chairmen of the 1954 Geneva Conference that:

> [On] 13 December 1960 Phoumi Nosavan launched attack on Vientiane capital Kingdom of Laos with obvious help of US and Thailand. Phoumi Nosavan was given assistance of moving troops through Thai territory. His troops together with a Thai contingent crossed Meking [Mekong] from Thai side to invade Vientiane.[56]

Even though no Thai official record has yet revealed Thailand's military involvement in Laos, it is clearly stated in declassified Department of State documents that Thailand supported Phoumi in the fighting at Vientiane.[57] The French also claimed that there were Thai military experts among Phoumi's troops, and that these Thai nationals participated in the battle of Vientiane.[58] Further-

53. Castle, *At War in the Shadow of Vietnam*, p. 24.
54. 'Welcoming the Expression of Friendship by the Royal Laotian Government', *Peking Review*, vol. 3, no. 48 (29 Nov 1960), pp. 10–11.
55. *SWB*, FE/472/B/3, NCNA, 23 Oct 1960.
56. Consulate-General in Hanoi to Foreign Office, DF 1015/1013 (15 Dec 1960), TNA: FO 371/152376.
57. *FRUS, 1958–1960, East Asia-Pacific region; Cambodia, Laos,* Vol. XVI, Memorandum of Discussion at the 470th Meeting of the National Security Council, 20 Dec 1960, p. 1014.
58. Dossier No. 26, 'Direction Asie-Océanie', Note: Internationalisation de la crise (7 Dec 1960), in Archives diplomatiques, Paris (Série: Asie-Océanie, Sous-série: Laos, Laotienne).

more, the British ambassador in Vientiane reported to the Foreign Office that Thailand provided direct military support to Phoumi's forces, including the participation of a full body of Thai troops and either the supply or transit of artillery tanks.[59] This undoubtedly confirms the Thai military involvement in the Vientiane attack. The "Thai military experts" and "Thai troops" referred to by the British and the French were likely to be the PARUs, who acted as military advisers in Phoumi's battalions.

Despite Phoumi's successful takeover of Vientiane, the situation in Laos remained complicated. There were now two governments, each claiming to be legitimate, each recognised by world superpowers, and each with its own army. The Soviet Union, the PRC and North Vietnam still extended full support to Souvanna Phouma in Phnom Penh, and for the remnant of his government in Laos. The United States, Thailand, South Vietnam, and several Western countries extended their support and recognition to the new government of Boun Oum.[60]

From here, minor conflicts between political factions in Laos turned into major conflicts between the external powers. Phoumi's rightist forces were backed by American aid and weapons, well-trained Thai military advisers, and Filipino technicians. Thai military airplanes were also supplied to Phoumi's forces, in addition to regular airlifts serviced by Air America, Inc., a civilian company secretly owned by the CIA.[61] At the same time, Moscow, Beijing and Hanoi gave unrelenting support and all necessities to the neutralists and the leftists. The joint Kong Le-Pathet Lao forces, whose bases were located on the Plain of Jars[62] in Xieng Khouang,

59. Vientiane to Foreign Office, DF 1015/990 (19 Dec 1960), TNA: FO 371/152375.

60. Britain delayed its recognition of the Boun Oum government. Foreign Minister to Prime Minister (23 Dec 1960), National Archives of Thailand (NAT): (2) Gor Tor 1.14/2, Box 2, Fol. 5.

61. *FRUS, 1958–1960, East Asia-Pacific region; Cambodia, Laos,* Vol. XVI, Commander-in-Chief, Pacific to the Joint Chiefs of Staff, 23 Dec 60, p. 1017.

62. The Plain of Jars (PDJ) gets its name from the thousands of stone jars, ranging from one to three metres in height, that lie scattered on the grassy upland plain in northern Laos. They are believed to have been made by people from an unknown ancient civilisation around 2000 years ago.

were supplied with military equipment and weapons by extensive Soviet airlifts. The Soviet Union's Deputy Foreign Minister Pushkin later told Averell Harriman that, with the exception of World War II, the airlift to Laos had been "the highest priority Soviet supply operation" since the 1917 revolution.[63] It was revealed by the Department of State in January 1961 that the Soviet Union flew at least 180 sorties to Laos between 15 December 1960 and 3 January 1961.[64] Apart from the Soviet Union, the People's Republic of China also extended its support to the Laotian neutralists, and hinted to the West that their military intervention in the Laos conflict would be met with retaliation.[65] As the foreign superpowers became fully engaged in the conflict, Laos had effectively been brought into the Cold War.

The exhilaration on the part of the Thais and the Americans after Phoumi's success in retaking Vientiane was short-lived. Kong Le's neutralist troops who had escaped from Vientiane unscathed in mid-December soon joined the forces of the Pathet Lao on the Plain of Jars (PDJ). The North Vietnamese took advantage of the confused situation and moved their troops into Laos to support the Pathet Lao.[66] Together, they expelled all the remnants of the rightist troops present in the PDJ and Xieng Khouang. The worst fear of the Thais and the Americans—that the neutralists and the communists would unite against the rightists—had come true.[67]

The seizure of the strategically important PDJ by Kong Le-Pathet Lao troops came as a severe blow to the Phoumist position in Laos. Surrounded in all directions by high, jagged mountains, the PDJ is the largest 'flat' area in northern Laos, with Vientiane

63. JFKL, Oral History Interview with W. Averell Harriman, 17 Jan 1965, by Arthur M. Schlesinger, Jr., Washington, D.C., p. 60; and Stevenson, *The End of Nowhere*, p. 119.

64. Department of State Bulletin, 23 Jan 1961, pp. 114–15.

65. *SWB*, FE/443/B/5, NCNA, 21 Sept 1960.

66. Dossier No. 26, 'Direction Asie-Océanie', Note: Internationalisation de la crise (7 Dec 1960), in Archives diplomatiques, Paris (Série: Asie-Océanie, Sous-série: Laos, Laotienne); and interview with Lair. According to French intelligence, there was evidence that the North Vietnamese troops started to move west towards Laos as early as 3 December 1960.

67. Interview with Lair.

to the south, Luang Prabang to the northwest, and North Vietnam to the east. The few roads available in northern Laos ran through or near the PDJ. Route 13, the only road linking the administrative capital of Vientiane and the royal capital of Luang Prabang, ran along the edge of the PDJ. Route 7 ran across the PDJ eastwards to the provinces of Xieng Khouang, Sam Neua, and then to North Vietnam. Therefore, the control of the PDJ by the neutralist-leftist troops not only threatened the land traffic between Vientiane and Luang Prabang, but also obstructed communication and transportation between the non-communist province of Xieng Khouang and the rest of Laos. With the neutralists, the Pathet Lao and the North Vietnamese uniting against the rightists, Phoumi's troops faced an uphill task to recapture the PDJ.

Despite the seriousness of the situation, Phoumi was overjoyed by his success in retaking Vientiane, and felt no urgency to capture the PDJ. He was, in fact, confident that the PDJ could be retaken in five days.[68] However, he did not launch an offensive to capture the PDJ until February 1961.[69] It was by then too late: the joint neutralist-communist forces, reinforced by supplies and advisers from Moscow, Beijing and Hanoi, had firmly established themselves on the PDJ. Phoumi's offensive soon turned into a perilously defensive mission.[70]

Fortunately, the Thais and the Americans had been directly involved in Phoumi's takeover of Vientiane, and were aware of Phoumi's weaknesses. They knew that the crux of Phoumi's low military performance was not just the lack of good leadership, but also the friendly, non-aggressive nature of the Lao Loum, the ethnic group that dominated the RLA's ranks. The majority of Lao Loum soldiers did not have the will to fight. As Bangkok and Washington did not want to introduce their ground troops into Laos for fear of damage to their public image and of possible

68. JFKL, Oral History Interview with Walt W. Rostow, 11 Apr 1964, by Richard Neustadt, Washington, D.C., p. 46.

69. Ibid.

70. Ibid., and interview with Lair.

retaliation by the Chinese People's Liberation Army (PLA), they decided to search for alternative local forces, which could fight better than the Lao Loum. Once again, the PARUs, who had acquired knowledge of different Laotian hill tribes from their day-to-day border operations, would assume an indispensable role in the conflict in Laos.

Enter Vang Pao

The PARUs started to establish small posts along the Mekong River opposite Laos in 1956. These border posts were usually manned by five men, whose work was mostly intelligence-collection. The station staff were free to cross the river and to talk to local people. Each month, PARU commander Pranet, frequently accompanied by Lair, would go to Thailand's northeastern border and visit PARU posts. It was during one of these visits that Pranet and Lair heard about Vang Pao, a promising major in the RLA and a prominent leader of the Hmong tribe in the PDJ area.[71]

Vang Pao was born in Nong Het, east of the PDJ, in 1931. During the last year of World War II, at the age of 14, he became a courier for French soldiers hiding from Japanese occupation troops in villages and caves in the PDJ area. When the French colonialists returned to Laos after the war, Vang Pao joined the national police and served the French colonial government. Even though he was treated poorly by his lowland Lao colleagues who believed that the hill tribes were racially inferior, Vang Pao's performance outdid that of the lowlanders. It was at the time when the French were fighting the Viet Minh that Vang Pao's extraordinary leadership and hit-and-run guerrilla tactics were acknowledged by the French masters. They selected him to join the Laotian military school. After his graduation from the officer school, Vang Pao rapidly rose through the ranks. By his late twenties, he had become a major in the RLA.[72]

71. Interview with Lair.

72. Interview with Vang Pao; and Warner, *Back Fire: The CIA's Secret War in Laos and Its Link to the War in Vietnam* (New York: Simon and Schuster, 1995), pp. 35–42.

As soon as Kong Le's forces had joined the Pathet Lao and expelled the remnants of the RLA from the area, the PARUs and the CIA decided to look for Vang Pao.[73] The Hmong were known for their superb fighting skills and aggressiveness. The mountains around the PDJ were one of the largest Hmong habitats in northern Laos. If the PARU and the CIA were able to recruit Vang Pao to their side, and could convince him to lead Hmong guerrillas around the PDJ, the occupation of northern Laos by the neutralist-Pathet Lao forces would be effectively challenged.[74]

The search for Vang Pao would prove, however, to be no easy task. At the time, it was believed that Vang Pao had successfully escaped from his post in Xieng Khouang when the communist troops took over, and had fled to the mountains around the PDJ. The PARUs and the CIA had difficulty contacting him, as all communication and transportation to Xieng Khouang had been severed by the occupying Pathet Lao forces. All major roads east of the PDJ had virtually been taken by the communists, and remnants of the RLA had had to flee to the mountains and countryside.[75]

Vang Pao's whereabouts would be disclosed by an Air America pilot, Ron Sutphin—the man who had transported Lair and big bags of kip to Phoumi in Savannakhet the previous September. It was fortunate that Lair met Sutphin in Vientiane one morning in early January. Sutphin told Lair that he had recently been sent to pick up the wives and children of Vang Pao from a remote location near the PDJ and fly them to safety in Luang Prabang. Lair asked Sutphin to pinpoint Vang Pao's location on the map. That afternoon Lair, Pranet, and a five-man PARU team were ready to be airborne in search of Vang Pao.[76] As there were no aeronautical finding aids in the helicopter, Lair and Pranet used the rivers to navigate. Once they got close to the area Sutphin had pointed out on the map, they spotted a man in a black Hmong suit. Landing at a small air strip nearby, Pranet spoke to the man and found

73. Interview with Lair.

74. Ibid.

75. Ibid.

76. Ibid.

that he knew the location of Vang Pao. Pranet and his five-man PARU team set off on foot in the direction given by the tribesman; Lair, who was not authorised to stay overnight in the countryside, returned to Vientiane.[77] The next morning Lair received a message from Pranet, which read: "Vang Pao and I talked most of the night. Come back as soon as you can. This is the guy we've been looking for!"

Lair joined Pranet two days later. Vang Pao told Pranet and Lair that there had been communist presence around the PDJ for some time. Pranet and Lair were delighted when they heard Vang Pao say that "we cannot get along with the communists. The Hmong's way of life is completely different from that of the communists. We have two choices, to leave Laos or fight them. If you give us weapons, we will fight."[78]

Arming the Hmong would, however, present a new dilemma. Since the Hmong and the lowland Lao did not get along well, what if the Hmong took up arms and rebelled against the Lao Government, like many hill tribes in Burma did against the central government in Yangon? If that happened, Laos would be in serious trouble. Vang Pao assured Pranet and Lair that the Hmong were loyal to the crown and wanted to live peacefully with the Lao Loum. They were happy to be a part of Laos and did not harbour any desire to secede from Laos.[79] Pranet and Lair took Vang Pao's word and returned to Vientiane with optimism. They had found the man they were looking for.[80]

Project Momentum

At the CIA office in Vientiane, Lair drafted a new programme to train and arm the Hmong. The PARUs would be an integral and indispensable part of his programme, as Lair believed the PARUs were the best trainers for the Hmong—certainly better than the

77. Ibid.
78. Ibid.
79. To look retrospectively, Vang Pao kept his word, and the Hmong never rebelled against the Royal Lao Government.
80. Interview with Lair.

Americans. The PARUs had been trained in all aspects of tropical guerrilla warfare, they were familiar with the terrain, they spoke the local language and could communicate directly with the Hmong, and above all, in Lair's words, "they were invisible". American trainers did not share these superb qualities of the PARUs.[81]

Lair's proposed programme was then submitted to his superiors in Washington. To Lair's surprise, this programme, named Project Momentum by the CIA's headquarters, was speedily approved. Sarit's government duly sanctioned the American decision, on the condition that Thai involvement in this programme would be kept covert. The Thais would provide the manpower while the United States would provide financial and equipment support. More and more five-man and ten-man PARU teams were gradually dispatched to Laos to train the Hmong. These teams included communications specialists, weapons and ammunition specialists, medical technicians, and combat instructors. The Hmong learned all kinds of hit-and-run guerrilla warfare tactics. The PARUs and their CIA colleagues were extremely impressed by the Hmong's courage, their willingness to fight, their great knowledge of local terrain, and their exceptional skills in mountain-climbing. The Hmong knew how to hit the enemy and run to safety. They could continue hiking and living off the land for several days.[82] By March 1961, 3000 Hmong had been trained, and the PARUs were asked to train them in how to operate more sophisticated weapons like mortars.[83] The project looked so promising that President Kennedy ordered a 33 per cent increase in the number of Hmong clandestine fighters by 1 April.[84]

By the middle of 1961, there were 13 PARU teams, totalling 99 men, training the Hmong guerrillas in Laos. According to Brigadier General Lansdale, an expert on guerrilla warfare from the

81. Ibid. Lair described the PARUs as "invisible" in the sense that the PARUs blended in well with the locals.

82. Interview with Lair; and interview with Vang Pao.

83. Belk to Bundy (15 Mar 1961), JFKL: NSF, Box 130, Fol. Laos, General.

84. Aide Memoire on Action in Laos (9 Mar 1961), JFKL, NSF, Box 130, Fol. Laos, General.

Pentagon, all PARU personnel dispatched to Laos were specially selected and screened, and were rated as being of high quality and outstanding combat performance, with exceptionally heroic and meritorious action. No wonder the United States asked the Thai government to increase the strength of the PARUs from 300 to 550.[85] Project Momentum had indeed gained an unstoppable momentum.

Conclusion

When back in November 1960 five PARU teams, totalling 25 men, were dispatched to Laos to assist Phoumi's battalions in an effort to retake Vientiane from Kong Le's forces, nobody at the time, not even the Thai ruling generals, could have imagined that it would be the beginning of an intervention that would last 15 years, and that would also culminate in the deployment in the early 1970s of the largest expeditionary mission in Thailand's contemporary history.

Indisputably, covert Thai intervention in Laos from 1960 to 1974 was vital to the survival of a non-communist government in Laos. The PARUs played an indispensable part in assisting the RLA to retake Vientiane in 1960. After that success, they assumed an even more important role in training Hmong tribesmen in guerrilla warfare, and successfully turning them into the most effective force the RLG had ever possessed.

The story does not end there. As the Indochina conflicts escalated from the mid-1960s, Thai covert intervention significantly expanded. Royal Thai Air Force pilots contributed tremendously to the destruction of enemy bases and supply lines in northern Laos. The introduction of RTA artillery units from the mid-1960s helped defend the RLG's advance strongholds against the communist onslaught. Later in the war, with the Hmong guerrilla forces depleted by years of fighting, Thai ground troops actively went to

85. Memorandum from Lansdale to Taylor, in *The Pentagon Papers*, pp. 643–9.

the front line and became the indispensable elements in resisting the Pathet Lao and the North Vietnamese forces.

Even though Laos eventually fell into communist hands in December 1975, Thai covert intervention in Laos was not useless. The presence of Thai irregulars in Laos had prolonged the life of Souvanna Phouma's regime, giving time for Thailand to improve its economy, to develop its remote areas, to educate its rural population, and to strengthen its military and the country's defence against communist threats. Moreover, the dispatch of Thai troops to Laos permitted Thai soldiers to gain first-hand combat experience from fighting with the North Vietnamese—something that they would not gain from their training. The reunified Vietnam would soon actively exert its influence over Laos and Cambodia and attempt to spread its influence across the borders into Thailand. Experts believe that Vietnam may have carried out an attack on Thailand if the Sino-Vietnamese War had not erupted. Clearly, the Thai military experience in Laos during the 1960s and early 1970s taught the Thai leaders that it was not China, but rather Vietnam, that posed the greatest threat to Thailand during the Cold War.

8

THE FATE OF NEUTRALISM IN CAMBODIA AND LAOS

Bruce Lockhart

Cambodia and Laos to some extent tend to be the 'also-rans' of the Cold War narrative in Southeast Asia, particularly from the American perspective, whereby the Second Indochina Conflict becomes simply the 'Vietnam War'. Cambodian history between 1945 and 1975 is often overshadowed by the horrors of the three-year Democratic Kampuchea regime which followed, while the conflicts which tore Laos apart during the same period fade into the obscurity that still characterises knowledge of that country in most of the world. Not only was the number of American deaths in these two countries infinitesimal compared to the tens of thousands of lives lost in Vietnam, much of the war itself (primarily bombings rather than ground operations) was shrouded in secrecy for years at a time. When these two countries are studied, all too often they are relegated to a secondary role vis-à-vis Vietnam—a "sideshow", as one authoritative analysis of US involvement in Cambodia termed it.[1] This chapter focuses on Cambodia and Laos after the Geneva Conference of 1954, and particularly on the issue of neutralism, which had relevance as a label and a diplomatic orientation for the two countries to a much greater degree than was the case for South Vietnam.

Sihanouk's Cambodia, 1954–1970

Cambodia between 1954 and 1970 was dominated by the towering figure of Prince Norodom Sihanouk, who almost single-handedly

1. William Shawcross, *Sideshow: Kissinger, Nixon and the Destruction of Cambodia* (New York: Simon and Schuster, 1979).

dictated his country's foreign policy and most of its domestic politics as well. It was Sihanouk who charted Cambodia's neutralist course from the time of independence, Sihanouk who navigated that course for the next 16 years, often through treacherous waters, and Sihanouk whose erratic and sometimes inept hand at the rudder eventually swamped his ship of state. He arguably represented Cambodia's 'best shot' at becoming and remaining the neutral oasis of peace that he wished it to be, yet in the end the fate that befell his own regime (in 1970) and his nation (in 1975) was to a large extent of his own making.

Cambodia's foreign policy during this period cannot be divorced from its domestic politics or from its geopolitical vulnerability. Although Sihanouk was widely credited with having provided the final push for independence through his 'royal crusade' in 1953–54, after independence he remained vulnerable to charges of collaboration with imperialism from opponents on the Left.[2] Not only had Sihanouk been put on the throne by French colonialism, he was now ready to accept American aid for his newly independent country. While doing so, therefore, he drew a clear distinction between aid and alignment, refusing to join SEATO and declaring himself a committed neutralist, particularly after a high-profile appearance at the Bandung Asian-African Conference in 1955.

For the first few years after independence, Sihanouk was able to maintain a reasonable balance between the Western and socialist blocs. Despite grumblings from Washington, he pursued relations with both Beijing and Hanoi, though initially refusing to establish formal diplomatic ties with either the Chinese or Vietnamese government as long as the two countries were divided. Cambodia was wooed not only by the PRC, but by the USSR, Yugoslavia, and

2. These included both liberal politicians and a group of Cambodian Communists who chose to participate legally in the Cambodian political process. Many of their comrades, who had fought the French with Vietnamese support, had relocated to Hanoi after the 1954 Geneva Accords.

numerous other governments outside the pro-American camp, and Sihanouk kept up a regular schedule of trips around the world. His wide-ranging diplomacy, combined with his ability to obtain aid from both blocs, gave considerable substance to his neutralist aspirations and contributed to the success of what is usually seen as modern Cambodia's 'Golden Age', however short-lived.

Sihanouk's deft diplomatic touch was much less sure when it came to his next-door neighbours, however, and a series of spats with Bangkok and Saigon gradually poisoned his relationship with Washington as well. Centuries of conflict and rivalry were not forgotten, and anti-Communism—a doctrine to which Sihanouk was profoundly attached where his own country was concerned, though not in his foreign relations—was not a sufficiently binding glue to cement ties among the three neighbours. Sihanouk cordially detested Thai Field Marshal Sarit Thanarat and South Vietnamese President Ngo Dinh Diem, and the feelings were mutual, particularly given Phnom Penh's overtures to Beijing and Hanoi. Thailand's seizure of the Preah Vihear Temple in 1958 and South Vietnamese border incursions only served to inflame tensions; and when both Sarit and Diem began to actively support anti-Sihanouk plots from rightist opponents, the late 1950s and early 1960s became a prolonged series of slanging matches escalating into diplomatic crises and, in the case of Thailand, a complete rupture in relations in 1961.

Willy-nilly the Americans were dragged into the fray. The degree of support for anti-Sihanouk elements from American military and/or intelligence officers in Thailand and South Vietnam is far from clear. Declassified correspondence makes it clear that US diplomats in Washington and Phnom Penh were not involved, but as developments in Laos during the same period would show, the left hand of the State Department did not always know what the right hands of the Department of Defense and Central Intelligence Agency were doing. Genuine pressure was exerted on the Diem and Sarit governments to end support for the rebels, but to no avail. Neither regime had any sympathy for Sihanouk and his neutralism, and it is quite likely that American officials in these countries were less than forceful in their protestations. (Sihanouk had few admirers among US diplomats or officers in neighbouring countries.)

Sihanouk was understandably angry over Thai and South Vietnamese support for his opponents, but he blamed the US as well. One of the many paradoxes in his thinking was that although he would never be anyone's puppet, he assumed that Sarit and Diem were just that. He became increasingly alienated from America, even after the change from the Eisenhower to the Kennedy administration led to a more flexible and somewhat less dogmatic foreign policy. Sihanouk issued ultimatums demanding that the US force Bangkok and Saigon to cease their support for rebel elements, and when Washington proved unwilling or unable to do so, Cambodia unilaterally terminated American aid in November 1963. The following month, the successive deaths of Diem, Kennedy and Sarit in the space of a few weeks led Sihanouk to make some injudicious remarks about all three men in a radio broadcast, provoking condemnation from Washington for his "barbaric" comments. This choice of words in turn so angered Sihanouk that he recalled the entire Cambodian diplomatic mission from the US. The relationship bumped along for over a year until 1965, when an insulting article in *Newsweek* magazine caused a full-fledged diplomatic rupture.

The Cambodian-US relationship was in many respects much more than bilateral; it was in a sense quadrilateral, since Bangkok and Saigon were implicated as well. This four-cornered relationship, while it did not completely nullify Sihanouk's neutralist ambitions, certainly undermined them. The key issues that provoked conflict among the four governments can be effectively summed up by the single word 'borders', which were significant in two important ways. At the diplomatic level, Sihanouk became obsessed with obtaining official recognition of Cambodia's borders from neighbours near and far. (This preoccupation was due partly to reasonably valid fears of possible Thai and/or South Vietnamese encroachment, and partly because of his failure to obtain guarantees of Cambodia's neutrality through an international conference as would be done for Laos in 1961–62.) At the geopolitical level, Cambodia's eastern border became a place of refuge for National Liberation Front (NLF) and People's Army of Vietnam (PAVN) forces—arguably the single most important development in the Indochina conflict as far as Cambodia was concerned.

For much of the 1960s, these two issues were accorded inverse importance in Phnom Penh and Washington. Sihanouk turned the recognition issue into a litmus test of other countries' goodwill, while playing down and even denying the importance of the Vietnamese troops' presence on his territory. Conversely, the US gave short shrift to his campaign for recognition of his borders, while becoming more and more upset over the sanctuary being given to their enemies. As Kenton Clymer has pointed out, Sihanouk's demand for recognition of his borders was fairly straightforward, and under other circumstances the US might have acquiesced from the start.[3] However, neither Bangkok nor Saigon was disposed to do so, and Washington was unwilling to irritate its closest allies in order to placate a neutralist increasingly perceived as flirting with the Communists. It was only when both sides were ready for a *rapprochement* in 1968–69 and the recognition issue became the only remaining obstacle to normalisation that the US agreed to Sihanouk's demand.

Sihanouk's position vis-à-vis the sanctuaries was much more delicate. Just when the first Vietnamese forces took refuge on Cambodian soil and just how actively Sihanouk acquiesced to their doing so are still subjects of debate, but for much of the Johnson administration, if not earlier, they were being officially tolerated by his government. Sihanouk had several motives for allowing these

3. Kenton Clymer, *Troubled Relations: The United States and Cambodia since 1870* (DeKalb: Northern Illinois University Press, 2007), p. 76.

sanctuaries to remain. First, and most significantly, the Cambodian army was not capable of driving them out. Second, while Sihanouk shared his people's traditional distrust of the Vietnamese, he was on good terms with Hanoi's leaders and certainly preferred them to Diem or any of his successors. He also thought that the revolution would eventually win in the South—though it took longer than he anticipated—and he wished to bet on the winning horse. Finally, although it is still unclear how much Sihanouk understood the dynamics of the relationship between the Vietnamese and Cambodian Communist movements, he may well have received assurances from Hanoi that they would restrain the opponents he had come to call the "*Khmers Rouges*".[4]

As mentioned above, Sihanouk's foreign policy was partially guided by domestic political developments. His pursuit of neutralism, particularly friendship with the socialist countries, served to disarm leftist critics, and his decision to gradually move away from the US seems to have received considerable support from many Cambodians. Compared to South Vietnam, Cambodia under Sihanouk remained closer to France than to the US; this situation only changed significantly after Lon Nol came to power in 1970. However, by the late 1960s the domestic scene had changed, and Sihanouk's foreign policy accordingly underwent a reorientation, leading to the re-establishment of ties with the US in 1969.

At least three important developments contributed to Sihanouk's tilt back towards the US. First, the Cultural Revolution in China had spilled over into Cambodia, spreading Maoist ideology among urban youth and provoking unrest in Phnom Penh. This severely damaged Sino-Cambodian relations and put paid to Sihanouk's traditional faith in the PRC as a disinterested friend

4. As Sihanouk tightened his grip in the 1960s, the Left had gradually been pushed off the political stage. A few future Khmer Rouge leaders remained in government positions for a time, but by the end of 1967 all had fled to the jungle. It is now known that Hanoi had in fact counselled restraint to their Cambodian comrades precisely because of Sihanouk's neutralism and because of the sanctuaries. This advice became a sore spot in relations between the two parties, particularly after the Khmer Rouge took up armed struggle against Sihanouk in 1967–8.

and protector. Second, from 1967–68 the combination of a more active Khmer Rouge insurgency and an ever-increasing Vietnamese presence in Cambodia's eastern provinces eroded Sihanouk's confidence in his ability to 'manage' either the domestic Left or his revolutionary neighbours. Finally, the strengthening of the political Right under Lon Nol, who became prime minister in 1966, exerted pressure on Sihanouk to tack right, all the more so because the deteriorating military situation meant that he needed to avoid further alienating the army, whose interests had been badly affected by the termination of American aid in 1963.

Although it is likely Sihanouk saw reconciliation with the US as a more balanced form of neutralism, in the end it amounted to the effective abandonment of that policy, and it came too late to save either his regime or his country. The US military had been preparing for an invasion of Cambodia to go after the Vietnamese sanctuaries, and the *rapprochement* with Washington postponed these plans—but only temporarily.[5] Although Sihanouk had indicated that he would conditionally accept 'hot pursuit' across the border with South Vietnam, the US took this consent as blanket approval for increasing military action, including bombing campaigns. Sihanouk's final year in power saw the steady escalation of the war along his eastern frontier as well as the erosion of his own power base. By March 1970, when he was overthrown in a coup led by Lon Nol and Prince Sirik Matak, Cambodia had been irreversibly drawn into the Indochina conflict and Sihanouk's dreams of an "oasis of peace" buffered by a policy of neutralism were long dead and buried.

Sihanouk in American eyes[6]

The diplomatic documents from Sihanouk's time in power reveal the very mixed emotions with which Washington viewed his often-

5. D.P. Chandler, *The Tragedy of Cambodian History: Politics, War and Revolution since 1945* (New Haven: Yale University Press, 1991), 172.

6. This section is based primarily on the declassified documents published in the *Foreign Relations of the United States* (*FRUS*) series for the period 1955–68. Declassified documents on Cambodia and Laos beyond

dramatic initiatives and his very public pursuit of a foreign policy which he believed to be in his country's best interests. Ironically, during the earliest years of Cambodia's independence there was actually a certain amount of both sympathy and comprehension on the part of the US for Cambodian neutralism, which was believed to reflect genuine nationalist sentiments. Sihanouk was sufficiently anti-Communist for American tastes and was expected to maintain a reasonable balance between East and West, and during these early years the likelihood for trouble with Cambodia's neighbouring governments appeared greater than the potential for internal subversion.[7]

Sihanouk was not without his critics in Washington, however, particularly when he began to manifest the more 'defiant' side of neutralism by visiting Beijing in early 1956. During a conversation at the time of this visit, Assistant Secretary of State Walter Robertson told the Cambodian ambassador bluntly that "such action, if not supporting Communism, at least gave the impression of such support", and asked why Phnom Penh could not follow the Thai and Philippine examples and take a stronger anti-Communist stance.[8] Sihanouk muddied the diplomatic waters further with his ill-fated visit to Manila, from which he returned protesting vociferously what he perceived as attempts to strong-arm him into joining SEATO. His increasing propensity to criticise both the amount and the nature of US aid provoked a strong response from the American military; CINCPAC Admiral Felix Stump suggested that "it is about time for the US to make some reaction other than turning the other cheek when neutralists and others spit in our face".[9]

the end of the Johnson administration have yet to be published. For an excellent study of Cambodian-US relations using both published and unpublished documents, see Clymer, *Troubled Relations*.

7. See, for example, Ambassador McClintock to State, 29 Apr 1955 (Document 199), National Intelligence Estimate, 16 Aug 1955 (Document 217), and McClintock to State, 12 Sept 1955 (Document 218), *FRUS*, 1955–57, vol. 21. Each *FRUS* volume will be cited in full at the first appearance; documents will subsequently be cited individually since the date will indicate which volume they appear in.

8. Memorandum of Conversation between Cambodian Ambassador and Asst. Secretary of State for Far Eastern Affairs, 10 Feb 1956 (Document 225).

9. Quoted in McClintock to State, 30 Mar 1956 (Document 230).

Under the Eisenhower administration there generally seems to have been more understanding of Sihanouk's position within the embassy in Phnom Penh than at Foggy Bottom. Robert McClintock, the first ambassador to Cambodia, is consistently said to have offended Sihanouk in particular and Cambodians in general through his behaviour.[10] However, on a number of occasions he defended the Prince's neutralism, particularly against criticisms from the US military and from the embassy in Bangkok, and attempted to downplay Washington's concerns that Cambodia was becoming "leftward [and] excessive[ly] neutralist".[11] McClintock maintained this stance after his reassignment to the State Department in Washington. In a May 1957 memo he argued at some length that Cambodia represented a "microcosm" of the issues faced by the US in dealing with decolonised countries around the world and that American policy there had "at least demonstrated the advantage of utilising the inert weight of neutralism as a counter-poise to communism".[12] The following year, too, the embassy prepared a position paper on the "desirability of making efforts to persuade [Phnom Penh] to abandon" neutrality but ultimately decided that the cons outweighed the pros.[13]

Neither Secretary of State John Foster Dulles nor Christian Herter, who would succeed him upon his death in 1959 and was already acting on his behalf during the final months of his life, had much sympathy for Sihanouk. Cambodia's decision to recognise the PRC in 1958 brought new turbulence to the relationship. Carl Strom, who had replaced McClintock in Phnom Penh, conveyed

10. Chandler, *The Tragedy of Cambodian History*, pp. 86–7; Milton Osborne, *Sihanouk: Prince of Light, Prince of Darkness* (St Leonards, NSW: Allen and Unwin, 1994), pp. 94, 103; Clymer, *Troubled Relations*, p. 32.

11. See, for example, McClintock to State, 11 May 1956 (Document 237) and McClintock to State, 31 May 1956 (Document 239), and McClintock to Chairman, Joint Chiefs of Staff, 27 July 1956 (Document 244 enclosure). The comment on Sihanouk's foreign policy is from Memorandum by Director of Office of Southeast Asian Affairs Young, 21 June 1956 (Document 240).

12. Memorandum by McClintock, Policy Planning Staff, 21 May 1957 (Document 255).

13. Chargé d'Affaires Kellogg to State, 18 Mar 1958 (Document 69), *FRUS*, 1958–60, vol. 16, downloaded from digital.library.wisc.edu./1711.dl/FRUS.

Washington's strong objections to Sihanouk but was told that "no Cambodian would ever believe [that the] Chinese were more dangerous than [the] Vietnamese."[14] Whatever the ambassador may have thought of the normalisation issue, he certainly recognised the truth of Sihanouk's assertion, and during the prolonged crisis with Bangkok and Saigon he consistently defended Cambodia against accusations from its neighbours, concluding that "despite Sihanouk's faults his removal from [the] Cambodian scene would cause serious instability and provide increased opportunities for Communists".[15]

The advent of the Kennedy administration, with Dean Rusk as secretary of state, brought the potential for a more stable relationship, as the State Department was generally better disposed toward Sihanouk than had been the case under Dulles or Herter. Sihanouk and Kennedy had several cordial meetings during the latter's first months in power, and both Rusk and William Trimble, the new ambassador in Phnom Penh, were sympathetic to Cambodia in its disputes with Saigon and Bangkok. As mentioned above, however, it was precisely these spats and what Sihanouk saw as American unwillingness to restrain its puppets that seriously damaged the relationship. Washington also stonewalled Sihanouk's desire for a Laos-style conference on Cambodia.[16] Both the embassy and Foggy Bottom spoke frequently of the need to reassure and soothe Sihanouk in order to keep relations on an even keel, but that was easier said than done.[17]

Sihanouk's cutting off of American aid and the nasty exchanges

14. Ambassador Strom to State, 25 July 1958 (Document 77).

15. Strom to State, 21 Nov 1958 (Document 89). Much of the correspondence in this volume of *FRUS* is devoted to the problems with Thailand and South Vietnam.

16. See State to Embassy Bangkok, 22 Aug 1962 (Document 89), Ambassador Strom to State, 7 Sept 1962 (Document 90), and documents 94–106, *FRUS*, 1961–3, vol. 23. Rusk's main concern was that a conference dealing with Cambodia on the heels of the Geneva Conference on Laos would "likely encourage extension of [the] conference concept to South Viet-Nam" (Document 89).

17. See, for example, Memorandum by National Security Council Staff Robert Johnson, 2 Nov 1961 (Document 77) and MAAG Cambodia Chief Scherrer to CINCPAC, 15 Nov 1961 (Document 80).

after Sarit's death threw Cambodian-US relations into a tailspin. Washington was less and less sympathetic to the Prince, particularly as the war in Vietnam heated up while he seemed to be flirting more and more with the Communists, talking seriously of recognising the Democratic Republic of Vietnam (DRV) and the National Liberation Front (NLF).[18] The issue of Vietnamese forces on Cambodian territory became increasingly contentious. When accusations about these sanctuaries first surfaced in 1961, the embassy had categorically rejected them, even though they came from Ambassador Frederick Nolting in Saigon.[19] By early 1965, though, the evidence for the bases was undeniable, and what the Joint Chiefs of Staff called Sihanouk's "pseudo-neutrality" was viewed as highly favourable to the Vietnamese revolutionary forces.[20]

After the diplomatic rupture of 1965, there were occasional attempts to repair the damage, although enthusiasm for this endeavour in Washington was somewhat mixed.[21] The issue of diplomatic *rapprochement*, however, was increasingly overshadowed by the military conflict. General William Westmoreland, commander of US forces in South Vietnam, in particular, was much more preoccupied with the possibility of sending B-52s across the Cambodian border than with the potential for sending envoys back to Phnom Penh.[22] Even as the two governments stumbled towards normalisation in 1968, there was a clear sense that Sihanouk's avowed neutralism now had little meaning. If in July the State

18. State Dept. Circular, 3 Dec 1964 (Document 148) and Memorandum from Director of Office of Southeast Asian Affairs to Assistant Secretary for East Asian Affairs, 18 Apr 1966 (Document 181), *FRUS* 1964–68, vol. 27, downloaded from www.state.gov/r/pa/ho/frus/.

19. Ambassador to State, 1 June 1961 (Document 70), Ambassador Nolting (Saigon) to State, 15 June 1961 (Document 71), Memo by Deputy Special Assistant for National Security Affairs Rostow to President, 23 Sept 1961 (Document 73), and MAAG Cambodia Chief Scherrer to CINCPAC, 15 Nov 1961 (Document 80).

20. Memo from JCS to Defense Secretary McNamara, 19 Dec 1966 (Document 198).

21. Clymer, *Troubled Relations*, chapter 5.

22. See, for example, Westmoreland to JSC, 5 Dec 1967 (Document 213), and Assistant Secretary of State for Far Eastern Affairs to Secretary of State, with attachment from Westmoreland, 27 May 1968 (Document 234).

Department could still raise the issue of "how we can most effectively move Cambodia back toward [a] position of true neutrality", a year-end memo from CINCPAC Admiral John McCain was less optimistic, stating bluntly that "Sihanouk has been of more value to the Communists as a 'neutralist' than as a declared ally".[23] By now, of course, Cambodia was being dragged full speed ahead into the war, and Sihanouk's final year in power witnessed the acceleration of this process. Neutrality and neutralism alike had died a slow and painful death.

Laos 1954–1975: Political developments

Laos's political evolution differed from Cambodia's in at least three crucial ways, each of which had an impact on its aspirations for neutralism. First, it had no single political figure able to dominate the scene to the degree that Sihanouk did in Cambodia. Prince Souvanna Phouma was in many ways the most important leader over the long term, and the figure around which various elements and factions rallied, but even at his strongest he did not wield the kind of power that Cambodia's leader did. Second, direct US involvement in Lao internal affairs was considerably greater than in Cambodia, where until 1970, at least, Americans had relatively little direct influence. Finally, the Lao Left—the Pathet Lao—remained a powerful political and military force throughout the two decades between 1954 and 1975.

The various Lao political forces are generally classified into three groups: Left, Neutralist, and Right. The Left, consisting of the Pathet Lao (now the Neo Lao Hak Xat, 'Lao Patriotic Front', fronting for the Vietnamese-trained Communist Party) and its allies, alternated between participation in the political process and withdrawal from that process, maintaining a separate power base in its 'liberated zone' of Sam Neua. The Neutralists, a more amorphous faction centred around Souvanna Phouma, emerged

23. Rusk to Embassy in Saigon, 8 July 1968 (Document 238), and CINCPAC to JCS, 18 Dec 1968 (Document 261).

as a separate grouping several years after independence but subsequently split into two factions, one of which threw in its lot with the Pathet Lao while the other gravitated towards the Rightists. The latter, composed of influential military officers and civilian politicians, remained consistently hostile to any compromise with the Pathet Lao and acted as a foil to the Neutralists.

A detailed narrative of political developments in Laos during this period would require considerably more space than this chapter can provide, so they will be summarised and divided into several phases. The first phase, lasting from the Geneva Conference through 1959, saw an extended effort to incorporate the Pathet Lao political and military forces into the Royal Lao Government (RLG) and its army. In 1957 a coalition government was formed with Souvanna Phouma as prime minister which incorporated several Pathet Lao leaders, including his half-brother Prince Souphanouvong, into the cabinet. This experiment failed, however, and the coalition broke down. The Pathet Lao members of the government were arrested and detained for several weeks before they escaped from prison, and the Communist-trained military units slipped away to rejoin their comrades in Sam Neua.

The second phase, from 1959 through 1962, was a chaotic one, following the rupture with the Pathet Lao and the rise of an influential group of Rightists under General Phoumi Nosavan, who enjoyed the backing of the US military and CIA. Phoumi undermined Souvanna Phouma's leadership but in so doing served as catalyst for the appearance of a more radical group of Neutralists under the leadership of Colonel Kong Le. For a period of time in 1960–61 Laos was effectively divided into three parts under the Leftist, Neutralists, and Rightists, until an international conference in Geneva, combined with a series of negotiations among the three factions, produced a second coalition government (again under Souvanna) in 1962.

The Provisional Government of National Union (PGNU) lasted in name until 1974, but this third phase was marked by prolonged civil war and further challenges to Souvanna Phouma from the Right. By mid-1964 the Leftist members of the government had once again left Vientiane for the liberated zone after a series of killings of Neutralist political figures. From that point onward, the government was tripartite in name only, being split between Souvanna and his followers on the one hand and the Rightists on the other. This period also saw the final division of the Neutralists, with Kong Le and his allies remaining loyal to Souvanna and his government while 'patriotic neutralists' further to the Left joined the Pathet Lao. The years between 1962 and 1974 brought a steady expansion of Pathet Lao-governed liberated zones at the expense of territory controlled by the RLG.

The final and briefest phase began in September 1973 with a protocol calling for another Provisional Government of National Union, which was formally established in April 1974. The next 20 months saw the progressive extension of Pathet Lao control over the organs of government. In 1975 a series of 'popular uprisings' in town after town provoked the flight of Rightist politicians and officers across the Mekong and culminated in the abdication of King Savang Vatthana and the establishment of the Lao People's Democratic Republic in December. Souphanouvong was president of the new regime and Souvanna Phouma retained a nominal position as Supreme Advisor, but from then onward the party, now called the Lao People's Revolutionary Party, was firmly in power.

The waxing and waning of Lao neutralism

Not surprisingly, the fate of neutralism as a foreign policy strengthened and weakened according to the fortunes of the Neutralist faction itself. During the first few years of independence, when the Eisenhower administration exercised a strong and conservative influence over Lao affairs and when the Neutralists had yet to coalesce as a solid political grouping, Vientiane's foreign relations were generally focused on the 'Free World' and neutral countries like Cambodia, India, and Burma. Of the 'Big Three' socialist powers, neither the PRC nor the DRV had formal ties with the RLG; the Soviet Union recognised the RLG in 1956 but was blocked by American pressure on the latter from actually establishing an embassy in Vientiane until 1960.[24]

This situation changed dramatically with the events of 1960, which catalysed an expansion of Vientiane's foreign relations with socialist countries. The coup by Kong Le in support of Souvanna Phouma led directly to the opening of a Soviet embassy and to Soviet airlifts for the Neutralists. From late 1960 through the formation of the 1962 coalition government, Souvanna's government was based at Khangkhay in Xieng Khouang (the Plain of Jars). Not only was it receiving aid from the socialist bloc, its proximity to the Pathet Lao liberated zone forged strong, though ultimately short-lived, links with the Neo Lao Hak Xat, and the Neutralists adopted the latter's position that the PRC and DRV should be officially recognised.

The formation of the 1962 PGNU was followed by the establishment of diplomatic relations with Beijing, Hanoi, and a number of European socialist countries, most of whom had already been providing aid to the Pathet Lao and/or Neutralist forces. These new relationships came at the cost of ties with Taiwan and South Vietnam but considerably expanded Laos's international circle of friends.[25] The gradual breakdown of the PGNU and the resumption of the military conflict in 1964 did not bring a rupture of the RLG's diplomatic relations with the socialist bloc, but the latter's support was increasingly given only to the Pathet Lao while the increasingly less Neutralist Vientiane government turned more and more to the United States.

The Lao language generally does not distinguish between 'neutrality' and 'neutralism'; the term *khwampenkang* is used for

24. Jean Deuve, *Le Royaume du Laos 1949–1965* (Paris: École Française d'Extrême-Orient, 1984), p. 195 note 16.

25. Ibid., pp. 228–9.

both. During the period of this study, the term was a 'buzzword' that appeared again and again in Lao political discourse and in the names of several parties and other movements, including the Lao Pen Kang (Neutral Lao) Party, which Souvanna Phouma himself founded. The bitter reality, however, was that although Laos might attain some kind of neutralist balance in its foreign relations—and indeed did so with relative success under the PGNU of 1962—genuine neutrality in the Indochina conflict was out of reach even before the last French guns were silenced by the Geneva Accords of 1954. By that point in time Laos had already been drawn into the struggle between the DRV and its enemies, and it would never succeed in extricating itself from this conflict during the decades that followed. Even before the Ho Chi Minh Trail became the North's main lifeline into the South, Laos's eastern border region was already a safe haven for DRV forces. More importantly, these same forces were fully committed to supporting the Pathet Lao in their struggle against the RLG.

Any objective account of the Lao civil war must assign equal responsibility to the US and the DRV for their respective parts in prolonging and escalating the conflict. Despite Hanoi's constant denials (and a surprising degree of silence on the subject even in accounts published in Vientiane long after the victory of the Revolution)[26], PAVN advisers and troops were present in ever-increasing numbers from 1954 onward. Their support for the revolutionary enemies of successive Vientiane regimes—whether

26. The presence of DRV 'volunteers' is almost completely omitted from two comprehensive studies of these events: Thongsa Xainhavongkhamdi et al., *Pavatsat Lao lem III 1893 theung pachuban* [History of Laos, Volume III, 1893 to the present] (Vientiane: Ministry of Education and Sports and Social Science Research Institute, 1989); and Ai Sulinyasaeng, *Salup songkham pativat potpoi sat khong kongthap lae pasason Lao (1945–1975)* [A summary of the revolutionary war of national liberation by the Lao army and people (1945–1975)] (Vientiane: Ministry of Defence, 2001). By contrast, the Vietnamese have published a lavishly illustrated trilingual history of Vietnamese involvement in the Lao revolution: *Quan he hu nghi, doan ket dac biet va hop tac toan dien Viet Nam-Lao/ Kanphuaphan mittaphap, khwamsamakkhi phiset lae kanhuammeu hopdan Vietnam-Lao/ Special friendship and solidarity, and comprehensive cooperation between Viet Nam and Laos* (Hanoi: Ministry of Culture, Sport, and Tourism, 2007).

headed by Souvanna Phouma or someone further to the Right—guaranteed that these regimes would continue to receive economic and military aid from the US and Thailand. The years of American bombing from 1964 onward were certainly more destructive than anything the DRV was capable of doing in Laos, but the long-term DRV support for the Pathet Lao was in a sense equally destructive in that it effectively forestalled any real resolution of the civil war. Not only did Vietnamese aid allow the Pathet Lao to maintain the fight for their vision of an eventual revolutionary regime which would leave the Right and Souvanna Phouma's Neutralists in the dustbin of history, it also empowered them to avoid making significant political or military compromises at any point in the endless rounds of negotiations and agreements that characterised this period of Lao history.

Souvanna Phouma and the Americans

Souvanna Phouma was a considerably less temperamental figure than Sihanouk, and certainly much less prone to making incendiary public statements or dramatic policy initiatives, and consequently he never generated the same degree of animosity or hostility among US policy-makers. However, during the early years of Lao independence, when the Eisenhower administration was attempting to consolidate anti-Communist governments around the region, Souvanna was seen as undesirable because he was too naive and too willing to make concessions to the Pathet Lao at a time when the crucial objective in American eyes was to keep them out of the Lao government at all costs. Souvanna believed that the Pathet Lao, particularly his brother Souphanouvong, who was the movement's most public face, were not Communists but rather nationalists who could be reintegrated into the national fold. The Americans' preferred Lao politician for most of the 1950s was Katay Don Sasorith, a half-Vietnamese Lao who was much more conservative than the Prince and who had, they believed, been disabused of his earlier illusions about the Pathet Lao.[27]

The US also had a very narrow definition of what was acceptable in terms of 'neutralism' for Laos. Writing in April 1956, Ambassador Charles Yost referred to "latent neutralism which is congenial to the Lao character and consonant with its power position", but he did not feel that Laos could "veer" too far in that direction, both because "Communist ambitions" were all too obvious and because the material support of the 'Free World' would be needed for the foreseeable future.[28] The US remained extremely sceptical, not to say suspicious, of excessive talk of either 'neutrality' or 'neutralism' when such talk involved the Communists, whether the Pathet Lao or outside powers.[29] Souvanna's willingness to visit China despite heated American objections set off alarm bells in Washington. However, Yost's successor, Graham Parsons, though himself not particularly well-disposed towards Souvanna, did make reassuring noises to the effect that the country was unlikely to wander very far down the Communist path. Dulles was of course unwilling to trust any leader who could waltz casually off to Beijing, and he urged the embassy to make it clear that "while US recognizes Lao desire remain independent and neutral, Laos should beware of real ChiCom intent in neutralizing Laos, which is ... to paralyze and reduce to vassalage small well-intentioned neighbor".[30] This point would be echoed again and again as the prospects of a coalition with the Pathet Lao grew more likely.

27. On the attitude towards the Pathet Lao of Katay and the Lao leadership in general, see Minister Yost to Dept. of State, 21 Jan 1955 (Document 265), and Minister Yost to Dept. of State, 3 May 1955 (Document 291), in *FRUS 1955–57*, vol. 21; on Souvanna Phouma's naïveté see Ambassador Yost to Dept. of State, 31 Mar 1956 (Document 348). Interestingly, Katay's mixed parentage is never mentioned in most sources; a detailed biography can be found in Tung Van, 'Katay Don Sasorith Thu tuong Lao goc Viet' [Katay Don Sasorith, the Lao Prime Minister of Vietnamese origins], *Tap chi Su dia* [Journal of History and Geography], 16 (1969): 121–32.

28. Yost to State, 6 Apr 1956 (Document 350). Yost also argued that the US "must give no solid grounds for allegations" of interference in Lao internal affairs, "dragooning the Lao Government into military pacts against its better judgment" or doing anything to prevent "peaceful coexistence" with its Communist neighbours. Since the first and last of these, at least, became cornerstones of US policy under Eisenhower, it's perhaps not surprising that Yost was replaced shortly afterward.

29. An explicit discussion of this issue can be found in Dulles to Ambassador Parsons, 7 Aug 1956 (Document 371).

30. See Memorandum from Director of Office of Southeast Asian Affairs, 4 Sept 1956 (Document 379).

During the political instability that preceded and followed the first coalition government, the US continued to look askance at Souvanna, preferring either Katay or the equally conservative Phoui Sananikone as an alternative leader. The coalition itself was anathema to Washington, of course, and the rise of Phoumi Nosavan and his Rightist faction to challenge Souvanna's government was pleasing to the Americans, especially after Leftist candidates performed dangerously well in elections held in 1958. Dulles in particular was optimistic about the potential of Phoumi's faction as a potential counterweight to Souvanna.[31] This enthusiasm was shared by his successor Herter, despite the increasingly vocal opposition of Horace Smith, who replaced Parsons as ambassador in early 1958. Smith found himself at the centre of a fairly serious policy split, as his superiors in Washington generally remained sympathetic to Phoumi's Rightists as they brought down first Souvanna and then Phoui. More crucially, Phoumi was supported—and considerably emboldened—by the military and CIA personnel attached to the embassy.[32]

Phoumi's and Souvanna's respective fortunes were gradually reversed during the period 1958–60. Smith had never been a fan of Phoumi's faction, as he was committed to constitutional government and was convinced—rightly, as it turned out—that they would be quite willing to resort to extra-constitutional means to seize and maintain power. Moreover, Smith believed that Phou-

31. Dulles to Ambassador Smith, 17 July 1958 (Document 185), *FRUS*, 1958–60, vol. 16, downloaded from digital.library.wisc.edu./1711.dl/FRUS.

32. This situation has been discussed in detail in several works: Bernard Fall, *Anatomy of a Crisis: The Laotian Crisis of 1960–1961* (Garden City, NY: Doubleday, 1969); Charles Stevenson, *The End of Nowhere: American Policy Toward Laos Since 1954* (Boston: Beacon Press, 1972); Arthur J. Dommen, *The Indochinese Experience of the French and Americans: Nationalism and Communism in Cambodia, Laos, and Vietnam* (Bloomington: University of Indiana Press, 2001); and Deuve, *Royaume du Laos*. For correspondence regarding the split within Laos-based US personnel, see, for example, Memorandum from Assistant Secretary of State for Far Eastern Affairs, 10 Nov 1959 (Document 288), Memorandum from Assistant Secretary of State for Far Eastern Affairs, 16 Nov 1959 (Document 293) and Herter to Smith, 21 Nov 1959 (Document 295). Smith's dissatisfaction with this situation is expressed in Smith to Assistant Secretary of State Parsons, 3 May 1960 (Document 340).

mi's Rightists ultimately represented a threat because they divided the anti-Communist elements. Phoumi's supporters, on the other hand, saw him as the only force powerful enough to keep Laos from falling to the Pathet Lao. Washington did authorise Smith to express the American preference for a constitutional and democratic government to the Lao elements concerned, but these warnings proved ineffective.[33]

The series of coups and countercoups that tore the country apart through 1959 and 1960, particularly the Kong Le seizure of power, left Washington increasingly ambivalent about Phoumi and effectively brought Souvanna Phouma back onto the radar screen at Foggy Bottom, even while Phoumi's star was still shining brightly at the Pentagon. Herter rather grudgingly told Smith's successor, Winthrop Brown, to pursue a better relationship with the Prince, even though the secretary of state himself continued to see Souvanna as excessively soft on Communism.[34] (CIA Director Allen Dulles went further, stating that the establishment of a government under Souvanna represented "the first step of a possible Communist take-over".[35]) By late 1960 the State Department was hoping to bring about some kind of alliance between Souvanna and Phoumi that would combine the former's moral authority with the latter's strength. Documents from this period are fraught with confusion as officials from the various government departments weighed all of the different possible scenarios. What it boiled down to, as White House staffer John Eisenhower put it, was that while hoping to reconcile the two men, "we hesitate to choose sides with neutralist Souvanna in the light of Phoumi's pro-US orientation".[36]

33. See, for example, Memorandum from Director of Office of Southeast Asian Affairs, 18 Dec 1959 (Document 305).

34. Herter to Brown, 18 Sept 1960 (Document 400). Herter believed that "if and when Souvanna gets firmly in [the] saddle ... this will be considered [a] US defeat".

35. Memorandum of NSC meeting, 18 Aug 1960 (Document 373). In the National Security Council meeting where Dulles expressed this view, C. Douglas Dillon of State was even harsher on Souvanna's ally Kong Le, who he said "sounds like a Castro Communist-type individual".

36. Paper prepared by Asst White House Staff Secretary, 13 Sept 1960 (Document 394).

As late as October, Herter was urging Brown to ask King Savang Vatthana to intervene, since Souvanna "from all indications is either unable, unwilling or ... actively conniving with the Communists to gradually hand over Laos".[37] Brown, however, was cautiously optimistic about Souvanna's potential to save the situation, seeing him as the "only rallying point left in [the] country".[38] Herter would do no more than "accept the inevitable" of cooperating with Souvanna "for reasons of expediency ... to maintain the façade of legality" for US action—hardly a ringing endorsement.[39] Foggy Bottom remained essentially unreconciled to the scenario of Souvanna returning to power for the long run, and it was only the change of administration in 1961 that brought about a change in Washington's official attitude.

This change was not immediate, however. As many scholars have noted, Laos was very high on Kennedy's list of priorities when he took office, though it is not known whether he shared Eisenhower's sentiments that "if it weren't for the neighboring countries and the effect on them, we ought to let Laos go down the drain".[40] Generally speaking, both Brown and Rusk remained highly doubtful that Souvanna Phouma was the right choice, even though they were gradually coming to accept that future governments might have to be more eclectic in composition than the US would have liked.[41] The problem was that the US was increasingly isolated in holding such a stance. As Kennedy himself commented perceptively in a March 1961 meeting, it "looked like all were in favour of Souvanna except us, and perhaps Thailand and South Vietnam, and that does not look like a very good lineup".[42]

37. Herter to Brown, 1 Oct 1960 (Document 412). The King was an active player in Lao politics, and various factions, including the US, looked to him as a potential arbitrator of conflict.

38. Brown to State, 5 Oct 1960 (Document 416)

39. Herter to Brown, 18 Oct 1960 (Document 432).

40. Memorandum of conference between President Eisenhower and President-Elect Kennedy, 2 Jan 1961 (Document 1), *FRUS, 1961–63*, vol. 24, downloaded from www.state.gov/r/pa/ho/frus/.

41. Report prepared by Inter-Agency Task Force on Laos, Jan 1961 (attachment to Document 10).

42. Memorandum of conference with President Kennedy, 9 Mar 1961 (Document 25).

During the early months of the new administration, the word 'neutrality' was being thrown around somewhat more freely than before. In the March meeting just mentioned, it was acknowledged that the US definition of neutrality in the Lao context had now changed from a "pro-Western and neutral" regime to one which was "anti-Communist but neutral".[43] This remark may seem somewhat like splitting hairs, but in fact Washington realised by now that it was going to be nearly impossible to keep Laos isolated from its socialist neighbours, so the key issues were how to 'manage' those relationships and whether Souvanna Phouma was the appropriate 'manager'.

Over the course of 1961 the State Department began to move ever so slowly in the direction of supporting Souvanna, particularly once the negotiations at Geneva had got under way. It was a very slow process, especially at the very top, as Rusk continued to stress that any support for Souvanna would be conditional on his willingness to "cooperate [in] achiev[ing] genuine[ly] neutral Laos but not one ordered by Communist dictation".[44] It was only when the Geneva Conference got under way that Washington's opinion began to change, driven by increasing disenchantment with the Vientiane government under Phoumi as well as the views of Averell Harriman, the veteran diplomat heading the American delegation at the negotiations, who was considerably more sympathetic to the Prince. By roughly August, it seems clear from the documents that the State Department accepted—though still reluctantly—the inevitability of a Souvanna-led government; by December Washington was debating the composition of Souvanna's future cabinet; and by March 1962 Ambassador Brown was actively lobbying Lao political figures on Souvanna's behalf.[45]

43. Ibid.

44. Rusk to Ambassador Brown, 14 Apr 1961 (Document 53).

45. See Memorandum from Secretary Rusk to President Kennedy, 29 Aug 1961 (Document 171), Rusk to Ambassador Brown, 30 Dec 1961 (Document 250), Vientiane Embassy to State, 10 Mar 1962 (Document 306). Brown's counterpart in Bangkok would later be mobilised to soothe Thai fears that Souvanna's government would be dominated by "pro-Communist" members; see Rusk to Bangkok Embassy, 16 June 1962 (Document 399).

From the establishment of the 1962 PGNU until the end of the RLG in 1975, Souvanna Phouma remained at the head of the government despite attempts to dislodge him by various opponents on the Right. The US remained convinced that only Souvanna could hold things together, and they stuck by him through successive rebellions by disgruntled officers, ranging from the fairly serious April 1964 coup attempt by an influential general to a brief initiative by an army colonel in February 1965, which the intrepid Ambassador Sullivan suppressed by mobilising a "half-stoned" Australian technician to cut the wires to the radio station.[46] Throughout this period the US steadfastly affirmed its support for Souvanna.

There were several reasons why Washington now remained fully committed to the Prince. First of all, they believed that as long as the tripartite government existed even in name—and such a government would almost have to be led by Souvanna—this would prevent a full break with the Pathet Lao that would in turn lead to a much more aggressive military posture on the latter's part. The legitimacy conferred on Souvanna's government by the Geneva Agreements, it was felt, would mean that the Pathet Lao would have to take the blame if it fell apart.[47] Second, the split within the Neutralist forces which began shortly after the formation of the PGNU and was complete by mid-1963 meant that the military units under Kong Le, whose loyalties had once been suspect, were now clearly alienated from the Pathet Lao and fighting for the RLG—as opposed to fighting for Souvanna alone during the earlier period when there were separate Neutralist and Rightist governments.[48] Finally, and perhaps most importantly, Sou-

46. Sullivan to State, 1 Feb 1965 (attachment to Document 162), *FRUS 1964–68*, vol. 28, downloaded from www.state.gov/r/pa/ho/frus/. For April 1964 see documents 22–39.

47. Memorandum by Director of Bureau of Intelligence and Research, 28 Aug 1962 (attachment to Document 421); 'Diplomatic Moves on Laos', Apr 1963 (attachment to Document 459); Ambassador Unger to State, 20 Apr 1964 (Document 29), Rusk to Ambassador Unger, 25 Apr 1964 (Document 37), Memorandum by Defense Secretary McNamara to President Johnson, 25 Apr 1964 (Document 38).

48. Ambassador Unger to State, 14 Apr 1963 (Document 453), Rusk to Ambassador

vanna himself became more stridently anti-Communist, openly denouncing the DRV's involvement in the civil war and giving at least tacit support to the American bombing campaigns in the Plain of Jars and along the southeastern Panhandle where the Ho Chi Minh Trail was located.[49]

Ultimately, however, American support was not strong enough to salvage the situation. The 'flip side' of the reliance on the Geneva Agreement for legitimacy was that Souvanna Phouma became "more and more solely the creature" of Geneva, and even the king admitted in March 1963 that the PGNU was "the result of an international process and was not suitable to anyone in Laos".[50] A CIA analysis in May that year concluded that a "viable neutralist solution" was not yet in sight, and the situation went downhill from there as the assassinations of neutralist figures and departure of most Pathet Lao members of the government destroyed the reality of a tripartite government. By April 1964, in the wake of the abortive coup attempt, another CIA report felt that recent events had dealt a death blow to the coalition and that "it is problematical whether it will be possible to preserve the tripartite coalition formula".[51]

From that point onward, internal American documents recognised that Souvanna's position was being increasingly undermined

Unger, 16 May 1963 (Document 470), CIA Special Report 'The Situation in Laos', 1 Nov 1963 (Document 490).

49. The US bombing campaigns in Laos were effectively two separate wars: one against the forces directly opposing the RLG in the Plain of Jars region and one along the Ho Chi Minh Trail in the southeastern Panhandle. Souvanna accepted the American military presence where the Plain of Jars operations were concerned, but he was much more ambivalent about the Panhandle operations, since they often involved American and/or South Vietnamese ground units, and for much of this period a sort of 'Don't ask, don't tell' policy was in effect. A good bit of the correspondence between Vientiane and Washington during the 1964–68 period relates to the question of just what Souvanna should and should not be consulted on. See, for example, Ambassador Unger to State, 1 Mar 1964 (Document 11) and Memo from President's Special Assistant Rostow to President Johnson, 19 Oct 1967 (Document 311).

50. Memorandum of conversation between King Savang Vatthana and President Kennedy, 27 Feb 1963 (Document 445); the "creature of Geneva" comment is from Paper by Director of Bureau of Intelligence Hilsman and Research and National Security Council Staffer Forrestal, Feb 1963 (Document 440).

51. CIA Memorandum, 29 Mar 1963 (Document 447) and CIA Memorandum, 22

by his anti-Communist stance and by the fact that the theoretically tripartite coalition now comprised only his Neutralists and the Rightists. After a certain point in time, the Pathet Lao essentially considered the Vientiane-based RLG as illegitimate or illegal.[52] As late as 1968, the US continued to argue that the Geneva Agreements were still in force. In apparent anticipation of a possible inclusion of Laos in the framework of the Paris peace talks, a State Department paper on the 'US Negotiating Position on Laos' affirmed that "since 1962, the United States has consistently supported the aims of the Geneva Agreements . . . to perpetuate Laos as a neutral national political entity serving as a buffer between Communist and non-Communist Asia".[53] An ultimately more accurate assessment, though, can be found in a 1966 report by Ambassador Sullivan: "As long as Souvanna is at hold [*sic*, helm?], we can also anticipate he will preserve *trappings* of tripartite government which visibly *symbolize* RLG fidelity to agreements of 1962."[54] Over the longer term, neither the 'trappings' of tripartism nor 'symbolic' adherence to the Geneva Agreements would have much value, and when Souvanna was once more called into service to head the final coalition government, his role was essentially to preside over the decline and fall of what remained of the RLG.

Apr 1964 (Document 33). It is significant that later party histories of the civil war specifically single out the 1964 coup attempt as signalling the end of the tripartite government, although they incorrectly claim it was a deliberate American strategy to sabotage that government. See Thongsa et al., *Pavatsat Lao*, pp. 336–7, 345; Ai, *Salup songkham*, p. 145.

52. Specifically noted in late 1968 as a "recent development" in Pathet Lao policy; Special National Intelligence Estimate 58-1-68, 31 Oct 1968 (Document 389). In 1974, one of many grievances expressed by Rightist politicians against the third and final PGNU agreement was the fact that it followed Pathet Lao policy in referring to the existing RLG as "the Vientiane government"; see the criticisms of the agreement in Un Xananikon, *Santiphap mai nai Phralatsanachak Lao* [New Peace in the Kingdom of Laos] (Vientiane: s.n., 1973).

53. State Dept. paper on negotiating position, late 1968 (Document 396). That this was not merely a public posture is confirmed by a similar statement in a top secret paper prepared earlier in the year, 'What the Enemy Has Not Done in Laos', enclosure to Under Secretary of State Katzenbach to Deputy Secretary of Defense Nitze, 8 May 1968 (Document 366).

54. Ambassador Sullivan to State, 18 Nov 1966 (Document 269); emphases added.

Conclusion

For the concluding section of this chapter, I shall attempt to make a clearer distinction between neutrality (as a position in a given conflict) and neutralism (as a broader foreign policy stance). As the sources for this study have made clear, Southeast Asians and Westerners alike during the Second Indochina War used the two terms if not completely interchangeably, then at least with a certain degree of semantic overlap. In order to assess the situation in Cambodia and Laos, however, it is necessary to evaluate each of the two concepts separately.

As described above, Sihanouk made a fairly successful go of neutralism during his early years in power, pursuing relations with friends near and far of various ideological stripes and obtaining aid from many different sources. A strong case can be made, though, that the Prince was ultimately done in by his famously 'mercurial' temperament and often impetuous words and actions. As a number of sources have noted, Sihanouk personalised not only his domestic politics but his foreign policy to an excessive degree.[55] It was arguably his *ad hominem* verbal attacks and his lurching from one diplomatic campaign to another that soured his most important relationship—with Washington—more than his flirtations with the socialist powers. The relative sympathy and goodwill that many Americans felt for him during the early years of his regime were gradually eroded, and those who defended Cambodia's interests against the encroachments by Bangkok and Saigon became increasingly isolated voices in the policy-making wilderness. The most appropriate epitaph for US-Cambodian relations during the Sihanouk era is perhaps an observation made by former secretary of state and long-time senior statesman Dean Acheson just a week before Kennedy's death: "Sihanouk would be a great

55. Excellent critical analyses of Sihanouk's foreign policies are in Osborne, *Sihanouk*, and Michael Leifer, *Cambodia: The Search for Security* (London: Pall Mall Press, 1967). For strongly anti-Sihanouk accounts from French observers of this period, see Charles Meyer, *Derrière le sourire khmer* (Paris: Plon, 1971) and Bernard Hamel, *Sihanouk et le drame cambodgien* (Paris: L'Harmattan, 1993).

guy, if he wasn't such a damned fool and didn't say so many crazy things."[56] Sihanouk famously quoted a French general during the decolonisation period who had referred to him as "*un fou de génie*" (a crazy genius), but in the eyes of many foreigners, genius was outweighed by eccentricity and even instability.[57] Successful neutralism requires the ability to walk a tightrope between competing blocs, but Sihanouk tended to slip and fall, and his ability to scramble back up and keep on walking diminished over time.

Neutralism in Laos was first mooted when Souvanna Phouma was in power in the 1950s, but it only became a reality in the early 1960s, particularly after the establishment of the second coalition government. In a fairly narrow sense Laos retained some degree of neutralism until the end of the RLG. Vientiane maintained diplomatic relations with both the DRV and the Republic of Vietnam (the latter re-established in 1964 after the earlier rupture), as well as with the PRC and the USSR, even while the socialist powers continued to maintain a strong presence in the Pathet Lao zone.[58] However, a neutralist stance in foreign policy became increasingly less meaningful as the tripartite structure of the 1962 government fell apart, as the Neutralist political and military forces dissolved into Leftist and Rightist factions, and, most importantly, as there were effectively two separate governments in Laos—one based in Vientiane and Luang Prabang and the other in Sam Neua—from 1964 until the establishment of the last PGNU in 1974. Perhaps

56. Memorandum of Telephone Conversation between Acheson and Deputy Assistant Secretary of State Rice, 14 Nov 1963 (Document 113).

57. Norodom Sihanouk, *Souvenirs doux et amers* (Paris: Hachette, 1981), p. 199. A number of the declassified documents in *FRUS* have been somewhat Bowdlerised where diplomats are making frank assessments of Sihanouk's personality and mental state.

58. Memorandum of Telephone Conversation between Acheson and Deputy Assistant Secretary of State Rice, 14 Nov 1963 (Document 113). Much still remains to be learned about Chinese ties with the Pathet Lao. The account of a high-ranking PRC cadre who spent several years there in the mid-1960s makes interesting reading, particularly his obvious disapproval of the extent to which the Vietnamese were running the show. According to him, Kaysone Phomvihan had gone to Beijing in October 1964 and specifically requested Chinese aid. See Hu Zhengqing, *Yige waijiaoguan de riji* [Journal of a Diplomat] (Jinan: Huanghe Chubanshe, 1991), p. 5.

most important was the bitter reality that each of these two governments had its own supporters and its allies, none of whom were about to abandon the cause.

If neutralism was problematic and at best ephemeral for Cambodia and Laos, despite the best efforts and intentions of Sihanouk and Souvanna, neutrality vis-à-vis the growing conflict in Vietnam was simply not a realistic prospect, for several reasons. The first and most fundamental factor was geographical proximity. The border between Cambodia and South Vietnam was simply too porous and the prospect of sanctuary on Cambodian territory too attractive—and, indeed, too necessary—for the revolutionary forces, and once the first NLF units took refuge on the other side of that border, the fate of Cambodian neutrality was effectively sealed. In the case of Laos, the close proximity of the DRV to the Pathet Lao liberated zone on the one hand, and the crucial strategic value of the Panhandle for the expansion of the Ho Chi Minh Trail on the other, meant that the Vietnamese and Lao conflicts became inextricably intertwined.

The second reason was the legacy of the Indochinese Communist Party, the predecessor of the Vietnamese, Cambodian, and Lao revolutionary movements. The Cambodian and Lao communist parties only came into existence as separate entities in 1951 and 1955 respectively and remained closely linked to their Vietnamese mentors. Even though neither the Lao nor the Cambodian revolutionaries were the puppets of Hanoi that their opponents tended to portray them as, for all parties concerned Indochina was a single battlefield.[59] (This solidarity would break down with the degradation of relations between the Vietnamese and the Khmer Rouge, but for the Pathet Lao it remained constant.) Just as the accusations of 'Northern aggression' in the South had little real mean-

59. Sihanouk routinely belittled the Khmer Rouge as instruments of "foreign masters", and the American documents throughout this period attribute almost no agency to the Pathet Lao. Similarly, the Lao party histories cited earlier assume that the US masterminded every political and military development in Laos.

ing in the context of the Vietnamese revolution, the expectation that agreements signed at Geneva or anywhere else could force the DRV to stop supporting its Lao comrades and withdraw its forces was unrealistic.

Finally, the mirror image of the second factor was the American commitment to Indochina as a region. Although South Vietnam remained the focal point of the US military effort, especially where ground forces were concerned, its neighbours were always on the American radar screen (figuratively at first and later literally, once the bombing campaigns began). Cambodia may have been to some extent a "sideshow" and Laos "the end of nowhere", as one author has put it,[60] but given the scale of the US involvement and the ferocity of the conflict in Vietnam, however, even a somewhat peripheral role in that conflict was sufficiently destructive to render any talk of 'neutrality' for either country desperate and ultimately meaningless.

60. Stevenson, *End of Nowhere*.

9

BEFORE THE QUAGMIRE: THE US ARMY AND SOUTHEAST ASIA

Brian M. Linn

'Why Vietnam?' remains the great and unanswerable question of the United States' military experience in Southeast Asia during the Cold War. Indeed, it is very difficult to even conceptualise the history of US military interest in Southeast Asia between 1947 and 1965 without immediately fitting it into a framework of the Vietnam War. But much as foreknowledge of World War II has shaped historical analysis of the inter-war period, so awareness of the looming tragedy of Vietnam has coloured interpretations of the US military experience in Southeast Asia in the early years of the Cold War. In both cases, the ensuing war became the military standard, the yardstick by which weapons, doctrines, individuals, training, organisation, and so forth are measured. Those who apparently predicted the oncoming war are praised as prescient outside-the-box thinkers, while those lacking a crystal ball, or preoccupied with resolving immediate problems, are dismissed as brass-hat reactionaries. Thus the blitzkrieg campaigns of 1939 and 1940 vindicate the armour advocates of the 1920s, and Mao's 1930s revolutionary warfare concepts are validated by North Vietnam's victory 40 years later.

But working backwards from the culminating event often blinds military historians to the strategic priorities of contemporary officers. Focusing only on the weapons or doctrines that proved most important in World War II obscures the issues that 1920s US Army officers believed important—harbour fortifications, beach and coast defence, etc.—many of which had little relevance by 1941. Similarly, the performance of doctrines, weapons, and individuals in the Vietnam War provides an unreliable measure of the 1950s US Army's understanding of Southeast Asia. This chapter represents a preliminary effort to study history forwards—to examine what officers in the US Army in the early Cold War thought about Southeast Asia.

The recent conflicts in Iraq and Afghanistan have led some prominent military and civilian pundits to warn that the US Army might be 'broken'—that it is, or will soon be, unable to function as a military organisation on any level, from its personnel system to its equipment. The ensuing debate over today's 'broken army' largely ignores the reality that virtually every war has 'broken' the US Army. World War II may have been one of the most shattering events in the army's history. Japan's unexpected surrender was followed by what one Army Chief of Staff referred to as "destructive demobilization", leaving the army "relatively impotent".[1] One future general fulminated, "In the warm glow of winning the Second World War, the American people deliberately destroyed the finest land force they ever created", with no thought to current national needs.[2] Another general recalled, "It had been a long, hard war. The whole nation had been behind it and now, everyone wanted to stop and go home immediately.... Let's face it, we did disintegrate."[3]

The human cost of this disintegration was considerable. Donald V. Bennett, returning from combat duty in Europe, was

1. J. Lawton Collins, 'U.S. Strategic Problems and the Development of the U.S. Armed Forces to Meet Them', Lecture at Imperial Defence College, London (27 May 1949), Dwight D. Eisenhower Library, Abilene, KS (hereafter DDEL): Speeches and Statements File (6), Box 42, J. Lawton Collins Papers. On the Cold War US Army, see Andrew J. Bacevich, *The Pentomic Era: The U.S. Army Between Korea and Vietnam* (Washington: National Defense University Press, 1986); Brian McAllister Linn, *The Echo of Battle: The U.S. Army's Way of War* (Cambridge, MA: Harvard University Press, 2007), pp. 151–92; Ingo Trauschweizer, *The Cold War U.S. Army: Building Deterrence for Limited War* (Lawrence: University Press of Kansas, 2008).

2. Donovan Yeuell, 'An Army That Can Fight', *Infantry Journal*, 63 (Dec 1948), p. 5.

3. George I. Forsythe Oral History, 1974, US Army Military History Institute, Carlisle, PA (hereafter MHI), vol. 1, p. 240.

reassigned to Japan in 1945. On leaving the troopship in Boston he was put on a train to Chicago with no heat, no water and no food for two days. When Bennett arrived, he found his promised leave was cancelled; he had been ordered to Oklahoma. He reached Oklahoma after another arduous journey and was reassigned to South Carolina with orders to report immediately. He spent his Christmas holiday driving to his new assignment only to be told the position was closed and he was longer needed. Bennett, having had enough, resigned his commission.[4] Bennett's Sinbadian voyages may have been extreme, but in the years following the war, millions of soldiers were similarly cast adrift. In August 1945 there were some 12 million Americans in uniform. Four months later nearly half had been discharged; by mid-1948 the army had fewer than 550,000 soldiers.[5] Or so it believed. According to one general officer, the service's paperwork was in such shambles that it was forced to institute a 'world-wide muster' day in 1946, ordering every soldier to get into formation to be counted. Even this drastic measure did not resolve the problem, since closer inspection revealed that many of the 'body count' forms were incorrectly filled out.[6] Even as it reeled from the trauma of demobilisation, the army struggled to meet the demands of post-war occupation and reconstruction, which required the army to deploy almost half its manpower overseas by mid-1948.

Congress refused to extend conscription, and in March 1947 the army lost access to its main source of manpower. This forced the army to compete for manpower with a booming post-war economy that paid unskilled factory workers twice what a soldier could make. Understandably, the best-educated and most technically competent left the ranks, leaving only the marginally competent 'career privates' and the resentful teenagers drafted in the last days

4. Donald V. Bennett Oral History, MHI, vol. 1, section 3, pp. 12–13. Bennett withdrew his resignation after finally being given a command and retired as a general.

5. Don Alan Carter, 'From G.I. to Atomic Soldier: The Development of U.S. Tactical Doctrine, 1945–1956', PhD dissertation, Ohio State University, 1987, p. 21.

6. William R. Desobry Oral History, 1977, MHI, vol. 1, section 4, p. 47.

of the war. In February 1946 the army secretary revealed that 50 per cent of the new recruits had enlisted only because it shortened their military obligation. He confessed, "Already many of our recruits are below the standard that should be set, [but] we dare not reject them for fear that better men will not be forthcoming."[7] The army exacerbated its own retention problems: as one senior officer confessed, "most of our inducements are all tending toward getting men out of the Army instead of re-enlisting".[8] The result was a clear decline in the quality of the enlisted ranks, a decline that was made worse by occupation duty and its attendant temptations of black-marketing and crime.[9]

A new mission: limited atomic war

The occupation forces soon found themselves drawn into local conflicts while simultaneously having to prepare for the growing threat of a third world war with the USSR. In Europe it appeared as if America's overseas land forces were little more than a tiny ceremonial guard who would be immediately swept away if the Red Army ever struck. To their superiors at home, it often appeared that the real enemies were, in no particular order, the atomic bomb, the Navy, the soon-to-be-independent Air Force, the political authorities, the newly formed defence intellectual community, the American public, and its own senior commanders. And in fact the army could not explain why—in an era of atomic bombs and intercontinental bombers—there was any need for anything beyond the smallest of ground forces. Even many who supported conscription looked to it as a means to provide education, trade skills, and

7. Robert P. Patterson to President, Subject: Increase in Pay for the Armed Forces (18 Feb 1946), in National Archives and Records Administration 2, College Park, MD (hereafter NARA2): Strategy and the Army Files, Folder 2, Box 1, Record Group 319.

8. Remarks of Gen. J. Lawton Collins, Background Material for the War Department Presentation to the Committee on the Armed Services (11 Feb 1947), Combined Arms Research Library, Fort Leavenworth, KS: N-15083-C.

9. Eugene P. Forrester Oral History, 1985, MHI, pp. 66–7. Ronald H. Spector, *In the Ruins of Empire: The Japanese Surrender and the Battle for Postwar Asia* (New York: Random House, 2007).

civic virtues rather than as the basis of a wartime army. Given the Soviet ground forces' overwhelming superiority in manpower and materiel, the first war plans asked the army in Europe to save itself by a precipitous and ignominious headlong retreat to England. The US Air Force was allocated the dominant role in these war plans, and American strategy was simple and direct: an all-out aerial atomic attack on Soviet cities, euphemistically termed 'general war'. Although President Dwight D. Eisenhower recognised such a war would immediately become a global holocaust, he reluctantly adopted this strategy of all-out atomic attack as his 'massive retaliation' policy. The US Navy had the vital role of defending the nation's commercial trade and attacking the enemy's periphery. But the army, other than fleeing to save itself, had no role in these plans. Or none until, perhaps, after the Soviet Union had been reduced to impotence, some surviving troops might be sent in to rebuild what was left. For officers who only a few years ago had fought the armies of fascist Germany and Japan, the new strategy consigning the army to the military dustbin was unacceptable.

Even before North Korean invaders turned the Cold War into 'hot war', army intellectuals began a two-pronged effort to undermine the United States' commitment to 'general war'. The first prong was an all-out attack on strategic nuclear warfare and Eisenhower's policy of 'massive retaliation'. Army critics decried this strategy as risky and ineffective. At worst, it risked a preemptive USSR attack on the United States' own cities, while at best it made a charred wasteland of the Soviet Union and unleashed international chaos. Army officers also claimed atomic warfare was immoral and inimical to the nation's long-term interests as leader of the 'Free World'. As General Lucius Clay told an air force audience in 1952, "the taking of an air bomb[ardment] to Russia until Russia herself has provoked total war will be inconsistent with the position of world leadership which we have assumed".[10]

10. Lucius D. Clay, 'Concept for Employment of Military Forces in Future War', Lecture, Air War College, 10 Apr 1952, Air Force Historical Research Agency, Maxwell Air Force Base, AL (hereafter AFHRA): K 239.716252-106.

The second part of the army effort was to invent and market a new form of warfare that would be far superior to the indiscriminate atomic holocaust of 'general war'. A 1950 guide summed up both the dilemma and the solution: "The Army, facing the probability of being out-numbered by the enemy ground forces, must have weapons systems for delivering mass destruction weapons against tactical targets." Only atomic weapons could "provide the shock effect" needed for American forces to defeat the Red Army masses.[11] But these atomic weapons could not be the air force's indiscriminate, city-destroying, multi-megaton thermonuclear bombs. Rather they were to be small-yield, highly accurate weapons that only targeted Soviet military formations, thus removing any possibility of the war escalating beyond the battlefield.

For much of the army, this concept of 'limited atomic war' soon became the be-all and end-all of both their professional and the service's existence. By the late 1950s the entire curriculum at the command and staff college was directed at atomic warfare. In 1957 the army reconfigured itself into 'Pentomic' divisions whose organisation, doctrine, and equipment all assumed that atomic weapons would be used in the next war. It soon unveiled a host of innovative, and sometimes bizarre, weapons for the atomic battlefield, including a 280 mm atomic cannon and a small, portable atomic mortar that could be used by infantry squads. Atomic warfare permeated service literature, from strategic studies to comic books. Although in retrospect the entire 'limited atomic war' experiments appear misguided, if not appalling, it is important to recognise the enormous institutional commitment it represented. The entire US Army's combat organisation, much of its budget, and, perhaps most importantly, its entire ideology of warfare were dedicated to this effort.

11. Combat Development Objectives Guide—Large Unit Operations (1954), NARA2: Box 33, Entry 55F, Record Group 337.

Southeast Asia in army thought

Although the United States Army had served as a colonial force in the Philippines since 1898, as an institution it gave very little thought to Southeast Asia before World War II. To army strategists, the Philippine islands were not so much an Asian as a Pacific possession. The army debate was between the 'imperialists', who supported a strong garrison in the Philippines and possible expansion into China, and the 'continentalists', who wished to withdraw from the Philippines and create an Alaska-Hawaii-Panama defence barrier. Not until very late in the 1930s did the United States government, and army commanders in the Philippines, begin to make contact with other Southeast Asian imperial powers for mutual defence against Japan.[12] During World War II the army's experience in Southeast Asia, barring the reconquest of the Philippines, was restricted largely to the all-but-forgotten China-Burma-India theatre. Afterwards, wartime agreements allocated the disarmament of Japanese troops to Great Britain, despite American misgivings about the re-imposition of colonial regimes.

At the start of the Cold War, most officers still regarded Southeast Asia as a peripheral region, of far less importance than Japan, China, or even Taiwan. But a variety of factors, both internal and external, led American strategists to shift their focus of containing communism from China to Southeast Asia, and in the process redefine the French struggle against the Viet Minh as an anti-communist crusade rather than a sordid imperialist conquest. In December 1949 the National Security Council submitted NSC 48/2, a paper outlining the threat posed by Soviet expansion into Southeast Asia and supporting US military, political, and economic assistance programmes to regimes under internal or external communist attack. The following April, President Harry S.

12. Brian McAllister Linn, *Guardians of Empire: The U.S. Army and the Pacific, 1902–1940* (Chapel Hill: University of North Carolina Press, 1997). Army priorities reflected those of the US government, whose State Department until 1953 titled the region the Philippine and Southeast Asia division.

Truman approved NSC 64, which recommended that "all practicable measures be taken to prevent further Communist expansion in Southeast Asia. Indochina is the key area of Southeast Asia and is under immediate threat."[13] When the Korean War broke out less than two months later, the American defence establishment perceived it as part of a general communist offensive in the Far East. It accelerated military aid to the French in Indochina even as Korea precluded the use of US Army forces there. In August 1950 Truman requested $4 million for military assistance; the final bill included $75 million for aid in "the general area of China".[14] American aid to the French for Indochina grew to $133 million in 1951, and with the American adoption of South Vietnam as a client, this grew to $446 million between 1955 and 1959. Despite being limited by the Geneva Accords to 342 advisers in South Vietnam, there were 732 American uniformed personnel assigned to Military Assistance Advisory Groups (MAAGs) in 1959. By 1961 there may have been 3200.[15]

From a very broad perspective, army perceptions of Southeast Asia appear to reflect those outlined in 1949–50 by President Truman, the Joint Chiefs of Staff, and the National Security Council. Army officers tended to regard Asia as one theatre of the Cold War, which was itself a global struggle between good and evil, freedom and tyranny, national survival and extinction. But army officers disagreed on a number of fundamental issues. Was the West losing or winning against the communist threat? Was a Soviet-American war inevitable, and if so, would it begin in Europe or

13. Office of Joint History, *History of the Joint Chiefs of Staff: The Joint Chiefs of Staff and the First Indochina War, 1947–1954* (Washington, D.C.: Office of the Chairman of the Joint Chiefs of Staff, 2004), p. 43.

14. Ibid., p. 54. Andrew J. Rotter, *The Path to Vietnam: Origins of the American Commitment to Southeast Asia* (Ithaca: Cornell University Press, 1987); Kathryn C. Statler, *Replacing France: The Origins of American Intervention in Vietnam* (Lexington: University of Kentucky Press, 2007).

15. Figures on US military assistance from Russell H. Fifield, *Southeast Asia in United States Policy* (New York: Frederick Praeger, 1963), pp. 103–4. On US military advising, see Ronald H. Spector, *The U.S. Army in Vietnam: Advice and Support: The Early Years, 1941–1960* (Washington, D.C.: US Army Center of Military History, 1983).

Asia? Could communists also be legitimate nationalists? Or was Colonel William O. Blandford correct when he wrote, in a 1952 Army War College paper, "Members of the Communist party in all nations are not members of a political power but rather the advance guard of Russian imperialism and are committed to the overthrow of the native government by fair means or foul"?[16] Was the primary threat the Soviet Union's strategic atomic arsenal or its ideologues, agents, subversives, and propagandists?[17] Or were the Soviet leaders realists who would not seek a war with the United States until they were sure they would win? General Lucius Clay acknowledged that "Stalin and his gang" might be successful for the next few decades, but "I do not believe that in any long drawn out period of world warfare of the type that we have now, that any but a free people can win it. And it has not yet been shown to me in any way how autocracy has been successful in overriding democracy."[18] But as some officers, such as Colonel William McKinley, maintained, "it is evident that the military and political position of the United States evidences many weaknesses, and that even the present position—unless it is somehow buttressed—will tend to weaken with time".[19] There were substantial differences as well between those who emphasised both the justice and the necessity of an immediate war with the Soviet Union, and those who argued, "Let us abandon foolish thoughts of wasting our blood and our resources on the endless steppes of Russia, in vain efforts to destroy all of the Russian armed forces.... Our children after us must live in this world. We do not want to create a vacuum and a chaos that will lay the seed of still another World War, nor do we

16. William O. Blandford, 'The Basis of Soviet Policies with Respect to the Far East', Army War College (hereafter AWC) student paper, MHI, 25 Mar 1952, p. 18.

17. Maynard N. Levenick, 'The Role of Free Governments, Parent and Colonial, in Communist Strategy', AWC student paper, 1 Apr 1953.

18. Clay, 'Concept for Employment'; Manton Eddy, 'Relationship of Land Power to Air Power', Lecture at AWC (1 Mar 1949), AFHRA: K 239.716249-28; Benjamin T. Ammons, 'The International Conferences at Yalta, Tehran, and Potsdam During World War II', AWC student paper, 24 Apr 1952.

19. William D. McKinley, 'The Struggle Between the United States and the USSR', AWC student paper, 1 Apr 1953, p. 19.

want to bleed our own nation white in the process."[20] There were officers who sought to use armed force to end the Cold War, and also those, such as Army Chief of Staff J. Lawton Collins, who insisted, "You've got to fight the cold war economically as well as militarily. If we don't improve the well-being of these people, communism is going to keep going, just as it did in China.... All we in the military can do is sort of a delaying action."[21]

In 1952 seven Army War College students wrote research papers on the topic, 'The Basis of Soviet Politics with Respect to the Far East'. Their views illustrate army attitudes in the early days of the Cold War. Officers agreed that the situation was critical: in the words of one student, "The USSR seeks control of the Far East as a stepping stone to the greater goal of world domination. This policy is being pursued under the unbending, ruthless leadership of the Kremlin."[22] They also dismissed any possibility that communist-led independence movements might reflect legitimate popular aspirations. Colonel Richard K. Boyd believed that "purely nationalistic aspirations sparked all the uprisings, but everywhere Moscow-trained leaders capitalized on them", so that most were now completely under Soviet control.[23] Colonel Roy Lasseter, Jr. saw Southeast Asia as "a tempting prize" in the global struggle between the United States and the USSR. If the region remained part of the 'Free World', it would seal communist expansion to the south and preserve vital natural resources. But, "Southeast Asia under Communist domination would furnish both defensive and offensive bases for military operations and further political and economic expansion". Lasseter recognised the differ-

20. Joseph C. Anderson, 'The Military Defeat of Russia', AWC student paper, 1 Apr 1953, p. 27; D.E. Beach, 'War Plan 1957', Lecture at AWC (29 Oct 1952), AFHRA: K 239.716252-117.

21. J. Lawton Collins, 'National Strategic Objectives', Lecture, AWC (20 Apr 1950), DDEL: Service School Speeches File (3), Box 43, J. Lawton Collins Papers.

22. Benjamin O. Turnage, Jr., 'The Basis of Soviet Policies with Respect to the Far East', AWC student paper, 24 Mar 1952, p. 27.

23. Richard K. Boyd, 'The Basis of Soviet Policies with Respect to the Far East', AWC student paper, 24 Mar 1952, p. 15. Haviland A.N. Connolly, 'US Security in the Far East-Pacific Ocean Area', AWC student paper, 15 Mar 1954.

ences between nationalists and communists. But while nationalism was "an evolutionary change" and generally a positive development, communists had infiltrated nationalist movements and were currently engaged in warfare in Indochina, Malaya, and the Philippines. Thus, although communists might claim to fight for nationalist goals, he believed "[e]very action taken and every technique and method used appear to be Soviet inspired and directed. There is little doubt that events in South East Asia will follow the same pattern of conquest by force and violence directly supported by Soviet Russia as has occurred in China and Korea."[24] These officer-students agreed with their colleagues, that Southeast Asia was vital to US interests, was under immediate threat by Russian-Chinese aggression, and required a substantial US commitment.

One rare dissenter was Colonel Theodore Hoffman. His 1958 student paper focused on the Philippines, where the Huk rebellion was apparently on the verge of defeat. Hoffman showed more awareness of the region's distinctiveness than most of his fellow officers. He warned that the US could not simply transpose the ideals and values of liberal capitalism on the region. Southeast Asia's most powerful ideology, he wrote, was nationalism, but even that was a contested term since, "cultural, social, religious, [and] ethnic differences have so diversified the inhabitants that no natural ties bind them together".[25] Rather than espousing the 'us versus them' view of his fellow officers, Hoffman considered it vital that the new governments avoid becoming economically dependent on the US. Instead, he stressed, the "exchange of trade, of culture, of education, of 'know-how', of mutual assistance among Southeast Asian countries must be promoted, encouraged, and led by the United States.... Our policies as a whole should tend to draw the nations together into a community with a common will and purpose."[26]

24. Roy Lasseter, Jr., 'The Basis of Soviet Policies with Respect to the Far East', AWC student paper, 24 Mar 1952, p. 22.

25. Theodore F. Hoffman, 'An Independent Philippine Republic Our Channel to Southeast Asia', AWC student paper, 19 Mar 1958, p. iii.

26. Ibid., p. 42.

Given their view of inevitable communist aggression, army officers strongly supported the idea of collective security in the region. And with President Eisenhower committed to reducing troop levels in Asia, it was vital that the United States find allies to provide manpower. But there was a consensus that SEATO was a flawed organisation incapable of fulfilling US goals.[27] Officers often contrasted SEATO with NATO: the latter had a unified command and a standing army, while SEATO had little more than a number of committees lacking any power to compel action. They dismissed SEATO's effort at joint manoeuvres in 1956 as a disaster. Lieutenant Colonel Davis W. Way's 1958 summation—"the alliance is weak and it is not accomplishing fully its intended purpose"—typified Cold War attitudes. Like several other commentators, Way noted that only three Asian nations belonged to the alliance and most regional governments were hostile or indifferent to it. Moreover, he found the SEATO treaty so vague he doubted it could be invoked to protect any nation in the region. Way concluded that SEATO's deterrent value lay almost entirely in the threat of United States retaliation, and he questioned whether the US could actually repel a communist attack without resorting to its atomic arsenal, itself of limited use.[28]

Many of Way's conclusions were echoed in a paper by his classmate, Lieutenant Colonel Francis M. Smith, entitled 'Military Strategy in Southeast Asia'. Like other officers, he warned against comparing SEATO to NATO and emphasised the area's complexity: "the SEATO environment is one of many currents—economies are not complementary and lack viability, nationalism and anticolonialism are widespread, and both Neutralism and Communism

27. Adrian St. John, 'SEATO: Strawman or Paper Tiger', AWC student paper, 25 Jan 1960; John DuV. Stevens, 'US Security in the Far East-Pacific Ocean Area', AWC student paper, 15 Mar 1954; Guy N. Blencoe, 'US Security in the Far East-Pacific Ocean Area', AWC student paper, 15 Mar 1954; Connolly, 'US Security'.

28. Davis W. Way, 'The United States Roles in the Southeast Asia Collective Defense Treaty (SEATO)', AWC student paper, 19 Mar 1958, p. iv; Frederick J. Kroesen, 'The Precarious Position of Thailand', AWC student paper, 15 Dec 1962.

are in competition with the collective security efforts represented by SEATO. Underlying all of these forces is a failure of the people to appreciate the Communist threat."[29] His detailed analysis of SEATO's armed forces convinced him that "in the absence of the deterrence to limited war provided by the United States policy of 'massive retaliation', local forces for defence against Communist aggression are inadequate and the availability of sufficient balanced forces from members outside the treaty area to cope with Communist aggression seems problematical."[30] In short, SEATO was a paper tiger: its ability to protect its members relied solely on the threat of United States atomic retaliation.

Lieutenant Colonel Hugh F. Queenin's 1960 War College thesis represented something of a recantation. Four years earlier he had published a generally positive article in the *Military Review* that concluded SEATO had adequate military power and that "in the event of overt Communist aggression" the US could "ensure the complete destruction of military targets without endangering unrelated civilian centers".[31] But by 1960 Queenin described SEATO as a dysfunctional alliance since its inception, and he was even more pessimistic about the long-term prospects for the region. SEATO was "only one element" in a regional security programme, and while the US could provide equipment and training, "the governments and peoples of Southeast Asia must be made to understand that they have to provide the will, initiative, and action necessary to overcome the Communist subversive activities".[32] The problem was that time was running out; such a profound transformation was unlikely to come before it was too late.

Queenin refuted the view of many Americans who regarded all 'Asians' as identical. Southeast Asia, he reminded them, contained

29. Francis M. Smith, 'Military Strategy in Southeast Asia', AWC student paper, 19 Mar 1958, p. ii.

30. Ibid., p. 38.

31. Hugh F. Queenin, 'The Military Implications of SEATO', *Military Review*, 35 (Feb 1956), p. 29.

32. Hugh F. Queenin, 'The Military Implications of the Southeast Asia Treaty Organization', AWC student paper, 25 Jan 1960, p. 57.

peoples of diverse races, religions, and socio-economic status, many of whom had long animosities with each other. Compounding the problem, the post-colonial 'ruling elite' maintained their power by suppressing dissidents and intimidating neighbours. Thus both historical and current conditions created political instability and "divisive separatism rather than cohesive regionalism".[33] Not only did Southeast Asian governments lack the will, or even the desire, to support each other, they lacked the means as well. In his view, most of the region's military forces were little more than constabularies incapable of defending their own territory from invasion—the only exception being North Vietnam. In his view, "[a]n act of overt Communist aggression, under current conditions, would probably result in the loss of major areas in Southeast Asia and logistic operations under such circumstances would almost be certainly be restricted to the ports of Saigon and Bangkok".[34] Given SEATO's inherent weakness, the growth of communist influence, and the "sociological incompatibility" of the region's peoples, Queenin concluded that the only solution was for the United States to "continue to demonstrate its willingness to participate in a 'limited war' defense of Southeast Asia. In so doing she must be prepared to overcome unfavorable reaction at home and abroad; and must be prepared to provide major ground forces ... to any SEATO action in the treaty area."[35]

Queenin joined many officers in criticising the Eisenhower administration's commitment to a strategy of 'massive retaliation', which essentially made nuclear weapons the first option in any conflict with the Soviet Union. In his view, SEATO's dependence on American logistical support made its members even more vulnerable to atomic attack than its opponents. The political effects of using atomic weapons would be catastrophic: the United States

33. Queenin, 'Military Implications', *Military Review*, p. 21.

34. Queenin, 'Military Implications', AWC student paper, p. 47.

35. Ibid., p. 57; William H. McKenzie III, 'Indochina: Center of Conflict', AWC student paper, 9 Mar 1962, p. 72; William O. Morgan, 'A SEATO Military Standing Force', AWC student paper, 7 Mar 1962.

would alienate not only the populations of Southeast Asia, but most of the world. Moreover, as Lieutenant Colonel Smith observed, 'massive retaliation' was only a bluff, since "it is most doubtful that any United States administration, or the American people, would be willing to risk an exchange of mass destructive weapons and all-out war in order to fulfill SEATO commitments".[36] Like other officers, Smith criticised atomic weapons' limited utility in Southeast Asian terrain. While they might be of some use against a Chinese or North Vietnamese invasion, "the most serious threat now seems to be of the covert type characterized by subversion and insurrection".[37] As Way noted, "the atomic era is the era for subversion, political infiltration and partisan warfare; and the doctrine of 'massive retaliation' may have little or no application as a continuing deterrent in Southeast Asia".[38]

If army officers subscribed to a bipolar, and increasingly pessimistic, view of Southeast Asia, they revealed a more balanced perspective when they wrote about the individual nations in the region. They might see the region in the context of a monolithic Cold War struggle between communism and the 'Free World', but when they examined the military situation in Indonesia, Malaysia, the Philippines, or Vietnam, they described unique and distinct cultural, personal, historical, and other distinguishing factors.

Students at the War College were remarkably consistent in their assessment of Indonesia. They recognised its instability and potential for civil war, its strategic importance, and the strength of its indigenous communist party. They were leery of direct American military involvement, and accepted both Indonesia's non-alignment policy and its refusal to join either the Soviet or American axis as rational choices. One 1954 student paper argued that neutrality was actually more beneficial to the US than an alliance; a 1963 paper was entitled 'Indonesia: A Case Study in Neutralism'. Army officers viewed Sukarno as a nationalist, not a commu-

36. Smith, 'Military Strategy', p. 31.
37. Ibid., p. 21.
38. Way, 'United States Roles', pp. 27–38.

nist, and recognised his skill at securing aid from both the Soviet Union and the United States without compromising his nation's own interests. By the 1960s they were confident that the Indonesian armed forces could defeat any communist uprising, a prediction that soon proved accurate.[39]

Cold War army perceptions of the Malayan Emergency are of special interest. Some historians argue that the US Army failed to apply the lessons of Malaya in Vietnam, thus implying that if the US had applied these lessons it would have secured South Vietnam's independence. To these advocates, the Malayan Emergency taught the importance of co-ordinating military and civil affairs, emphasising local security forces and police, restraints on firepower, small-unit patrolling, and extensive intelligence operations. Others claim that the US Army was over-influenced by the Malayan example—and that the US lost the war because it listened to the British instead of following its own distinct American Way of War based on firepower, going all out against the enemy, and other iconic values.[40]

With such speculation on both sides, it is interesting to see how little attention the US Army's intellectual community actually devoted to studying the counterinsurgency campaign in Malaya. During the entire period the Emergency was fought, not a single student at the War College chose to write his thesis on this topic. Nor did the army high command direct the War College to incorporate the lessons of Malaya into the curriculum. In the army's professional journals throughout the 1950s and into early

39. Walter E. Tardy, 'The Strategic Importance of Indonesia', AWC student paper, 18 Feb 1957; Blencoe, 'US Security'; Arthur S. Hyman, 'Indonesia: A Case Study in Neutralism', AWC student paper, 8 Mar 1963; Frank E. Burgher, 'Indonesia: The Soviet Threat', AWC student paper, 8 Mar 1963. For the perspective of a US Marine Corps officer, see Carl W. Hoffman, 'Indonesia: At the Crossroads', AWC student paper, 10 Feb 1961.

40. John Nagl, *Learning to Eat Soup with a Knife: Counterinsurgency Lessons from Malaya and Vietnam* (Chicago: University of Chicago Press, 2005); Sam Sarkesian, *Unconventional Conflicts in a New Security Era: Lessons from Malaya and Vietnam* (Westport, CT: Greenwood Press, 1993); Harry G. Summers, Jr., *On Strategy: The Vietnam War in Context* (Washington, D.C.: Government Printing Office, 1981).

1961, analysis of Malaya was largely confined to a paragraph or two in the 'professional notes' section. The few published articles were mostly by British officers who were veterans of the conflict. One exception was a 1963 analysis by Lieutenant Colonel William F. Long, who examined Malaya, the French defeat in Indochina, and the Madagascar and Kenyan campaigns for common denominators in counterinsurgency. Long acknowledged Malaya was a successful campaign, but in comparing it with Indochina, he noted that in both cases "the most significant fact is that the insurgents succeeded in bringing about an effective degree of independence, either directly or as a result of reform and concessions by the colonial powers, regardless of the outcome of military operations".[41] To Long, the key lessons of Malaya were Britain's ability to maintain civil authority and political control of the countryside, to provide security for the population, and to undertake necessary economic reforms. These all resulted in separating the hard-core guerrillas from the population. But at least as far as the army's professional education system was concerned, there is little evidence that the Malayan Emergency significantly influenced American thinking about guerrilla warfare, communist insurgency, or Southeast Asia.

American officers were far more familiar with political, economic, and military conditions in the Philippines than anywhere else in Southeast Asia, a reflection of the army's decades of garrison service in the archipelago. They shared Lieutenant Colonel Guy N. Blencoe's 1954 assessment that "the Philippines are strategically essential to the U.S. in that they constitute one of the key positions in our front line of defense in the Pacific".[42] The Philippines were also important because, in the words of a 1962 Command and General Staff College lecture, of ideological reasons. They provided "dynamic disproof of any charges of imperialism that may be leveled against the United States" and served as inspi-

41. William F. Long, 'Counterinsurgency: Some Antecedents for Success', *Military Review*, 43 (Oct 1963): 90–7, quotations on pp. 91–2. R.L. Clutterbuck, 'Malaya: A Case Study', *Military Review*, 43 (Sep 1963): 63–78.

42. Blencoe, 'US Security', p. 9.

ration for "democratic nations throughout the world".[43] Yet some army officers questioned whether US interests were being served by an alliance with dysfunctional, corrupt, and often repressive governments. They noted the Philippines' deep economic problems, its double-digit unemployment, and its ethnic and religious divisions and wondered if it could survive. Surprisingly, some officers blamed the United States for continuing the colonial relationship. A 1958 AWC student committee noted the US was currently providing over $600 million in aid and essentially underwriting the costs of the Philippine armed forces. The students argued it would be beneficial for both the US and the Philippines "to have the Filipinos throw off the shackles of dependence on the United States".[44] Colonel Hoffman noted that while the US emphasised its role in creating Philippine democracy, "our policies have been inconsistent in that we emphasized political independence on the one hand and economic dependence on the other". Hoffman urged cutting US aid to $75 million and investing it in training for administrators, scientists, and educators, who could then help the rest of Southeast Asia. In his view, "Our main costs will not be in money and personnel, but in patience, in understanding, in effort to learn about these people of the area, in determination to assist without seeking tangible gain in return."[45]

The US Army studied guerrilla warfare in the Philippines more than any other conflict, with the possible exception of Vietnam. Some officers fought alongside Filipino guerrillas during the reconquest of 1944–45; some had even encountered the communist Hukbalahap, or Huks, in Luzon. After the war, the Huks, now renamed the People's Liberation Army (HMB), rose up against

43. Instruction Circular 7: Area Studies, Command and General Staff College, 8 Oct 1962, NARA2: Box 34, RG 337.

44. Course 1, Course 2, Committee 1, AY 1958–1959, 'Southeast Asia and United States, Policy Problems' (31 Oct 1958), MHI: Box 1958/1959-2.

45. Hoffman, 'An Independent Philippine Republic', p. 45. On army distaste for Philippine politics, see 14th Radio Broadcasting and Leaflet Battalion, 'Psychological Warfare Area Handbook for Philippines', 1957, NARA2: Box 92, E UD-7, RG 550.

the government and for almost a decade controlled much of Central Luzon. The United States sent both financial and military assistance as well as several expert advisers. One of these, Air Force Colonel Edward Lansdale, would become famous (or infamous) as Filipino defence minister Ramon Magsaysay's counterinsurgency expert. Another veteran, Russell Volckmann, helped write the army's counterinsurgency doctrine in the 1950s. Despite the general Cold War mentality of the officer corps, and the lack of analytical papers, there was surprising sympathy for the Huks, or at least for the peasantry who were in arms. In 1950 Chief of Staff Collins declared, "The Huks are not Commies, not by any manner or means. They try to do something about the poor conditions in the Philippines."[46] There was also a consensus that the Huk rebellion was a unique event—caused more by the failings of the Philippine government then by any appeal of communism to the Filipino peasantry. Colonel Donald McGrain's 1956 War College thesis criticised the officers and soldiers of the Philippine armed forces for acting as "occupation forces rather than combat forces" and dismissed the federal police as "lazy, incompetent, or corrupt".[47] Both the government and the armed forces persisted in viewing the Huks as bandits, whereas the population "believed in the HMB cause and saw it as a hope for a better existence where previously no hope had existed at all".[48]

McGrain, like other American officers, idealised Magsaysay as a pro-American nationalist who stood up to the communists and the corrupt landlords, politicians, and military officers. Indeed, the Filipino president soon became an iconic figure against whom all other Southeast Asian leaders were compared—and inevitably fell short. But the implications of this hero worship were not lost on Long, who commented it was "a disturbing observation . . . that men of Magsaysay's caliber have also been on the other side".[49]

46. Collins, 'National Strategic Objectives'.

47. Donald MacGrain, 'Anti-Dissident Operations in the Philippines', AWC student paper, 26 Mar 1956, p. 13.

48. Ibid., p. 14.

49. Long, 'Counterinsurgency', 91.

The Cold War army intellectuals' interpretation of the narrative of the Huk rebellion shaped their analysis; the perceived lessons of the Philippine experience essentially confirmed the army's current counterinsurgency doctrine. In the words of one analyst, "in the end, the Hukbalahap military forces were beaten to the ground—leaving aside the effect of the civic action programmes—largely by more orthodox means".[50] Officers downplayed the harshness of the Philippine military's operations against the peasantry, choosing to focus on the benevolent civic reform policies that Magsaysay and his supporters publicised.[51] Thus the limited study that officers devoted to the Huk rebellion may have actually hampered the army's ability to appreciate the challenge of communist guerrilla warfare later in Indochina.

In the estimation of army officers in the 1950s, much of the outcome of the Cold War in Southeast Asia hinged on what two War College faculty—John M. Palmer and Richard Stilwell—termed "The Indochina Contest."[52] Writing under a directive from the army staff, the two colonels conceded that North Vietnam was a formidable opponent: its population was "vigorous and martial", its army "battle tested and good", and its "leadership dedicated and experienced. No matter how one looks at it, Ho Chi Minh still has the stature of a national hero."[53] In contrast, South Vietnam was in a "state of political chaos", and the American and French aid programmes were ineffective. In their view, the US should either pull out of Vietnam and focus on Cambodia and Thailand, or "deploy its first team to that area" and fully commit itself to the new government of Ngo Dinh Diem and to creating a viable army. In their view, "the objective is to establish stability and national security. Imposition of sophisticated Western style democratic methods and procedures has no part in this emergency program!"[54] Thus, like

50. Robert Ross Smith, 'The Hukbalahap Insurgency', *Military Review*, 45 (Jun 1965): 41.

51. Andrew J. Birtle, *U.S. Army Counterinsurgency and Contingency Operations Doctrine, 1942–1976* (Washington, D.C.: Center of Military History, 2006), pp. 55–69.

52. John M. Palmer and Richard G. Stilwell, 'The Indochina Contest', AWC Faculty Study, 28 Oct 1954, MHI.

53. Ibid., p. 38.

54. Ibid., p. 39.

their political superiors, Palmer and Stilwell focused on the immediate and the tactical.

The Palmer-Stilwell report mirrored the views of most army officers in the 1950s: a mixture of insistence on Vietnam's importance and resignation at the weakness of its government and military. Thus one 1958 AWC student committee, after criticising Diem and the Vietnamese army's incompetence and brutality, concluded, "whether we like it or not, this exposed salient in the Free World has become a showcase for what American friendship, support, and material aid can do in Asia".[55] Colonel Donald Clayman, also writing in 1954, declared that "control of Indochina is the key to domination of all Southeast Asia" and the struggle there had "world-wide political and psychological implications which make a Communist defeat imperative".[56] Clayman viewed the conflict as a legitimate anti-colonial reform movement that had been corrupted: "the majority of the Indochinese supporting the Viet Minh are not Communists, they support the Communist forces because they desire freedom and are intensely Anti-French." French military operations had been "ineffective" because most Vietnamese "have a strong dislike of the French and do not trust them".[57] Yet despite his pessimism about France's chances of success, Clayman urged the United States to provide more aid to the French so that they could "gain a decisive victory".[58] His reasoning presaged the 'domino' principle. The region was not only vital for its natural resources, but also crucial in terms of prestige. "[D]efeat in Indochina would render Western political, economic, and diplomatic activities ineffective throughout the whole area."[59] At the same time, he urged Americans to "make a comprehensive study of the operations in Indochina" as a means of defeating similar revolutionary wars in other areas.[60]

55. Course 2, Committee 2, 'Southeast Asia and United States, Policy Problems' (31 Oct 1958), AY 1958–59, MHI: Box 1958/1959-2.
56. Donald C. Clayman, 'The Strategic Importance of Indochina', AWC student paper, 31 Mar 1953, p. 36.
57. Ibid.
58. Ibid., p. 38.
59. Ibid., p. 37.
60. Ibid., p. 38.

But some officers opposed further expansion of US military presence in Vietnam and were harshly critical of American support to France. In 1954 Colonel Guy Blencoe argued, "aid to the French in Indochina appears to the Asians more like an extension of the yokes of colonialism which they are all trying to throw off, than an honest effort to permit their participation in the civil rights programmes, and the economic and social reforms which we aim to sponsor".[61] A year later, Lieutenant Colonel William F. Lewis argued, "US observers (military and civilian) showed themselves to be not impervious to the American propensity for wishful thinking" in their support for French plans and "emphasized the importance of manpower and materiel in order to continue the French in the struggle. Not too much was said about the factor of relative spirit." With the French now departed from Vietnam, the US was repeating their mistakes—supporting an unpopular regime, creating an indigenous military force in its own army's image, and ignoring political solutions in favour of military ones. In his view, "The Vietminh proved that a well-led and indoctrinated guerrilla force is more than a match in this sort of terrain for a better equipped US-type organization, less well-led and indoctrinated." As such, "the only fit adversary for a specially trained and politically inspired force" such as the Viet Minh was "another such force. That means effective planning and the primary role to indigenous forces. Foreign advisors should be strictly in the background.... Foreign organization, equipment, and techniques must be boldly adjusted to the terrain and the people."[62] The American advisers were not only mistaken in their efforts to produce a South Vietnamese clone of the US Army, they were also doing a poor job of securing popular support: "Living like 'Roman conquerors' in a foreign land is not calculated to build mutual trust and enduring friendship."[63]

61. Blencoe, 'US Security', p. 15; Connolly, 'US Security'.
62. William F. Lewis, 'National Policy for Limited War', AWC student paper, 14 Mar 1955, p. 28.
63. Ibid., p. 37.

Lewis's comments underscore the diversity of army thought about Vietnam and the lack of consensus on crucial issues, including their perception of Ngo Dinh Diem. Palmer and Stilwell's 1954 report highlighted this ambivalence: Diem "may not be the best man available, but he has the basic attributes which warrant our support".[64] A 1958 AWC student committee noted the US was pouring as much as $2 million a day into South Vietnam, with the result that "South Vietnam has a spurious, artificial prosperity". But despite US efforts to portray it as a democracy, "actual leadership remains largely in [Diem's] hands and a very small immediate group around him, whom he trusts".[65] Lieutenant Colonel William Harris, who believed South Vietnam was "a showcase of American aid in Southeast Asia", described Diem as personally popular, especially with the peasants, and "a courageous, crusading, militant foe of the Communists". In his view, "future United States policy must provide for continued support of Diem because no alternative, no other man, can hope to lead the people as Diem has led them."[66] But another officer, noting Diem's "police state methods", his use of "repression and reprisal", and the widespread popular disgust with his regime, commented that "[o]n balance, the Government of Vietnam presents its people with a social order whose effects are hardly distinguishable from those in North Vietnam".[67] A year later, Colonel Cornelius A. Murphy was even more outspoken: "Even if the communist threat were disregarded, it has become obvious that Diem is not the kind of leader which the United States should support in order to expand our philosophy in the world."[68] Murphy's opinion, shared by some of his colleagues, was that it was time for the United States to "arrange for the installa-

64. Palmer and Stilwell, 'Indochina Conflict', p. 42.

65. Course 2, Committee 1, 'Southeast Asia and United States'.

66. William J. Harris, 'Vietnam: A Showcase of American Aid in Southeast Asia', AWC student paper, 10 Feb 1961, p. 46.

67. Robert C. Dennison, 'The Importance of South Vietnam', AWC student paper, 5 Feb 1962, p. 24.

68. Cornelius A. Murphy, 'Vietnam: Villainy in the Villages', AWC student paper, 8 Mar 1963, p. 42.

tion of a suitable president in the Republic of Vietnam".[69]

In 1957 Lieutenant General Carter Magruder lectured War College students about how the army planned to fight a hypothetical 'limited war' in South Vietnam. Envisioning a North Vietnamese attack, Magruder predicted the South Vietnamese forces would retreat in good order as the US Navy quickly interdicted the enemy's supply routes along the coast. The army would immediately airlift a paratroop division and a contingent of advisers for the South Vietnamese, building up to three divisions within two months and 300,000 soldiers within six months. Over a third of these troops would be deployed on logistical duties, creating the supply and transport infrastructure to allow the combat forces to come to grips with the enemy. The army would also deploy four long-range-missile battalions equipped with low-yield tactical atomic weapons. Not only would these weapons prevent any repetition of Dien Bien Phu, they could shatter any North Vietnamese concentrations. Yet Magruder emphasised, "we would not want to make casualties of a lot of Vietnamese" and that "judging by the experience of the French, it is doubtful if atomic weapons ... would be decisive".[70] Despite being unable to use the army's much-vaunted new tactical atomics, Magruder was confident that if the logistic problems were resolved, the army, with minimal help from the South Vietnamese, would soon be victorious.

Although almost all army officers agreed that Indochina was crucial to the security of the 'Free World' and that a communist takeover would be a disaster, they disagreed on the wisdom of committing American forces to protect South Vietnam. Similarly, officers consistently disagreed over whether the growing communist guerrilla resistance in South Vietnam was due to such internal factors as the corruption of the South Vietnamese government and

69. Ibid., p. iii; Robert J. Delaney, 'Republic of Vietnam: Can We Win?' AWC student paper, 6 Mar 1964; Dennison, 'Importance'; E.A. Rudquist, 'The True Reflection of South Vietnam', AWC student paper, 9 Mar 1962.

70. Carter Magruder, 'Army Logistics', Lecture at AWC (15 Feb 1957), AWC Lectures AY 1956–57, MHI.

the ineptitude of its armed forces or to external aggression from North Vietnam. In retrospect, it is clear that even those who supported military intervention n South Vietnam were uncertain of its results. Many of their conclusions anticipated the problems the United States would encounter in its efforts to defend South Vietnam. Palmer and Stilwell emphasised that "one of the great lessons of Indochina is that one cannot win political victories by military battles alone"—a 'lesson' that has still not been assimilated by much of the US Army even four decades after its precipitate withdrawal from Vietnam.[71] Lewis noted that US officers displayed "a propensity for wishful thinking" and focused too much on firepower and materiel, and too little on ideology, politics, and motivation.[72] Clayman recognised that, "Determined guerrilla forces can successfully combat an organized army in rough and undeveloped terrain provided the have the sympathy and cooperation of the local population."[73] Long's 1963 analysis of recent counterinsurgency campaigns led him to conclude, "Stage one, the winning of an effective degree of population support, is the critical stage." Governments that could couple political and economic reforms with effective military action could render the insurgency stillborn, but "it is doubtful that an outside power can be effective in a people's war once stage one consolidation is accomplished by the insurgents".[74] Within three years, the US commander in Vietnam, determining that the Viet Cong and North Vietnamese had reached the 'third stage' of conventional warfare, would commit US forces into battle.

Conclusion

The US Army in the 1950s, and particularly its experience in Southeast Asia, has generally been regarded as setting the stage—or

71. Palmer and Stilwell, 'Indochina Conflict', p. 37; Conrad C. Crane, *Avoiding Vietnam: The U.S. Army's Response to Defeat in Southeast Asia* (Carlisle, PA: Strategic Studies Institute, 2002).

72. Lewis, 'National Policy', p. 28.

73. Clayman, 'Strategic Importance of Indochina', p. 36.

74. Long, 'Counterinsurgency', 97.

mapping the pathway—for the inevitable commitment of ground forces to South Vietnam and the ensuing Vietnam-American War. So it is important to recognise that US Army officers who studied Southeast Asia in the 1950s did not know they would be fighting there a few years later. Their priorities were elsewhere—particularly fixing what they perceived was a 'broken army' on the brink of irrelevance. The entire decade of the 1950s was devoted to this rebuilding process—an enormous effort requiring a new concept of warfare based on a great land campaign in Central Europe.

The army intellectual community's view of the world as a giant battleground between the US and the Soviet Union shaped their analysis of the Southeast Asian region—particularly when it came to geopolitics and SEATO. Army analysis of the region also provided an opportunity to directly attack the Eisenhower administration's policy of deterrence through strategic nuclear weapons. When studying individual nations or specific events, officers could often recognise that a rigid bipolar Cold War ideological framework did not apply, and demonstrated an appreciation for complexity, ambiguity, and nationalism. Thus, for example, they recognised that Indonesia's neutrality policy was legitimate and that the Huks were not all dupes of Moscow.

But predictably, by the end of their essays they would try to fit these individual exceptions within the broad construct of worldwide Soviet-American rivalry. This was especially true of Indochina, where despite recognising South Vietnam's internal problems—both political and military—and despite recognising that other regions and other priorities were clearly more important, army officers almost inevitably blamed North Vietnam for South Vietnam's problems and insisted the US must confront what they perceived as a global communist menace emanating from Moscow. Even more alarming, with few exceptions they failed to reconcile the US Army's focus on large-scale atomic war in Central Europe with the challenge of fighting in the Southeast Asian environment. Because these contradictions were never resolved, or even challenged, there is a myopic sort of cognitive dissonance running through army intellectual thought in the 1950s. Or, for those interested in more traditional interpretations, it is well to remember Sun Tzu's admonition: "If you know neither the enemy nor yourself, you will succumb in every battle."

10

WHAT'S IN IT FOR US? RETHINKING THE BRITISH DEFENCE COMMITMENT TO SINGAPORE AND MALAYSIA FROM MACMILLAN TO WILSON

Malcolm H. Murfett

Timing is crucial in politics. What might be popular and prestigious in one era can become a rejected anachronism in another. Imperialism and empire, those much-vaunted tokens of power in the post-1870 period, reeked of exploitation and abuse by the time World War II ended in 1945. Freedom from foreign oppression thereafter became a touchstone of the nationalist movements around the world as colonial states sought to undo the shackles imposed upon them by the European powers in the distant past when the former were weaker and the latter stronger than was the case in the mid-20th century.

While decolonisation might be ignored for a time, ultimately it would have to be confronted. Clement Attlee, arguably one of the more discerning British prime ministers of the 20th century, had foreseen the nature of the problem in 1942: "The colonial problem will not be solved by a combination of an eye to business and humanitarian sentiment. Nor on the other hand will it be solved by looking backwards and imagining that we can recreate the conditions of a past age."[1] As far as Attlee was concerned, the British would have to relinquish "sentimental imperialism" in

1. Ronald Hyam, *Britain's Declining Empire: The Road to Decolonization 1918–1968* (Cambridge: Cambridge University Press, 2006), p. 94.

favour of taking a more realistic approach. This was much easier said than done even for Attlee, who saw nothing grievously wrong with the concept of empire as long as it was administered justly and progressively. No matter how virtuous and assiduous the mother country may have been, however, Attlee (described by Michael Foot as 'the sphinx') acknowledged that self-government was bound to come to these colonial territories sooner or later.[2]

Despite recognising that decolonisation would be a force to be reckoned with in the coming years, Attlee—like others of his ilk—had no wish to see the UK's influence disappear entirely off the map East of Suez.[3] Ironically, that fear of retreating British power was arrested temporarily on his watch as Chin Peng and the Malayan Communist Party (MCP) forced the government in London to tackle the Malayan Emergency head-on in Southeast Asia.[4] Worse was to follow for the Western democracies as Mao's rise to power in China and the activities of Kim Il Sung and Ho Chi Minh in Korea and Vietnam respectively suggested that the critical momentum lay with the communists and nationalists along the Asian littoral of the Pacific Rim. While neither Attlee nor his immediate successor, Churchill, considered themselves to be Far Eastern experts, both were as loath as the Americans and the French to see the 'domino theory' played out in this region.[5]

An emotive factor at the best of times, decolonisation was always likely to raise the temperature of the global Cold War. It

2. Attlee to Cripps and Pethick-Lawrence (22 Dec 1945), The National Archives of the UK (hereafter TNA): PREM 8/59, cited in ibid.

3. Malcolm H. Murfett, *In Jeopardy: The Royal Navy and British Far Eastern Defence Policy 1945–1951* (Kuala Lumpur: Oxford University Press, 1995), pp. 22–4.

4. Ibid., pp. 41–154; see also Anthony Short, *In Pursuit of Mountain Rats: The Communist Insurrection in Malaya* (Singapore: Cultured Lotus, 2000); C.C. Chin and Karl Hack (eds), *Dialogues with Chin Peng: New Light on the Malayan Communist Party* (Singapore: Singapore University Press, 2004).

5. Churchill's comments to the British diplomat Pierson Dixon on 2 May 1953 about the current crisis in Laos are instructive in this regard since they applied not only to that state but to much of Indochina: according to his official biographer, Churchill complained that he had been able "to remain ignorant about these outlandish areas all his life; it was hard that they had come to tease him in his old age." Martin Gilbert, *Churchill: A Life* (New York: Henry Holt and Co, 1991), p. 911.

did so spectacularly in the aftermath of Eden's wretched mishandling of the Suez crisis in 1956. His provocative and indefensible behaviour in Egypt undermined British morale, prestige and leadership in the most graphic way possible, exposed Western duplicity in the Middle East and North Africa, and boosted Afro-Arab nationalism.[6] In many ways it was the worst of all possible strategic scenarios for those ostensibly running things in London. Any coupling of 'Great' and 'Britain' seemed like a sad joke, as cringing embarrassment and conspicuous hypocrisy went hand in hand in those days of excess. Eden's sudden departure from Downing Street in January 1957 didn't put an end to the affair. If anything it encouraged the accelerated break up of the British Empire. Whatever lingering deference to H.M.G. there might have been after World War II promptly evaporated as the magnitude of the British failure at Suez came to be fully appreciated and the unravelling of the old empire began.[7]

Post-Suez defence policy

Harold Macmillan, whose dramatic U-turn on Suez had left his premier little room for manoeuvre in November 1956, was handed what looked to be a thoroughly poisoned chalice when Eden resigned suddenly at the outset of the new year. Appearances can be deceptive, however, and the new premier was to breathe astonishing new life into what had looked like the electoral corpse of the Tories, with the 'You've never had it so good!' era of blatant domestic consumerism in the years thereafter. Even before he had been dubbed 'SuperMac' by cartoonists for this act of staggering resuscitation in the late 1950s, Macmillan's resilient self-confidence was much in evidence. His recent experience at the Treasury had

6. Keith Kyle, *Suez* (New York: St Martin's Press, 1991), pp. 500–563; Wm. Roger Louis and Roger Owen (eds), *Suez 1956: The Crisis and Its Consequences* (Oxford: Oxford University Press, 1991).

7. Hyam, *Britain's Declining Empire*, pp. 241–326; Anthony Gorst and Lewis Johnman, *The Suez Crisis* (London: Routledge, 1997), pp. 147–69; David Carlton, *Britain and the Suez Crisis* (Oxford: Basil Blackwell, 1988), pp. 82–112.

made him uncomfortably aware that the UK was living well beyond its means. He sensed that overseas expenditure offered much scope for reform and economising. From the outset, therefore, he was determined to do something radical to cut away surplus expenditure and construct a global defence strategy that mixed maximum effectiveness with minimum cost. It may have sounded like wishful thinking, but the new incumbent of 10 Downing Street was prepared to try and execute such a mission. He chose the blunt and intemperate Duncan Sandys as the right-wing architect of this policy.[8] If Sandys possessed a soft touch it was rarely, if ever, seen in public. Indeed, he seemed to work on the principle that it was his way or the highway (Nehru once tellingly remarked that Sandys reminded him of the sort of Englishman who used to put him in jail).[9]

As minister of defence Sandys was given the liberty of shaking up the entire defence establishment and his White Paper of 1957—referred to by more than just the press corps as 'the Sandys Axe'—sought a phasing out of the national service obligation and, even more controversially, expressed a marked preference for scaling down conventional forces (and some military bases overseas) in favour of much greater reliance upon the nuclear deterrent. Publication of the paper caused a furore in the UK, not least from those in the Royal Navy who couldn't see where they fitted into future British war planning and were aghast to see the RAF assuming the lead in the projection of strategic power through the exercise of the nuclear option.[10] Upon closer inspection, however, this headlong pursuit of dramatic change in defence policy was far from revolutionary. This was particularly true in the case of the defence com-

8. An old Etonian and Oxford graduate, Sandys was a member of the Conservative Party's right-wing Establishment faction known as the Monday Club. Malcolm H. Murfett, John N. Miksic, Brian P. Farrell and Chiang Ming Shun, *Between Two Oceans: A Military History of Singapore From First Settlement to Final British Withdrawal* (Kuala Lumpur: Oxford University Press, 1999), pp. 294–6.

9. Hyam, *Britain's Declining Empire*, p. 246.

10. Murfett et al., *Between Two Oceans*, pp. 294–6.

mitment to the Middle and Far East, which somehow remained in place despite the need for global cost-cutting. Foreign policy considerations—especially the need to preserve Western interests in these areas—won out over economic virtue. As a result, therefore, the UK's place in the sun was maintained. It would not be required to surrender any of its military bases in Singapore, at least in the short to medium term. Indeed Singapore's importance to it was underscored as both a supply centre and a focal point for any future reinforcements that might be needed in the region.[11]

Nonetheless, imbibed with Treasury orthodoxy, Macmillan's desire for a shrinking bottom line was such that he was not merely content with a reworking of British defence posture overseas, he also wished to focus upon the stewardship of the British colonial empire. As a result, he commissioned a number of far-reaching reports that examined the vital link between resources and commitments over the approaching 1960s. Sir Patrick Dean, a leading Foreign Office mandarin, was given the task of collating the information that flowed in from a variety of sources.[12] Dean's report revealed a depressing picture of wilting British power around the globe in the years to come. This lent credence to the belief that preservation of the 'special relationship' with the US was vital—indeed as a departmental minute put it, "the core of our foreign policy".[13] In association with that fundamental aim, Dean's report stressed the need to keep Sino-Soviet power at bay in the following decade. This was also a good deal easier said than done since the two major communist powers were capable of causing all kinds of strife for the Western democracies in far-flung parts of the world. What, for instance, did it mean for Southeast Asia?

11. Brian Farrell in his discerning essay, 'Old Wine in a New Bottle: Singapore and British Defence Policy 1945–1962', notes that Singapore's role remained "pivotal" in the Sandys review. Ibid.

12. Sir Patrick Dean was at the time deputy under-secretary of state at the Foreign Office. He went on to become the UK's representative to the United Nations (1960–64) and ambassador to the US (1965–69).

13. Minute by Peter Ramsbotham (22 Sept 1959), No. 72, TNA: FO 371/143707, cited in Hyam, *Britain's Declining Empire*, p. 255.

While the 'wind of change' began blowing vigorously in Africa from 1957 onwards, the situation in Southeast Asia was more measured and less extreme. Macmillan's government seemed more in control of developments in this region, buttressed as it was by a series of defence agreements made with other powers in recent years. It was not altogether an illusory feeling. Apart from the geographical area of ANZAM (Australia, New Zealand and Malaya) formalised into a system of defence in 1953 and to which was added the establishment of the Commonwealth Far East Strategic Reserve (CSR) in 1955, the creation of SEATO (Southeast Asia Treaty Organization) in 1954 and AMDA (Anglo-Malayan Defence Agreement[14]) in 1957 suggested an integrated and viable structure that would restrict opportunities for the communists to cause mayhem within the region.[15] Unfortunately, much of this defence network looked appreciably better on paper than it did in practice.[16] This was especially true of SEATO, whose real importance to successive British governments lay in the political leverage it was thought to give them in the corridors of power in Washington D.C.[17]

14. AMDA became the Anglo-Malaysian Defence Agreement after the creation of Malaysia on 16 September 1963.

15. It is interesting to note that the establishment of the Commonwealth Strategic Reserve (CSR) in the shape of the 28th Commonwealth Brigade was the first example of a joint Commonwealth force to be formed in peacetime. Chin Kin Wah, *The Defence of Malaysia and Singapore: The Transformation of a Security System 1957–1971* (Cambridge: Cambridge University Press, 1983); L.D. MacLean, *ANZIM to ANZUK: An Historical Outline of ANZAM* (Canberra: Department of Defence, 1992); Leszek Buszynski, *SEATO: The Failure of an Alliance Strategy* (Singapore: Singapore University Press, 1993).

16. Ambiguity was never far from the scene not least because Singapore was considered to be a British, not a SEATO, military base. It was a moot point as to where this left the Federation of Malaya, which wasn't even a SEATO member. It was one of those issues that remained a tricky question and could potentially flare up at any time and compromise London's relations with Kuala Lumpur. Chin, *The Defence of Malaysia and Singapore*, p. 56.

17. SEATO comprised the US, UK, Australia, France, New Zealand, Pakistan, the Philippines, and Thailand. Its dominant raison d'être was that it formed a bloc of military powers within the Southeast Asia region which would come together to confront any Sino-Soviet threat to the region. For instance, by 1960 the British government realised that the RAF had the potential to fly up to three squadrons of V bombers with their payload of nuclear weapons to Singapore for use either as a strategic nuclear deterrent or as a strike force against China should it become necessary to do so. Nonetheless, a specific commitment to utilise the UK's nuclear deterrent hadn't been included in any detailed

No longer the economic treasure trove of yore and now under a wily leader, the Cambridge graduate, Tunku Abdul Rahman, whom the British had somewhat belatedly come to trust, Malaya was ushered towards independence with the minimum of fuss or regret on 31 August 1957, despite the fact that the Tunku was distinctly unimpressed with the concept of SEATO and disinclined to join it.[18] While this decision was regarded as unfortunate, the Tunku's virulent anti-communism couldn't be faulted and remained a continuing comfort to the British and the Commonwealth in the years to come.[19]

In sharp contrast, across the causeway to the south lay the quintessential fortress colony of Singapore, with 32,000 British troops stationed on an island the size and shape of the Isle of Wight. This military complex with its regional naval base was seen by Eden's Colonial Secretary Alan Lennox-Boyd as still being of cardinal importance to British defence and foreign policy East of Suez. As such, the most the minister was prepared to do was to allow the local Singaporean politicians a measure of limited internal self-government (from February 1955), but considered any early prospect of full independence as being utterly delusional. Like a prized sporting asset, Singapore was not for sale at any price and probably wouldn't be for many years to come. For Lennox-Boyd, the cabinet and the British Chiefs of Staff's (COS) pro-

SEATO planning at this stage. SEATO's development of Plan 4, as Brian Farrell graphically reveals in his essay in this volume, became far more strident in the period from 1961 to 1962. Nonetheless, according to Buszynski, SEATO was weak and vulnerable as an alliance from the outset. "If deterrence was its primary function ultimately it did not deter, if defence was its function it was never given an opportunity to defend." Buszynski, *SEATO*, pp. ix–xi; David Easter, *Britain and the Confrontation with Indonesia 1960–1966* (London: Tauris Academic Studies, 2004), pp. 7–8.

18. According to Chin Kin Wah, the Tunku's lack of enthusiasm for SEATO reflected a much wider Malayan disdain for it: "The fact remained that, in Malayan perception, membership of SEATO was strategically unnecessary, politically unpopular and generally ineffective." Chin, *The Defence of Malaysia and Singapore*, p. 31. See also Murfett et al., *Between Two Oceans*, pp. 308–10.

19. T.N. Harper, *The End of Empire and the Making of Malaya* (Cambridge: Cambridge University Press, 1999), pp. 348–56; Peter Dennis and Jeffrey Grey, *Emergency and Confrontation: Australian Military Operations in Malaya and Borneo 1950–1966* (St Leonards, NSW: Allen & Unwin in association with the Australian War Memorial, 1996), pp. 99–100.

found distrust of the left-leaning Chinese politicians in Singapore was such that the fear of communist subversion in this melting pot of cultures was very real. They decided, therefore, that the colonial authorities must retain control over the apparatus of internal security on the equatorial island for the foreseeable future. All the leading figures in London were as one in being determined that Singapore "must not become an independent Chinese outpost at the strategic heart of South-East Asia".[20]

This sentiment remained uppermost in British eyes even though the People's Action Party's electoral success in 1959 ushered a dynamic young man of formidable intelligence into power as prime minister of Singapore. Another Cambridge graduate, could the young, brash Lee Kuan Yew be trusted to accommodate himself to Western interests and keep the communists at bay (both internally and externally) in the same way that the more avuncular Tunku had done in the Federation of Malaya since independence? Only time would tell.[21] From London's perspective, however, the communist threat to the region remained as threatening as ever and the 'domino theory' seemed to be just as relevant at the start of the 1960s as it had been when President Eisenhower had mentioned the principle for the first time at a news conference in April 1954.[22]

Whatever the future held for the British in Southeast Asia, the way forward was likely to be far more problematic unless they

20. David Marshall, the chief minister of Singapore, was distinctly unimpressed with the little constitutional progress that the British were able to offer him. In a wonderful parting shot, he ultimately rejected their overtures as "Christmas pudding with arsenic sauce" and promptly resigned. Hyam, *Britain's Declining Empire*, pp. 201–2. See also C.M. Turnbull, *A History of Modern Singapore 1819–2005* (Singapore: NUS Press, 2009), pp. 262–5.

21. After the PAP's victory in the 1959 Singapore general election, the British announced plans to increase significantly the military complex on the island. General Sir Richard Hull was quoted in *Dawn* (21 July 1959) as indicating: "We are not building these just temporarily. This is a permanent base." Part of this infrastructural build-up came in extending the Tengah airbase at a cost of £2.5 million. Chin, *The Defence of Malaysia and Singapore*, pp. 44–5.

22. President Eisenhower's News Conference, 7 Apr 1954, *Public Papers of the Presidents: Dwight D. Eisenhower, 1954* (Washington, D.C.: Government Printing Office, 1960), pp. 382–3.

mended and improved their 'special relationship' with the Americans.[23] Macmillan tried hard to rescue Anglo-American relations, which had been badly fractured by the Suez crisis, but his concerted efforts at rehabilitating a North Atlantic liaison with the Eisenhower administration were not rewarded with much more than modest success for the remainder of the decade and his earnest championing of summitry (regarded in a lukewarm manner by the policy-makers in Washington) fell apart in the aftermath of the U-2 incident of 1 May 1960. Fortunately things would change greatly for the better once John F. Kennedy was sworn in as the 35th president of the United States in January 1961. Despite their generational and other differences, a strong personal bond was quickly established between these two able statesmen. An odd couple, they nonetheless shared something of the same vision that weakness and vulnerability within their spheres of interest needed to be urgently addressed.[24]

The 'Grand Design'

Southeast Asia was an obvious case in point. Macmillan believed that the UK couldn't afford to service what could become a bottomless financial pit by being dragged into yet another regional morass now that the Malayan Emergency had been brought to an end. Partly for this reason he became increasingly receptive to the so-called 'Greater Malaysia' scheme mooted by the Tunku and Lee—albeit for starkly different motives—in the early 1960s.[25]

23. Peter Lowe, *Contending with Nationalism and Communism: British Policy Towards Southeast Asia, 1945–65* (Basingstoke; Palgrave Macmillan, 2009), pp. 215–43.

24. Matthew Jones, *Conflict and Confrontation in South East Asia, 1961–1965* (Cambridge: Cambridge University Press, 2002), pp. 23–8.

25. While it is nowadays asserted that the initiative for 'Greater Malaysia' came from the leading figures in Kuala Lumpur and Singapore, Malcolm MacDonald had been sympathetic to such a scheme as early as 1947. Tan Tai Yong, *Creating 'Greater Malaysia': Decolonization and the Politics of Merger* (Singapore: Institute of Southeast Asian Studies, 2008), pp. 3–4; Hyam, *Britain's Declining Empire*, p. 293; John Subritzky, *Confronting Sukarno: British, American, Australian and New Zealand Diplomacy in the Malaysian-Indonesian Confrontation, 1961–5* (Basingstoke: Macmillan, 2000), pp. 26–8.

Macmillan's stance on this scheme, aided and abetted by Lord Selkirk, the commissioner-general for South-East Asia, proved to be well in advance of some of his cabinet colleagues (especially Iain Macleod) and senior members of the diplomatic corps (primarily Sir William Goode) who were less convinced that it would solve the unique issue of Singapore, ensure the continued viability of the three disparate British territories on the island of Borneo (Brunei, North Borneo and Sarawak), and create a stable bloc of anticommunist powers in the region as the prime minister and his supporters evidently imagined it would.[26] Macleod's reservations were justified by the marked lack of enthusiasm for the 'Grand Design' exhibited by the three Borneo territories (especially the oil-rich sultanate of Brunei) and by the very hostile reception that this scheme received at the hands of the leading politicians in both the Philippines (who felt they had a good constitutional case for annexing North Borneo) and most especially in the vast archipelago of Indonesia, where the mercurial President Sukarno had designs on all three of the island territories.[27]

Flamboyant and opportunistic, Sukarno was well aware of the rich possibilities that potentially lay in wait for him in this era of regional decolonisation as the former European masters began to retreat from the scene. Patient when he needed to be, Sukarno skilfully acquired West Irian from Dutch control in August 1962 before turning his attention to the Tunku's scheme for a 'Greater Malaysia'.[28] It soon became obvious that he regarded this project as a classic case of neo-colonialism—a disingenuous scheme of only 'virtual' independence that had been 'cooked up' in London with a willing accomplice (the Tunku) who would administer the 'fraud-

26. Easter, *Britain and the Confrontation with Indonesia,* pp. 6–21.

27. Ibid., pp. 22–44; Hyam, *Britain's Declining Empire*, pp. 293–4.

28. Jones, *Conflict and Confrontation,* pp. 31–60. In London the Foreign Office (FO) had few doubts about Indonesia's long-term ambitions, describing them as probably aiming at "uniting all the Malaya-speaking [*sic*] people of South East Asia in a Greater Indonesia." See also the FO contribution to the Joint Intelligence Committee's Report on 'Future Indonesian Intentions' forwarded by A.S. Fair (Commonwealth Relations Office) to E.V. Vines (Canberra), FR.39/2 (10 Oct 1962), TNA: DO 169/67.

ulently' enlarged state on behalf of his silent partner in Whitehall.[29] Sukarno wasn't prepared to countenance this consolidation of a British client's power in the region and his vitriolic dislike of 'Greater Malaysia' was articulated in an increasingly acerbic campaign that left everyone in the region and well beyond in no doubt as to where he stood on this issue.[30]

While Sukarno waged his propaganda offensive against the mooted 'Greater Malaysia', matters on the island of Borneo deteriorated markedly in the coming months and culminated in a short-lived rebellion in Brunei in December 1962.[31] According to intelligence gathered in Singapore by the Joint Intelligence Committee (Far East), Indonesian complicity in the staging of this revolt was unmistakable. Lord Selkirk didn't need any further prompting to inform the Macmillan government that it shouldn't underestimate their Javanese foe, for he could prove to be a formidable enemy: "We are up against a man with much of the instability and lust for power of Hitler."[32] It was a frightening parallel if Selkirk was right. Sukarno clearly had territorial ambitions that were encouraged by the existing geopolitical situation along this part of the equator, but whether he was Hitlerian seems rather exaggerated and smacks of Eden's denunciation of Nasser for being a cross between the disreputable Mussolini and his megalomaniacal partner in crime, the late German Führer.[33]

29. A.J. Stockwell, 'Malaysia: The Making of a Neo-Colony', *Journal of Imperial and Commonwealth History*, vol. 26, no. 2 (1998): 138–56; John D. Legge, *Sukarno: A Political Biography* (Singapore: Archipelago Press, 2003), pp. 406–17.

30. Selkirk to FO, No. 374 (19 Dec 1962), TNA: PREM 11/4346; Jones, *Conflict and Confrontation*, pp. 98–121; Percy Craddock, *Know Your Enemy: How the Joint Intelligence Committee Saw the World* (London: John Murray, 2002), pp. 210–11.

31. A.J. Stockwell (ed.), *British Documents on the End of Empire*, Series B, Volume 8, *Malaysia* (London: Stationery Office, 2004), pp. 411–24, 431–2; Tan, *Creating 'Greater Malaysia'*, pp. 151–87.

32. Easter, *Britain and the Confrontation with Indonesia*, pp. 26–9, 57; Craddock, *Know Your Enemy*, p. 213.

33. Even Eden was more inclined to compare Nasser to Mussolini than to Hitler. See Scot Macdonald, *Rolling the Iron Dice: Historical Analogies and Decisions to Use Military Force in Regional Contingencies* (Westport, CT: Greenwood Press, 2000), pp. 115–44; Lindsay Frederick Braun, 'Suez Reconsidered: Anthony Eden's Orientalism and the Suez Crisis', *The Historian*, vol. 65, no. 3 (2003): 535–61.

Konfrontasi

While maybe not in their league, Sukarno could still prove to be a very considerable thorn in the side of Western interests in the Southeast Asian region. Supported and seemingly egged on by his foreign minister, Subandrio, the Indonesian president showed every appearance of assuming that role and more in the weeks that followed the collapse of Azahari's attempted coup in Brunei. Subandrio's announcement of *Konfrontasi* (Confrontation) on 20 January 1963 gave formal notice that Indonesia was determined to kill off the Malaysia project before it could be legally launched.[34] This certainly wasn't a New Year's resolution that Macmillan's government wished to hear. Being thrust onto the front line between the Indonesians and the newly emerging state of Malaysia was regarded as anathema in cabinet circles. At this stage, however, it couldn't be certain that the destructive intentions of the Indonesians would match their inflammatory rhetoric.[35] It took a few more weeks to resolve that issue, but the answer came with the eruption of armed raids across the Kalimantan border with Sarawak in April 1963.[36]

For a time during the early summer of 1963 diplomatic overtures were made by Jakarta to both Manila and Kuala Lumpur for a regional concept which came to be known as Maphilindo. Although both the American and Australian administrations were delighted with this initiative, Macmillan's government in London regarded the proposed confederation as a "complete sham" and opposed it from the outset as just a means to end British influence

34. Easter, *Britain and the Confrontation with Indonesia,* pp. 22–37. See also Background memos on Indonesia for talks between Lord Home and Dean Rusk (24 Sept 1963), TNA: FO 371/169906.

35. Boasting an army of 300,000, 400 aircraft and a navy that was predominantly Soviet-equipped, the Indonesians posed a considerable threat to any of the indigenous regional powers in Southeast Asia. Pressure was applied by the Indonesians early in February when they twice sent gunboats into Malayan waters and two of their bomber missions came within 64 km of Singapore before turning back. Chin, *The Defence of Malaysia and Singapore,* pp. 67–9; Dennis and Grey, *Emergency and Confrontation,* pp. 181–4; Murfett et al., *Between Two Oceans*, pp. 313–15.

36. Andrew Gilchrist (British Ambassador to Indonesia) to FO, 322 (19 Apr 1963), 346 (24 Apr), 382 (2 May), TNA: CO 1030/1502.

in the region. Its negative attitude was based on the fact that there had been no let-up in *Konfrontasi* on the island of Borneo as talks on Maphilindo had progressed elsewhere. This was clearly in line with the pledge given privately by General Abdul Haris Nasution, the Indonesian defence minister, to fight on until the British military were finally driven out of Singapore.[37] Confirmation of this intention was provided in mid-August by the analysis of first-grade intelligence received in London that clearly indicated the Indonesians had used Maphilindo as a means to further their own strategic aims and that *Konfrontasi* was designed not just to thwart Malaysia's territorial plans but also lead to the rejection and repudiation of British power in the region as a whole. As a result, the UK was alerted to the likelihood that Operation *A* (guerrilla warfare in Borneo) would escalate in the coming months.[38]

Knowing that the Americans had no wish to interfere in what was seen as a strictly British sphere of influence, Macmillan's government was left with no option but to respond militarily to these admittedly small-scale armed incursions. Nonetheless, it had to tread warily since it didn't wish to be pulled into an attritional conflict that might take years to resolve and cost an inordinate amount of money that it could ill afford to pay. Worse still, while Sukarno might be personally offensive—and according to the distinctly unimpressed Tunku "a helpless sex maniac … incapable of rational thought on politics"—he still headed a state of 97 million people that the Kennedy administration didn't wish to alienate or humiliate since this might drive the Indonesian president into the arms of the Communist Party of Indonesia (PKI) and the political

37. Gilchrist to FO (7 June 1963), TNA: FO 371/169903, DH 1062/40; FO to Washington (8 July 1963), TNA: PREM 11/4348, cited in Subritzky, *Confronting Sukarno*, pp. 57–61, 65–6.

38. Apparently, the Malaysian military attache in Jakarta had managed to obtain a copy of the minutes of a meeting held on 14 August 1963 between Subandrio, Nasution and Magenda, the Chief of Intelligence Indonesian Combined Forces Staff, in which these matters were discussed openly. Andrew Gilchrist (British Embassy, Djakarta) to FO, 897 and 898 (16 Aug 1963), TNA: CO 1030/1529. Easter, *Britain and the Confrontation with Indonesia*, pp. 59–60.

embrace of the People's Republic of China in Beijing.[39] In essence, this meant that for geopolitical reasons, if nothing else, the British were obliged to defend 'Greater Malaysia' and fight a guerrilla war against Sukarno's forces with the minimum of fuss and triumphalism—not an easy proposition even in the pre-Ted Turner and CNN era of instant journalism.[40]

'Greater Malaysia' and its problems

In the summer of 1963 the 'Greater Malaysia' project was in danger of being derailed as much from within as from without. While the Tunku wished to acquire the Borneo territories, not least for the large oil reserves in Brunei, he was much less keen on incorporating Singapore into the enlarged state. As he vacillated on whether he could trust his southern Chinese-dominated neighbour, Lee Kuan Yew's provocative behaviour and incessant demands seemed to reinforce the Tunku's considered opinion that assimilating Singapore would prove to be both extremely contentious and profoundly unsatisfactory. To complicate matters further, the economic jewel in the new crown of 'Greater Malaysia'—Brunei—was far from enthusiastic about sharing its oil wealth with anyone and its sultan remained unconvinced about the merits of his future role and the preservation of his privileges in the newly enlarged state.[41]

Anything less than 'Greater Malaysia' made little sense to either the Commonwealth Relations Office or the Colonial Office in London and the intemperate Duncan Sandys, who had resurfaced successively in both ministries as Macmillan's trusted lieutenant and chief enforcer for his 'pet project'. Sandys, typically

39. Easter, *Britain and the Confrontation with Indonesia*, pp. 59–60, 68; Subritzky, *Confronting Sukarno*, pp. 56–63.

40. While the Americans didn't wish to alienate the Indonesians, Robert Kennedy, the attorney-general in both his brother's administration and that of his successor LBJ, confided in the British ambassador in Washington that "there was no one whom he disliked more or trusted less" than Sukarno. Sir David Ormsby-Gore to FO, 153 (14 Jan 1964), TNA: DEFE 13/631. See also Jones, *Conflict and Confrontation*, pp. 235–40, 268–73.

41. Tan, *Creating 'Greater Malaysia'*, pp. 172–82; Craddock, *Know Your Enemy*, pp. 212–13. See also Minute by E.H. Peck (21 June 1963) on FO memo 'Malaysia' by P.A. Warner (21 June 1963), TNA: FO 371/169703.

dismissive of local objections and infuriated by Lee Kuan Yew's machinations, even went so far as to instruct Sir Varyl Begg, the British Commander-in-Chief Far East, to draw up an outline plan for a coup d'etat in Singapore on the morning of 16 September 1963 involving the arrest of Lee and his ministers, and the seizure of Radio Singapore and the vernacular press.[42] Begg was unenthusiastic about this *démarche*, recognising that it would be a hazardous operation necessitating 14 major units just to maintain control of the Lion City alone, leaving him with no reinforcements for deployment to Borneo should the Indonesians take the opportunity to step up their guerrilla activity while the British were engaged in subduing the unruly Singaporeans. Moreover, if the British seized control of Singapore to protect their military bases on the island, their action would prove Sukarno's point about neo-colonialism incontrovertibly and thereby pose a whole slew of long-term financial and military ramifications for those in Whitehall. Faced with the probability of doing far more harm than good by resorting to direct rule, Sandys was obliged to swallow his pride and rely instead upon forceful diplomacy to bring 'Greater Malaysia' into being.[43]

Sandys's innate and bludgeoning superiority—summed up in the culturally indefensible observation, "we couldn't allow the susceptibilities of the headhunters to wreck the project"—appalled the Tunku, who was made of finer stuff and didn't appreciate being bullied by anyone, let alone a remnant of the old colonial order.[44] By the same token, the Tunku didn't take kindly to either

42. Easter, *Britain and the Confrontation with Indonesia,* pp. 61–2.

43. In his *New York Times* obituary of the 'headless man' Sandys (published on 27 Nov 1987), Mark A. Uhlig suggested that Macmillan's right-wing cabinet colleague subscribed to the theory that "if you can't convince them, batter at them until they agree out of sheer weariness." In citing an unnamed press account of 1964, Uhlig indicated that Sandys had kept the delegates to the Malaysian independence talks in 1963 "up all night again and again, until they finally slumped together in blinking unity."

44. Resenting the irksome treatment he had received at Sandys's hands in these negotiations, the Tunku came to loathe the colonial secretary. Easter, *Britain and the Confrontation with Indonesia,* p. 62; Hyam, *Britain's Declining Empire*, p. 296.

Lee's hectoring brinkmanship or the Sultan of Brunei's persistent unwillingness to subsume his state's future with that of 'Greater Malaysia'. Despite the pressure exerted by Sandys and Selkirk, Macmillan's 'Grand Design' evolved into something short of what the premier envisaged and created a constitutional compromise that gave the authorities in Kuala Lumpur both more and less than what they ideally wanted.[45]

Indonesia's fury at what had transpired was swiftly felt. On the same day that the Federation of Malaysia was founded on 16 September 1963, 10,000 demonstrators appeared on the streets of Jakarta. Frustrated after marching to the old Malayan compound with the intention of presenting a resolution to its ambassador and finding him absent, the mob stormed to the newly erected British embassy building some streets away and began stoning it. After smashing all of its 938 plate-glass windows, some of the protesters managed to clamber into the embassy compound, tear down the union flag, tow away Ambassador Gilchrist's official car and burn both while the Indonesian police looked on from a discreet distance, doing nothing to prevent the mayhem.[46] Tension was ratcheted up to incendiary levels when Malaysia not only broke off relations with both Indonesia and the Philippines (17 September) but added insult to injury by allowing a group of UMNO youth members to attack the Indonesian embassy in Kuala Lumpur, insult Sukarno and tear down the Garuda emblem from the gates of the embassy, bearing it off to the Tunku, who supposedly stamped on it and told the enthusiastic crowd of supporters to bury it. Such a

45. The Federation of Malaysia was founded on 16 September 1963. Singapore, Sabah (North Borneo) and Sarawak were added to the existing Malayan state but Brunei remained outside this new grouping in an independent existence. Tan, *Creating 'Greater Malaysia'*, pp. 172–82. See also Tan's chapter 'The "Grand Design" British policy, Local Politics, and the Making of Malaysia, 1955–1961' in Marc Frey, Ronald W. Pruessen, and Tan Tai Yong (eds), *The Transformation of Southeast Asia: International Perspectives on Decolonization* (Armonk, NY: M.E. Sharpe, 2003), pp. 142–60.

46. Further direct action against British interests occurred elsewhere within the republic on 16 September, including the destruction of their consulate at Medan in Sumatra. Jones, *Conflict and Confrontation*, pp. 195–7.

besmirching of national pride was bound to have further repercussions and they were not long in coming. A day later (18 September) busloads of young activists returned to the windowless British embassy once more, ransacked it and set fire to both the contents and the building. But this was merely an hors d'oeuvre to the string of attacks in the next few days on anything British, especially their economic and commercial interests throughout Indonesia (worth roughly £160–200 million), which were taken over ostensibly to 'protect' them from hostile forces, and the severing of all trade with Malaysia (21 September), designed, of course, to damage the new Federation's entrepôt trade—most particularly that flowing into and out of Singapore. Just to add a little rhetorical spice to the mix, Sukarno went on record on 25 September as predicting that Indonesia would "*ganyang* Malaysia" (gobble Malaysia raw) because it was a hated example of neo-colonialism.[47]

Maphilindo had clearly suffered a sudden and traumatic death. Its demise was a relief to the authorities in London even if those in Canberra and Washington bitterly regretted its passing and blamed Sandys for killing it off altogether.[48] Whatever hopes Macmillan may have invested in the new Malaysian Federation, the 'Grand Design' was never intended to lead to a rupture of relations with Indonesia let alone a war with that nation. Unfortunately, the concept of a 'Greater Malaysia' had clashed with Sukarno's plan to unite all Malay people as well the indigenous inhabitants of New Guinea to form a 'Greater Indonesia'—an aim that enabled him domestically to keep some kind of precarious balance between the

47. Ibid., pp. 198–200; Easter, *Britain and the Confrontation with Indonesia*, pp. 32, 62; Merle C. Ricklefs, *A History of Modern Indonesia Since c. 1200*, 4th edition (Basingstoke: Palgrave Macmillan, 2008), p. 311.

48. British concern about American support for an "Asian solution" to *Konfrontasi* as expressed by Robert Kennedy is evident in the telegram FO to British Ambassador in Washington, 962, 'Mr. Robert Kennedy and Malaysia' (21 Jan 1964), TNA: DEFE 13/631. A year later Sir Andrew Gilchrist, the British ambassador in Jakarta, starkly revealed the difference in approach in a scathing summary of Maphilindo, denouncing it in the following terms: "As for Maphilindo, the answer is dead, for ever and a day. When, may I ask, did it ever live, except as a predatory and imperialistic gleam in Sukarno's eye?" Gilchrist to E.H. Peck (FO), 1046/65 (6 Jan 1965), TNA: FO 371.181490. See also Subritzky, *Confronting Sukarno*, p. 66.

army and the PKI.[49] Apart from wistfully hoping that Sukarno's well-documented kidney problems might take him permanently from the scene within the next five years, the British policy-makers were left with few options about how to deal with him.[50]

Ironically, it was Macmillan's health that was the first to fail. While he may well have seen himself as the godfather of 'Greater Malaysia,' his premiership barely survived its subdued inauguration. In early October 1963, on the eve of the Tory party conference, he was taken ill. After being classically misdiagnosed with inoperable prostate cancer, he decided to resign immediately as prime minister. There was much sleight of hand and action behind the scenes before a new leader emerged in the shape of the 14th Earl of Home, who shortly thereafter contrived to disclaim his peerage and contest a safe House of Commons seat at Kinross and West Perthshire as Sir Alec Douglas Home.[51] Home's brief, prosaic premiership ran along the lines of business as usual and contrasted markedly with what was going on elsewhere.[52] Shortly

49. A FO memo drawn up for the overseas representatives of the British government is instructive in this regard: "Although Sukarno is not a Communist he admires Communist methods and has worked consistently to turn Indonesia into an authoritarian state on Marxist lines. Visits to Soviet Russia and China in 1956, when he was lavishly feted, are said to have inspired the 'Guided Democracy' he inaugurated in 1967. Although Sukarno's personal position still largely depends on preserving a balance between the army and the PKI it has been evident for some little time that he is moving steadily towards the left and relying more and more on the PKI. It was in fact the PKI which first urged Sukarno to pursue active confrontation against Malaysia...." FO to Overseas Reps of the UK Government, 218, Guidance (18 May 1965), TNA: DEFE 25/212. See also earlier FO memos: 'Talking Points for Mr. Rusk' (24 Sept 1963), TNA: FO 371/169906; 'The Views of President Soekarno on Certain Major Issues of Policy', D.O.(O) (63) 8 (10 Dec 1963), TNA: DEFE 7/2390.

50. Easter, *Britain and the Confrontation with Indonesia,* pp. 31, 69–71. Meanwhile, in lieu of natural attrition, the British had to rely upon hardware to cope with Sukarno's regime. According to the naval historian Eric Grove, they maintained a fleet of about 50 ships in Malaysian waters during *Konfrontasi,* including two strike carriers, HMS *Victorious* and HMS *Centaur,* the commando carrier, HMS *Bulwark,* two guided-missile destroyers, HMS *Kent* and HMS *Hampshire,* 17 destroyers and frigates, five submarines, and nearly a dozen minesweepers. Eric J. Grove, *Vanguard to Trident: British Naval Policy Since World War II* (Annapolis: Naval Institute Press, 1987), pp. 266–7.

51. Far from being in terminal decline, Macmillan remained active as chancellor of Oxford University until he died at the age of 92 on 29 December 1986. Kenneth O. Morgan, *Britain Since 1945: The People's Peace* (Oxford: Oxford University Press, 2001), pp. 213–36.

52. R.A. Butler (FO) to Sir Alec Douglas Home (Prime Minister), 'British and

after its start Home's administration was greeted with the appalling news of President Kennedy's assassination in Dallas and his premiership concluded in October 1964 with the disclosure of the success of the PRC's first atomic device and the unrelated ousting of Nikita Khrushchev from the Kremlin.[53] His narrow defeat at the polls in the autumn of 1964 seemed tame in comparison with these momentous happenings on the world's stage. Nonetheless, while lacking the dynamism of the Sino-Soviet dramas, the abandonment of 13 years of Tory rule in the UK was not without some significance of its own.[54]

Wilson's first term in office, 1964–1966

Where would the Labour government of Harold Wilson, nursing an overall majority of just four seats, fit into the new overall strategic picture? And would things change significantly as far as British foreign and defence policy East of Suez was concerned?[55] Appeasement was ruled out since it was thought that the existing Indonesian leadership would see it as a gesture of weakness and become even more truculent than ever. Lacking an effective alternative strategy, the British and their Australasian allies were forced to engage in a covert, as well as costly, war of attrition in a bid to overcome *Konfrontasi*.[56] Successful though these operations were—Denis Healey was to describe the defeat of the Indonesians

American Strategic Interests in Area of South East Asia and the Indian Ocean', PM/64/51 (20 Apr 1964), TNA: PREM 11/4907.

53. Denis Healey, *The Time of My Life* (London: Michael Joseph, 1989), p. 250; Harold Wilson, *The Labour Government 1964–70* (London: Pelican, 1974), p. 23.

54. Vastly experienced on the foreign stage, Home had realised the underlying danger of *Konfrontasi*. "We must defend Malaysia of course; but it will help neither Malaysia nor ourselves, nor the Western cause in general, if in the course of defending Malaysia we drive Indonesia into the arms of communist Russia or China. It is probably considerations of this sort that make our friends and allies less than wholehearted in our support." This summed up the American position splendidly. John Subritzky, 'Britain, Konfrontasi, and the End of Empire in Southeast Asia, 1961–65' in Kent Fedorowich and Martin Thomas (eds), *International Diplomacy and Colonial Retreat* (London: Frank Cass, 2001), p. 216.

55. Morgan, *The People's Peace*, pp. 239–76.

56. *Konfrontasi* certainly lived up to the grim financial predictions made of it: the UK committed over 60,000 troops and 80 warships to this struggle and the cost to Far East Command grew from £70 million to £250 million in 1966. According to Subritzky,

"as one of the most efficient uses of military force in the history of the world"—the whole issue masked a grave, long-term economic dilemma for any British government. It had been highlighted by a Defence and Oversea Policy Committee memorandum issued in September 1964 while Home and the Tories remained in Downing Street.[57] This policy document had found that fully 15 per cent of the British defence budget went on maintaining a military base in Singapore and keeping troops in Hong Kong at a time when Southeast Asia provided only 3 per cent of British trade and under 6 per cent of their investment revenue—a figure put into context by the fact that it was less than that generated by British involvement in Latin America![58]

Obviously, economic virtue alone couldn't explain this conundrum. Geopolitical considerations continued to exert a decisive influence over British policy in the region and would remain so until *Konfrontasi* was finally wound up. While maintaining an active presence in Southeast Asia to assist the democratic cause in resisting encroaching communism certainly helped to foster better Anglo-American relations, the cost of doing so was uncomfortably high and was arguably unsustainable for the long-term future given the economic mess that the British government found itself in. After all, an enticing aspect of 'Greater Malaysia' had been the hope (increasingly forlorn) that economies of scale would work in favour of the new state and reduce the UK's overseas expenditure. What hadn't been on the drawing board was that the new state would spawn a guerrilla war in the region and force the British to scrap any lingering thoughts of saving money on supporting these former colonies and instead require H.M.G. to devote

the struggle was costing British taxpayers £1 million a day in early 1965. Fortunately, the toll on the armed forces was not as severe: 114 Commonwealth forces were killed and 181 wounded in this three-year ordeal. In comparative terms it was a small sacrifice when set alongside the losses sustained by the US in its epic struggle with the Viet Cong. Murfett et al., *Between Two Oceans*, pp. 313–15; Subritzky, *Confronting Sukarno*, pp. 198–9.

57. Easter, *Britain and the Confrontation with Indonesia*, p. 193; Healey, *Time of My Life*, p. 289.

58. Easter, *Britain and the Confrontation with Indonesia*, pp. 110–12.

large sums of money so as to keep them from being subjugated by their large and hostile neighbour. Short of withdrawing from the region, which was politically unacceptable all the while *Konfrontasi* lasted, the British were left with no alternative but to continue to fight and to pay.[59]

Whatever the new British premier (who was to go on record as musing that he saw the British frontier as being drawn up along the borders of the Himalayas) and Denis Healey, his self-confident and rather abrasive minister of defence, may have wished to do about British power projection in the mid-60s, the grim reality was that the new administration was beset by an economic crisis far worse than its leading members had even suspected.[60] A £800 million balance of payments deficit indicated that a systemic problem was at hand and that something needed to be done to correct what seemed to a sinking ship of state. An obvious remedy—devaluation—offered itself to the former economics don from New College, Oxford, but that controversial solution was rejected out of hand. Wilson's adamant refusal to go down that particular route (arguably born more out of political motives than economic ones) and instead seek alternative ways of getting out of this economic mess, would eventually fail three years later and cost the British exchequer over £1 billion—a sum equal to its entire reserves of gold and convertible currencies.[61] Meanwhile, trapped in a fundamental disequilibrium between discharging its foreign and political obligations and not possessing the means to pay for them, the Wilson government found itself caught between the proverbial

59. As Craddock indicates, it didn't help that the British and the Americans hadn't seen eye to eye with each other on Indonesia since the 1950s. Craddock, *Know Your Enemy*, pp. 219–20.

60. John Darwin, *Britain and Decolonisation: The Retreat from Empire in the Post-War World* (London: Macmillan, 1988), p. 291; David Reynolds, *Britannia Overruled: British Policy and World Power in the Twentieth Century* (London: Longman, 1991), pp. 226–31.

61. Diane B. Kunz, '"Somewhat Mixed Up Together": Anglo-American Defence and Financial Policy during the 1960s' in Robert D. King and Robin W. Kilson (eds), *The Statecraft of British Imperialism: Essays in Honour of Wm. Roger Louis* (London: Frank Cass, 1999), pp. 213–32; P.L. Pham, *Ending 'East of Suez': The British Decision to Withdraw from Malaysia and Singapore 1964–1968* (Oxford: Oxford University Press, 2010), pp. 34–57.

rock and a hard place. Neither Healey nor Wilson wished to pull back from East of Suez, but playing such a world role had serious consequences and whatever defence reviews might be fashioned and weapons systems and platforms sacrificed, the reality was that until *Konfrontasi* was concluded, major savings remained pipe dreams rather than reality.[62]

The 'Special Relationship'

Although Wilson was anxious to keep on good terms with the latest occupant of the White House, President Lyndon B. Johnson and his close advisers were far from convinced that the British premier was entirely straightforward. Could he really be trusted or was he just the latest in a long line of disingenuous British individuals whose self-interest came well before any deep-seated commitment to Anglo-American relations?[63] Again, only time would tell. Wilson and his delegation's visit to Washington in early December 1964 proved to be better and more amicable than expected, but it still left the Johnson administration in little doubt that the premier regarded any kind of active British military intervention in Vietnam as being beyond the pale.[64] No matter what the British offered in exchange—strategic involvement on Borneo and a continuing military presence in Malaysia (Singapore) to keep *Konfrontasi* from spilling over into a more exaggerated conflict—the suspicion that the Americans expected more than H.M.G. was prepared to give them in Southeast Asia lingered long after the British team returned to London.[65]

62. Expenditure on Singapore alone in 1964–65 was estimated by the Ministry of Defence at £210 million, as compared to £199 million on Europe and £75 million on Aden. Easter, *Britain and the Confrontation with Indonesia,* p. 117.

63. Even Governor Franklin Delano Roosevelt had been wont to complain in 1932: "Every time we have taken the British into our confidence they have given us a trimming." Jeffrey Steinberg, 'FDR's 1932 Victory over London's Wall Street Fascists', *Executive Intelligence Review,* 4 Apr 2008, p. 10.

64. Lowe, *Contending with Nationalism and Communism*, pp. 82, 150–7, 231; Jones, *Conflict and Confrontation*, p. 286.

65. On 7 December 1964 Secretary of State Dean Rusk set out the American view of the UK's importance to the US: "The United Kingdom fulfilled a strategic function in many parts of the world which the United States could not attempt; and because they

Maintenance of a strong British presence East of Suez was the minimum requirement of the 'special relationship', even though the refusal by the British to provide any combat troops in the Vietnam imbroglio was probably the true, if unspoken, litmus test applied by Johnson to measure the depth of their friendship.[66] Nonetheless, having to make do with less than the ideal had often been a daily fact of congressional life for the Texan Democrat. Clearly some things hadn't changed even though he was now occupying the White House. Therefore, the president was prepared to accommodate Wilson's politically driven defence policy agenda as long as the British retained a regional presence in Southeast Asia.[67] But could the British, in debt to the IMF, be even expected to continue in Southeast Asia once *Konfrontasi* ended? A clue of sorts was provided by the rather bland Michael Stewart, Gordon Walker's successor at the Foreign Office, in a discussion with Dean Rusk in May 1965. At their meeting, Rusk had urged the British not to withdraw from the region because the US couldn't fulfil the role of the world's policeman on its own. For his part, the undemonstrative Stewart had confirmed that the Labour government was undertaking a fresh defence review, adding ominously: "we might have to stop spreading the butter so thin...."[68] How thin it was became evident only a few weeks later.

could do this, with relatively small forces, the value of their contribution extended beyond the immediate local impact—in particular it had a kind of 'multiplier' effect by enabling the greater power of the United States to be deployed in areas which might otherwise by largely inaccessible to it." Thomas Alan Schwartz, *Lyndon Johnson and Europe: In the Shadow of Vietnam* (Cambridge, MA: Harvard University Press, 2003), p. 71; Saki Dockrill, *Britain's Retreat from East of Suez: The Choice between Europe and the World?* (Basingstoke: Palgrave Macmillan, 2002), pp. 66–75.

66. McGeorge Bundy, the national security advisor, intimated to President Johnson on 28 July 1965 that "a British Brigade in Vietnam would be worth a billion dollars at the moment of truth for Sterling." Schwartz, *Lyndon Johnson and Europe*, pp. 79–80.

67. In a meeting held in Washington on 8 December, Patrick Gordon Walker, the British foreign secretary, told Dean Rusk that the UK had 8000 troops in Borneo and a total of 20,000 in Malaysia. As far as Gordon-Walker was concerned, this was a military commitment comparable to the US troop presence in Vietnam. See PMV(W) (64) 4th mtg., cited in Jones, *Conflict and Confrontation*, p. 286.

68. Kunz, '"Somewhat Mixed Up Together"', p. 215; Schwartz, *Lyndon Johnson and Europe*, p. 76.

As the economic woes besetting the UK intensified during the early summer of 1965, the Americans led an international rescue effort that provided $1.4 billion to prop up the pound and prevent its devaluation. In doing so the Johnson administration sought a substantial quid pro quo from the Wilson government in the shape of at least a 10-year defence commitment East of Suez.[69] As long as it didn't involve Vietnam—an absolute political no-go area for the UK—Wilson didn't have difficulty in signing on to remain in the region. He hadn't wanted to leave it precipitously in any case.[70] But could he justifiably countenance an open-ended British commitment to remaining East of Suez if the overall economic situation in the UK didn't improve? Moreover, what might happen if the top secret and highly successful *Claret* operations (cross-border raids in Kalimantan) actually led to the winding down of the counterinsurgency conflict with Indonesia?[71]

A gathering of leading government ministers in mid-June at Chequers (the prime minister's weekend retreat in Buckinghamshire) addressed these issues and the necessity of making substantial cuts to the defence budget. Just how painful these were ultimately going to be was revealed by Wilson at a cabinet meeting on 15 June 1965 when he spoke of an agreement to cut defence expenditure by 16 per cent (£400 million) by 1969–70. While the government didn't wish to abandon any specific theatre commitment momentarily, it seemed only a matter of time before the British withdrew from their bases at Aden and, once *Konfrontasi* had been resolved, Singapore too.[72]

69. Ibid., pp. 216–18; Dockrill, *Britain's Retreat from East of Suez*, p. 115.

70. Clive Ponting, *Breach of Promise: Labour in Power 1964–1970* (London: Hamish Hamilton, 1989), pp. 47–54.; Dockrill, *Britain's Retreat from East of Suez*, pp. 105–21; Pham, *Ending 'East of Suez'*, pp. 70–87.

71. While the British were clearly winning in Borneo, the same could not be said of the situation in Sumatra and the Riau islands, where the Indonesians had developed a significant amphibious capacity. Easter, *Britain and the Confrontation with Indonesia*, pp. 124–5, 127, 135–7, 156, 171, 181, 191, 194–5, 197; Ian Pfennigwerth, *Tiger Territory: The Untold Story of the Royal Australian Navy in Southeast Asia from 1948 to 1971* (Kenthurst, NSW: Rosenberg, 2008), pp. 150–219.

72. Dockrill, *Britain's Retreat from East of Suez*, pp. 103–4, 134–7.

Singapore banished from Malaysia

If the Wilson government thought it may have finally taken ownership of its defence and economic problems, it was soon swiftly disabused of that notion. Out of the blue—the Joint Intelligence Committee (Far East) didn't even get a whisper of it—the Tunku and Lee Kuan Yew parted company, and Singapore was cast adrift from Malaysia on 9 August 1965.[73] Tension between the two had been evident from the outset but a 'Little Malaysia' and an independent Singapore were just about the last things the Wilson government wanted to defend. Separation meant that British colonial defence strategy in Southeast Asia from the Macmillan premiership onwards was now utterly compromised and a huge stimulus had been given to their regional opponents.[74] Needless to say, the news of Singapore's forced exit from Malaysia was greeted enthusiastically in Jakarta as "the first fruit of confrontation".[75] In Sukarno's circle at least the belief gained ground that more 'harvesting' would be bound to follow as *Konfrontasi* continued and neo-colonialism was shown up for what it was. For a time the overall picture became very confused; news filtered through that the Tunku was prepared to make overtures to Sukarno to end the war—much to the horror of the Americans, whose attitude to Sukarno had changed 180 degrees—and Lee Kuan Yew added to the prevailing bleakness with an ungracious anti-colonial tirade in which he declared he could "kick the British out of their bases in 24 hours" if he wanted to.[76] As a threat it had a distinctly hollow sound.

73. Turnbull, *A History of Modern Singapore,* pp. 282–95

74. Albert Lau, *A Moment of Anguish: Singapore in Malaysia and the Politics of Disengagement* (Singapore: Times Academic Press, 1998); Easter, *Britain and the Confrontation with Indonesia,* pp. 136–55.

75. "Indonesians found it hard to conceal the glee they felt about Singapore's withdrawal from Malaysia. Ganis Harsono indicated that 'Indonesia had always said that Malaysia was not a viable entity and this was now proved. Indonesia could say to the United Nations I told you so.'" Sir Andrew Gilchrist to FO, 1727 (9 Aug 1965), TNA: PREM 13/589. See also Easter, *Britain and the Confrontation with Indonesia,* p. 149.

76. Howard Jones, the long-term US ambassador to Indonesia, had been sympathetic to Sukarno. His replacement in 1965 by Marshall Green was hugely significant. Green thought Sukarno posed a serious threat to Western interests and the sharply revised US policy to Jakarta reflected this attitude of antipathy towards the Indonesian president. Subritzky, *Confronting Sukarno*, pp. 167–70.

John Rob, the UK high commissioner to Singapore, described it as "a real blunder", but the damage was done. Singapore was in no position to do without either the British military spending on the island or the jobs that it directly or indirectly generated. Threatening to banish the British when they provided 20 per cent of Singapore's GDP was, therefore, crass in the extreme. Sensing he had gone too far, Lee wrote to Wilson on 23 August indicating that his government realised that it needed the British military for its own survival: "Singapore is the linchpin of South-East Asia. If your bases are out of Singapore, Democratic socialists are out also. We have no death wish."[77]

A 'black swan' turns up

Because of their unpredictability, so-called 'black swans' always manage to give a shock to the system and the Untung coup in Jakarta on 1 October did just that. Although the violent coup quickly collapsed in disarray, a bloody aftermath saw perhaps 500,000 communist members, fellow travellers and other suspects die as the PKI was smashed as a political force in Indonesia.[78] Intentionally or unintentionally, the Untung coup had a number of major consequences. Apart from the civilian slaughter it unleashed, the coup led to the rise of Major-General Soeharto and the eventual fall of Sukarno and Subandrio; it also had a massive counterrevolutionary impact upon Indonesian foreign policy, with the new government seeking a closer understanding with the West; and it laid, too, the groundwork for the formal end to *Konfrontasi* on 11 August 1966, a campaign which had been costing the UK anything in the region of £1–2 million a week.[79] Such an extraordinary transformation in

77. J.V. Rob (UK High Commissioner in Singapore) to Sec. of State for Commonwealth Relations (Arthur Bottomley), 'Singapore: Foreign Policy since Independence' (30 Dec 1965), CRO Ref: 2PG41/80/2 (24 Jan 1966), TNA: PREM 13/1833; Philip Ziegler, *The Authorised Life of Lord Wilson of Rievaulx* (London: Weidenfeld and Nicolson, 1993), pp. 210–11.

78. Ricklefs, *A History of Modern Indonesia*, pp. 318–21, 327; Legge, *Sukarno*, pp. 431–58; Easter, *Britain and the Confrontation with Indonesia*, pp. 156–73.

79. Michael Stewart opted for the larger figure and Denis Healey the smaller one. Easter, *Britain and the Confrontation with Indonesia*, pp. 174–92.

favour of the Anglo-Americans convinced the conspiracy theorists that the West must have been involved in the coup in some way. Over the course of the past four decades, however, no 'smoking gun' has been found to link either Washington or London with the coup. Even though it helped both governments enormously, it seems they and/or their security services didn't orchestrate the coup or assist in its successful crushing. Whether Soeharto helped to engineer the coup, only to extinguish it once his rivals had been killed, is still a moot point. What is clear, however, is that he seized his opportunity to eliminate the plotters, crush the communists and remove Sukarno from a position of decisive power.[80] This 'black swan' came as a most unlikely gift for the British. From being bewildered and downcast at the expulsion of Singapore from Malaysia and fearing that *Konfrontasi* was likely to drag on interminably and pose perennial obstacles to British economic recovery, an almost surreal solution to the Indonesian question lay at hand. It was a gift that the Wilson government was unlikely to spurn.

Healey leads the charge

What would this remarkable but still highly fluid situation in Southeast Asia mean for British defence policy in the short to medium term? Denis Healey put forward a somewhat ambiguous answer in his Defence White Paper of February 1966. Despite cancelling the new aircraft carrier (CVA 01) which the Royal Navy had hoped to deploy East of Suez, Healey opted instead to buy 50 long-range and land-based 'swing-wing' tactical fighter aircraft (F-111A) from the Americans. According to Healey, these were supposed to do the same job as the TSR-2 (the British-made vertical take-off, tactical strike and reconnaissance aircraft jettisoned in 1965) and the carrier, but at a cheaper price.[81] This had cer-

80. Ricklefs, *A History of Modern Indonesia*, pp. 327–33.

81. There was a delicious irony in this situation given that much of the development work on the 'swing-wing' technology had been carried out by a team of aeronautical engineers led by Sir Barnes Wallis (of Dambuster fame) at the British firm of Vickers in the UK. Once the British government had opted to develop the BAC-designed TSR-2, it

tain obvious financial attractions as well as reassuring those who wanted the British to retain a military presence East of Suez well into the next decade. On 23 January 1966 the Defence and Oversea Policy Committee (OPD) wrestled with the contentious future of the Singapore military base. Healey indicated the British and their American and Australian allies did not see eye to eye on the subject:

> ... while we regarded Singapore as a base from which we conducted military operations and which local difficulties might increasingly make untenable, they saw it as a potential communist stronghold akin to Cuba, and feared that our withdrawal would leave a vacuum which would very soon be filled by Communist China."[82]

He remarked that any talk of a British withdrawal was likely to cut little ice with the authorities in either Canberra or Washington and that a more suitable tack was to suggest to their allies that the British were perfectly prepared to remain in Singapore with a much reduced set of forces, provided Lee's government was content for them to do so and didn't insist on restricting their freedom of action in the use of these forces in the region.[83]

Shortly afterwards, the combative defence secretary found himself explaining the rationale for the latest White Paper to those members of the Commonwealth likely to be affected by its conclusions. Addressing the National Press Club in Australia, Healey indicated reassuringly to his hosts: "We have no intention of ratting on any of our commitments. We intend to remain and shall remain fully capable of carrying out all the commitments we have

decided to give the designs for the 'swing-wing' plane to the US National Aeronautics and Space Administration (NASA) in 1958, which used them in the design and development of the F-111A! See *Flight International*, vol. 84, no. 2854 (21 Nov 1963), www.thunder-and-lightnings.co.uk/tsr2/history.html.

82. OPD(66), 8th Mtg. (23 Jan 1966), TNA: CAB 148/25.

83. Healey even ruefully suggested that if the British were to retain the base against their better judgment, their allies should pay them for so doing! Ibid.

at the present time, including those in the Far East, the Middle East and Africa. We do intend to remain in the military sense a world power."[84]

Two days later in Singapore, he informed Lee Kuan Yew that it was the cabinet's intentions to keep a military presence in the region for an indefinite period of time, although the size of their forces on the island was likely to be reduced once *Konfrontasi* had been brought to an end. This didn't come as any surprise to Lee because Wilson had recently intimated to him that the number of British servicemen in Singapore might in future be cut by 50 per cent.[85] Healey went on, however, to gain the prime minister's undivided attention by confessing that the stealth and secrecy shown by Malaysia and Singapore in effecting their secession in August 1965 had taught his government a lesson and had led it to approach the Australians with a view to arranging alternative base facilities in Western Australia as an insurance policy against any future pre-emptive move that might be taken against British interests in Southeast Asia. A little nonplussed by the nature of this rebuke, Lee replied that the British had no reason to fear that Singapore would conspire against it—unlike the Malaysians and the Indonesians or the PRC in the longer term—and indicated his preference for the British military to remain on the island rather than see them replaced by the more disputatious Americans. According to Lee, because the odds of the Malaysians launching a coup against his PAP government were greater than those faced by any African leader (a touch hyperbolic, one suspects), the British should deter the Tunku's government in Kuala Lumpur from carrying out such an act. Healey remained unruffled by Lee's dark vision of the immediate future and advised the prime minister to recruit more Gurkhas if he felt uneasy about the security situation on the island![86]

84. Miles Hudson, 'East of Suez', Old Queen Street Paper, No. 9, Conservative Research Department, 27 Apr 1969, p. 9.

85. Lee Kuan Yew, *From Third World to First: The Singapore Story, 1965–2000* (Singapore: Times Media, 2000), p. 47.

86. Note of meeting between Healey and Lee Kuan Yew (4 Feb 1966), TNA:

Wilson's second term

After handsomely winning the general election in March 1966, Wilson's Labour government could now look forward to a sustained spell in office. Lee Kuan Yew was anxious lest this comprehensive victory might have persuaded the Wilson government to think of taking a bold gamble with its force structure in the Far East. It was already well known that those on the left wing of the Labour Party, such as Richard Crossman, Michael Foot, Ian Mikardo and Frank Allaun, amongst others, were all for a complete withdrawal East of Suez for ideological as well as economic reasons. Lee was more concerned with a report that the volatile George Brown (Wilson's deputy) was leading a group within the cabinet that sought a phased withdrawal sooner rather than later.[87] Seeing this as a distinct possibility, Lee took himself off to London to query those in charge about the rumours he had heard from afar. Healey did his best to allay Lee's fears at their meeting on 22 April: "H.M.G. had come to the conclusion, taking account of the policies of the U.S. and Australian Governments, that the best course would be to retain our facilities in Singapore, so long as we were welcome there, even though the forces based on the spot might not have a very active role once confrontation had died down."[88] Despite rehearsing these reassuring signs of the UK's long-term commitment to Singapore, Healey cautioned Lee that relations between Singapore and Malaysia and the policies they might pursue were bound to have an effect on future British policy in Southeast Asia. Appreciating this fact, Lee mentioned in reply that he had discussed the possibility of a British withdrawal

PREM 13/1833. Healey passed on his impressions gained from talking to Harold Holt and Lee to the OPD upon his return from the Far East and Australasia. He concluded that it would be a mistake for British troops to leave Malaysia and Singapore before it was necessary to do so since such a withdrawal might lead to hostilities between the two neighbouring countries and to "a state of chaos which would make it necessary for us to return, at far greater cost." OPD(66), 12th Mtg. (11 Feb 1966), TNA: CAB 148/25.

87. Wilson, *The Labour Government 1964–70*, p. 276.

88. Record of Meeting between Denis Healey and Lee Kuan Yew, London (22 Apr 1966), TNA: PREM 13/1832.

with his Malaysian counterpart and had found the Tunku quite sanguine over the prospect. "The Tunku had taken the line that there was nothing serious to worry about since the West needed Malaysia and Singapore more than the latter needed the West, arguing that it was enough that they should take an anti-Communist line."[89]

In his conversation with Wilson a few days later, Lee reiterated his by now well-known sentiments on the bases issue, namely, that he wished the British to remain for as long as it was economically feasible for them to do so since he believed even a "phased withdrawal" would induce the moral, economic and political rot to set in. He confided, however, that the presentation of this policy to the outside world was all-important as Singapore could ill afford to be denounced as a stooge of the West.[90] George Brown painted an altogether bleaker picture of the British East of Suez policy when he met Lee shortly afterwards at a gathering of the Socialist International in Stockholm. Irascible and indiscreet, Brown admitted that if he had his way the British would immediately withdraw from Southeast Asia, sourly pointing out that it was only American money propping up the pound that kept the UK in the region.[91]

Lee's concern that further economic misfortune might seal the fate of the British presence in Southeast Asia was not wide of the mark and two crippling blows—a 6½-week seamen's strike that began in May and yet another speculative attack on sterling that followed in July—did much, in Kenneth Morgan's words, to blow the recently re-elected government off course. Under immense pressure to cut back on public expenditure, Wilson was forced on 20 July to introduce a draconian package of deflationary measures designed to save £500 million by the end of the next financial year. A saving of £100 million was supposed to be made from the

89. For his part, Lee appreciated that his personal survival depended upon the success of the policy he followed and therefore he was hoping to establish a far more stable relationship with the authorities in Kuala Lumpur than had existed hitherto. Ibid.

90. Conversation between Harold Wilson and Lee Kuan Yew, London (25 Apr 1966), TNA: PREM 13/1832.

91. Lee, *From Third World to First,* p. 51.

defence budget and this not surprisingly roused the left-wingers in the party to demand that the government should call it a day in the Far East and return home.[92] Healey duly embarked upon another whirlwind tour of Southeast Asia explaining to his Malaysian and Singaporean hosts that military cut-backs were vital and that British forces in the two countries would be reduced to the level that they would have been without *Konfrontasi.* What this ambiguous new figure would be was revealed by the defence secretary in the House of Commons on 3 August when he disclosed that 10,000 troops were to be withdrawn from Borneo once the Indonesian government called off its cross-border war.[93]

Further defence cuts

This was still not enough for the Treasury and in the aftermath of the sterling crisis Callaghan mounted yet another raid on the services by demanding that the Defence Review Programme, agreed to only six months before, be cut by another £200–300 million. Deep cuts of this nature brought about a fundamental shift in British defence policy and Healey was grudgingly forced into devising an entirely new defence plan that could make further substantial savings in the defence estimates over the next quinquennium on the basis of yet more troop cuts and reduced overseas commitments. At Chequers in late October he gave a few of his senior ministerial colleagues a sense of what these reforms might eventually entail.[94] By 9 December when the matter came before the OPD, Healey had been joined by George Brown in preparing a joint paper on the subject. In essence, it called for a 50 per cent reduction in Far East Command and cuts of roughly a third in

92. Morgan, *The People's Peace,* pp. 239, 254–5, 263–6.

93. *Konfrontasi* ended in Aug 1966 but the Commonwealth troop withdrawal took longer than expected and wasn't finished until April 1967. Dockrill, *Britain's Retreat from East of Suez*, p. 169; Murfett et al., *Between Two Oceans*, pp. 318–19; Lee, *From Third World to First,* p. 51.

94. According to Wilson, Healey professed himself ready to propose an "approximate terminal date" for British deployment East of Suez. Wilson, *The Labour Government 1964–70*, p. 381.

both the British forces based in the Middle East and in Europe. Richard Crossman, known to be unsympathetic to retaining any sort of military presence East of Suez, grumbled that a total withdrawal from the Far East did not appear to be even on the cards. "On the contrary, the whole assumption was that we are there for ever because it is necessary to keep a British military presence in the Far East to sustain our membership of the four-power agreement with Australia, New Zealand and the U.S.A."[95] Joined by Callaghan, however, Healey and Brown finally got their way and a study was commissioned of what would be involved in a total British withdrawal from the Far East.[96] While cabinet support for the maintenance of any kind of East of Suez role cooled even further, Wilson remained stoically wedded to the concept for the time being and reassured President Johnson to that effect in late November.[97]

Withdrawal from East of Suez

By the time the Working Party of the OPD reported in March 1967, another champion of the East of Suez policy had been lost to the cause. In casting around for sufficient economies to satisfy the rampant Treasury, the defence secretary, an erstwhile status-quo man, now informed Wilson that he had seen the light and considered there was no longer any realistic alternative to halving all British forces in Malaysia and Singapore by 1970–71 and withdrawing them completely by 1975–76.[98] Although no longer doubting the necessity of withdrawing from Southeast Asia, Healey knew

95. Crossman hinted darkly that this was the result of personal commitments Wilson had already made with President Johnson. Callaghan was evidently of the same opinion and had openly articulated the point in the OPD meeting on 9 December. Richard Crossman, *The Diaries of a Cabinet Minister, Vol. II* (London: Hamish Hamilton and Jonathan Cape, 1976), pp. 155–7.

96. Dockrill, *Britain's Retreat from East of Suez*, pp. 174–5.

97. Ibid., pp. 176–7; Pham, *Ending 'East of Suez'*, p. 132.

98. Report of the OPD(Official) Committee's Defence Review Working Party, OPDO (DR) (67)16 (20 Mar 1967), TNA: FCO 24/25; Minutes of OPD(67) 14th Mtg. (22 Mar 1967), TNA: CAB 148/30. See also Memorandum by George Brown and Denis Healey, 'Defence Expenditure Studies', C(67)40 (31 Mar 1967), TNA: CAB 129/128.

that convincing all the interested parties that this was unavoidable was likely to be a very fraught affair. "Although our allies might well be willing to see us reduce the size of our deployment in the Far East, they attached importance to our maintaining a presence of some kind and particularly to our not saying publicly that we intended to withdraw completely."[99] Much finesse would therefore be needed by those charged with revealing the strategic truth, or as much of it as possible, to the UK's allies and friends.

George Brown, the British foreign secretary, was hardly the type of emissary that the Wilson government needed—calm, unruffled, phlegmatic—to bring bad news to an American administration that had enough of its own, bogged down as it was in Vietnam with no easy way out from that military quagmire. Brown could be a most intemperate fellow. He was bright, passionate and boisterous. If he drank, and he did, his virtues receded as his eloquence dimmed. To use and convert an old descriptive epigram, when Brown was good, he was very good; when he was bad, he was appalling.[100] Fortunately, on this occasion when the SEATO council members gathered in Washington, Brown performed creditably. While all accepted the plan to reduce British forces in Malaysia and Singapore by 50 per cent by 1970–71, everyone was implacably opposed (none more so than the Australians) to a total British withdrawal from the two states by the mid-1970s. Moreover, Brown was left under no illusions that the Americans had any intention of taking up the slack left by a British withdrawal from the region. It was plain they wouldn't. Despite the concerns of the Allies, Brown was neither discouraged nor overawed by what he had encountered in Washington and felt that the government should press ahead with its plans for a total withdrawal regardless of foreign opposition.[101]

99. Confidential Annex, OPD(67), 15th Mtg. (14 Apr 1967), TNA: CAB 148/30.

100. Healey describes Brown in virtually the same way. See his reference to the "immortal Jemima" in Healey, *The Time of My Life*, p. 297.

101. Records of Brown's meetings in Washington are recorded in TNA: PREM 13/1384. See also Confidential Annex, OPD(67) 17th Mtg. (21 Apr 1967), CAB 148/30.

There is nothing like the zealousness of a recent convert, and a confident Healey was to demonstrate the validity of this assertion on his flying mission to Singapore and Kuala Lumpur in late April. Actually, the grim news he had to impart didn't come as a surprise to either Lee or the Tunku, since they had learnt the substance of it from cables they had received from Harold Holt and Keith Holyoake, who had been in Washington with George Brown. As a result, Healey was relieved to find that the two former adversaries were both "more helpful and constructive" than he had any right to expect.[102] Upon his return to London, he wanted to build on this goodwill and urged his ministerial colleagues to be sensitive to the concerns of Lee, in particular, who was anxious that announcement of any plans for a total withdrawal might undermine confidence in Singapore's economic future. Healey got his way. At the OPD meeting of 12 May, the critics of the East of Suez policy wanted full disclosure of a final withdrawal immediately; but the moderate pragmatists, with Wilson in the van, won the day with an astute, if somewhat disingenuous, call for cautious restraint since various governments and alliance obligations were involved and time was needed to settle these issues. A fudged compromise, much as Crossman had earlier predicted, thus emerged and the UK put off the fateful day of reckoning once more.[103]

Despite drawing comfort from what he now saw as the inescapable logic of a total withdrawal, Healey was forced to admit in a cabinet memorandum of 23 May that the UK's allies were "strongly opposed" to any announcement of this intention once the Defence Expenditure Studies were completed in July 1967 because of the grave political consequences it might have within the region and especially in Singapore, which still remained very dependent upon an active British presence in its economy.[104] As if on cue a letter

102. Confidential Annex, OPD(67), 19th Mtg. (12 May 1967), TNA: CAB 148/30; Healey, *The Time of My Life*, p. 290; Lee, *From Third World to First*, p. 52.

103. Confidential Annex, OPD(67), 19th Mtg. (12 May 1967), TNA: CAB 148/30; Crossman, *Diaries of a Cabinet Minister, II*, p. 313.

104. Memo by Healey, 'Defence Expenditure Studies: Consultation on Defence Policy', C(67)81 (23 May 1967), CAB 129/130.

from Lee arrived in Downing Street a few days later, warning Wilson that the communists in the PRC and in North Vietnam would be jubilant at the prospect of a total British withdrawal from the region: "If it is in Britain's interests to make public now what Britain intends to do in 1975, perhaps you will not be unmindful of the price to be paid by all who live in South and South East Asia and others outside who have made a commitment to prevent the area going chaotic and Communist."[105]

Before Lee and Goh Keng Swee, his combative minister of defence, arrived in London in June for further talks on the matter, the Six-Day War had exploded in the Middle East. Apart from changing the overall complexion of the Arab-Israeli dynamic, the war's disruption of trade and shipping undermined the shaky pound once more and did much to confirm the UK's unwanted status as 'the sick man of Europe'.[106] Upheaval in the Levant and throughout the Suez Canal formed an unenviable backdrop to an acrimonious series of talks that opened with the Singaporean delegation on 22 June. If Herbert Bowden, the Commonwealth Secretary, seemed ill at ease and played for time, Healey's candour could hardly be faulted. He advised Lee and his team that the British military presence in Singapore on 31 March 1971 would be 32,000 and that all of these troops would have left the city state by "about April 1975". Given that all locally employed civilians would have had their contracts terminated by the summer of 1975, the British military presence in Southeast Asia would amount to a small-scale, naval amphibious unit with no accompanying ground troops or air forces. Upon hearing this, Lee was incensed. He summed up the British position flawlessly: "Alarming statements alternated with stout words, while the impression grew that Britain was ratting on

105. Letter from Lee Kuan Yew to Harold Wilson, 26 May 1967, circulated for cabinet consideration as C(67)87 (29 May 1967), TNA: CAB 129/130.

106. Wilson had little difficulty in claiming subsequently that the Six-Day War was "the biggest contributing factor to the devaluation which came five months later." Wilson, *The Labour Government 1964–70*, p. 513.

her commitments because of financial difficulties."[107] He promised he would have even harsher words to say when he met a host of backbench Labour MPs in the House of Commons on 26 June:

> Nobody in his right mind expected Britain to hold the main burden of maintaining peace in South East Asia.... The only role required of the British... was to hold the base area. Who could attack it? No one knew when China would be able to do so. They had told Ho Chi Minh to hang on for seven years. To announce a decision to withdraw completely from the mainland would be for Britain to hand over victory before battle had been joined. This would be utter madness.[108]

While Lee and Goh complained about the fecklessness of the Wilson government and shopped around for as much aid and compensation from it as possible, the Lord President of the Council Richard Crossman decided that the Singaporeans and their moral blackmail had to be resisted. According to his diary entry, the left-wing intellectual—well known as being a 'little Englander'—decided to meet fire with fire. He told Lee, "It is in the interest of Great Britain to get out of the Far East as fast as we possibly can. Our presence may be useful to you but it isn't useful to us. We mustn't have a strategy beyond our economic strength."[109] Lee was stunned by Crossman's forthright views, but the latter was unabashed and pressed the Singaporean prime minister to declare what the absolute minimum time period for a complete British withdrawal would be. Lee admitted that they would need five years to bring this military involvement to an end. Crossman was exultant and swiftly prepared a cabinet memorandum urging his ministerial colleagues to insist upon a complete evacuation of the Asian mainland within five years.[110]

107. Note of a Meeting at the Commonwealth Office (22 June 1967), TNA: PREM 13/1832.
108. Ibid.
109. Crossman, *Diaries of a Cabinet Minister, Vol. II*, pp. 399–400; Lee, *From Third World to First*, p. 55.
110. Memo by Crossman, 'Defence Withdrawals', C(67)116 (4 July 1967), CAB 129/131.

Defence White Paper

Healey's Defence Draft White Paper made its first appearance in the OPD on 3 July and contained few surprises except for the large amount of aid that the Ministry of Defence was proposing to set aside as compensation for Malaysia and Singapore both before and after total withdrawal. Crossman was again to the fore in getting this sent back for downward revision of the proposed cost structure.[111] When the Supplementary Statement on Defence Policy was eventually published on 18 July its reception at home was raucous, with the Tory opposition making political capital out of what it saw as the crass decision to name a date for withdrawal and the left-wing Labour MPs irritated by the government's failure to bring that date forward by several years. As for the UK's friends and military allies abroad, only the Tunku appeared reasonably satisfied by the news. There was a marked lack of enthusiasm emanating from the corridors of power in Washington, Canberra, Wellington and, naturally, Singapore on this subject. *The Economist* was particularly unimpressed, using an editorial to rubbish the notion that military redeployment might lead to some sort of economic salvation and a leading article to describe the defence plans as both "cavalier" and "provocative". Under the title 'Good Luck, Harry, Good Luck, Tunku', the influential weekly suggested that by fixing a timetable for a total withdrawal the UK was providing an unwitting invitation to the enemies of Malaysia and Singapore to begin planning an insurrection against them.[112]

Although the Conservative peers of the realm managed to inflict a defeat on the government (85-61) in a debate on the bill in the House of Lords on 25 July, it was in truth merely a glancing blow. Wilson won where it mattered most—in the House of

111. Cabinet Memorandum, 'Defence: Draft White Paper', C(67)117 (4 July 1967), TNA: CAB 129/131. See also accompanying cabinet memoranda on the same and related subjects: C(67)118; C(67)119; C(67)121 (4 July 1967), TNA: CAB 129/131; OPD(67) 25th Mtg. (3 July 1967), TNA: CAB 148/30; Crossman, *Diaries of a Cabinet Minister, II*, pp. 406–7.

112. *The Straits Times*, 19, 20 and 24 July 1967; *The Times*, 20 and 21 July 1967; *The Economist*, 22 July 1967.

Commons—a couple of days later, even though 19 of his own party abstained from voting on the issue.[113] As far as both Healey and Wilson were concerned, the mid-70s withdrawal date was now irrevocable and they agreed a final evacuation could take place any time from 1973 to 1977.[114]

Devaluation and after

Unfortunately, that wasn't the end of the story. After an autumn confronting a crippling dock strike and watching the UK's trade figures go through the floor in October, the pressure on sterling became overwhelming and the exchange rate of $2.80=£1 could no longer be sustained. After vainly searching for a last-minute financial reprieve in early November, Wilson and Callaghan were forced to admit that they had run out of all options and only devaluation remained. Both men saw it as a political catastrophe, which indeed it seemed to be in those days of fixed exchange rates. On 18 November 1967 Wilson announced the 14.3 per cent devaluation in a special broadcast to the nation—a sound bite of which was to haunt him for the rest of his political career. Along with the reduction in the exchange rate to $2.40=£1 came a package of deflationary measures, including a further cut of £100 million from the defence budget.[115]

113. The government motion approving the Defence White Paper was passed on 27 July by 297 votes to 230. *The Times*, 26 July, 28 July 1967.

114. Meanwhile, Wilson was prepared to offer Lee £1.5 million immediately in special aid for the current financial year 1967–68. Lee politely accepted this offer but took the opportunity to press for other short-term budgetary and financial assistance so as to enable the Singaporeans to establish new industrial investments. Text of Lee Kuan Yew's reply to Harold Wilson's Telegram of 4 Aug 1967 (tel. no. 683) contained in Cypher/Cat A: Singapore (BHC) to Commonwealth Office, tel. no. 554 (25 Aug 1967), TNA: PREM 13/1833; *The Straits Times*, 29 July 1967.

115. Kenneth O. Morgan, *Callaghan: A Life* (Oxford: Oxford University Press, 1997), pp. 268–76. Morgan captures the essence of the prime minister's performance on this occasion in the phrase "extraordinary chutzpah." It was a satirist's dream to try and claim that despite the 14.3 per cent fall in the value of sterling, the pound in the pocket of the British people was somehow worth the same as before devaluation! It was a gaffe that fuelled the growing suspicions of those who distrusted this gifted, but troubled, figure. Morgan, *The People's Peace*, p. 275; Pham, *Ending 'East of Suez'*, pp. 201–7.

Downcast by devaluation which he had always opposed, Callaghan resigned as chancellor of the exchequer at the end of November 1967 and was succeeded by the son of a South Wales miners' agent—the Balliol graduate, Roy Jenkins. Never having been a devotee of the East of Suez policy, the new man at the Treasury unerringly fell upon overseas defence policy as a vehicle for a whole slew of economies he was proposing to implement in order to get the economy back on track. He duly informed Healey at lunch on 14 December that the date for the total withdrawal of British forces from Southeast Asia would have to be brought forward and the next day he confided in Wilson that he hoped to accelerate the withdrawal to 1970–71.[116] Rebuffed by General de Gaulle's emphatic '*Non*' to the latest British application to join the Common Market, Wilson readily agreed to Jenkins's new timetable for pulling back from East of Suez and assured him that he was determined to get cabinet approval for these measures so that they could be presented to parliament when it reconvened in mid-January.[117]

Cabinet approval was hardly in doubt, but convincing their allies that these economies were vital for the UK would not be so easy for Wilson's ministers. George Thomson, the secretary of state for Commonwealth affairs, found that out to his cost when he flew to Southeast Asia and the Australasian dominions in early January to brief the various government leaders on the fateful news. It was not well received. In Kuala Lumpur Thomson found the Malaysian ministers Tun Razak and Tan Siew Sin "nonplussed and gravely disturbed" by his disclosures. Razak indicated that the communists would be encouraged by the speedier withdrawal, while the Tunku, describing himself as "sad and gravely disappointed", went

116. Roy Jenkins, *A Life at the Centre* (London: Macmillan, 1991), pp. 222–3.

117. Wilson had become a late convert to pulling back from East of Suez. As his biographer Philip Ziegler reveals in *The Life of Lord Wilson*, p. 211, at one stage in the mid-1960s he had held the view, "To abandon a Commonwealth ally like Singapore might one day prove inevitable, but only as a last resort...." Three years later he was to declare that "clinging on to the East of Suez role had been one of his worst mistakes as Prime Minister." See also Pham, *Ending 'East of Suez'*, pp. 207–36.

further by stating on the following day that without British military assistance, Malaysia "would be defenceless". It was clear that the Malaysians felt that they had been "seriously let down" by what they had always seen as a "staunch friend and ally".[118] If Thomson's experience had been uncomfortable in KL, the mood would darken further in Singapore. There he met Lee for an hour alone and found the prime minister "fighting mad" about the unilateral decision the British had made to stage an accelerated withdrawal from the region. An expected firestorm of criticism became even more volcanic as the two of them traded verbal blows with each other—accusations of broken promises and blackmail, selfishness, threats to leave the Sterling area, and other retaliatory action ebbed and flowed as the evening wore on. Dinner was served with Lee's cabinet ministers present and the recriminations continued. Thomson reported later that his officials had never before experienced such a systematic campaign of pressurisation as they endured from Lee and his highly organised and militant team of ministers on this occasion. Thomson went on to state that in his opinion the Singaporean prime minister was in "a near-hysterical and unpredictable state".[119] Anxious to be heard before any public declaration could be made on this subject, Lee flew to London to lobby both the government and the opposition on Singapore's behalf.[120]

Before battle could be joined in Downing Street, however, George Brown had what he was to describe as "a bloody unpleasant meeting" in Washington on 11 January 1968 with Dean Rusk. It was clear that the US secretary of state was highly contemptuous of the Wilson government's inept handling of its East of Suez policy and indicated his resentment of the "acrid aroma of the fait accompli" in which the final decision to quit was couched. In expressing

118. Telegram no. 21, Thomson to Wilson (7 Jan 1968); tel. nos 22 and 23, Thomson to Wilson (8 Jan); C(68)13 (9 Jan), TNA: CAB 129/135.

119. Telegram no. 26, Thomson to Wilson (8 Jan 1968); tel. no. 32, Thomson to Wilson (9 Jan); Memo by Michael Stewart (First Secretary of State), C(68)15 (11 Jan); Memo by Thomson, C(68)23 (15 Jan), TNA: CAB 129/135.

120. Lee, *From Third World to First*, p. 58.

his "deep distress" about the abandonment of the UK's international role, he reminded his British colleague that H.M.G. should live up to its name: "for God's sake be Britain," he declared.[121] Brown didn't take kindly to a civics class from his opposite number, but he could hardly have expected anything less. While President Johnson weighed in with his own personal message of dismay, the Texan sensed that the Wilson government's mind was made up on the issue.[122]

Whether it was or not, the Singaporean prime minister was determined to try and secure a better deal for his tiny island republic. He met Wilson on 14 January for more than five hours and urged him and his leading ministerial colleagues to extend the withdrawal deadline beyond 31 March 1971. Lee obviously hoped that Singapore's paramount security concerns—he was wont to describe them as literally "a matter of life and death"—might be such as to persuade the Wilson government to postpone the military withdrawal by a couple of years. That was always likely to be an ambitious and perhaps unattainable target, but he conceded that even a few months' grace would be in his country's best interest.[123] George Thomson, who had recently endured a very torrid time with Lee and his ministerial team in Singapore, couldn't fault the passion and intensity of the Singaporeans and thought it would be both diplomatic and appropriate to give the recently independent city state a little breathing space by extending the deadline for withdrawal by a year. In the vital cabinet meeting of 15 January, in which the final decision would be ratified, the animated discussion showed the stark divisions that had been formed between the ministers on the controversial clauses of the revised defence review. It

121. Telegram no. 54, Brown to Stewart (11 Jan 1968), attachment to 'Singapore and Malaysia: Far East', C(68)22 (12 Jan), TNA: CAB 129/135.

122. Dockrill, *Britain's Retreat from East of Suez*, pp. 204–5; Karl Hack, *Defence and Decolonisation in Southeast Asia: Britain, Malaya and Singapore 1941–1968* (London: Curzon, 2001), p. 286.

123. Meeting between Lee and Wilson (14 Jan 1968), TNA: PREM 13/2081. See also correspondence between the two leaders (15–16 Jan), TNA: FCO 46/43. Lee, *From Third World to First*, pp. 58–62.

soon became evident that the final vote was likely to be a very close one and it took a last-minute intervention from Wilson to settle the matter. He proposed a compromise arrangement by which the military withdrawal would be deferred for nine months and take effect only after 31 December 1971.[124] After gaining cabinet approval for these measures, Wilson went before a packed parliamentary chamber on 16 January 1968 to explain what his government had decided to do about its East of Suez policy.[125]

Nine months may have been a short reprieve for the Singaporeans, but at least it was something to show for Lee's vigorous efforts at bearding the British in their den.[126] Having bought a little time for himself, Lee also took solace in the fact that another general election would have to be fought in the UK before the spring of 1971 at the very latest. If Edward Heath and the Conservatives were able to oust Wilson and the Labour government at the polls, the future for Singapore might become a little rosier since the Opposition had bitterly attacked the pull-back from East of Suez and the Tory leader had written to him personally supporting his stand on the issue.[127] Moreover, in the two-day parliamentary debate on the defence review, Iain Macleod, the former Tory colonial secretary and a leading member of Heath's front-bench team in the Commons, pledged that a future Conservative government would review the accelerated withdrawal from the Far East

124. Cabinet 7th Mtg. (15 Jan 1968), TNA: CAB 128/43; Crossman, *Diaries of a Cabinet Minister, II*, p. 650.

125. Wilson announced that the British military withdrawal from the Persian Gulf would also take place on 31 December 1971 and that the Royal Navy's aircraft carriers would be phased out in the 1970s after the various military withdrawals from East of Suez had been effected. He also indicated that the 50 F-111A strike aircraft which Healey had ordered from the US to replace the British-built TSR-2 would also be cancelled at a saving of £400 million. Lord Longford, Lord Privy Seal and Leader of the House of Lords, was the only cabinet minister to resign on the issue. *Official Report, Parliamentary Debates (House of Commons) Fifth Series*, vol. 756, cols 1578–82, 16 Jan 1968; *The Times*, 17 Jan 1968.

126. Lee, *From Third World to First*, pp. 58–62; Turnbull, *A History of Modern Singapore*, pp. 308–9.

127. *The Times*, 11 and 19 Jan 1968; *The Straits Times*, 16 Jan 1968; Malcolm H. Murfett, '"The Times they are a-Changin": Britain's Military Commitment to Singapore, 1967–1971' in Brian P. Farrell (ed.), *Churchill and the Lion City: Shaping Modern Singapore* (Singapore: NUS Press, 2011), pp. 139–73.

and might reverse the decision if necessary.[128] It seemed prudent, therefore, for Lee to pin his faith on the Tories—the old party of empire—not to let the Singaporeans down in their hour of need as Wilson and the socialists had done to friends and allies alike in the Far East and across the Pacific. Surely, the Tories could be trusted not to rat on their obligations, couldn't they? Once again the future would reveal all.[129]

So what can be made of this episode in British defence and foreign policy? Various possibilities seem to exist: Does it represent an unnecessary betrayal? Is it safe to describe it as a commonsense withdrawal? Would it be unfair to call it an undignified scuttle? What about a bit of all three?

128. *The Straits Times*, 19 Jan 1968.

129. Lee, *From Third World to First*, pp. 64–5; Hack, *Defence and Decolonisation in Southeast Asia*, pp. 287–8. For the knock-on effects of the British withdrawal as far as SEATO was concerned, see Buszynski, *SEATO*, pp. 126–35.

11

BENEFICIARY OF THE COLD WAR: SOEHARTO AND THE 'NEW ORDER' IN INDONESIA, 1966–1990

Dewi Fortuna Anwar

The rise of the 'New Order' government in Indonesia in 1966 and the political longevity of its supreme leader, Soeharto—who ruled with an iron fist for the next 32 years—owed much to the geopolitical setting of the Cold War and the strategic place Indonesia occupied within it. With its uncompromising anti-communist credentials, Soeharto's 'New Order' government—which replaced Sukarno's 'Guided Democracy', a period of growing communist influence at home and close relations with China—gained the support of the United States and its allies till the end of the Cold War. They regarded Indonesia, the largest country in Southeast Asia, as an important anti-communist bulwark in the region. As a "de facto ally" of the United States,[1] notwithstanding Indonesia's nominally non-aligned status, the 'New Order' government was able to pursue domestic and regional goals that would have been difficult, if not impossible, to achieve in any other circumstance; and shielded from international censure by powerful friends in Washington and other Western capitals, the government was able, especially during its early years, to get away literally with murder in its attempts to consolidate the powers of the Indonesian state, with President Soeharto at the apex.

1. See Juwono Sudarsono, 'Indonesia and the United States, 1966–1975: an inquiry into a de facto alliance association', PhD thesis, London School of Economics and Political Science, 1979.

In the years following Indonesia's independence in 1945, a plurality of centrifugal forces had threatened on many occasions to tear apart the new republic's national unity, territorial integrity and economic viability. The primary goal of the 'New Order' government was to strengthen the Indonesian state in relation to these forces. There were striking similarities between Soeharto's 'New Order' and the Netherlands East Indies colonial state, as Benedict Anderson has pointed out, for both were equally obsessed with internal security and order and with enlarging the role and control span of the state vis-à-vis societal forces at large.[2] In its determined pursuit of national resilience as the basis for a strong state, the 'New Order' government ruthlessly destroyed or marginalised elements that it regarded as threatening or inimical to the envisioned national order, while rewarding and co-opting others that were willing to toe the line.

The 'New Order' system of governance—underpinned on the one hand by a military-dominated authoritarian regime that systematically carried out human rights abuses as a matter of security policy, and on the other hand by a large infusion of foreign investment and access to export markets—could only have been possible in the enabling environment of the Cold War. Once the Cold War ended, the violations of human rights would bring harsh criticism and sanctions from the international community. But throughout the 1960s, instead of making Indonesia an international pariah, the killings of large numbers of communists almost immediately paved the way for a large influx of capital from Western countries and Japan, which set Indonesia on the road to becoming one of the 'Asian Tiger' economies. Moreover, as communist countries such as China and Vietnam were not yet part of the global market economy, Indonesia was able to enjoy access to international capital and markets without too much competition.

2. Benedict Anderson, 'Old State, New Society: Indonesia's "New Order" in Comparative Historical Perspective', *Journal of Asian Studies*, XLII, no. 3 (May 1983): 477–96.

This chapter looks at how Soeharto and the 'New Order' government made use of and benefited from the Cold War in four key areas: first, in the army's destruction of the Indonesian Communist Party (PKI) and the subsequent rise and consolidation of an army-dominated political structure; second, in Indonesia's peaceful rise as the *primus inter pares* in ASEAN, with close foreign-policy and defence ties with the West; third, in Indonesia's annexation of East Timor with the tacit support of the major Western powers; and fourth, in the 'New Order' government's sustaining of an authoritarian developmental state over a fairly long span of time.

Destruction of the PKI and rise of an army-dominated political structure[3]

On 30 September 1965, six high-ranking Indonesian army officers, including the Army Chief of Staff General Ahmad Yani, were brutally killed. According to the official account given by the Indonesian army immediately after the event, known in Indonesia as G30S (Gerakan 30 September) or Gestapu/PKI, the killing of the generals was done by the PKI, to prevent an army strike against the PKI in the event of President Sukarno's death. This army version of the event has been adopted as the official account in Indonesian history books, up to the present day. Foreign scholars have offered different interpretations, however, mostly casting doubt that the PKI was really behind the event. Some accounts argue that the coup was basically an internal army affair, as the leader of the coup, Lieutenant Colonel Untung, was an army officer and a member of the Presidential Guard. Others have pointed fingers at Soeharto, the primary beneficiary of the whole affair, as the real mastermind, for by killing the most senior generals Soeharto's rise to the top became unchallenged, and by pinning the blame on the PKI the army could wipe out its most dangerous political oppo-

3. Much has been written about the circumstances surrounding the political rise of General Soeharto, the establishment of the 'New Order' government and its political structure. This chapter will only highlight two interrelated issues, namely the destruction of the Indonesian Communist Party and its followers by the Indonesian army and its supporters, and the role of the United States.

nent almost unhindered. The fact that Untung had been a subordinate of Soeharto's when they were serving in the Diponegoro division in Central Java, that Untung met Soeharto shortly before the fateful evening, that Soeharto was not on the list of the generals killed, and that the PKI offered no resistance when the army moved against it, indicating that the PKI was probably taken unawares, have led many analysts to question the official version of the Gestapu affair.[4]

While the circumstances surrounding the coup have remained contested, the countercoup by the army immediately afterward has not been disputed (except in the number of people killed). Lieutenant General Soeharto, commander of the Army Strategic Reserves Command (KOSTRAD), quickly rallied his troops and rounded up the coup-plotters. Blaming the killing of the generals on the PKI and distributing photos of the badly mutilated and decomposing bodies dug up from Lubang Buaya, a well near the Air Force base Halim Perdanakusuma, with accompanying stories of the sadistic cruelty of the women's wing of the PKI, the Gerwani, who allegedly tortured the officers, Soeharto was able to rouse general repulsion towards the PKI.[5] In a few months between 1965 and 1966 the army together with vigilante groups of Muslim youths hunted down members and affiliates of the PKI and their families, including women and children, in the PKI strongholds in Central and East Java. Estimates of the number of people killed

4. One of the earliest analyses was Benedict Anderson and Ruth McVey, *A Preliminary Analysis of the October 1, 1965 Coup in Indonesia* (Ithaca: Cornell University Press, 1971), which hinted at Soeharto's role in the conspiracy. Because of this publication Anderson and McVey were blacklisted by the 'New Order' government for many years. See also Brian May, *The Indonesian Tragedy* (London: Routledge and Kegan Paul, 1978) and Rex Mortimer, *Indonesian Communism Under Sukarno* (Ithaca: Cornell University Press, 1974).

5. The author remembers as a primary school pupil in West Sumatra being shown photos of the decomposed bodies of the generals and the alleged horrors being inflicted on them by the Gerwani. Although 'Gerwani' is simply the short-form of Gerakan Wanita Indonesia (Indonesian Women's Movement), until today it carries a fearsome connotation in Indonesia. In West Sumatra, where the PKI was not strong, little was known about the massive killings being carried out in Java, and probably few actually cared to think about it.

range from 250,000 to over one million. Whatever the true figure, the bloodshed that took place, and which marked the transition from Sukarno's 'Old Order' to Soeharto's 'New Order', is undoubtedly one of the most horrific acts in recent history.

Yet, the tragedy has not been widely talked about or reported in the international media except in left-wing publications. In Indonesia naturally there has been a complete blackout about the whole episode since the army proceeded to dominate Indonesian politics for over three decades and imposed strict censorship over the media and publications in general, as well as on writings that could be brought into the country. Most Indonesians who grew up under the 'New Order' have only known the official version of the Gestapu affair. Lately, after the fall of Soeharto, a few Indonesian historians have begun to question this official interpretation. However, even now attempts to revisit the 1965–66 events have been met with fierce resistance by a number of groups and individuals who were active in the anti-communist movement in the mid-1960s, such as Islamic organisations and former student activists.[6] What is even more noteworthy, however, is the tacit silence of the Western media about the bloody event in Indonesia when it occurred. In fact, mainstream reporting generally put a positive spin on the wholesale destruction of communism and the concomitant rise of the army-dominated anti-communist government in Indonesia, which quickly oriented Jakarta away from Beijing towards the West. One commentator highlighted in a scathing article the difference in the way the Western, mostly American,

6. Recently Asvi Warman Adam, a historian from the Indonesian Institute of Sciences (LIPI), wrote and talked about the need to redress the wrongs committed against the PKI members who were killed and their surviving relatives who suffered various hardships under the 'New Order'. As a result he has been accused of being a communist sympathiser by a number of people, and a group of them belonging to an Islamic organisation came looking for him at LIPI, though happily he was away at the time. The men were met by the vice-chairman of LIPI, formerly a prominent student leader, who convinced them that Asvi was not a communist, only a scholar. Thus nearly 20 years after the end of the Cold War and several years after the fall of Soeharto the issue of communism in Indonesia is still a very touchy subject.

press reported the genocide committed by Pol Pot and the Khmer Rouge in Cambodia and the massacres of the PKI and its followers by the Soeharto regime in Indonesia.[7] In fact, the word 'massacre' was hardly ever applied to the massive and systematic killings of the PKI members and followers. Of course one can argue that Cambodia, which afterwards became a desolate land wracked by internal conflicts, cannot be compared to Indonesia under the 'New Order', which for all its shortcomings did transform Indonesia from a least-developed country to a lower-middle-income country with a respectable regional and international standing. Yet the point is taken that the killings of large numbers of communists in Indonesia were considered a 'good thing' by the predominant Western media and by the policy-makers in major Western capitals, notably Washington.

The generally supportive attitude of the United States and other Western countries towards Soeharto's action against the communists cannot be divorced from the Cold War conflict between communism and capitalism. From the end of the 1950s to the fall of Sukarno and the decimation of the PKI, Indonesia seemed to be all but lost to communism, at least in the eyes of Washington. The 1958 regional rebellions of the military commanders in West Sumatra and North Sulawesi in collaboration with leaders of the Islamic Masyumi Party and the Indonesian Socialist Party (PSI), which received covert American support because of the rebels' strong anti-communist outlook, had been defeated easily by the central government in Jakarta.[8] These rebellions marked the end of Indonesia's first experiment with parliamentary democracy[9] and paved the way for the establishment of Sukarno's 'Guided Democracy', which tried to bring together the different political forces

7. Edward S. Herman, 'Good and Bad Genocide: Double standards in coverage of Soeharto and Pol Pot', *Extra!* (Sep/Oct 1998), www.fair.org/extra/9809/Soeharto.html.

8. See Audrey R. Kahin and George McTurnan Kahin, *Subversion as Foreign Policy: The Secret Eisenhower and Dulles Debacle in Indonesia* (New York: The New Press, 1995).

9. Herbert Feith, *The Decline of Constitutional Democracy in Indonesia* (Ithaca: Cornell University Press, 1962).

under a more consensual form of government firmly guided by President Sukarno. He devised a new political ideology known as 'Nasakom', which united nationalism, religion and communism. The PKI was formally brought into the power structure of the 'Guided Democracy', which was thus characterised by an uneasy alliance between the anti-communist army and the PKI—as well as Sukarno, who tried to stay at the top by balancing the one against the other.[10] The two anti-communist parties, Masyumi and PSI, were banned because of their involvement in the regional rebellions. By the early 1960s the PKI had emerged as the largest communist party outside of Communist China and the Soviet Union, and seemed to be growing in influence as Indonesia espoused radical foreign policies, such as the Confrontation against Malaysia in 1963–65,[11] and the creation of a Jakarta-Phnom Penh-Hanoi-Peking-Pyongyang Axis in 1965, which brought Indonesia closer into the communist camp than ever before.

Much has been written about the Indonesian military, especially the army, which rose to political prominence from the late 1950s and became the dominant political force in the 'New Order' government.[12] Through its role in the revolutionary struggle for independence against the returning Dutch colonial power in 1945–49, the army saw itself as the guardian of the state, while the political instability under successive civilian governments during the parliamentary democracy in the 1950s further instilled in the military a rather poor opinion of political parties and politicians in general. The army as an organisation had also developed a strong enmity towards the communists ever since the 1948 communist rebellion in Madiun under its leader, Muso, who challenged the

10. Herbert Feith, 'Dynamics of Guided Democracy' in Ruth T. McVey (ed.), *Indonesia* (New Haven: Yale University Press, 1963), pp. 309–409.

11. J.A.C. Mackie, *Konfrontasi: The Indonesia-Malaysia Dispute, 1963–66* (Kuala Lumpur and Oxford: Oxford University Press, 1974).

12. See, among others, Harold Crouch, *The Army and Politics in Indonesia* (Ithaca: Cornell University Press, 1988), Ulf Sundhaussen, *The Road to Power: Indonesian Military Politics, 1945–1967* (Kuala Lumpur and Oxford: Oxford University Press, 1982).

leadership of President Sukarno. The Muso rebellion took place when the new Republic of Indonesia, proclaimed on 17 August 1945, was struggling for its very survival against the determined Dutch onslaught. Thus in the eyes of the army the communists were traitors to the nationalist cause.

The failure of parliamentary democracy—in part due to the activities of President Sukarno, who chafed at his essentially ceremonial role—and the problems within the army that contributed to the regional rebellions, paved the way for the military as a whole to become involved in politics. The army could not as yet openly challenge the authority of President Sukarno, whose stature and prestige before his political disgrace in 1965 was such that every political force deferred to him. Both the PKI, who needed Sukarno's patronage and protection against powerful enemies, and the army, which with its control over the means of violence actually had an independent power base of its own, paid deference to Sukarno, known as the Great Leader of the Revolution. With its 'Middle Way' doctrine, in which the army would neither take over political power nor stand aloof from politics, the army became a powerful partner in the triangular power relations of the 'Guided Democracy'. The viability of the 'Guided Democracy' clearly solely depended on President Sukarno and it was quite evident from the outset that the army and the PKI would be engaged in a deadly conflict to become the sole heir of Sukarno.

Many army officers had received training in the United States, and with the army's generally anti-communist outlook, it was quite natural that Washington pinned its hopes on the army to ensure that the communists would not come to control Indonesia. While the army was just as nationalistic as most other political forces in Indonesia, so that its anti-communism would not necessarily make it into a formal ally of the United States, the army clearly looked to Washington for concrete support in the former's campaign to exterminate the PKI, and the latter was more than willing to oblige. It has been revealed in recent years that the US embassy in Jakarta had compiled an extensive list of PKI leaders, cadres and sympathisers at the national, regional and local levels—data that the army did not possess. Based on this American list, the army and its equally anti-communist supporters, particularly Islamic youth organisations, were able to hunt down and kill the suspected communists by the thousands. The United States also provided a communications system that greatly assisted the army's mopping-up operations against the PKI members.[13]

Thus with the full backing of the United States—though the nature of its actual role in the killing of the communists was not fully known until recently declassified documents were released, and then reclassified due to their explosive content—the Indonesian army was finally able to destroy the PKI and remove President Sukarno from power.[14] The army became the unchallenged political force in Indonesia and quickly legitimised its political role by institutionalising the 'Dual Function' doctrine, which stated that the military was both a security force and a social-political force. This doctrine went beyond the scope of the earlier 'Middle Way' doctrine, in which the military would not dominate politics.[15] The 'New Order' government clearly placed the military, especially the army, as the most dominant political force. During the more than three decades of the 'New Order', military officers occupied strategic positions in the government, from president, several vice-presidents, cabinet ministers, ambassadors down to regents and mayors. The military was allocated seats in the House of People's Representatives and the People's Consultative Assembly, occupied strategic positions in state-owned enterprises, and basically controlled almost all aspects of Indonesian public life between 1966 and 1998.

13. See Kathy Kadane, 'Ex-agents say CIA compiled death lists for Indonesians. After 25 years, Americans speak of their role in exterminating Communist Party', *San Francisco Examiner*, 20 May 1990, and *Washington Post*, 21 May 1990.

14. See Peter Dale Scott, 'The United States and the Overthrow of Sukarno, 1965–1967', *Pacific Affairs*, 58, no. 2 (Summer 1985): 239–64.

15. See Ian MacFarling, *The Dual Function of the Indonesian Armed Forces: Military Politics in Indonesia* (Canberra: Australian Defence Studies Centre, 1996).

With the destruction of the PKI and the triumph of the anti-communist forces led by the army, the right-versus-left ideological conflict in Indonesia had in fact come to an end by early 1966. Nevertheless the 'New Order' regime continued to milk the anti-communist scare throughout its rule to silence critics, especially those who fought against social and economic exploitation and inequity. The Soeharto government also continued to reap dividends for its anti-communist purges from Washington and its allies throughout most of the 'New Order' period, particularly in the form of political support, access to defence technologies, economic aid, investment and market opportunities.

Indonesia's peaceful rise as the *primus inter pares* in ASEAN

Sukarno's foreign policy had not merely alarmed the United States and its allies due to Jakarta's increasing tilt towards China, it had also made Indonesia a feared regional bully—one that tried to force its will on its smaller neighbours. Prior to the rise of the 'New Order' government, with its anti-communist and pro-economic development outlook, Indonesia was basically out of step with its immediate maritime neighbours. While Indonesia adhered to a strongly non-aligned foreign policy, which later veered much closer to the communist camp, all of its immediate neighbours were allied one way or another with the West. To the south, Australia and New Zealand were both members of the US-led alliance, ANZUS; Sukarno's bellicose policy clearly alarmed Canberra, which always feared the threats coming from or through the Indonesian archipelago. Malaysia, formerly Malaya, and Singapore were still closely linked to Britain, which continued to retain bases in its former colonial territories. The Philippines and Thailand were both members of the US-led military alliance, SEATO (Southeast Asia Treaty Organization). While Sukarno with his strongly independent and often anti-Western foreign policy rhetoric undoubtedly felt that Indonesia was being encircled by hostile neo-colonialist and neo-imperialism forces, for their part these neighbouring countries felt equally threatened by Indonesia's confrontationist policy. It should also be borne in mind that in the early 1960s Indonesia had become the most powerful military power in Southeast Asia after procuring massive quantities of weapons from the Soviet Union.

Throughout most of his rule Sukarno was relatively successful in playing off one major contestant of the Cold War against another to extract the most benefits for Indonesia. Washington, while covertly supporting the anti-Jakarta regional rebellions in the late 1950s, also tried to maintain fairly close relations with Jakarta throughout this period, so that Indonesia would not completely be won over by the other side. Nevertheless, on one matter Washington would not oblige Indonesia, namely Indonesia's repeated requests to procure modern arms from the United States, arms that Jakarta wanted to use in its struggle to liberate West Irian (West Papua) from the Dutch. West Irian had been excluded from the sovereignty transfer agreement between the new Republic of Indonesia and the Netherlands, signed in December 1949, with the understanding that the two countries would reach a peaceful settlement over this territory at a later date. Successive efforts by Indonesia to persuade the Netherlands to resolve the West Irian dispute through negotiations failed and when similar efforts to get the United Nations to support Indonesia's position also failed in 1957, Sukarno decided to seize West Irian by force. Indonesia nationalised Dutch assets, expelled Dutch nationals, and between 1958 and 1961 began to build up its offensive military capability to launch an attack on the Dutch position in West Irian.

Indonesia turned first towards the United States for arms, but since the Netherlands was an ally of the US in NATO, Washington was unwilling to sell Indonesia arms that were clearly intended to be used against the Dutch. Moreover, President Eisenhower and Secretary of State John Foster Dulles, who regarded neutrality in the Cold War as immoral, viewed Sukarno with suspicion. The US was willing to sell a small amount of arms to Jakarta, but not the warships and fighter aircraft that Indonesia wanted.[16] Between 1958 and 1965 the United States transferred about US$431 million worth of arms to Indonesia—comprising *inter alia* two transport aircraft, 14 helicopters, 5 landing ships, and 35 P-51D Mustang fighter aircraft—which were expected to satisfy Indonesia's defence-modernisation needs without giving it an offensive capability. Indonesia, however, was not satisfied with the American arms transfers and simultaneously turned to the Soviet Union. Moscow was more than happy to oblige, and in the same period transferred US$3,396 million worth of arms to Indonesia, comprising *inter alia* 28 transport aircraft, 32 bomber aircraft, 123 MIG fighter aircraft of various types, 12 submarines, 121 anti-ship missiles of various types and 24 bomber aircraft.[17] The arms purchases from the Soviet Union between 1958 and 1965 were the largest in Indonesia's history—unmatched since in terms of both the money spent and the types and quantities of weapons procured.

This massive procurement of arms from the Soviet Union alarmed Washington sufficiently for it to put pressure on the Netherlands to cede West Irian to Indonesia. The new Kennedy administration helped to broker a deal that led to the signing of an agreement between the Netherlands and Indonesia at the UN headquarters in New York in August 1962. Under this agreement the Netherlands would transfer West Irian to the United Nations Temporary Executive Administration (UNTEA), which would administer the territory until its transfer to Indonesia in mid-1963, while Indonesia must hold a plebiscite to determine the final position of West Irian at a later date. In 1969 Indonesia held a consultation amongst the Papuan tribal elders, who overwhelmingly voted for West Irian to be part of Indonesia. Although many pro-democracy activists and supporters of the Free Papua Movement later denounced the consultation process as not really democratic,

16. Discussions about this event can be found in Kahin and Kahin, *Subversion as Foreign Policy*.

17. SIPRI Trend Indicator Values (TIVS) expressed in US dollars at constant 1990 prices.

the UN accepted the result and Indonesia's sovereign jurisdiction over West Irian was internationally recognised. The Cold War competition had undoubtedly benefited Indonesia in its national struggle to secure the return of West Irian from Dutch control.

Fresh from its victory over West Irian, Indonesia under Sukarno launched a Confrontation against the newly formed Malaysian Federation in 1963. Sukarno had watched with suspicion the development of the Malaysian Federation plan—which would bring together the Malayan Peninsula, Singapore and the British North Borneo territories of Sarawak, Sabah and Brunei (though Brunei decided in 1962 not to join the planned Federation)—regarding it as a British imperialist plot to retain influence in its former colonies, especially as British bases would continue to be maintained. His antipathy to the presence of foreign bases stemmed from the time of the regional rebellions, when the rebels received logistics support from the British bases in Malaya and Borneo and the US Clark Air Base in the Philippines. At the same time some in Indonesia were worried that by including Singapore the new Malaysian Federation would be dominated by the ethnic Chinese population. In May 1963 Sukarno held talks with Malayan Prime Minister Tunku Abdul Rahman, in which an understanding was reached whereby Indonesia would accept the Federation if a plebiscite in North Borneo showed that the people supported it. When the Tunku signed an agreement in London in early July 1963 that the Malaysian Federation would be established on 31 August 1963, before the result of the plebiscite was known, Sukarno accused the Tunku of a breach of faith and reacted by launching in late July a 'Crush Malaysia' campaign. A regional forum, Maphilindo—comprising Malaya, the Philippines and Indonesia, which had been launched in Manila earlier in July 1963 to foster closer cooperation between the three predominantly Malay nations—could not prevent the dispute between Jakarta and Kuala Lumpur from escalating.[18]

18. See Mackie, *Konfrontasi*.

To explain the *Konfrontasi*, as the campaign was popularly called in Indonesia, a number of scholars have mainly looked at the dynamics of Indonesian domestic politics under the 'Guided Democracy'. Franklin Weinstein, for instance, argued that Indonesia's confrontationist foreign policy served certain domestic political functions for each of its main protagonists—Sukarno, the army and the PKI—each using the political agitation and the limited military campaign carried out against Malaysia to consolidate its own hold on power. Sukarno was able to indulge in rousing public speeches to unite the fractious political forces against a common external enemy, the PKI was able to mobilise supporters and organise large public rallies, while the army was able to justify its continued large defence spending while demonstrating its patriotism and loyalty to President Sukarno. The army furthermore did not want the PKI to gain an advantage through the political agitation that the *Konfrontasi* atmosphere afforded opportunities for.[19]

Some, however, have argued that Indonesia's Confrontation against Malaysia was driven by Jakarta's territorial ambitions in North Borneo, notwithstanding Sukarno's claim that Indonesia had no such ambitions. While Indonesia vehemently denied that it had territorial designs on its neighbouring countries, one would probably concur with Michael Leifer's argument that Indonesia's policy towards its immediate neighbours had been driven by two contradictory impulses, namely a sense of regional entitlement on the one hand and vulnerability on the other.[20] Leifer argued that as the largest country in Southeast Asia, Indonesia expected to be consulted and its views taken into account on matters affecting the region as a whole. At the same time its large size, porous borders and limited capability to defend its boundaries had also instilled in Indonesia a deep feeling of vulnerability vis-à-vis the neighbouring territories, which could be used to launch an attack

19. Franklin B. Weinstein, *Indonesia Abandons Confrontation: An Inquiry into the Functions of Indonesian Foreign Policy* (Ithaca: Cornell University Press, 1969).

20. Michael Leifer, *Indonesia's Foreign Policy* (London: George Allen & Unwin, 1983).

or subversive activities against Indonesia. In the case of Indonesia's Confrontation against Malaysia, Sukarno probably genuinely viewed the Malaysian Federation as a British imperialist plot to encircle the independent-minded Republic of Indonesia. At the same time it was also clear that Jakarta felt entitled to be consulted by Kuala Lumpur on such important an matter as the formation of the Malaysian Federation. Indonesia, with its revolutionary history, immense size and strategic location, clearly viewed itself as a leading country in Southeast Asia, and under Sukarno Jakarta was willing to enforce its will through political and military confrontation.

Sukarno's search for regional primacy to enhance Indonesia's national security ironically produced the opposite results. Indonesia became isolated regionally, surrounded by mostly hostile powers, while internationally it was pushed into much closer relations with a few radical communist countries such as China and North Korea. All of these developments exacerbated the domestic tensions between the PKI and the army, particularly as the army saw that the *Konfrontasi* benefited the PKI more, by pushing Indonesia closer to the left. Thus even before Sukarno was impeached—he had been appointed president for life—by the provisional People's Consultative Assembly in 1966, General Soeharto had already started a secret negotiation with Malaysia to bring *Konfrontasi* to an end.

Soeharto's 'New Order' government pursued a substantially different policy from that of Sukarno's 'Guided Democracy'. Soeharto and the army were much more concerned about internal threats to national security than threats from outside, and focused its policy on ways to reduce these threats as well as on strengthening the capacity of the state to govern the country. While Sukarno had pursued a 'lighthouse' foreign policy to put Indonesia on the world map and to confront its enemies, often at the expense of economic development at home, Soeharto emphasised economic development as the best way to strengthen the Indonesian nation-state. Unlike Sukarno, who regarded neo-colonialism and neo-imperialism as the main threats to Indonesian security, Soeharto viewed communism, which could exploit poverty and social inequality, as the major threat. Even as China was regarded by the 'New Order' government as the most immediate external threat, it was the possibility of ideological subversion coming from China that most concerned Jakarta, rather than military threats per se. Thus the military-dominated 'New Order' government extolled the importance of developing national and regional resilience, which did not put too much emphasis on military power. National resilience was to be achieved through a comprehensive security approach that combined strict political control with rapid economic growth and improvement of welfare, which would in turn contribute towards the development of regional resilience; regional resilience would also be attained through regional cooperation and a good-neighbour policy.

Far from regarding its immediate neighbours as 'neo-imperialist puppets', as Sukarno did, the 'New Order' government shared a similar strong anti-communist outlook with them. This made it possible for Jakarta to transform its earlier confrontational foreign policy to one of regional cooperation. Soeharto's foreign policy towards Southeast Asia, which culminated in the establishment of the Association of Southeast Asian Nations (ASEAN) on 8 August 1967, was primarily driven by his desire to focus on Indonesia's internal development free from external distractions. The internal focus of the 'New Order' differed markedly from Sukarno's efforts, which often used external adventures to avoid having to address intractable domestic problems. Nevertheless, in terms of his envisioned regional order, Soeharto was not fundamentally different from Sukarno: he sought to reduce the influence of extra-regional powers and at the same time enhance the ability of the regional members to be masters in their own house.[21] In such a regional

21. See Howard Warshawsky, 'From Confrontation to Cooperation: The influence of domestic forces on Indonesian foreign policy', PhD thesis, University of Virginia, 1974.

order, Indonesia, as the largest member, would clearly occupy the position of first amongst equals—without having to assert itself too much, which in fact could be counterproductive. Soeharto's desired regional order was made possible by the fact that there was no imminent external security threat to worry about. Notwithstanding Indonesia's rejection of security alliances, Jakarta clearly benefited from the presence of the US forward military deployment in the region against possible communist threats from the north. As a result, Indonesia felt no urgent need to divert scarce resources towards the development of a huge defence force.

Indonesia's shift from confrontation to a good-neighbour policy with Malaysia—which was followed immediately by participation in the establishment of ASEAN—was due to at least three main reasons. First, the 'New Order' government needed to foster a peaceful and friendly regional environment so that Indonesia would not have to worry about the security of its borders or fear threats from the neighbouring countries, thus enabling it to concentrate on its domestic priorities. During the *Konfrontasi*, large numbers of Indonesian troops had been stationed along the Indonesian-Malaysian border in Kalimantan, which clearly put pressure on the national budget. Second, Indonesia needed to show to the wider international community, particularly prospective donors and investors, that Jakarta was truly committed to becoming a peaceful member of the region and fully focused on its own internal development. Third, cooperation with countries that shared its concerns about the communist danger, including the perceived threat from China, helped to enhance Indonesia's overall sense of security vis-à-vis the wider region, even though ASEAN was never intended as a security alliance.[22]

As noted earlier, while their approaches were fundamentally different, Sukarno and Soeharto in fact shared a very similar vision of the regional order and Indonesia's position in such an order.

22. Dewi Fortuna Anwar, *Indonesia in ASEAN: Foreign Policy and Regionalism* (Singapore: Institute of Southeast Asian Studies, 1994).

Soeharto's anti-communism did not make him less nationalistic than Sukarno when it came to the appropriate role of foreign military powers in Southeast Asia. This was clearly seen in the 1967 Bangkok Declaration establishing ASEAN, which stipulated, at Indonesia's insistence, that foreign military bases were temporary in nature and should not be used to threaten the other member countries—even though Soeharto, unlike his predecessor, clearly did not feel immediately threatened by these bases. While all of the other original members of ASEAN were linked in security alliances with Western powers, ASEAN issued the Declaration on the Zone of Peace, Freedom and Neutrality (ZOPFAN) of Southeast Asia in 1971, which also emphasised the region's desire to be free of external interventions at the height of the Cold War. At the first ASEAN summit in Bali in February 1976 the association formally adopted Indonesia's development credo of national and regional resilience, as can be seen from the Declaration of ASEAN Concord (Bali Concord I).

By veering to the right in the Cold War and developing close cooperation with its non-communist neighbours, Indonesia under the 'New Order' government succeeded in achieving two strategic outcomes. First, as Indonesia's potential as a regional troublemaker was duly recognised, its subsequent good-boy policy became doubly appreciated not just by the immediate neighbouring countries but also by the United States and its allies, such as Japan, which invested heavily in Indonesia's economic development. These countries regarded Indonesia as a lynchpin of regional stability in Southeast Asia worthy of their support. Indonesia had frozen its diplomatic relations with China and while it continued to maintain diplomatic relations with the other communist countries these became cool and distant. The United States, which in the earlier period had been reluctant to sell massive quantities of modern arms to Indonesia, began to be Indonesia's most important arms supplier from 1970 onward—up until Washington imposed an arms embargo in the wake of the Santa Cruz incident in East

Timor in November 1991.[23] Although still less than the total worth of arms transferred by the Soviet Union in the late 1950s and 1960s, between 1970 and 1990 Indonesia procured US$2,151 million worth of arms from the United States, including 16 F-5E Tiger-2 combat aircraft.[24] Second, Indonesia's deliberately low-profile policy in ASEAN was also appreciated by the other members. Sensitive of its earlier image as a regional bully, Indonesia under Soeharto followed the Javanese strategy of *tut wuri handayani*, or 'leading from behind', in ASEAN. Yet there was little doubt that President Soeharto, especially as he became one of the longest-serving leaders in ASEAN, was highly respected, and Jakarta's wishes were generally deferred to by the other members of ASEAN. In short, throughout the 'New Order' period Indonesia was usually seen as the *primus inter pares* in ASEAN.

Annexation of East Timor

Another important indication of the great benefits enjoyed by Soeharto's 'New Order' government due to the strategic environment of the Cold War was Indonesia's annexation of East Timor at the end of 1975 without encountering any significant international opposition. The small Portuguese colony of East Timor, which shares Timor Island with the Indonesian territory of West Timor—part of the East Nusa Tenggara Province—had never been claimed by Indonesia when it fought for independence from the Dutch. The new Republic of Indonesia claimed only the former territory of the Netherlands East Indies, which included West Irian, but not East Timor nor the British North Borneo territories, which also shared land borders with Indonesian provinces in Kalimantan. Suggestions by some of the early nationalist leaders,

23. On 12 November 1991, Indonesian soldiers fired on East Timorese pro-independence protesters at the Santa Cruz cemetery, killing several people, which led to international condemnation of Indonesia, particularly from Western countries.

24. SIPRI Trend Indicator Values (TIVS) expressed in US dollars at constant 1990 prices.

such as Muhammad Yamin, for the formation of Indonesia Raya, or 'Greater Indonesia', which would include not just the Netherlands East Indies territories but also the adjacent colonised Malay territories of Malaya, Sabah and Sarawak, as well as the Portuguese colony of East Timor, were quashed by other nationalist leaders, who argued that Indonesia would not be an expansionist state. While Indonesia fought hard to reclaim West Irian from the Dutch as part of the Netherlands East Indies patrimony, and also launched a Confrontation against Malaysia over the incorporation of Sabah and Sarawak into the Malaysian Federation, it generally ignored East Timor. Even during the fiery anti-colonialist rule of Sukarno, Indonesia did not consider the presence of the Portuguese in East Timor, right in the middle of the Indonesian archipelago, as a threat.

Jakarta's general indifference towards East Timor changed dramatically when Portugal left East Timor precipitately after the right-wing government in Lisbon was overthrown by a leftist military revolt in April 1974. The new government in Lisbon was inclined towards decolonisation and this attitude encouraged nationalist movements in East Timor to seek independence. Three political groups emerged: the Timorese Democratic Union (UDT), supported by Timor elites and senior Portuguese colonial administrators; the Revolutionary Front for an Independent East Timor (Fretilin), a left-leaning party supported by younger East Timorese and lower-level colonial officials; and the Timorese Popular Democratic Association (Apodeti), which was for integration with Indonesia. The Fretilin enjoyed the greatest popular support amongst the three political groups and pushed for a quicker independence. In January 1975 they formed an alliance with the UDT, but because of the UDT's concerns about the Fretilin's communist outlook, the alliance collapsed in May. Fearing a Fretilin takeover, the UDT launched a coup to drive Fretilin supporters out of Dili, the capital, in August; in September the Fretilin launched a counterattack. With most of the Portuguese administrators fleeing to the island of Atauro, the Fretilin had de facto control over most of East Timor.[25]

While Indonesia initially supported the right of East Timor to be independent, the 'New Order' government clearly did not welcome the prospect of an independent East Timor under the left-leaning Fretilin, concerned undoubtedly that a communist power might be invited to build its base there. Concerns about growing communist influence in the region had been heightened by the defeat of the American troops in Vietnam in mid-1975, leaving Vietnam and later the whole of Indochina under communist sway. Indonesia did not immediately send troops to intervene in the civil war in East Timor because of concerns about possible international reaction. Instead, it conducted secret infiltrations into East Timor, launched anti-Fretilin propaganda, and mobilised support for pro-Indonesian integration amongst the followers of the UDT and Apodeti. On 28 November the Fretilin declared the independence of East Timor and on the very next day Indonesia extracted a 'declaration of integration' from the representatives of the UDT and the Apodeti. Indonesia launched a full-scale invasion of East Timor almost immediately after the visit of US President Gerald Ford and State Secretary Henry Kissinger to Jakarta on 6 December 1975.

It was always widely understood that Indonesia's annexation of East Timor had the blessing of the United States and other major Western powers, notwithstanding the later criticism and condemnation that came from these sources. The Western powers, including Australia, were equally worried about the emergence of a communist enclave in the middle of the Indonesian archipelago, so they were probably quite relieved to have Jakarta solve this problem. In any case the 'New Order' government till the end of the Cold War did not encounter too much difficulty from West-

25. William Burr and Michael L. Evans (eds), 'East Timor Revisited: Ford, Kissinger and the Indonesian Invasion, 1975–76', *National Security Archive Electronic Briefing Book*, no. 62 (6 Dec 2001), www.gwu.edu/-nsarchiv/NSAEBB/NSAEBB62/.

ern governments over its integration of East Timor. The criticisms that it did face came from Western non-governmental organisations protesting human-rights abuses committed by the Indonesian military in East Timor.

Recently declassified documents from the Gerald R. Ford Presidential Library, released to the National Security Archive, reveal clearly the relationship between Ford and Soeharto. A number of documents, including the minutes of the meeting between Ford and Soeharto in Jakarta, indicate that the US was fully cognizant of Indonesia's intentions to take over East Timor and raised no objection to this plan. In fact, both the American president and the secretary of state fully understood Indonesia's security concerns and desire to have East Timor firmly under Jakarta's control. The only requests by the visiting American leaders were that American arms not be used in the invasion, as this would violate US laws on the lawful use of arms, and that the invasion be carried out after President Ford had returned to the United States.[26]

Such an understanding and acceptance of a country annexing another country by the United States—Soeharto had in fact earlier hesitated to encroach on East Timor openly until he had the green light from Washington—was only possible in the Cold War years. Once the Cold War was over, Indonesia's rule over East Timor came under increasing criticism from Western governments. As mentioned earlier, the United States imposed an arms embargo on Indonesia in the wake of the Santa Cruz incident, in which several pro-independence East Timorese demonstrators were killed by Indonesian troops in November 1991. From that point onward Indonesia's position in East Timor became increasingly untenable, and a year after the fall of Soeharto, his successor, B.J. Habibie, allowed the East Timorese to vote for their independence through

26. Document 4, Embassy Jakarta Telegram 1579 to Secretary State, 6 December 1975 [Text of Ford-Kissinger-Soeharto Discussion], Secret/Nodis (24), Gerald R. Ford Library: Kissinger-Scowcroft Temporary File, Box A 3, Country File, Far East-Indonesia, State Department Telegrams 4/1/75–9/22/76. Burr and Evans, 'East Timor Revisited'.

a UN-sponsored referendum. The US arms embargo was only fully lifted in 2005, after Indonesia had become a fully fledged democracy and the military had been removed from politics.

An authoritarian developmental state

The establishment of the anti-communist military-led 'New Order' government in Indonesia has been seen by many as a victory of the United States over its competitors in gaining the friendship of the largest country in Southeast Asia during the ideologically competitive Cold War period. In the eyes of many critics American deep interests in Indonesia were primarily driven by the former's desire to have free access to the latter's rich natural resources, such as oil and various minerals. Sukarno had been hostile to foreign economic interests and in fact nationalised Dutch-owned assets in the late 1950s over the West Irian dispute. Under the more radical nationalist outlook of the 'Guided Democracy', especially with the growing influence of the PKI, Indonesia's overall economic policy and attitude towards foreign direct investment, which would mostly come from Western countries and Japan, were not conducive for business to say the least. Sukarno openly stated that he was not too interested in the economy; and a focus on economic development, which would have necessitated more sober politics, fiscal discipline and close cooperation with the major industrialised countries, would certainly have cramped Sukarno's revolutionary style. It was therefore not surprising that the United States tried various means to undermine Sukarno throughout the 1950s and early 1960s. Although the regional rebellions in the 1950s were not secessionist movements that sought independence from Jakarta, as Kahin and Kahin showed, Washington certainly entertained the idea of partitioning Indonesia so that Sukarno and his leftist policy would be confined to resource-poor Java, while the well-endowed Outer Islands would come under the control of a new, non-communist regime backed by the United States.[27]

27. Kahin and Kahin, *Subversion as Foreign Policy*.

In a highly critical article entitled 'Ford Country: Building an Elite for Indonesia', David Ransom argued that immediately after Indonesian independence, the United States had begun to cultivate members of the Indonesian elite whose nationalist ideology was more moderate than that of Sukarno and more open to close economic cooperation with the West. Ransom highlighted the important role played by the PSI (Indonesian Socialist Party) leader, the economist Sumitro Djohohadikusumo, who later joined the regional rebellions after Sukarno began nationalising Dutch holdings in 1957. As early as 1949 Sumitro explained to an American audience in Washington D.C. that "his kind of socialism included 'free access to Indonesian resources' and 'sufficient incentives' for foreign corporate investment".[28] After the defeat of the regional rebels, Sumitro went overseas to live in self-imposed exile and only returned to Indonesia after the rise of Soeharto, to become one of the chief architects of the Indonesian economy under the 'New Order'. Sumitro became the doyen of a new crop of Indonesian economists dubbed the 'Berkeley Mafia', for most of them had been trained as economists in the 1950s and early 1960s at the University of Berkeley with scholarships from the Ford Foundation, who managed the Indonesian economy throughout most of the 'New Order' period. Ransom argued that Ford had launched its efforts to create a modernising elite for Indonesia from 1954 involving tertiary institutions in the United States such as MIT, Cornell, Berkeley and Harvard to "remold the old Indonesian hierarchs into modern administrators, trained to work under the new indirect rule of Americans".[29] Regardless of the possible motivations of the United States and its various public and private agencies such as Ford, it would clearly be a gross simplification to argue that the 'New Order' government was established to serve American interests. What is probably more correct is that the Indonesian

28. David Ransom, 'Ford Country: Building an Elite for Indonesia' in Steve Weissman (ed.), *The Trojan Horse: A Radical Look at Foreign Aid*, revised edition (Palo Alto: Ramparts Press, 1975), pp. 93–116.

29. Ibid.

military's worldview and strategy of controlling and developing Indonesia converged with the strategic and economic interests of the United States so that both profited from their association with each other.

As mentioned at the beginning of this chapter the 'New Order' government was primarily concerned with maintaining security and order, controlling the centrifugal forces that threatened to pull it apart, and concentrating power in the hands of the central government. To achieve these objectives Soeharto pursued a double-prong strategy of political stability and economic development—which were regarded as indivisible. Economic development could only be carried out if there was political stability, and political stability could only be maintained if there was sufficient economic development which would make it possible to improve public welfare and remove the root causes of social discontent and radicalism.

In reaction to the ideological competition and frenetic politicisation of the earlier period, the 'New Order' government tried to depoliticise the political system by, among other measures, tightly limiting the number and controlling the activities of political parties and forcing every organisation to accept the national ideology, Pancasila. Civil and political rights were restricted, and opponents of the government were often jailed. The military permeated every facet of public life from the capital down to the village level, quashing dissent before it could become a major problem to the state. All of these state-security measures were justified on the grounds that they were necessary for maintaining a politically conducive environment in which rapid economic development could take place.[30] In this respect, Indonesia followed a policy similar to many other authoritarian developmental states in East Asia dur-

30. See, among others, Dwight Y. King, 'Indonesia's "New Order" as a Bureaucratic Polity, a Neopatrimonial Regime, or a Bureaucratic Authoritarian Regime: What Difference Does it Make?' in Benedict Anderson and Audrey Kahin (eds), *Interpreting Indonesian Politics: Thirteen Contributions to the Debate* (Ithaca: Cornell Modern Indonesia Project, 1982).

ing the Cold War, such as South Korea, Taiwan and Thailand, all of whom were strongly anti-communist in nature. In Indonesia any criticism of the government's often harsh policies, especially in relation to land acquisition or labour exploitation, was liable to being labelled as communist subversion and therefore likely to incur harsh punishment.

Throughout the Cold War period the wider strategic environment enabled regimes such as Soeharto's 'New Order' to flourish and become a respectable member of the regional and international community. Frequent reports about human rights abuses, particularly in East Timor, Aceh, and Papua, but also generally throughout Indonesia, and the practices of Pancasila democracy, which were widely acknowledged to be less than democratic, did not diminish the attraction of Indonesia in the eyes of its many Western supporters. The 'New Order' government did in fact deliver on its promise of making Indonesia a relatively stable country with a vibrant economy, which contributed positively to the peace and stability of its immediate region. By introducing a new foreign investment law in 1967 that allowed foreign capital to invest in various economic sectors, including oil, gas and mining industries, which came to be dominated by American companies, Indonesia embarked on several decades of rapid economic growth, which only temporarily came to a halt during the Asian financial crisis in the late 1990s.

Between 1976 and 1996, according to Thee Kian Wie, rapid and sustained economic growth in Indonesia led to a sharp reduction in the incidence of poverty from 40 to 11 per cent.[31] This enviable economic performance was made possible because of the prudent management by the mostly American-trained technocrats who were given almost a free hand to do their job by Soeharto and shielded from the possible distracting effect of politics. These technocrats and other supporters of the authoritarian devel-

31. Thee Kian Wie, 'Indonesia's Economic Performance under Soeharto's New Order', *Seoul Journal of Economics*, vol. 20, no. 2 (2007).

opmental state had argued that for a developing country like Indonesia democracy was an unnecessary luxury; the 'immature' people needed a firm hand to control and guide them so that they could devote their energy to improving their economic welfare. This anti-democratic and developmental ideology was dominant throughout most of the Cold War period, not just in Indonesia but also amongst the major Western donors and investors who were quite content to witness Indonesia's emergence as one of the new Asian economic miracles.

It took the end of the Cold War and the rise of new international priorities, such as democracy and human rights replacing concerns about ideology and security, for the symbiotic relationship between Soeharto and the major Western countries to come to an end. Starting from the 1991 Santa Cruz incident in East Timor, Soeharto's standing in Washington and in other major Western capitals began to go downhill. From then on the United States, among others, began to cultivate new Indonesian elites who could be partners in pushing for the democratisation of Indonesia and challenging the legitimacy of the 'New Order' political construction.

12

THE COLD WAR IN HINDSIGHT: LOCAL REALITIES AND THE LIMITS OF GLOBAL POWER

Merle C. Ricklefs

During the Cold War, unquestionably great powers loomed over Southeast Asia. The US and USSR, principal poles of the divided world after World War II, wielded real influence in the region and around the world. China, though preoccupied with internal problems, was never entirely absent from the political calculations of Southeast Asian leaders (and would become more so in the 1980s as Deng Xiaoping's reforms brought greater development). In this political climate, several Southeast Asian states came to be directly connected with the Cold War powers: Thailand and the Philippines, as members of SEATO; the South Vietnamese, with their American backing; and the North Vietnamese, with their Communist supporters. But these obvious cases tend to overshadow other, less significant consequences of the great powers' influence. We may still ask to what extent the competition among the great Cold War powers shaped the affairs of the Southeast Asian states: what was the direction of causation, where did agency lie, and what were the limits of the great powers' powers during the Cold War?

Causation, agency and control

These issues are part of a larger historical topic in two contexts. In the context of Southeast Asian history, it was a common assumption of colonial-era historiography that the colonial powers set the agenda and the colonised peoples responded. As the colonial era has receded in time, this stereotype has largely disappeared from Southeast Asian historical studies. There is no doubt that the colonial period and the colonial powers were important, but we now see more clearly that Southeast Asians retained much room for manoeuvre and that their powers of agency were not entirely lost. We have come to think of the colonial period more as a time of interaction, synthesis and partnership. The same may now be true of our views of the Cold War, already more than two decades behind us. If so, then reconsidering the impact of the Cold War can contribute to our understanding of the tenacity and ongoing agency of local politics, local issues and local leaders.

The second context is that of global geopolitics. World history teems with aspirant global hegemons. We need only think of Alexander the Great in the 4th century BCE, or of Pope Alexander VI, the Spanish and the Portuguese in the 16th century imagining that they could divide the globe between two Catholic states, to recognise that pretensions to global hegemony are hardly new. The colonial period was full of boundaries agreed on maps by colonial powers whose writ was hardly—or not at all—recognisable where those lines lay on the ground. The Cold War was part of this pattern, as each 'bloc' looked at the world in terms of where its influence or intervention could be decisive. The pattern was replicated more recently in triumphalist American rhetoric about the "end of history" and aspirations to international dominance that followed the Cold War. Looking again at the Cold War period itself should convince us, as does earlier history, that there are major constraints on the capacity of aspirant hegemons to set the agenda, to control the direction of causation or to know the consequences of their policies. This is a lesson not just for historians, but for policymakers in every age.

The Cold War, in hindsight, had its greatest impact in Southeast Asia at its beginning and—perhaps—at its end. At both times, world politics seemed in flux, old certainties no longer applied, new kinds of relationships seemed possible. It was unclear just how the world was going to work—both in the latter half of the 1940s as well as in the early 1990s. Thus were created circumstances in which political actors might miscalculate their environment, but might also find new opportunities. Between those two periods, Southeast Asian states and policy elites approached the Cold War as a fact of life, a context that had to be acknowledged. Indeed, rather than the Cold War powers restraining Southeast Asians' freedom of manoeuvre, generally the latter exploited the context to maintain their power of agency. It was arguably the great powers themselves whose flexibility of policy were restricted by the application of their Cold War strategic assessments, doctrines and priorities. These were such as to amount at times to ideological blinkers that probably made it difficult for them to recognise strategic opportunities. In other words, the Cold War in Southeast Asia demonstrates again—as do countless episodes from Alexander the Great to the colonial period—that power does not always, in fact frequently does not, add up to control.

The beginning: Cold War geopolitics, 1945–1950

In late 1945 the United States was the most powerful state in the world—victorious over its enemies, richer than in 1939, stronger militarily than any other state, the world's first and only nuclear-armed nation, without a peer in world politics or history. The Western European states were devastated and exhausted by the war and dependent on US economic aid for recovery. The Soviet Union—America's future competitor—was similarly heavily damaged by the war and concentrating on creating a secure zone in Eastern Europe under its domination, but also recovering rapidly. Over 1945–46 the US and its allies became convinced that they faced a new threat in the form of Soviet expansion in Europe, an idea given greater public recognition in Churchill's famous speech of March 1946 in Fulton, Missouri, in which the term 'Iron Curtain' was born.

Events in 1948 confirmed in US eyes that an aggressive 'Communist bloc' campaign for hegemony was not confined to Europe.

The Communist coup d'etat in Czechoslovakia and the Berlin Blockade confirmed the depth of conflict in the European theatre. These events seemed to be paralleled in East and Southeast Asia: the rebellion of the Red Flag Communists in Burma (the White Flag Communists having been in rebellion since 1946); the outbreak of the so-called 'Emergency' in Malaya; the advances of the Hukbalahap guerrillas in the Philippines; and Mao's advances in China. In the following year, the Soviet nuclear test of August 1949 and Mao's declaration of the People's Republic of China in October intensified the anxieties of the Americans and their allies. A Soviet-led Communist empire appeared to be advancing aggressively on a world scale, and was nuclear-armed like the Americans. American strategic thinking was now dominated by the idea that a 'Cold War' was under way, pitting an American-led 'Free World' against a Soviet-led 'bloc'. The defence of the United States and its allies therefore depended on 'containing'—and if possible turning back—the threat posed by that bloc.

Within Southeast Asia, it was American strategic doctrines and actions that were most important throughout the Cold War. This was because in fact the United States' presence was far stronger there than that of either the PRC or USSR. The PRC had the weight of population on its side, but could never match American economic, technological or military power. The USSR was more of a match, but given the distances from Soviet territory to Southeast Asia and American capacity to dominate shipping lanes, Soviet power could never be projected there on a par with that of the US. In any case, American, Chinese and Soviet histories gave these states differing priorities. For the USSR, Central Europe and Central Asia were the sources of the greatest threats to the Soviet heartland and therefore received the greatest priority in strategic thinking. For the Chinese, the greatest threats had always come from their Inner Asian frontiers, where they now bumped into the Soviet Union; Chinese policies had only rarely involved projecting power by sea or overland into Southeast Asia. PRC priorities continued to follow this pattern, although they were now somewhat complicated by the presence of the fled Chiang Kai-shek government in Taiwan, where it survived under American protection. For the Americans, however, the Western Pacific and East Asia had long been a significant area, where commercial interests were committed and power was projected via a powerful navy. American possession of Hawaii, along with the American colonial period in the Philippines, the continued American military presence there, and the post-war US occupation of Japan, all reflected this priority. Thus, for the Americans, events in Southeast Asia were closer to historical strategic priorities than was true of the USSR. For the PRC, Southeast Asia gained greater strategic importance in this period precisely because of the American presence and the threat of American-led 'containment'.

American policy saw the struggle against Communism as universal—domestic as well as international. Hence the American domestic political furore over China being 'lost' to the Communists—as if it had ever been America's to lose—which, along with other events, sparked the McCarthyism of the 1950s. American television and politics of the 1950s promoted the idea of an all-pervasive threat of Communist espionage and sabotage within the country and abroad. Later, the launching of the Soviet *Sputnik* satellite in 1957 produced still further American anxieties that the presumed American technological lead no longer existed. There followed the claims of a 'missile gap' that served John F. Kennedy well in his 1960 presidential campaign. So the Cold War in Southeast Asia as a theatre of major American strategic thought and political commitment was driven by both domestic and foreign policy considerations.

Southeast Asia and the developing Cold War, 1945–1950

Within Southeast Asia, the array of US-USSR-PRC strategic and political thought and priorities had its greatest impact over the period 1945–50 in Vietnam and Indonesia. A consideration of the diametrically opposite outcomes in those two areas can tell us a great deal about this early period, when much remained uncertain about just how the world was going to work and while American global predominance was still evident.

In September 1945, Ho Chi Minh declared the Democratic Republic of Vietnam (DRV) in Hanoi. During the war his Viet Minh guerrillas had worked with the American Office of Strategic Services (OSS) and when the DRV was declared, signs of OSS sympathy were to be seen. The DRV declaration quoted the American Declaration of Independence of 1776. During the war, President Roosevelt had displayed considerable hostility to French intentions to reoccupy Indochina and preferred the idea of a United Nations trusteeship—although what that might amount to was far from clear. These ideas died with Roosevelt in April 1945.

Upon the Japanese surrender, British-commanded South-East Asia Command (SEAC) forces occupied Vietnam south of the 16th parallel and allowed the French to return and reoccupy the towns. Chiang Kai-shek's forces reoccupied Vietnam north of the 16th parallel, but had no long-term interest in the region. They concentrated on looting anything of value and then turned the area over to the French in February 1946. The French and DRV sides made some efforts at negotiations, but there was distrust and bad faith on both sides and fighting broke out in December 1946.

What position the Americans would take in this conflict was crucial to both sides. For the Americans, the choice was fairly straightforward. Europe was the top priority in the thinking of President Truman and the State Department. There, the issue was how to keep France on the 'Free World' side and strong, and at this time it was conventional wisdom that colonies were a source of strength, for no European power had yet been drained by fighting to retain a colony in Asia. Those resisting French reoccupation—mainly Ho and his Viet Minh—were Communists, and in the context of the emerging Cold War, that was a decisive issue in US thought. The European priority therefore won and American sympathy was on the French side.

The Americans' sympathy for the French was translated into support of their military action in Vietnam—really as one part of a wider anti-Communist strategy in Asia. In June–July 1950, as the Korean War erupted, President Truman took three related steps: he ordered the US Navy to block the Straits of Taiwan to prevent PRC action against Chiang's government in Taiwan; authorised the use of American forces in Korea; and allocated major funding to support French military action in Vietnam. By 1953, the United States was covering some 80 per cent of French military costs there. Arguably, for the Americans this war was never about Vietnam itself; it was about France, China and the USSR. The war in Korea was something more than just a 'proxy war', in the sense that American, Russian and Chinese forces were directly engaged from 1950 and the war was fought near the borders of the USSR and PRC. The Vietnam War had crucial differences. While American combat forces eventually became directly involved in Vietnam, there were never significant Soviet or Chinese combat forces there. The PRC provided a rear base, materiel and advisers for the Viet Minh in the early 1950s, but Chinese support was limited, not least because of the PRC's entanglement in Korea. Moreover, China was a very poor country, rich only in people. The Soviet Union was far stronger by 1950, but it was difficult for it to send military supplies to the Vietnamese Communists given the distances involved. So if American wealth and power were ever to prevail in a 'hot' version of the Cold War, its best prospects were in Vietnam.

The motivations of the main actors in the Vietnam conflict c. 1945–50 were clear. For Ho and his supporters, the goal was independence and the creation of a Communist-dominated state. Non-Communists would either collaborate or be eliminated. These aims, it should be emphasised, long pre-dated the Cold War. The French aim was to re-establish the French Indochina colony and thereby regain national wealth and prestige after war, defeat, occupation, collaboration and liberation at the hands of others. This aim also pre-dated the Cold War. For the French, the anti-Communism of American Cold War doctrine provided an opportunity to manoeuvre the Americans into supporting their cause.

The US had two potentially conflicting ideologies. One predated the Cold War, being American anti-imperialism. This was a powerful tradition and had been reflected in Roosevelt's ideas of UN trusteeships for former European colonies after the war. The other American ideology was anti-Communism, which the Cold War reinforced, and this time anti-Communism trumped anti-imperialism. Those resisting French reconquest were Communists, so American support went to the French. This also saw the beginning of the American search for non-Communist nationalists, who could reconcile America's policy dilemma between anti-Communism and anti-imperialism, but this search met little success in Vietnam.

Hence it was the US whose analysis and actions were constrained by Cold War doctrine. Pressuring the French and DRV to achieve some sort of accommodation was never a realistic policy objective to the Americans. France was too important in Europe to offend and the main opposition to the French in Vietnam were Communists. Thus began over two decades of frustration and terrible costs for the US, as the hegemon that had fought World War II on two fronts, and had won it almost single-handedly in the Pacific, found itself facing the limits of its hegemony in a smallish country stretched narrowly along the South China Sea. Meanwhile the DRV and French pursued objectives far older than the Cold War, the French using Cold War thought to their advantage, Ho and his followers pursuing their goals despite the additional difficulties of doing so in the midst of the Cold War.

The Indonesia story was very different and even more clearly instructive about the years between 1945 and 1950. In August 1945 Sukarno and Hatta declared independence. At this stage there was a political and military vacuum in the archipelago. Japan had surrendered but the Allied forces under SEAC who were to accept that surrender had not yet reached Indonesia. This vacuum gave the Indonesian revolutionaries—which in many cases meant locally formed groups of youth activists—the chance to take control of the main cities and public facilities, particularly in Java and Sumatra. It was some time, however, before news of the declaration of independence reached some more remote parts of the archipelago.

In September SEAC troops arrived in Java and Sumatra and faced an Indonesian republican fait accompli. SEAC's commanding general, Lord Mountbatten, treated the republican administrations that he faced as the de facto governments, but conflicts nevertheless arose. They came to a head in the bloody Battle of Surabaya in November 1945. The SEAC forces prevailed there, inflicting major losses on the Indonesian side, but lost their commanding officer. The British decided at this stage that exit would be prudent and allowed the Dutch to resume control of major cities over late 1945 and early 1946. In eastern Indonesia, Australian forces under SEAC took the Japanese surrender and facilitated a quick Dutch restoration there, where in any case the revolution had more shallow roots.

Indonesian-Dutch negotiations followed. As in Vietnam, there was distrust and bad faith on both sides and the agreements failed. In July 1947 the Dutch felt able—and indeed obliged by mounting costs—to take military action. This was dubbed a 'police action' on the grounds that it took place within sovereign Dutch territory, a view utterly rejected by the Indonesian Republicans. Dutch forces gained control of all of the deepwater ports of Java, Madura, much of Sumatra (where there were much-needed oil, coal and rubber stocks) and part of East Java (where sugar was stockpiled).

At this stage, Australia—now under Chifley's Labor government—drew the attention of the UN Security Council to the Indonesia conflict. The Americans were uncomfortable about the Australian action, and indeed suspected Chifley's government of leftist inclinations, but did not attempt to block this action. India and the USSR also expressed support for the Indonesians.

At this stage no one knew whether the UN would have teeth. The Soviets had already begun to use their veto power to block Security Council decisions, but the UN was nevertheless still thought to be potentially powerful. In 1950–53 it did, in fact, fight a war in Korea, although that was because the USSR made the mistake of walking out of the meeting rather than casting a veto. So in 1947, UN attention to the Indonesian conflict was thought likely to be a development of significance. The Security Council called for a ceasefire in Indonesia, a vote on which the US abstained. Again the Americans faced the policy dilemma of deciding between their anti-imperialist and anti-Communist instincts (for there were obvious leftists in the Indonesian government), and between their interest in Europe and their interest in Asia. In this latter context, it was to the disadvantage of the Dutch that they were of far less significance in European politics than the French.

The anti-imperialist versus anti-Communist dilemma of the Americans was resolved by developments in Indonesia in 1948. The Indonesian Communist Party (PKI) leader Muso returned after years of exile in August 1948 and set about unifying Indonesian leftists under the leadership of the party. The following month PKI activists took control in Madiun and Muso declared a new Indonesian Republican government, formally initiating a Communist rebellion against the Republic led by Sukarno and Hatta. Communist activists took over many other towns in East Java as well. In the areas they held, they attacked and killed enemies, including Islamic religious leaders. Sukarno ordered the Indonesian military to crush the rebellion. Although there was considerable leftist sympathy within the regular military, Sukarno's influence and the threat posed by PKI to the republic—while Dutch forces stood watching at nearby ceasefire lines—proved decisive. The Siliwangi Division led the assault on Madiun. Muso and others were killed and the uprising was crushed. Perhaps some 8000 were killed in these events and the PKI was destroyed as a political force until the 1950s.

In the crushing of the Communist uprising by the Indonesian Republic, the Americans found what they wanted—the combination that resolved their policy dilemma—for here were unquestionably anti-Communist nationalists. Indeed, the Indonesian Republican forces had gone into battle against and cut down Communists, so their anti-Communist credentials could not be doubted in Washington. When the Dutch now attempted a second 'police action' in December 1948, they won a military victory but gained a political disaster. They took most of the remaining Republican territory and captured Sukarno and most of the cabinet. The Republican military, however, broke up into smaller guerrilla units and harassed Dutch forces wherever they could. The civilian population and even the governments of Dutch-created 'federal states' protested. In the diplomatic realm, the Dutch now encountered solid opposition both in the UN and from the US. Since the Dutch economy was heavily dependent on American aid for recovery, in the end the Dutch had no choice but to give in and accept the inevitability of Indonesian independence. They restored the Indonesian government to its capital in Yogyakarta, agreed a ceasefire, entered into negotiations in the Netherlands and acknowledged Indonesian independence in December 1949.

Thus it was that, unlike in Vietnam, Cold War assessments worked to the advantage of the Indonesian revolutionaries. The unique geopolitical circumstances of the late 1940s—American predominance, emerging conflict between a 'Free World' and a 'Communist bloc', the possibility that the UN would really be a force of significance in world affairs—along with the sanguinary Indonesian demonstration of anti-Communist nationalism and the Indonesians' own tough resistance to the Dutch, all came together to bring independence to the nation. Had this not been so, we might reasonably guess that the Dutch would have faced what the French, and after them the Americans, faced in Vietnam: a long, bloody, resource-sapping war. If the Americans, with all their immense wealth and power, could not in the end defeat Ho's revolutionaries, what prospect of victory would the small nation have over the vastly larger Indonesian archipelago? So perhaps it was not only the Indonesians but also the Dutch who benefited from the Cold War, hastening as it did their exit from Indonesia.

Burma won independence from the British in January 1948 not through a revolution, but by threatening one. The UK was then under the Attlee Labour government rather than Churchill's Conservatives—who might have chosen to fight in Burma—and the British withdrew as they also withdrew from India. This was the culmination of events reaching back into the colonial period and was uninfluenced by Cold War issues.

Thailand had never been colonised but faced a delicate situation after the war. The government of Phibun Songkhram had signed a treaty with Japan, declared war on the UK and US and taken bordering territories previously occupied by French Indochina and the British Burma and Malaya regimes. Although Thai diplomats abroad had maintained friendly relations with the British and American governments in the name of a 'Free Thai' movement, and although Phibun was no longer in power at war's end, the British were nevertheless hostile to the Thai government. Thailand recognised the dominant trend in world affairs and sought US support. The Americans indeed persuaded the British to compromise in return for the northern Malay states being restored to Malaya and Shan areas being returned to Burma, and for substantial cheap sales to them of Thai rice. The tension to be resolved in the Thai case was between the two closest allies of the Western world, the Americans and the British, not something deriving from the growing Cold War. Later the Thai alliance with the US led Thailand to be one of the only two countries in Southeast Asia to join SEATO in the mid-1950s.

Laos and Cambodia were entangled on the fringes of the developing Vietnam conflict. They gained various forms of semi-independence under French influence and control, but in fact neither was able to chart its own destiny so long as the Vietnam conflict continued. Even after that they were trapped by the complicated geopolitical realities of their positions, caught between more powerful Vietnam to the east and Thailand to the west. Laos and Cambodia, in effect, shared something like the painful historical experience of Poland in Europe, a circumstance long pre-dating the Cold War.

As far back as 1934, the independence of the Philippines had been scheduled for July 1946. The entire process of moving from American colonial rule to independence had roots in American anti-imperialist instincts and was done as an exercise in partnership. Despite World War II happening in the meantime, the scheduled date was met. The Philippines' connections with the US made it, along with Thailand, one of only two Southeast Asian states to sign up to SEATO in the 1950s.

The British re-established themselves in their territories in Malaya, Singapore and Borneo with little difficulty. The US trusted the British to do the right thing—which was whatever the British thought it to be. Nationalist movements were weak or non-existent there. Immediately after the war, bloody inter-ethnic conflict between Malays and Chinese broke out in Malaya, conflict that carried political nuances since the Malayan Communist Party was overwhelmingly Chinese. These events culminated in the 'Emergency' of 1948. The policy priority for the British in 1950 was to defeat the MCP, not to grant independence. For the US, events in Malaya were consistent with its worldview. Here were Communists in rebellion while close allies were fighting to put them down, and there was no conflict with American anti-imperialist thought because the British were promising to move Malaya towards independence, which in fact they did in the course of the 1950s, with independence coming to Malaya in 1957.

Southeast Asia in the middle years of the Cold War, c. 1950–1989

American and Soviet strategic thought altered in no way that was significant for Southeast Asian states in the middle years of the

Cold War. For those states, the Cold War was a condition of life, a geopolitical reality to be lived with and, so far as possible, manipulated to their advantage. It was not something that restricted their range of action—except of course in the case of those states directly embroiled in the war in Vietnam.

The Cold War did not prevent Burma's transition from an electoral democracy to a military dictatorship, which proclaimed the 'Burmese way to socialism'. It did not prevent, indeed it assisted, the Thai elite to remain dominant. Thailand was the non-Indochinese Southeast Asian state most directly involved in the 'hot war' in Vietnam. This involvement reflected far older issues, in particular the Thai-Vietnamese competition for hegemony over the intervening territories in Laos and Cambodia, a conflict reaching back to before colonial times. For the Thais, the US engagement in Vietnam provided useful support for their long-term strategic interests.

Clearly the Cold War—even in its 'hottest' version—did not prevent the Vietnamese Communists from pursuing their goals. They pursued their land reform programmes of the 1950s and by 1975 had won the war against the South Vietnamese, the Americans and their allies. In the other Indochina states of Laos and Cambodia, ultimate outcomes were also contrary to American wishes or capacity to control. Both fell to Communist regimes in 1975. The victory of the genocidal Khmer Rouge regime under Pol Pot in Cambodia was arguably facilitated by American actions during the Vietnam War.

When Vietnam invaded Cambodia in late 1978, American policy-makers faced a new dilemma. Were they more opposed to the Communist state in Vietnam that had only recently defeated them, or to the unspeakably murderous Communist state in Pol Pot's Cambodia? It was decided that the primary enemy was the Vietnamese. So the US now became a clandestine supporter—along with the PRC—of Khmer Rouge resistance to the Vietnamese. Some Cold War, we might say, with the US and PRC now secretly collaborating to support one of the bloodiest regimes ever to rule in Southeast Asia. We should note *en passant* that Nixon had made his trip to China in 1972 and that PRC-US relations were set upon a sometimes rocky road towards normalisation thereafter. Thus, Cold War categories were indeed looking somewhat dog-eared by this time. The Southeast Asian states that had come together to form ASEAN in 1967 also backed the Khmer Rouge against the Vietnamese. In this they were led by Thailand as the 'front-line state', and the state—as noted above—with a long history of competition with Vietnam over the intervening territories. This was despite misgivings on the part of ASEAN's largest member, Indonesia, where the military had considerable respect for and contacts with the Vietnamese, Vietnam and Indonesia being the only two states in Asia who fought armed revolutions for independence after World War II.

The Philippines was also involved in the 'hot war' in Vietnam and US bases in the Philippines played important roles. This was the Southeast Asian state most closely connected to the US by history, economics and politics. But that connection and the Cold War conflicts did not prevent the collapse of its electoral democracy into the dictatorship of Marcos in 1972. Marcos, of course, justified his regime to the Americans on the grounds that he was anti-Communist and thereby manoeuvred the US into supporting a non-democratic, repressive and massively corrupt government. Again, a policy dilemma for the US was resolved as Cold War doctrines demanded: American support for democracy in the Philippines for the previous seven decades was discarded in the name of anti-Communism. The US could not reform the Marcos regime and in the end could not justify supporting it. It could only offer Marcos refuge in Hawaii when he was overthrown by the 'People Power' movement in 1986.

In Indonesia, American influence and Cold War thinking could not prevent the leftward drift of the Sukarno regime and the rise to prominence of the PKI in the course of the 1950s and early 1960s, or the launching of Indonesia's armed 'Confrontation' against Malaysia in 1963. In 1965–66 the PKI was eliminated in the worst blood-letting in Indonesian history, but the causes of that were domestic in nature, despite occasionally absurd American claims that the Indonesians were only emboldened to stand up to Communism because the US was doing so in Vietnam. The subsequent Soeharto regime was like the Marcos regime in many respects and successfully manipulated Cold War ideas to its advantage. It, too, was non-democratic, repressive and massively corrupt, and again anti-Communism trumped support of democracy in American policy. All was not bleak during the Soeharto years, of course: the US was pleased—as were Indonesians—at the economic development achieved by that regime. But the key to ongoing US friendship was Indonesia's anti-Communism.

The US was also pleased at the Indonesian regime's apparent containment and domestication of Islamic political forces. This was an issue of growing significance in American strategic thought after the Iranian Islamic revolution of 1979. When the USSR invaded Afghanistan in that same year, Islamism added a new layer of policy dilemmas to those already thrown up by the Cold War. Cold War priorities again prevailed and the US decided to support Mujahideen resistance to the Soviets. The consequences for America in future years of a strengthened and better-armed Islamist movement in Afghanistan and Pakistan were ignored, underestimated or just not foreseen—another example of the inevitable limits to the prescience of global players.

American influence could not, however, restrain the Soeharto regime's increasing dysfunctionality, corruption and oppression, any more than the PRC's previous influence during the Sukarno period could stop Soeharto freezing relations with China or prevent attacks on Chinese diplomatic and private property in Indonesia. Furthermore, although the United States, and indeed many other states and analysts, approved of the regime's containment of Islamist politics at national level, in fact the Soeharto period was a time of deepening Islamic religious influence across Indonesian society generally and of an increasingly Islamic religious style within the military. This was driven by domestic forces and no external power could have any influence here.

For its part, the Soeharto regime successfully manipulated Cold War doctrines to its advantage, most notably in 1975. Indochinese states had just fallen to Communist regimes. As the Portuguese colonial regime collapsed into civil war in East Timor, Indonesia launched a colonial-style (and badly managed) invasion and takeover. Soeharto justified this as a strike to prevent Fretilin—a radical leftist organisation—gaining power in East Timor. US President Gerald Ford and Secretary of State Henry Kissinger visited Jakarta just before the invasion and indicated that they understood Jakarta's position.

The only significant exception to this pattern took place in the later 1970s. Jimmy Carter was elected US president in 1976 after a campaign in which human rights issues were emphasised. The Indonesian government was then holding (according to the estimate of Amnesty International) some 55,000–100,000 political prisoners, detained without trial since the coup attempt of 1965. After first attempting sham releases (in fact relocation to what were meant to be permanent incarceration camps) to assuage American pressure, in the end Soeharto had to give in. By the end of 1980, thc government had in fact released all prisoners whom they felt could not be put on trial. This time American pressure indeed caused the Indonesian government to do something it did not wish to do, but it is worth noting that this was the only major issue in US-Indonesian relations in this period where something other than anti-Communism was a top American priority.

Malaya, Singapore, Brunei, Sarawak and Sabah were areas of primarily British influence. In 1955 elections were held in Malaya and it became independent in 1957. Singapore, Brunei, Sarawak and Sabah were more complicated cases, mainly because of ethnic complexities, and, in the Borneo territories, low levels of political development. Matters were further complicated by the UK's wish to bring its colonial responsibilities to an end and its 1968 announcement that it would withdraw from military bases East of Suez in 1971 (although in fact some small contingents did remain thereafter). Before then a 'Grand Design' (as the British called it) had brought Singapore, Sarawak and Sabah with peninsular Malaya into the state of Malaysia in 1963. Brunei stood outside this arrangement as an independent sultanate. In 1965 Singapore and Malaysia went their separate ways. None of these decisive events was significantly a Cold War issue. The USSR and PRC were not major calculations in these affairs, except insofar as some people continued to fear that Southeast Asian Chinese—in this case, primarily meaning the Chinese of Singapore—were in some way inherently pro-PRC. Undoubtedly there were Communist Chinese activists, particularly in Singapore and Malaysia, but as a general rule there was limited evidence to support this stereotype before the end of the Cold War and still less after it.

In 1967 Malaysia, Singapore, Thailand, the Philippines and Indonesia formed ASEAN. Indonesia's Soeharto—still new to power—was one of the major initiators of the new organisation. ASEAN was welcomed by the US but it arose mainly from regional aspirations. One of its main purposes was to rehabilitate Indonesia as a responsible regional actor, as well as to encourage economic and cultural cooperation among these non-Communist states. In practice, although its charter ruled out military cooperation, ASEAN also provided a framework within which bilateral military cooperation agreements interlocked to provide something of a regional security structure. The ASEAN nations were seeking regional cooperation and stability in part as a way to counter great-power influence in the region. This element of the agenda became abundantly clear after the Cold War came to an end, whereupon an ASEAN Free Trade Area was created in 1992, Vietnam became a member (1995), Laos and Burma joined (1997) and finally Cambodia did as well (1999). Brunei had already joined in 1984. ASEAN thus became a Southeast-Asia-wide grouping—unconcerned about whether a member was Communist or not—in search of an independent voice in a world of greater powers.

Southeast Asia at the end of the Cold War

There is an inherent logical difficulty in arguing that the absence of one thing might have caused another. Nevertheless, it is possible that the end of the Cold War was of significance at least in Indonesia. The Soeharto regime was accustomed to the Cold War context and adept at manipulating it to the regime's advantage. Oppression, extravagant corruption and the colonial conquest of East Timor had all been condoned by the US because the regime was a pillar of anti-Communism in Southeast Asia. After the Cold War was over, however, the US no longer saw a need to prop up objectionable regimes just because they were anti-Communist. We might guess that, had the 1997–98 financial crisis struck 15 years before, the US would have done all it could to bolster the Soeharto regime. Perhaps it could not have succeeded in such an effort. After all, it could not win the Vietnam War or keep Marcos in power in 1986. Whatever the case, the US conspicuously neglected to offer the decrepit Soeharto regime its support in 1997–98 and indeed encouraged Soeharto to go. The regime fell for essentially domestic reasons, and there was no longer a Cold War context which it might invoke in the hope of external support.

Elsewhere in Southeast Asia, the international context of course continued to matter. After the Cold War, the US was even more the dominant global hegemon with influence in Southeast Asia, although over the years PRC influence grew. Dramatic events followed. The boom years of 1990–97 produced new middle classes in much of the region. Vietnam embraced Doi Moi—'renovation'. Even impoverished Laos and Cambodia saw improvements. Burma, or Myanmar, as the regime preferred, remained corrupt, oppressive and poorly developed—the only Southeast Asian state not to win benefits from a decade of development. There followed the economic crisis of 1997–98, a decade of patchy recovery and then the global crisis beginning in 2008. In all these events, of course, the global context mattered, but arguably Southeast Asian states were no more influenced by that context than, say, the nations of Europe were.

Conclusion

The Cold War mattered in Southeast Asia, but we should not overestimate how much it mattered. For most of the period of the Cold War, for most Southeast Asian policy-makers, it was a fact of life, an ever-present context, like the weather. Most Southeast Asian states were able to use the Cold War to maintain their freedom of manoeuvre and to achieve their objectives. Many of the issues that motivated Southeast Asian politics long pre-dated the Cold War and had domestic roots.

Ironically, the main exception to such generalisations, the state that was most profoundly constrained by and in the end destroyed in the context of the Cold War, was the United States' most dependent dependency, the Republic of (South) Vietnam. No other state in Southeast Asia had so much direct US support both in funding and in military force. Its opponent, the DRV, received far less from its poorer Communist Cold War allies. Yet, by 1973 the US knew that it was beaten in Vietnam and by 1975 the RVN had been destroyed by the DRV forces. This conflict, too, might be traced back to historical conflicts between states located in northern and southern Vietnam, but the Vietnam War was the conflict most clearly—and hotly—a part of the Cold War. Yet there, the most powerful of the Cold War states could not prevail.

The Vietnam case brings to our attention the issue raised early in this chapter, whether the great powers' Cold War strategic assessments, doctrines and priorities were such as to amount at times to ideological blinkers. Historical counterfactuals are not always worth pursuit, but we may nevertheless ask what might have happened if in 1945 or 1950 or 1955 the US had said to the

French that they would be stronger without Vietnam, and to Ho Chi Minh that he was welcome to have whatever domestic political and economic system he wanted so long as his state was not a tool for PRC or USSR expansion. Could the normalisation of US-Vietnamese relations that in fact came about from 1995 onwards have been achieved in 1945 or 1950 or 1955? Was it impossible for the US to consider such options because of the inflexibility of its Cold War analysis? In the complex realities of the 50 years between 1945 and 1995, perhaps the US could not have taken a course other than it did. But we may still wonder.

In Southeast Asia, the reigning global Cold War doctrines were imperfectly aligned with local realities. They were also, in fact, of doubtful utility for the great powers of the Cold War. We have repeatedly seen how limited was the capacity of the most powerful of the powers, the US, to influence events on the ground and how much freedom local players found to pursue their own agendas. And we can see why this was so. Political realities in Southeast Asia—as is common in the rest of the world—were a mix of interacting local interests, local players and local issues (often with long histories behind them) on one side, intersecting with global powers and issues on the other, giving rise to specific political dynamics on the ground. Complexity was of the essence of these dynamics, but the ideas of the great powers smacked of simplicity. We may also guess why in the USSR and USA—and perhaps also in the PRC—leaders had trouble accepting the salience and complexity of local matters when they looked at their global chess-boards. In the wake of the colonial period and World War II, they may have found it difficult to imagine the extent to which recently colonised people who now ran shaky new states would reassert the historical agency which had been theirs long before Europeans and Americans came conquering, would defend their own views and aspirations, and would stand firm against the pretensions to hegemony by the global players whom they confronted.

The interaction of the global Cold War and local realities in

Southeast Asia brought opportunities for some but demanded great costs from many, both in Southeast Asia and in the homelands of the global players, particularly the US. Looking back, it is hard to imagine that any of the major players—except presumably the elite of the RVN and the Soeharto and Marcos clans—can regret that the Cold War is a thing of the past.

SELECT BIBLIOGRAPHY

PRIMARY SOURCES

Official records

Archives New Zealand (ANZ):

EA 1, W 2668
LONB, 106/7/1

Australian War Memorial (AWM):

122/69/2016

Combined Arms Research Library, US (CARL):

General J. Lawton Collins, Background Material for the War Department Presentation to the Committee on the Armed Services, 11 February 1947.

Dwight D. Eisenhower Library (DDEL):

General J. Lawton Collins Papers

National Archives of Australia (NAA):

A 1209/23
A 1209/1961
A 1209/1962
A 1838, TS 688

The National Archives of the UK, Public Records Office (TNA):

CAB 21/4431
CAB 128/43
CAB 129/128
CAB 129/130–31
CAB 129/135
CAB 131/1644–45
CAB 134/24
CAB 148/25
CAB 148/30
CAB 159/35
CAB 159/37
CAB 163/22
CO 1030/925
CO 1030/972–73
CO 1030/977–80
CO 1030/1502
CO 1030/1529
DEFE 4/137
DEFE 7/2382
DEFE 7/2390
DEFE 13/542
DEFE 13/631
DEFE 25/212
DO 169/25–26
DO 169/67
DO 169/30
DO 169/249
FCO 15/393
FO 371/143707
FO 371/169703
FO 371/169903
FO 371/169906
FO 371/181490
PREM 8/59
PREM 11/3277
PREM 11/3418
PREM 11/4346
PREM 11/4348
PREM 11/4907
PREM 13/589
PREM 13/1832–33
PREM 13/2081

US Army Military History Institute (USAMHI):

Oral Histories
Bennett, Donald V.
Desobry, William R.
Forrester, Eugene P.
Forsythe, George I.

Army War College Student Papers
Ammons, Benjamin T. 'The International Conferences at Yalta, Tehran, and Potsdam During World War II', 24 April 1952.
Anderson, Joseph C. 'The Military Defeat of Russia', 1 April 1953.
Blandford, William O. 'The Basis of Soviet Policies with Respect to the Far East', 25 March 1952.
Blencoe, Guy N. 'US Security in the Far East-Pacific Ocean Area', 15 March 1954.
Boyd, Richard K. 'The Basis of Soviet Policies with Respect to the Far East', 24 March 1952.
Burgher, Frank E. 'Indonesia: The Soviet Threat', 8 March 1963.
Clayman, Donald C. 'The Strategic Importance of Indochina', 31 March 1953.
Connolly, Haviland A.N. 'US Security in the Far East-Pacific Ocean Area', 15 March 1954.
Delaney, Robert J. 'Republic of Vietnam: Can We Win?' 6 March 1964.
Dennison, Robert C. 'The Importance of South Vietnam', 5 February 1962.
Harris, William J. 'Vietnam: A Showcase of American Aid in Southeast Asia', 10 February 1961.
Hoffman, Carl W. 'Indonesia: At the Crossroads', 10 February 1961.
Hoffman, Theodore F. 'An Independent Philippine Republic Our Channel to Southeast Asia', 19 March 1958.
Hyman, Arthur S. 'Indonesia: A Case Study in Neutralism', 8 March 1963.
Kroesen, Frederick J. 'The Precarious Position of Thailand', 15 December 1962.
Lasseter, Roy, Jr. 'The Basis of Soviet Policies with Respect to the Far East', 24 March 1952.
Levenick, Maynard N. 'The Role of Free Governments, Parent and Colonial, in Communist Strategy', 1 April 1953.
Lewis, William F. 'National Policy for Limited War', 14 March 1955.
MacGrain, Donald. 'Anti-Dissident Operations in the Philippines', 26 March 1956.

McKenzie, William H., III. 'Indochina: Center of Conflict', 9 March 1962.
McKinley, William D. 'The Struggle Between the United States and the USSR', 1 April 1953.
Morgan, William O. 'A SEATO Military Standing Force', 7 March 1962.
Murphy, Cornelius A. 'Vietnam: Villainy in the Villages', 8 March 1963.
Queenin, Hugh F. 'The Military Implications of the Southeast Asia Treaty Organization', 25 January 1960.
Rudquist, Eric A. 'The True Reflection of South Vietnam', 9 March 1962.
Smith, Francis M. 'Military Strategy in Southeast Asia', 19 March 1958.
St. John, Adrian. 'SEATO: Strawman or Paper Tiger', 25 January 1960.
Stevens, John DuV. 'US Security in the Far East-Pacific Ocean Area', 15 March 1954.
Tardy, Walter E. 'The Strategic Importance of Indonesia', 18 February 1957.
Turnage, Benjamin O., Jr. 'The Basis of Soviet Policies with Respect to the Far East', 24 March 1952.
Way, Davis W. 'The United States Roles in the Southeast Asia Collective Defense Treaty (SEATO)', 19 March 1958.

Faculty Study
Palmer, John M. and Richard G. Stilwell. 'The Indochina Contest', 28 October 1954.

US National Archives and Records Administration (USNARA):
Combat Development Objectives Guide—Large Unit Operations, 1954, Record Group 337.
Strategy and the Army Files, Record Group 319.

Printed sources

Baviera, Aileen and Lydia Yu-Jose (eds). *Philippine External Relations: A Centennial Vista*. Manila: Foreign Service Institute, 1998.
Dennis, Peter and Jeffrey Grey. *Emergency and Confrontation: Australian Military Operations in Malaya and Borneo 1950–1966*. St Leonards, NSW: Allen & Unwin in association with the Australian War Memorial, 1996.
Enverga Report on the Exploratory Mission to the Socialist Countries in 1967. Manila: Congress of the Republic of the Philippines, 1968.
Foreign Relations of the United States, 1955–1968 [*FRUS*]. Washington: Government Printing Office. Vol. XVI (East Asia-Pacific Region: Cambodia, Laos), downloaded from digital.library.wisc.edu./1711.dl/FRUS;

Vol. XXI (East Asian Security: Cambodia, Laos); Vol. XXIII (Southeast Asia); Vol. XXIV (Laos), downloaded from www.state.gov/r/pa/ho/frus/; Vol. XXVII (Mainland Southeast Asia: Regional Affairs), downloaded from www.state.gov/r/pa/ho/frus/; Vol. XXVIII (Laos), downloaded from www.state.gov/r/pa/ho/frus/.

Goldsworthy, David (ed.). *British Documents on the End of Empire.* Series A. Volume 3, *The Conservative Government and the End of Empire, 1951–1957, Part II: Politics and Administration*. London: HMSO, 1994.

Office of Joint History. *History of the Joint Chiefs of Staff: The Joint Chiefs of Staff and the First Indochina War, 1947–1954*. Washington, D.C.: Office of the Chairman of the Joint Chiefs of Staff, 2004.

Official Report, Parliamentary Debates (House of Commons), Fifth Series.

The Pentagon Papers: Senator Gravel Edition. Volumes 1–2. Boston: Beacon, 1971–72.

People's Action Party. *Sixth Anniversary Celebrations Souvenir.* Singapore: PAP, 1960.

Philippine Diplomacy: Chronology and Documents 1972–1981. Manila: Foreign Service Institute, 1981.

Philippine Treaty Series. Quezon City: University of the Philippines Law Center, 1968.

Public Papers of the Presidents: Dwight D. Eisenhower, 1954. Washington, D.C.: U.S. Government Printing Office, 1960.

Report of Singapore Constitutional Conference held in London in March and April 1957. Cmd 147, para 48(d). London: HMSO, 1957.

Roxas, Manuel A. *Speeches, Addresses and Messages as President of the Philippines.* Manila: Bureau of Printing, 1954.

Singapore Legislative Assembly Debates, 1958–63.

Stockwell, A.J. (ed.). *Malaysia, British Documents on the End of Empire.* Series B: Volume 8. London: HMSO, 2004.

The 30-Year War 1945–1975, Volume 1: 1945–1954. Hanoi: The Gioi Publishers, 2000.

Vietnam Documents and Research Notes, Number 76, 'Forty Years of Party Activity'.

SECONDARY SOURCES

Abdul Rahman Putra, Tunku. *Lest We Forget: Further Candid Reminiscences.* Singapore: Eastern Universities Press, 1983.

Abdullah C.D. *Memoir Abdullah C.D.* Petaling Jaya: SIRD, 2007.

Abraham, Collin. *'The Finest Hour': The Malaysian-MCP Peace Accord in Perspective.* Kuala Lumpur: SIRD, 2006.

Abueva, Jose V. *Ramon Magsaysay: A Political Biography*. Manila: Solidaridad Publishing House, 1971.

Ai Sulinyasaeng. *Salup songkham pativat potpoi sat khong kongthap lae pasason Lao (1945–1975)* [A summary of the revolutionary war of national liberation by the Lao army and people (1945–1975)]. Vientiane: Ministry of Defence, 2001.

Albert, Carlos L. 'The War Next Door: A Filipino at Borneo Frontline.' *Philippines Herald*, 6–10 July 1965 (reprinted by Malaysia's Department of Information).

Aldrich, Richard J. *The Key to the South: Britain, the United States, and Thailand during the Approach of the Pacific War, 1929–1942.* New York: Oxford University Press, 1993.

Alias Chin Peng. *My Side of History*, as told to Ian Ward and Norma Miraflor. Singapore: Media Masters, 2003.

Ambrose, Stephen. *Rise to Globalism: American Foreign Policy Since 1938*. Harmondsworth, Middlesex: Penguin Books, 1971.

Anderson, Benedict. 'Old State, New Society: Indonesia's New Order in Comparative Historical Perspective', *Journal of Asian Studies*, vol. XLII, no. 3 (May 1983).

Anderson, Benedict and Audrey Kahin (eds). *Interpreting Indonesian Politics: Thirteen Contributions to the Debate*. Ithaca: Cornell Modern Indonesia Project, 1982.

Anderson, Benedict and Ruth McVey. *A Preliminary Analysis of the October 1, 1965 Coup in Indonesia*. Ithaca: Cornell University Press, 1971.

Andrew, Christopher and Vasili Mitrokhin. *The Mitrokhin Archive II: The KGB and the World.* London: Allen Lane, 2005.

Ang Cheng Guan. 'Vietnam in 1948: An International History Perspective', *Kajian Malaysia*, vol. 27, nos 1 and 2 (2009).

Anwar, Dewi Fortuna. *Indonesia in ASEAN: Foreign Policy and Regionalism*. Singapore: Institute of Southeast Asian Studies, 1994.

Arcellana, Emerciana Yuvienco. *The Social and Political Thought of Claro Mayo Recto*. Manila: National Research Council of the Philippines, 1981.

Bacevich, Andrew J. *The Pentomic Era: The U.S. Army Between Korea and Vietnam.* Washington, D.C.: National Defense University Press, 1986.

Baker, Chris (tr.). 'An Internal History of the Communist Party of Thailand' (first drafted 1974, updated 1978), *Journal of Contemporary Asia*, 33:4, 2003.

Baker, Chris and Pasuk Phongpaichit. *A History of Thailand.* Cambridge: Cambridge University Press, 2005.

Ban Nghien Cuu Lich Su Dang Trung Cong. *Nam Muoi Nam Hoat Dong Vua Dang Cong San Viet Nam.* Hanoi: Nha Xuat Ban Su That, 1982.

Batson, Benjamin A. *The End of the Absolute Monarchy in Siam.* Singapore: Oxford University Press, 1984.

Birtle, Andrew J. *U.S. Army Counterinsurgency and Contingency Operations Doctrine, 1942–1976.* Washington, D.C.: Center of Military History, 2006.

Bradley, Mark Philip. *Imagining Vietnam and America: The Making of Postcolonial Vietnam, 1919–1950.* Chapel Hill: University of North Carolina Press, 2000.

Braun, Lindsay Frederick. 'Suez Reconsidered: Anthony Eden's Orientalism and the Suez Crisis', *The Historian*, vol. 65, no. 3 (2003).

Brimmell, J.H. *The Malayan Communist Party: A Short History.* Singapore: Donald Moore, 1956.

Burr, William and Michael L. Evans (eds). 'East Timor Revisited: Ford, Kissinger and the Indonesian Invasion, 1975–76', *National Security Archive Electronic Briefing Book No. 62*, 6 December 2001.

Busch, P. *All the Way with JFK? Britain, the US and the Vietnam War.* Oxford: Oxford University Press, 2003.

Buszynski, Leszek. *SEATO: The Failure of an Alliance Strategy*. Singapore: Singapore University Press, 1983.

Carlton, David. *Britain and the Suez Crisis.* Oxford: Basil Blackwell, 1988.

Carter, Don Alan. 'From G.I. to Atomic Soldier: The Development of U.S. Tactical Doctrine, 1945–1956.' PhD dissertation, Ohio State University, 1987.

Carver, Michael. *Tightrope Walking: British Defence Policy Since 1945.* London, Hutchinson, 1992.

Castle, T.N. *At War in the Shadow of Vietnam: U.S. Military Aid to the Royal Lao Government 1955–1975.* New York: Columbia University Press, 1993.

Chandler, David P. *The Tragedy of Cambodian History: Politics, War, and Revolution Since 1945.* New Haven: Yale University Press, 1991.

Charney, Michael W. *A History of Modern Burma*. Cambridge: Cambridge University Press, 2009.

Chen Jian. 'China and the First Indo-China War, 1950–54.' *China Quarterly*, no. 133 (March 1999).

———. *Mao's China and the Cold War.* Chapel Hill: University of North Carolina Press, 2001.

Chen, King C. *Vietnam and China 1938–1954.* Princeton: Princeton University Press, 1969.

Chin, C.C. and Karl Hack (eds). *Dialogues with Chin Peng: New Light on the Malayan Communist Party.* Singapore: Singapore University Press, 2004.

Chin Kin Wah. *The Defence of Malaysia and Singapore: The Transformation of a Security System 1957–71*. Cambridge: Cambridge University Press, 1983.

Clutterbuck, Richard L. 'Malaya: A Case Study.' *Military Review*, 43 (September 1963).

Clymer, Kenton. *Troubled Relations: The United States and Cambodia since 1870*. DeKalb: Northern Illinois University Press, 2007.

Comber, Leon. 'The Origins of the Cold War in Southeast Asia: The Case of the Communist Party of Malaya (1948–1960)—A Special Branch Perspective.' *Kajian Malaysia*, vol. 27, nos 1 and 2 (2009).

———. *Malaya's Secret Police 1945–60: The Role of the Special Branch in the Malayan Emergency*. Singapore: Institute of Southeast Asian Studies, 2008.

Craddock, Percy. *Know Your Enemy: How the Joint Intelligence Committee Saw the World.* London: John Murray, 2002.

Crane, Conrad C. *Avoiding Vietnam: The U.S. Army's Response to Defeat in Southeast Asia.* Carlisle, PA: Strategic Studies Institute, 2002.

Crosby, J. 'The Failure of Constitutional Government in Siam.' *Asiatic Review*, 39, 140 (October 1942).

———. 'War and Militarism in Siam.' *Great Britain and the East,* 61, 1726 (24 June 1944).

Crossman, Richard. *The Diaries of a Cabinet Minister, Volume II.* London: Hamish Hamilton and Jonathan Cape, 1976.

Crouch, Harold. *The Army and Politics in Indonesia.* Ithaca: Cornell University Press, 1988.

Cullather, Nick. *Illusions of Influence*. Stanford: Stanford University Press, 1994.

Darwin, John. *Britain and Decolonisation: The Retreat from Empire in the Post-War World.* London: Macmillan, 1988

Deery, Philip. 'Britain's Asian Cold War?' *Journal of Cold War Studies,* 9:1 (2007).

Deuve, Jean. *Le Royaume du Laos 1949–1965*. Paris: École Française d'Extrême-Orient, 1984.

Diplomatic Agenda of Philippine Presidents, 1946–1985. Manila: Foreign Service Institute, 1985.

Dockrill, Michael. *British Defence Since 1945*. Oxford: Blackwell, 1989.

Dockrill, Saki. *Britain's Retreat from East of Suez: The Choice between Europe and the World?* Basingstoke: Palgrave Macmillan, 2002.

Domingo, Benjamin B. *The Making of Filipino Foreign Policy*. Manila: Foreign Service Institute, 1983.

———. *The Re-making of Philippine Foreign Policy*. Quezon City: Asian Center, University of the Philippines, 1993.

Dommen, Arthur J. *Conflict in Laos: The Politics of Neutralization.* New York: Frederick A. Praeger, 1964.

Dommen, Arthur J. *The Indochinese Experience of the French and Americans: Nationalism and Communism in Cambodia, Laos, and Vietnam*. Bloomington: University of Indiana Press, 2001.

Duiker, William J. *The Communist Road to Power in Vietnam.* Boulder: Westview Press, 1996.

——. *U.S. Containment Policy and the Conflict in Indochina.* Stanford: Stanford University Press, 1994.

Easter, David. *Britain and the Confrontation with Indonesia 1960–1966.* London: Tauris Academic Studies, 2004.

Elliot, David W.P. *The Vietnamese War: Revolution and Social Change in the Mekong Delta 1930–1975*. Armonk, NY: M.E. Sharpe, 2007.

Fall, Bernard. *Anatomy of a Crisis: The Laotian Crisis of 1960–1961*. Garden City, NY: Doubleday, 1969.

Feith, Herbert. *The Decline of Constitutional Democracy in Indonesia*. Ithaca: Cornell University Press, 1962.

——. 'Dynamics of Guided Democracy', in Ruth McVey (ed.), *Indonesia.* New Haven: Yale University Press, 1963.

Fifield, Russell H. *Southeast Asia in United States Policy.* New York: Frederick Praeger, 1963.

Fineman, Daniel. *A Special Relationship: The United States and Military Government in Thailand, 1947–1958*. Honolulu: University of Hawaii Press, 1997.

Frankum, Ronald B. *The United States and Australia in Vietnam 1954–1968: Silent Partners*. Lewiston, NY: Edwin Mellen, 2001.

Freedman, Lawrence. *The Evolution of Nuclear Strategy*. New York: St Martin's Press, 1983.

Furuta, Motoo. 'The Indochina Communist Party's Division into Three Parties: Vietnamese Communist Policy towards Cambodia and Laos, 1948–1951', in Takashi Shiraishi and Motoo Furuta (eds), *Indochina in the 1940s and 1950s.* Ithaca: Cornell Southeast Asia Program, 1992.

Gaiduk, Ilya V. *Confronting Vietnam: Soviet Policy Toward the Indochina Conflict, 1954–1963*. Stanford: Stanford University Press, 2003.

Gilbert, Martin. *Churchill: A Life.* New York: Henry Holt and Co, 1991.

Goldstein, M.E. *American Policy Towards Laos.* Cranbury, NJ: Associated University Presses, Inc., 1973.

Gorst, Anthony & Lewis Johnman. *The Suez Crisis.* London: Routledge, 1997.

Goscha, Christopher E. 'Courting Diplomatic Disaster? The Difficult Integration of Vietnam into the International Communist Movement (1945–1950)', *Journal of Vietnamese Studies*, vol. 1, nos 1–2 (Feb/Aug 2006).

Goscha, Christopher E. *Thailand and the Southeast Asian Networks of the Vietnamese Revolution, 1885–1954*. Richmond: Curzon, 1999.

Grove, Eric J. *Vanguard to Trident: British Naval Policy Since World War II.* Annapolis: Naval Institute Press, 1987.

Hack, Karl. *Defence and Decolonisation in Southeast Asia: Britain, Malaya and Singapore 1941–68*. Richmond: Curzon, 2001.

Hamel, Bernard. *Sihanouk et le drame cambodgien*. Paris: L'Harmattan, 1993.

Han Fook Kwang, Warren Fernandez and Sumiko Tan, *Lee Kuan Yew: The Man and His Ideas.* Singapore: Singapore Press Holdings and Times Editions, 1998.

Harper, T.N. *The End of Empire and the Making of Malaya.* New York: Cambridge University Press, 1999.

Hartendorp, A.V.H. *History of Industry and Trade of the Philippines.* Manila: American Chamber of Commerce of the Philippines, 1958.

Healey, Denis. *The Time of My Life.* London: Michael Joseph, 1989.

Herman, Edward S. 'Good and Bad Genocide: Double standards in Coverage of Suharto and Pol Pot.' *Extra!* September/October 1998. Downloaded from www.fair.org/extra/9809/suharto.html.

Horowitz, R.S. *The Ramparts We Watch.* Derby: Monarch Books, 1964.

Hu Zhengqing. *Yige waijiaoguan de riji* [Journal of a Diplomat]. Jinan: Huanghe Chubanshe, 1991.

Hudson, Miles. 'East of Suez.' Old Queen Street Paper, No. 9. London: Conservative Research Department, 27 April 1969.

Hyam, Ronald. *Britain's Declining Empire: The Road to Decolonization 1918–1968.* Cambridge: Cambridge University Press, 2006.

Ito, Yuko. 'Postwar U.S. Military Policy Toward the Philippines and the "Japanese Factor", 1945–1951', in Ikehata Setsuho and Lydia Yu-Jose (eds), *Philippines-Japan Relations*. Quezon City: Ateneo de Manila University Press, 2003.

Jenkins, Roy. *A Life at the Centre.* London: Macmillan, 1991.

Jocano, F. Landa. *Philippines-USSR Relations*. Metro Manila: NDCP Foundation, 1988.

Jones, Matthew. *Conflict and Confrontation in Southeast Asia, 1961–65: Britain, the United States and the Creation of Malaysia.* Cambridge: Cambridge University Press, 2002.

——. 'Creating Malaysia: Singapore Security, the Borneo Territories, and the Contours of British Policy, 1961–63.' *Journal of Imperial and Commonwealth History*, 28, 2 (2000).

——. 'Up the Garden Path? Britain's Nuclear History in the Far East, 1954–1962.' *International History Review*, XXV, 2 (June 2003).

Kadane, Kathy. 'Ex-agents say CIA compiled death lists for Indonesians. After 25 years, Americans speak of their role in exterminating Communist Party.' *San Francisco Examiner*, 20 May 1990, and *Washington Post*, 21 May 1990.

Kahin, Audrey R. and George McTurnan Kahin. *Subversion as Foreign Policy: The Secret Eisenhower and Dulles Debacle in Indonesia.* New York: The New Press, 1995.

Kerkvliet, Benedict J. *The Huk Rebellion: A Study of Peasant Revolt in the Philippines*. Berkeley: University of California Press, 1977.

King, Dwight Y. 'Indonesia's New Order as a Bureaucratic Polity, a Neopatrimonial Regime, or a Bureaucratic Authoritarian Regime: What Difference Does it Make?' in Benedict Anderson and Audrey Kahin (eds), *Interpereting Indonesian Politics: Thirteen Contributions to the Debate*. Ithaca: Cornell Modern Indonesia Project, 1982.

Kissinger, Henry. *Nuclear Weapons and Foreign Policy*. New York: W.W. Norton, 1969.

———. *Years of Upheaval.* London: George Weidenfeld and Nicolson, 1982.

Kunz, Diane B. '"Somewhat Mixed Up Together": Anglo-American Defence and Financial Policy during the 1960s', in Robert D. King and Robin W. Kilson (eds), *The Statecraft of British Imperialism: Essays in Honour of Wm. Roger Louis.* London: Frank Cass, 1999.

Kwa Chong Guan, Derek Heng and Tan Tai Yong. *Singapore: A 700-Year History—From Early Emporium to World City.* Singapore: National Archives of Singapore, 2009.

Kyle, Keith. *Suez.* New York: St Martin's Press, 1991.

Landon, K.P. *Siam in Transition.* London: Oxford University Press, 1939.

Lau, Albert. *The Malayan Union Controversy, 1942–48.* Singapore: Oxford University Press, 1990.

———. *A Moment of Anguish: Singapore in Malaysia and the Politics of Disengagement.* Singapore: Times Academic Press, 1998.

Lawrence, Mark Atwood. *Assuming the Burden: Europe & the American Commitment to War in Vietnam.* Berkeley: University of California Press, 2005.

Lee Kuan Yew. *The Battle for Merger.* Singapore: Government Printing Office, 1962.

———. *From Third World to First: The Singapore Story, 1965–2000.* Singapore: Times Media, 2000.

Legge, John D. *Sukarno: A Political Biography.* Singapore: Archipelago Press, 2003.

Leifer, Michael. *Cambodia: The Search for Security*. London: Pall Mall, 1967.

———. *Indonesia's Foreign Policy*. London: George Allen and Unwin, 1983.

Liang, Chi-shad. *Burma's Foreign Relations: Neutralism in Theory and Practice.* Westport, CT: Praeger, 1990.

Lich Su Quan Doi Nhan Dan Viet Nam, Tap I. Hanoi: Nha Xuat Ban Quan Doi Nhan Dan, 1977.

Linn, Brian McAllister. *The Echo of Battle: The U.S. Army's Way of War.* Cambridge, MA: Harvard University Press, 2007.

——. *Guardians of Empire: The U.S. Army and the Pacific, 1902–1940.* Chapel Hill: University of North Carolina Press, 1997.

Long, William F. 'Counterinsurgency: Some Antecedents for Success', *Military Review*, 43 (Oct 1963).

Lopez, Salvador P. 'New Directions in Philippine Foreign Policy', *Army Journal*, June 1977.

Louis, Wm. Roger and Roger Owen (eds). *Suez 1956: The Crisis and its Consequences.* Oxford: Oxford University Press, 1991.

Lowe, Peter. *Contending with Nationalism and communism: British Policy Towards Southeast Asia, 1945–65*. Basingstoke: Palgrave Macmillan, 2009.

Mabon, David W. 'Elusive Agreements: The Pacific Pact Proposals of 1949–1951.' *Pacific Historical Review*, May 1988.

Macapagal, Diosdado. *The Philippines Turns East*. Quezon City: Mac Publishing House, 1966.

Macdonald, Scot. *Rolling the Iron Dice: Historical Analogies and Decisions to Use Military Force in Regional Contingencies.* Westport: Greenwood Press, 2000.

MacFarling, Ian. *The Dual Function of the Indonesian Armed Forces: Military Politics in Indonesia.* Canberra: Australian Defence Studies Centre, 1996.

Mackie, J.A.C. *Bandung 1955: Non-Alignment and Afro-Asian Solidarity.* Singapore: Didier Millet, 2005.

——. *Konfrontasi: The Indonesia-Malaysia Dispute, 1963–1966.* Kuala Lumpur and Oxford: Oxford University Press, 1974.

MacLean, L.D. *ANZIM to ANZUK: An Historical Outline of ANZAM.* Canberra: Department of Defence, 1992.

Madrona, Severo Canete, Jr. 'Respectable Independence: The Foreign Policy of Carlos P. Garcia, 1957–1961.' Unpublished MA History thesis, University of the Philippines, 2002.

Malaya, J. Eduardo and Jonathan Malaya (eds). *So Help Us God: The Presidents of the Philippines and their Inaugural Addresses*. Manila: Anvil Publishing, 2004.

McMahon, Robert J. 'The United States and Southeast Asia in an Era of Decolonization, 1945–1965', in Marc Frey, Ronald W. Pruessen and Tan Tai Yong (eds), *The Transformation of Southeast Asia: International Perspectives on Decolonization.* Singapore: Singapore University Press, 2004.

McVey, Ruth. *The Calcutta Conference and the Southeast Asian Uprisings*. Ithaca: Cornell Modern Indonesia Project, 1958.

Meyer, Charles. *Derrière le sourire khmer*. Paris: Plon, 1971.

Meyer, Milton W. *A Diplomatic History of the Philippine Republic: The First Years, 1946–1961*. Claremont: Regina Books, 2003 [1965].

Miller, Harry. *The Communist Menace in Malaya*. New York: Praeger, 1955.

Moore, R. 'Where Her Majesty's Weapons Were.' *Bulletin of the Atomic Scientists*, 57, 1 (2001).

Morgan, Kenneth O. *Britain Since 1945: The People's Peace*. Oxford: Oxford University Press, 2001.

——. *Callaghan: A Life*. Oxford: Oxford University Press, 1997.

Murfett, Malcolm H. *In Jeopardy: The Royal Navy and British Far Eastern Defence Policy 1945–1951*. Kuala Lumpur: Oxford University Press, 1995.

——. '"The Times they are a-Changin": Britain's Military Commitment to Singapore, 1967–1971', in Brian P. Farrell, *Churchill and the Lion City: Shaping Modern Singapore*. Singapore: NUS Press, 2011.

Murfett, Malcolm H., John N. Miksic, Brian P. Farrell and Chiang Ming Shun. *Between Two Oceans: A Military History of Singapore from 1275 to 1971*. 2nd edition. Singapore: Marshall Cavendish Editions, 2011.

Nagl, John. *Learning to Eat Soup with a Knife: Counterinsurgency Lessons from Malaya and Vietnam*. Chicago: University of Chicago Press, 2005.

Nguyen Khac Vien. *Vietnam: A Long History*. Hanoi: Gioi Publishers, 1993.

Ohno, Takushi. *War Reparations and Peace Settlement: Philippines-Japan Relations, 1945–1956*. Manila: Solidaridad Publishing House, 1986.

Osborne, Milton. *Sihanouk: Prince of Light, Prince of Darkness*. St Leonards, NSW: Allen and Unwin, 1994.

Osornprasop, Sutayut. 'Thailand and the American Secret War in Indochina, 1960–1974.' PhD thesis, University of Cambridge, 2006.

Pfennigwerth, Ian. *Tiger Territory: The Untold Story of the Royal Australian Navy in Southeast Asia from 1948 to 1971*. Kenthurst, NSW: Rosenberg, 2008.

Pham, P.L. *Ending 'East of Suez': The British Decision to Withdraw from Malaysia and Singapore 1964–1968*. Oxford: Oxford University Press, 2010.

Piyaphan, B. *Lao nai krung Rattanakosin* [The Lao in early Bangkok]. Bangkok: Samnakngan kongtoon sanap sanun kanwijai, 1998.

Pobre, Cesar P. *History of the Armed Forces of the Filipino People*. Quezon City: New Day, 2000.

Ponting, Clive. *Breach of Promise: Labour in Power 1964–1970*. London: Hamish Hamilton, 1989.

Poulgrain, Greg. *The Genesis of Kronfrontasi: Malaysia, Brunei, Indonesia, 1945–65*. London: Hurst, 1998.

Prados, John. *Operation Vulture.* New York: Ibooks, Inc, 2002.

Pye, Lucian W. *Guerrilla Communism in Malaya: Its Social and Political Meaning.* Princeton: Princeton University Press, 1956.

Quan he hu nghi, doan ket dac biet va hop tac toan dien Viet Nam-Lao/ Kanphuaphan mittaphap, khwamsamakkhi phiset lae kanhuammeu hopdan Vietnam-Lao/Special friendship and solidarity, and comprehensive cooperation between Viet Nam and Laos. Hanoi: Ministry of Culture, Sport, and Tourism, 2007.

Queenin, Hugh F. 'The Military Implications of SEATO', *Military Review*, 35 (February 1956).

Randolph, R.S. *The United States and Thailand: Alliance Dynamics, 1950–1985.* Berkeley: Institute of East Asian Studies, University of California, 1986.

Ransom, David. 'Ford Country: Building an Elite for Indonesia', in Steve Weissman (ed.), *The Trojan Horse: A Radical Look at Foreign Aid*. Revised edition. Palo Alto: Ramparts Press, 1975.

Reynolds, David. *Britannia Overruled: British Policy and World Power in the Twentieth Century.* London: Longman, 1991.

Ricklefs, Merle C. *A History of Modern Indonesia Since c. 1200.* 4th edition. Basingstoke: Palgrave Macmillan, 2008.

——— (ed.). *A New History of Southeast Asia.* Basingstoke: Palgrave Macmillan, 2010.

Romulo, Carlos P. *The Meaning of Bandung*. Chapel Hill: University of North Carolina Press, 1956.

———. Report on the Peace Treaty with Japan. Unpublished, 1951.

Rotter, Andrew J. *The Path to Vietnam: Origins of the American Commitment to Southeast Asia.* Ithaca: Cornell University Press, 1987.

Salamanca, Bonifacio S. *Towards a Diplomatic History of the Philippines*. Quezon City: University of the Philippines Press, 1996.

Sarkesian, Sam. *Unconventional Conflicts in a New Security Era: Lessons from Malaya and Vietnam.* Westport: Greenwood Press, 1993.

Schwartz, Thomas Alan. *Lyndon Johnson and Europe: In the Shadow of Vietnam.* Cambridge, MA: Harvard University Press, 2003.

Scott, Peter Dale. 'The United States and the Overthrow of Sukarno, 1965–1967', *Pacific Affairs*, 58, no. 2 (Summer 1985).

Shamsiah Fakeh. *Memoir Shamsiah Fakeh: Dari AWAS ke Rejimen Ke-10.* Petaling Jaya: SIRD, 2007.

Shawcross, William. *Sideshow: Kissinger, Nixon and the Destruction of Cambodia*. New York: Simon and Schuster, 1979.

Short, Anthony. 'Correspondence', *Journal of Southeast Asian Studies*, 1, 2 (September 1970).

Short, Anthony. *In Pursuit of Mountain Rats: The Communist Insurrection in Malaya.* Singapore: Cultured Lotus, 2000.

Sihanouk, Norodom. *Souvenirs doux et amers*. Paris: Hachette, 1981.

Simmonds, E.H.S. 'The Evolution of Foreign Policy in Laos.' *Modern Asian Studies*, vol. II, I (1968).

Smith, Ralph B. 'China and Southeast Asia: The Revolutionary Perspective', *Journal of Southeast Asian Studies,* XIX, 1 (1951).

Smith, Robert Ross. 'The Hukbalahap Insurgency', *Military Review*, 45 (June 1965).

Sodhy, Pamela. 'America's Melby Mission to Southeast Asia in 1950: The Case of Malaya', *JEBAT* (History Journal of the Universiti Kebangsaan Malaysia), 18 (1990).

Sopiee, Mohamed Noordin. *From Malayan Union to Singapore Separation: Political Unification in the Malayan Region, 1945–65*. Kuala Lumpur: Penerbit Universiti Malaya, 1974.

Spector, Ronald H. *In the Ruins of Empire: The Japanese Surrender and the Battle for Postwar Asia.* New York: Random House, 2007.

———. *The U.S. Army in Vietnam: Advice and Support: The Early Years, 1941–1960.* Washington, D.C.: US Army Center of Military History, 1983.

Statler, Kathryn C. *Replacing France: The Origins of American Intervention in Vietnam.* Lexington: University of Kentucky Press, 2007.

Steinberg, Jeffrey. 'FDR's 1932 Victory over London's Wall Street Fascists.' *Executive Intelligence Review*, 4 April 2008.

Stenson, M.R. *Industrial Conflict in Malaya: Prelude to the Communist Revolt of 1948.* Oxford: Oxford University Press, 1970.

Stevenson, C.A. *The End of Nowhere: American Policy Toward Laos Since 1954.* Boston: Beacon Press, 1972.

Stieglitz, Perry. *In A Little Kingdom*. Armonk, NY: M.E. Sharpe, 1990.

Stockwell, Anthony J. *British Policy and Malay Politics During the Malayan Union Experiment, 1945–48.* Singapore: Malaysian Branch of the Royal Asiatic Society, 1979.

———. 'Chin Peng and the Struggle for Malaya.' *The Journal of the Royal Asiatic Society,* 6:1 (2006).

———. 'Malaysia: The Making of a "Grand Design."' *Asian Affairs,* XXXIV, no. III (November 2003).

Stockwell, Anthony J. 'Malaysia: The Making of a Neo-Colony?' *Journal of Imperial and Commonwealth History*, 26, no. 2 (1998).

Stockwell, Anthony J. '"A Widespread and Long-Concocted Plot to Overthrow Government in Malaya?" The Origins of the Malayan Emergency.' *Journal of Imperial and Commonwealth History*, 21:3 (September 1993).

Stowe, Judith A. *Siam Becomes Thailand: A Story of Intrigue.* London: C. Hurst and Co, 1991.

Stuart-Fox, Martin. *Buddhist Kingdom, Marxist State: The Making of Modern Laos*. Bangkok: White Lotus, 1966.

Stubbs, Richard. *Hearts and Minds in Guerrilla Warfare: The Malayan Emergency 1948–1960.* Singapore: Oxford University Press, 1989.

Subritzky, John. 'Britain, Konfrontasi, and the End of Empire in Southeast Asia, 1961–65', in Kent Fedorowich and Martin Thomas (eds), *International Diplomacy and Colonial Retreat.* London: Frank Cass, 2001.

———. *Confronting Sukarno: British, American, Australian and New Zealand Diplomacy in the Malaysian-Indonesian Confrontation, 1961–5*. Basingstoke: Macmillan, 2000.

Sudarsono, Juwono. 'Indonesia and the United States, 1966–1975: an inquiry into a de facto alliance association.' PhD Thesis, University of London, London School of Economics and Political Science, 1979.

Summers, Harry G., Jr. *On Strategy: The Vietnam War in Context.* Washington, D.C.: Government Printing Office, 1981.

Sundhaussen, Ulf. *The Road to Power: Indonesian Military Politics, 1945–1967.* Kuala Lumpur and Oxford: Oxford University Press, 1982.

Suwannathat-Pian, K. *Thailand's Durable Premier: Pibul through Three Decades, 1932–1957.* Oxford: Oxford University Press, 1995.

Tan Tai Yong. *Creating 'Greater Malaysia': Decolonization and the Politics of Merger.* Singapore: Institute of Southeast Asian Studies, 2008.

———. 'The "Grand Design" British Policy, Local Politics, and the Making of Malaysia, 1955–1961', in Marc Frey, Ronald W. Pruessen and Tan Tai Yong (eds), *The Transformation of Southeast Asia: International Perspectives on Decolonization.* Armonik, NY: M.E. Sharpe, 2003.

———. 'Singapore's Story: A port city in search of hinterlands', in Arndt Graf and Chua Beng Huat (eds), *Port Cities in Asia and Europe.* London: Routledge, 2009.

Tarling, Nicholas. *Nations and States in Southeast Asia.* Cambridge: Cambridge University Press, 1998.

———. '"Some Rather Nebulous Capacity": Lord Killearn's Appointment in Southeast Asia', *Modern Asian Studies*, 20, 3 (1986).

Thee Kian Wie. 'Indonesia's Economic Performance Under Suharto's New Order.' *Seoul Journal of Economics,* vol. 20, no. 2 (2007).

Thompson, Virginia. *Thailand: New Siam.* New York: Institute of Pacific Relations, 1941.

Thompson, Virginia and Richard Adloff. *The Left Wing in Southeast Asia.* New York, William Sloane, 1950.

Thongsa Xainhavongkhamdi et al. *Pavatsat Lao lem III 1893 theung pachuban* [History of Laos, Volume III, 1893 to the present]. Vientiane: Ministry of Education and Sports and Social Science Research Institute, 1989.

Trauschweizer, Ingo. *The Cold War U.S. Army: Building Deterrence for Limited War.* Lawrence: University Press of Kansas, 2008.

Tung Van. 'Katay Don Sasorith Thu tuong Lao goc Viet' [Katay Don Sasorith, the Lao prime minister of Vietnamese origins], *Tap chi Su dia* [Journal of History and Geography], 16 (1969).

Turnbull, C.M. *A History of Modern Singapore 1819–2005*. Singapore: NUS Press, 2009.

Un Xananikon. *Santiphap mai nai Phralatsanachak Lao* [New peace in the Kingdom of Laos]. Vientiane: s.n., 1973.

Vellut, J.L. *The Asian Policy of the Philippines, 1954–1961*. Canberra: Department of International Relations, Research School of Pacific Studies, Australian National University, 1965.

Vongvichit, P. *Nai Kwam Song Jam kong Phoumi Vongvichit* [In the memory of Phoumi Vongvichit], translated by Pitsanoo Janwitan. Bangkok: Nation Books International, 2003.

Warner, Roger. *Back Fire: The CIA's Secret War in Laos and Its Link to the War in Vietnam.* New York: Simon and Schuster, 1995.

Warshawsky, Howard. 'From Confrontation to Cooperation: The Influence of Domestic Forces on Indonesian Foreign Policy.' PhD Thesis, University of Virginia, 1974.

Weinstein, Franklin B. *Indonesia Abandons Confrontation: An Inquiry into the Functions of Indonesian Foreign Policy.* Ithaca: Cornell University Press, 1969.

'Welcoming the Expression of Friendship by the Royal Laotian Government', *Peking Review*, vol. 3, no. 48. (29 November 1960).

White, Nicholas. 'The Business & Politics of Decolonization: The British Experience in the Twentieth Century.' *Economic History Review*, 53, 3 (2000).

Wilson, Harold. *The Labour Government 1964–70*. London: Pelican, 1974.

Yano Toru. 'Who Set the Stage for the Cold War in Southeast Asia?' in Yonosuke Nagai and Akira Iriye (eds), *The Origins of the Cold War in Asia.* Tokyo: University of Tokyo Press, 1977.

Yeo Kim Wah. *Political Development in Singapore, 1950–55*. Singapore: Singapore University Press, 1973.

Yeo Kim Wah and Albert Lau. 'From Colonialism to Independence, 1945–65', in Ernest Chew and Edwin Lee (eds), *A History of Singapore.* Singapore: Oxford University Press, 1991.

Yeuell, Donovan. 'An Army That Can Fight', *Infantry Journal*, 63 (December 1948).

Zhai, Qiang. *China and the Vietnam Wars, 1950–1974*. Chapel Hill: University of North Carolina Press, 2000.
Ziegler, Philip. *The Authorised Life of Lord Wilson of Rievaulx*. London: Weidenfeld and Nicolson, 1993.

Media

Abdul Rahman, Tunku. Speech in Parliament, 16 October 1961.
Beach, D.E. 'War Plan 1957.' Lecture at US Air War College, 29 October 1952.
Clay, Lucius D. 'Concept for Employment of Military Forces in Future War.' Lecture at US Air War College, 10 April 1952.
Collins, J. Lawton. 'National Strategic Objectives.' Lecture at US Air War College, 20 April 1950.
Collins, J. Lawton. 'U.S. Strategic Problems and the Development of the U.S. Armed Forces to Meet Them.' Lecture at Imperial Defence College, London, 27 May 1949.
Eddy, Manton. 'Relationship of Land Power to Air Power.' Lecture at US Air War College, 1 March 1949.
Eisenhower, Dwight D. News conference, 7 April 1954.
Goh Chok Tong. Prime minister's National Day Rally speech at the University Cultural Centre, National University of Singapore, 19 August 2001.
Lee Kuan Yew. Radio broadcast, 25 September 1961.
Lee Kuan Yew. Speech at luncheon of the Singapore National Union of Journalists, 24 May 1963.
Magruder, Carter. 'Army Logistics.' Lecture at US Army War College, 15 February 1957.

Newspapers and periodicals

Dawn
The Economist
The New York Times
Siam Rath
Straits Echo
The Straits Times
Sydney Morning Herald
The Times

NOTES ON THE AUTHORS

ANG CHENG GUAN is associate professor and head of humanities and social studies education at the National Institute of Education, and adjunct senior fellow of the S. Rajaratnam School of International Studies, at the Nanyang Technological University, Singapore. He specialises in the Cold War diplomatic history of Southeast Asia and the Indochina wars. His works include *Vietnamese Communist Relations with China and the Second Indochina Conflict, 1956–1962* (1997); *The Vietnam War from the Other Side: The Vietnamese Communists' Perspective* (2002); its sequel, *Ending the Vietnam War: The Vietnamese Communists' Perspective* (2004); and most recently, *Southeast Asia and the Vietnam War* (2010).

DEWI FORTUNA ANWAR straddles the worlds of academia, political activism and government. She currently serves as the deputy secretary for political affairs to the vice-president of the Republic of Indonesia, and was assistant minister for foreign affairs 1998–99. She obtained her Phd from Monash University in 1990, and is primarily based at the Indonesian Institute of Sciences' Research Center for Politics, where she is a research professor. Dewi is also chairman of the Institute for Democracy and Human Rights at the Habibie Center, a private think-tank based in Jakarta. She has written widely on Indonesia's foreign policy, its democratisation, and regional political and security issues.

CHEAH BOON KHENG was professor of history at the Universiti Sains Malaysia in Penang until his retirement. Since then he has taken up visiting professorships at the Australian National University in Canberra, the Institute of Southeast Asian Studies in Singapore, and the National University of Singapore. His books include *The Masked Comrades: A Study of the Communist United Front in Singapore and Malaya, 1945–1948* (1979); *Red Star Over Malaya: Resistance and Social Conflict During and After the Japanese Occupation, 1941–1946* (1983); *From PKI to the Comintern, 1924–1941: The Apprenticeship of the Malayan Communist Party* (1992); and *Malaysia: The Making of a Nation* (2002).

Brian P. Farrell teaches military history at the National University of Singapore, where he has been working since 1993. He has published extensively on his principal research interests, including the military history of the British Empire and of the West in Asia. Major publications include *The Basis and Making of British Grand Strategy 1940–1943: Was There a Plan?* (1998); *Between Two Oceans: A Military History of Singapore from 1275 to 1971* (co-author; 1st edition 1999, 2nd edition 2011); *The Defence and Fall of Singapore 1940–1942* (2005); *Malaya 1942* (2010); and *Churchill and the Lion City* (editor, 2011). His current projects include a study of the Indonesian Confrontation 1962–66.

Ricardo Trota Jose is professor of history at the University of the Philippines Diliman. He obtained his bachelor's and master's degrees in history at the University of the Philippines, and his PhD from the Tokyo University of Foreign Studies. He specialises in military and diplomatic history, particularly Philippines-Japan relations. Among his publications are *The Philippine Army, 1935–1942* (1992); a volume on the Japanese occupation of the Philippines in the 10-volume *Kasaysayan: The Story of the Filipino People* (1998); and *The Book on the Japanese Occupation: World War II and the Japanese Occupation* (editor, 2006).

Brian McAllister Linn obtained his PhD from Ohio State University in 1985 and joined the department of history at Texas A&M University in 1989; in 2009 he was awarded the Ralph R. Thomas professorship in liberal arts. He has been an Olin fellow at Yale University, the Harold K. Johnson visiting professor of history at the Army War College, and a Fulbright fellow at the National University of Singapore. From 2009 to 2011 he was president of the Society for Military History. His publications include *The U.S. Army and Counterinsurgency in the Philippine War* (1989); *Guardians of Empire: The U.S. Army and the Pacific, 1902–1940* (1997); *The Philippine War, 1899–1902* (2000); and *The Echo of Battle: The Army's Way of War* (2007).

Bruce Lockhart was trained in linguistics and history at Cornell and Yale universities, completing his PhD in Southeast Asian history at the former. His three countries of specialisation are Vietnam, Laos, and Thailand; the topics that particularly interest him are monarchy and modern historiography. His publications include *The End of the Vietnamese Monarchy* (1993); *Historical Dictionary of Vietnam* (co-author, 2006); *A New History of Southeast Asia* (co-author, 2010); and *The Cham of Vietnam: History, Society, and Art* (co-editor, 2011). He is currently working on a history of the modern Thai monarchy.

Malcolm H. Murfett did his doctorate on Anglo-American relations at New College, Oxford, and worked for five years as the research assistant to the Earl of Birkenhead on the officially commissioned life of Winston Churchill. He joined the department of history at the National University of Singapore in 1980, and was elected a fellow of the Royal Historical Society in 1990. His publications include *Fool-proof Relations: The Search for Anglo-American Naval Cooperation During the Chamberlain Years, 1937–1940* (1984); *In Jeopardy: The Royal Navy and British Far Eastern Defence Policy 1945–1951* (1995); *Between Two Oceans: A Military History of Singapore from 1275 to 1971* (co-author; 1st edition 1999, 2nd edition 2011); *Naval Warfare 1919–1945* (2009); *Imponderable But Not Inevitable: Warfare in the 20th Century* (2010).

Sutayut Osornprasop graduated with first class honours from Chulalongkorn University, and obtained his MPhil and PhD from the University of Cambridge. He won the Gates Cambridge Scholarship to pursue his doctorate study, resulting in his dissertation on 'Thailand and the American Secret War in Indochina, 1960–1974'. At the 2006 LSE-GWU-UCSB Graduate Conference on the Cold War, he won the Best Paper prize. Now with the World Bank as a human development specialist, his work focuses on social-sector research and project management in Southeast Asia.

Merle C. Ricklefs is professor emeritus of the Australian National University and a fellow of the Australian Academy of the Humanities. A scholar of the history and current affairs of Indonesia, he was formerly director of the Research School of Pacific and Asian Studies at the Australian National University and professor of history at the National University of Singapore. His books include *Jogjakarta Under Sultan Mangkubumi, 1749–1792* (1974); *War, Culture and Economy in Java, 1677–1726* (1993); *The Seen and Unseen Worlds in Java, 1726–49* (1998); *Polarising Javanese Society: Islamic and Other Visions c. 1830–1930* (2007); *A History of Modern Indonesia* (4th English edition, 2008); and *A New History of Southeast Asia* (co-author, 2010).

Tan Tai Yong is a historian and currently vice-provost at the National University of Singapore and director of the Institute of South Asian Studies. He has written extensively on the history of South Asia, Southeast Asia and Singapore, and his recent books include *The Aftermath of Partition in South Asia* (co-author, 2000); *The Transformation of Southeast Asia: International Perspectives on De-colonisation* (co-editor, 2003); *The Garrison State* (2005); *Partition and Post-Colonial South Asia: A Reader* (co-editor, 2007); *Creating 'Greater Malaysia': Decolonisation and the Politics of Merger* (2008); and *Singapore: A 700-Year History—From Early Emporium to World City* (co-author, 2009).

INDEX

Figures in subscript point to footnotes, and are given only for pages where the indexed term does not also appear in the main text.